"Peter Rudnytsky is not only our best scholar (i.e. thorough in reading, meticulous in research, and innovative in interpretation), he is the most enjoyable as well. His writing style is a seamless blend of historical documentation, behind-the-scenes glimpses of our pioneers, theoretical argument, juicy trivia, lament, and unexpected revelations. Unmasking the personal determinants of puzzling impasses and impressive advances in the theoretical evolution of our field, Rudnytsky dazzles us with his investigative zeal."

Salman Akhtar, *International Journal of Psychoanalysis*,
Professor of Psychiatry, Jefferson Medical College,
and Training and Supervising Analyst,
Psychoanalytic Center of Philadelphia

Mutual Analysis

Sándor Ferenczi's mutual analysis with Elizabeth Severn—the patient known as R.N. in the *Clinical Diary*—is one of the most controversial and consequential episodes in the history of psychoanalysis. In his latest groundbreaking work, Peter L. Rudnytsky draws on a trove of archival sources to provide a definitive scholarly account of this experiment, which constitutes a paradigm for relational psychoanalysis, as Freud's self-analysis does for classical psychoanalysis.

In Part 1, Rudnytsky tells the story of Severn's life and traces the unfolding of her ideas, culminating in *The Discovery of the Self*. He shows how her book contains disguised case histories not only of Ferenczi and Severn herself—and thereby forms an indispensable companion volume to Ferenczi's *Clinical Diary*—but also of Severn's daughter Margaret, an internationally acclaimed dancer whose history of childhood sexual abuse uncannily replicated Severn's own. Part 2 compares Severn to Clara Thompson and Izette de Forest as transmitters of Ferenczi's legacy, sets the record straight about Ferenczi's final illness, and reveals how Severn went beyond Freud and Groddeck in her capacity as Ferenczi's analyst. Finally, in Part 3, Rudnytsky delineates the contrast between Freud and Ferenczi as men and thinkers and makes it clear why he agrees with Erich Fromm that Ferenczi's example demonstrates how Freud's attitude need not be that of all analysts.

The first comprehensive study of Ferenczi's mutual analysis with Severn, this book is a profound reexamination of Ferenczi's relationship to Freud and an impassioned defense of Severn and Ferenczi's views on the nature and treatment of trauma. It will appeal to psychoanalysts and psychotherapists, especially to relational analysts, self psychologists, and trauma theorists.

Peter L. Rudnytsky is Professor of English at the University of Florida and Head of the Department of Academic and Professional Affairs as well as Chair of the Committee on Confidentiality of the American Psychoanalytic Association. Coeditor of the History of Psychoanalysis series for Routledge and the Psychoanalytic Horizons series for Bloomsbury, he has edited Severn's *The Discovery of the Self* in the Relational Perspectives series and received the Gradiva Award for *Reading Psychoanalysis: Freud, Rank, Ferenczi, Groddeck*.

Relational Perspectives Book Series

Series Editors: Adrienne Harris, Steven Kuchuck & Eyal Rozmarin
Founding Editor: Stephen Mitchell
Editor Emeritus: Lewis Aron

The Relational Perspectives Book Series (RPBS) publishes books that grow out of or contribute to the relational tradition in contemporary psychoanalysis. The term *relational psychoanalysis* was first used by Greenberg and Mitchell[1] to bridge the traditions of interpersonal relations, as developed within interpersonal psychoanalysis and object relations, as developed within contemporary British theory. But, under the seminal work of the late Stephen A. Mitchell, the term *relational psychoanalysis* grew and began to accrue to itself many other influences and developments. Various tributaries—interpersonal psychoanalysis, object relations theory, self psychology, empirical infancy research, feminism, queer theory, sociocultural studies and elements of contemporary Freudian and Kleinian thought—flow into this tradition, which understands relational configurations between self and others, both real and fantasied, as the primary subject of psychoanalytic investigation.

We refer to the relational tradition, rather than to a relational school, to highlight that we are identifying a trend, a tendency within contemporary psychoanalysis, not a more formally organized or coherent school or system of beliefs. Our use of the term *relational* signifies a dimension of theory and practice that has become salient across the wide spectrum of contemporary psychoanalysis. Now under the editorial supervision of Adrienne Harris, Steven Kuchuck and Eyal Rozmarin, the Relational Perspectives Book Series originated in 1990 under the editorial eye of the late Stephen A. Mitchell. Mitchell was the most prolific and influential of the originators of the relational tradition. Committed to dialogue among psychoanalysts, he abhorred the authoritarianism that dictated adherence to a rigid set of beliefs or technical restrictions. He championed open discussion, comparative and integrative approaches, and promoted new voices across the generations. Mitchell was later joined by the late Lewis Aron, also a visionary and influential writer, teacher and leading thinker in relational psychoanalysis.

Included in the Relational Perspectives Book Series are authors and works that come from within the relational tradition, those that extend and develop that tradition, and works that critique relational approaches or compare and contrast them with alternative points of view. The series includes our most distinguished senior psychoanalysts, along with younger contributors who bring fresh vision. Our aim is to enable a deepening of relational thinking while reaching across disciplinary and social boundaries in order to foster an inclusive and international literature.

A full list of titles in this series is available at www.routledge.com/Relational-Perspectives-Book-Series/book-series/LEARPBS.

1 Greenberg, J. & Mitchell, S. (1983). Object relations in psychoanalytic theory. Cambridge, MA: Harvard University Press.

Mutual Analysis

Ferenczi, Severn, and the Origins of Trauma Theory

Peter L. Rudnytsky

Routledge
Taylor & Francis Group
LONDON AND NEW YORK

First published 2022
by Routledge
4 Park Square, Milton Park, Abingdon, Oxon OX14 4RN

and by Routledge
605 Third Avenue, New York, NY 10158

Routledge is an imprint of the Taylor & Francis Group, an informa business

© 2022 Peter L. Rudnytsky

The right of Peter L. Rudnytsky to be identified as author of this work has been asserted in accordance with sections 77 and 78 of the Copyright, Designs and Patents Act 1988.

All rights reserved. No part of this book may be reprinted or reproduced or utilised in any form or by any electronic, mechanical, or other means, now known or hereafter invented, including photocopying and recording, or in any information storage or retrieval system, without permission in writing from the publishers.

Trademark notice: Product or corporate names may be trademarks or registered trademarks, and are used only for identification and explanation without intent to infringe.

British Library Cataloguing-in-Publication Data
A catalogue record for this book is available from the British Library

Library of Congress Cataloging-in-Publication Data
Names: Rudnytsky, Peter L., author.
Title: Mutual analysis: Ferenczi, Severn, and the origins of trauma theory / Peter L. Rudnytsky.
Description: Abingdon, Oxon; New York, NY: Routledge, 2022. | Series: Relational perspectives series | Includes bibliographical references and index.
Identifiers: LCCN 2021025693 (print) | LCCN 2021025694 (ebook) | ISBN 9781032133836 (hbk) | ISBN 9781032133829 (pbk) | ISBN 9781315280134 (ebk)
Subjects: LCSH: Ferenczi, Sándor, 1873–1933. | Severn, Elizabeth. | Psychoanalysis.
Classification: LCC BF109.F47 R83 2022 (print) | LCC BF109.F47 (ebook) | DDC 150.19/5—dc23
LC record available at https://lccn.loc.gov/2021025693
LC ebook record available at https://lccn.loc.gov/2021025694

ISBN: 978-1-032-13383-6 (hbk)
ISBN: 978-1-032-13382-9 (pbk)
ISBN: 978-1-315-28013-4 (ebk)

DOI: 10.4324/9781315280134

Typeset in Times New Roman
by Apex CoVantage, LLC

Also by Peter L. Rudnytsky

Formulated Experiences: Hidden Realities and Emergent Meanings from Shakespeare to Fromm (2019)

ed., *The Discovery of the Self: A Study in Psychological Cure*, by Elizabeth Severn (2017)

Rescuing Psychoanalysis from Freud and Other Essays in Re-Vision (2011)

ed., *Her Hour Come Round at Last: A Garland for Nina Coltart* (with Gillian Preston) (2011)

ed., *Psychoanalysis and Narrative Medicine* (with Rita Charon) (2009)

Reading Psychoanalysis: Freud, Rank, Ferenczi, Groddeck (2002)

ed., *Psychoanalyses/Feminisms* (with Andrew M. Gordon) (2000)

Psychoanalytic Conversations: Interviews with Clinicians, Commentators, and Critics (2000)

ed., *Ferenczi's Turn in Psychoanalysis* (with Antal Bókay and Patrizia Giampieri-Deutsch) (1996)

ed., *Freud and Forbidden Knowledge* (with Ellen Handler Spitz) (1994)

ed., *Transitional Objects and Potential Spaces: Literary Uses of D. W. Winnicott* (1993)

The Psychoanalytic Vocation: Rank, Winnicott, and the Legacy of Freud (1991)

ed., *Contending Kingdoms: Historical, Psychological, and Feminist Approaches to the Literature of Sixteenth-Century England and France* (with Marie-Rose Logan) (1990)

ed., *The Persistence of Myth: Psychoanalytic and Structuralist Perspectives* (1988)

ed., Ivan L. Rudnytsky, *Essays in Modern Ukrainian History* (1987)

Freud and Oedipus (1987)

To Carlo Bonomi and Franco Borgogno

*"Voi credete
forse che siamo esperti d'esto loco;
ma noi siam peregrin come voi siete."*

—Dante, *Purgatorio*, canto ii

> Dear Dr Severn
>
> I apologize for the delay of my answer, it was caused by a short visit in Vienna.
>
> It is of course impossible to give any definite opinion upon a case "ab invisis"; but your strong wish for finishing the analysis made a rather favourable impression on me from the therapeutic point of view.
>
> I certainly never advise to take technical instruction alone, the only real technical study being one's own analysis. But the duration of the latter is always uncertain.
>
> The cases which are now under my care do not permit me to fix the date of the beginning of a new analysis. I hope to be in the position to do it; 2 or 3 weeks.
>
> At any rate you could reconsider after these short informations your plans and write me again; I hope I can give you then a more concrete answer.
>
> Very sincerely yours
>
> S. Ferenczi
>
> Budapest, 6. March 1925
> IV. Nagydiófa u. 3.

The first known contact between Ferenczi and Severn. Ferenczi declines to offer an opinion on her case "sight unseen" (*ab invisis*), but states that her "strong wish for finishing" her analytic journey with him bodes well. He adds that analysis cannot be learned by "technical instruction alone," but only by undergoing "one's own analysis," though he is unable to predict how long that might take. Severn arrived in Budapest less than a month after Ferenczi wrote this letter.

© Boston Psychoanalytic Society and Institute Archives

Contents

Acknowledgments	xiii
Note on Sources	xv
Prelude: Ferenczi's Secret Life	1

PART 1
Conceptions — 27

1	Traces of a Life	29
2	The Metaphysical Calling	44
3	Much Farther Than Freudianism	62
4	The Psychoanalytic Severn	69
5	The Case of Ferenczi	88
6	Mother and Daughter	101

PART 2
Contexts — 133

7	Polygamous Analysis	135
8	The End of the Affair	160
9	Ferenczi's Sanity and the "Blood-Crisis"	172
10	Kissing Papa Ferenczi	183

11 Beyond Groddeck	197
12 The Evil Genius	210

PART 3
Consequences 219

13 For No Assignable External Reason	221
14 Roux's Needle	245
15 The Antitraumatic in Freud	264
16 New Veins of Gold	286
Finale: A Whole Soul	312
References	320
Index	337

Acknowledgments

This book would not have been possible without the friendship and support I have received from my fellow pilgrims in the International Sándor Ferenczi Network. In addition to those named in the dedication, I have been especially buoyed by the kindness of Giselle Galdi, the fidelity of Aleksandar Dimitrijevic, the acuity of Gianni Guasto, and the generosity of Judit Székács-Weisz. Antal Bókay paid me the salary of a Hungarian professor long ago. B. William Brennan and Christopher Fortune answered my queries with exemplary graciousness, as did Alan Barnett, Mario L. Beira, John Boyle, Gabriele Cassullo, Patricia Everett, Gerald Gargiulo, Philip Kuhn, Simon Partridge, and Steven Stern. Adrienne Harris stands as godmother to this book, as she did to its elder sibling in the Relational Perspectives series, my edition of Elizabeth Severn's *The Discovery of the Self*. Lewis Aron was taken from us all too soon.

I again owe a debt of gratitude to Kathleen Meigs, who first spotted the disguised case histories of Ferenczi and Severn herself in *The Discovery of the Self* and then generously left it to me to share her revelation with the world.

Rainer Funk gave me an electronic key to the Fromm Archives in Tübingen. My thanks go also to Jeffrey M. Flannery and Bruce Kirby of the Manuscript Division at the Library of Congress in Washington, D.C.; Bryony Davies of the Freud Museum in London; Danielle Castronovo at the Library of the Performing Arts in New York City; and John Leonard of the Chicago Psychoanalytic Institute. The letter reproduced as the frontispiece was serendipitously brought to my attention by Anna Borgos, who has published it with an introduction in *Imágó Budapest*. It was made available by Olga Umansky from the archives of the Boston Psychoanalytic Society and Institute, where it was found inside a copy of Ferenczi's *Final Contributions* donated by S. Louis and Kathleen Mogul, and it appears by permission of Judith Dupont.

Kate Hawes has been a steady hand at the helm of Routledge. This is the third book on which I have been fortunate to have Autumn Spalding as my production manager at Apex Co-Vantage. A sabbatical leave from the University of Florida in 2015–16 allowed me to make substantial headway on the writing. At earlier stages, I have presented my work in progress at a symposium of the Ferenczi Center at the New School in September 2015; at the Chicago Psychoanalytic Institute in May 2017; and at conferences of the International Sándor Ferenczi Society in Toronto in May 2015 and in Florence in May 2018. In March 2020, when life still seemed normal, I was honored to share the fruits of my research with members of the Inner Circle Seminar convened by Anthony Stadlen in London. Gabriela Gusita and the participants in our Ferenczi study group remind me why I love psychoanalysis.

Cheryl belongs to a class of which she is the only member.

Note on Sources

I have attempted to document all quotations and references as scrupulously as possible. In addition to published sources, I have utilized materials in the Fromm Archives (Tübingen), the Freud Archives (Library of Congress), the Freud Museum (London), the Elizabeth Severn Archives (Library of Congress), and the Margaret Severn Collection (Library of the Performing Arts). Where citations are not provided in the text for unpublished items, they will be found listed in the bibliography. I likewise scoured the Internet to learn what I could about the life and family history of Elizabeth Severn. While I believe that the story I am about to tell is factually accurate, I apologize to the reader for not being able to furnish the address for every scrap of information I managed to track down on the web. All translations from German or French not otherwise credited are my own, and all italics in quotations not said to be added appear in the original texts, while the reverse is true of ellipses. Connoisseurs of George Eliot will discern my homage to her "home epic."

Prelude
Ferenczi's Secret Life

If the "Ferenczi renaissance" may be said to have been sparked by the publication of his *Clinical Diary*—the private journal Ferenczi kept in 1932, the year before his death at the age of fifty-nine—first in French in 1985, followed in 1988 by the German original and the English translation, then I hope that the 2017 publication of my edition of Elizabeth Severn's *The Discovery of the Self: A Study in Psychological Cure*, which had been out of print and forgotten by all but a handful of specialists since 1933, may do the same in just proportion for Severn, and thereby help to inaugurate a "second wave" of Ferenczi studies in contemporary psychoanalysis.[1]

As I recounted in my introduction to Severn's book, although she initially became a minor celebrity as the patient known in the *Diary* by the initials "R.N.," presumably because of the last two letters of her surname, with whom Ferenczi conducted his experiment in mutual analysis, the real breakthrough came with the discovery by Kathleen Meigs that Severn had in *The Discovery of the Self* provided a disguised case history of Ferenczi—as well as of herself as though she were one of her own patients—and thereby bequeathed to posterity "the other side of the story" of the experience of mutual analysis.

This book contains the echo of that thunderclap. In the course of my research, I realized that Severn also included a disguised case history of her daughter Margaret, an internationally acclaimed dancer, whose history of childhood sexual abuse uncannily paralleled Severn's own. Thus, in addition to being an indispensable companion volume to the *Clinical Diary*, and for that reason alone one of the most important texts in the history of psychoanalysis, *The Discovery of the Self* opens a window on the intergenerational transmission of trauma with fascinating vistas for any psychoanalytic scholar or clinician. It transpires that Margaret was indeed her mother's analytic patient and that she also had a modicum of analysis with Ferenczi. Although late in her life Margaret destroyed the priceless cache of her mother's letters from Budapest, she made up for this loss in part with her 3,099-page autobiography, *Spotlight: Letters to My Mother* (1988). Together with the interviews given by Elizabeth Severn and Clara Thompson to Kurt R. Eissler, this compulsively readable typescript constitutes the most valuable external source for what went on between Ferenczi and Severn, as well as offering a firsthand account of the history of the Severn family—or, rather, of the Brown and Heywood families.

During my own prolonged gestation period, Arnold W. Rachman has weighed in with the first book on Severn, aptly titled *Elizabeth Severn: The "Evil Genius" of Psychoanalysis* (2018). Through the mediation of a friend, Rachman in 2003 purchased the Elizabeth Severn Papers from Peter Lipskis, who had become Margaret Severn's literary executor upon her death in 1997. In 2013, an initial donation of materials pertaining to Elizabeth Severn was made publicly available at the Library of Congress, followed in 2018 by a second portion pertaining to Margaret Severn. Rachman has thereby performed a great service to Severn scholarship, and there are valuable nuggets to be gleaned from his book. Unfortunately, however, it is riddled with so many misspellings and typographical errors as to be maddening, and so many blunders as to forfeit the reader's trust.[2]

There can be no doubt that Ferenczi's willingness to enter into a mutual analysis with Severn is one of the most controversial episodes in the history of psychoanalysis, which has been roundly denounced by conservative commentators. In the view of Glen O. Gabbard (1995), after the "rather remarkable series of boundary violations" (p. 1,122) that ensued when Ferenczi took into analysis and then proceeded to fall in love with Elma Pálos, the elder daughter of his married lover Gizella Pálos, he "went on to engage in other forms of boundary violations" by commencing a mutual analysis "with four female American patients" (p. 1,125). Even after being urged by Emanuel Berman (1997) to be mindful of the "crucial difference" between "critically evaluating experimental treatment methods and stigmatizing them in toto as boundary violations" (p. 570), Gabbard (1997) held his ground, reiterating that "to regard mutual analysis as something other than a boundary violation strains credulity" because Ferenczi's willingness to participate in a "role reversal" constitutes "a direct exploitation of the patient, in that the patient's needs are completely subordinated to the analyst's need for help" (pp. 571–72). Harold P. Blum (2004), who succeeded Eissler as Executive Director of the Sigmund Freud Archives, concurs that Ferenczi engaged in "egregious and mutually destructive acting out of transference and countertransference," which is "evident in

the cases of 'mutual analysis' with Clara Thompson at the beginning of the clinical diary and Elizabeth Severn at the end" (p. 11), while Karen Maroda (1998) repeats a libel originating with Ernest Jones when she alleges that his "highly unorthodox treatment" of Severn casts "a shadow not only over Ferenczi's clinical judgment, but also his sanity" (p. 115).

The first thing to point out are the factual errors of Ferenczi's detractors. Far from it being true that Ferenczi conducted mutual analysis with Thompson, let alone with four patients, Thompson envied Severn for being granted this privilege by Ferenczi.[3] As Ferenczi wrote in the opening entry to the *Clinical Diary*, dated January 7, 1932, "*In one case* the communication of the content of my own psyche developed into a form of mutual analysis from which I, the analyst, derived much profit" (Dupont, 1985, p. 3; italics added), a statement corroborated by Thompson (1952a) when she told Eissler that Ferenczi had "*a patient*" (p. 2; italics added) whom he permitted to analyze him. Gabbard (1995) again goes astray in asserting that Ferenczi "abandoned mutual analysis" after "a few months" (p. 1,125). To be sure, the *Diary* documents Ferenczi's conflicts about the mutual analysis, which caused him to proceed by fits and starts, but that he never aborted it is proved by the final entry, dated October 2, 1932, where he records Severn's tribute to their work together: "From *my* analysis she expects insight into the *personal* (independent of her), historical determinants of my behavior toward patients—and thus definitive detachment. What will *remain*, she hopes, is a *reciprocal* 'honorable' recognition of mutual achievement, of having coped *with such a case*" (Dupont, 1985, p. 214).

These errors expose the unreliability of the fault-finders, and it is telling that Severn's name goes unmentioned by Gabbard. But the crux of the matter is whether the mutual analysis constituted "a direct exploitation of the patient" because Ferenczi "completely subordinated" Severn's needs to his own "need for help." Now, it cannot be denied that Ferenczi was still in search of the healing he had not received from his two previous "analyses," such as they were, with Freud and Groddeck. Indeed, he makes no bones about the fact that he "derived much profit" from becoming Severn's patient. But what the critics overlook is that, far from being an "exploitation" of Severn, in temporarily ceding the role of analyst Ferenczi was actually placing her needs above his own. As he writes, it was because Severn sensed "feelings of hate" in him, and began insisting that "her analysis would not make any progress unless I allowed her to analyze those hidden feelings in me," that he "decided to make this sacrifice," but only after having "resisted this for approximately a year" (Dupont, 1985, p. 99). It is legitimate to question Ferenczi's judgment, but not his motives, which were to do what was in the best interest of his patient, even though it required a great "sacrifice" from himself. As Anthony Bass (2015) has put it, "he realized that his patient needed to give him the psychoanalysis he needed to give her the psychoanalysis that she needed" (p. 12).

Ferenczi's love triangle with Gizella and Elma Pálos, a drama that unfolded in 1911 and 1912, needs to be considered separately from his leap of faith two decades later with Severn, although they are routinely coupled by those who want to make a case against him. The requisite rejoinder has been offered by Berman (2004a):

> Although Ferenczi's early entanglement with Elma was indeed an impulsive and destructive boundary violation in which the analyst lost control of his therapeutic task, mutual analysis—based on the egalitarian yearnings so prominent in Ferenczi's personality, which indeed had a certain role in his falling in love with Elma—is a much more thoughtful, deliberate, and controlled experiment, conducted under continual self-criticism.
>
> (p. 53)

An apparent link between these episodes is supplied by Thompson, the subject of Freud's notorious reprimand of Ferenczi in December 1931 for his "kissing technique," as can be seen when Blum cites both Thompson and Severn as examples of Ferenczi's "egregious and mutually destructive acting out of transference and countertransference," or when Gabbard (1995) claims that Ferenczi's "technique included kissing and hugging the patient" (p. 1,125). Although there is no evidence that Ferenczi ever engaged in sexual intercourse with Elma, he did, as Berman acknowledges, definitely commit a boundary violation by our contemporary standards, as can be seen in a letter from Elma to Michael Balint on May 7, 1966:

> All in all after a few sessions Sandor got up from his chair behind me, sat on the sofa next to me and, considerably moved, kissed me all over and passionately told me how much he loved me and asked whether I could love him too. Whether or not it was true I cannot tell, but I answered "yes" and—I hope—I believed so.
>
> (qtd. in Berman, 2004b, p. 514)

In addition, on December 19, 1917, Ferenczi admitted to Freud that he "gave way to a kiss" with a "very poor, very beautiful, very intelligent" female patient, a lapse he describes as "the repetition of the case of Elma," which resulted in a catastrophe when this other young woman shot herself to death because "she had wanted to love *the man* and not only *the doctor* in me" (Falzeder and Brabant, 1996, p. 253).

Ferenczi's conduct in these earlier cases is certainly not above reproach. But his basic integrity is attested by the fact that, even with the patient who committed suicide, he did not attempt to conceal what had happened. Both Freud and Gizella Pálos were apprised of his confusion and ambivalence with respect to Elma, and they endorsed Ferenczi's ill-advised decision to take her into analysis. Because Freud was in the position of ultimate authority in this situation, he arguably bears a greater responsibility for what happened than Ferenczi himself. Indeed, not only did Freud place unremitting pressure on Ferenczi to choose the mother over the daughter, he himself took Elma into analysis for three months and then sent her back for a second stint on Ferenczi's couch. As Berman (2004b) observes in his indispensable account of Ferenczi's triangle, Freud's "detailed . . . reports to his friend about Elma's analysis" were, "by today's standards, highly unethical" (p. 496); and both Freud and Ferenczi were blind "to the cruelty of the experiment" with Elma, as well as to "the hopeless double bind created by making analytic openness the precondition for marriage with the analyst" (p. 499). In the end, Elma married the Norwegian-born American art critic and photographer John Laurvik in 1914—from whom she separated a decade later, though they never divorced (p. 508)—and Sándor married Gizella in 1919.

Even in his worst moments, therefore, Ferenczi's lapses were due to weakness rather than malevolence, and he never engaged in "a direct exploitation of the patient." If that charge is to be leveled against anyone, it should be against Freud, whose conduct in the "Frink affair" is one of the most sordid chapters in the history of psychoanalysis.[4] In brief, Horace Frink, one of the founders of the New York Psychoanalytic Society, was in analysis with Freud for approximately seven months in two installments in 1921 and 1922. While in analysis with Freud, Frink was having an affair with his own patient, Angelika Wertheim Bijur, an immensely wealthy bank heiress. Just as Freud had steered Ferenczi away from Elma and toward Gizella Pálos, so, even more reprehensibly, he urged both Frink and Bijur, both of whom were married, to divorce their respective spouses and marry each other, which they did on December 27, 1922. Freud's matchmaking ended with Frink consumed with guilt over the death of his abandoned wife Doris in May 1923—the death of Abraham Bijur a year earlier had removed the primary obstacle to his union with Angelika—and then plunging into a major depression, leading to repeated suicide attempts and hospitalizations, as his marriage to Angelika unraveled. By the spring of 1925 the once ecstatic adulterers were themselves divorced.

In condoning Frink's adultery, Freud took it for granted that it involved sexual relations with his patient. Freud wrote to Thaddeus Ames, the analyst of the justifiably outraged Abraham Bijur, on October 9, 1921:

> I had to explain to Frink what his internal difficulties were and did not deny that I trust it the good right of every human being to strive for sexual gratification and tender love if he saw a way to attain them, both of which he had not found with his wife. When he grew uncertain with his mind, I had to take the side of his repressed desires, and in this way become the advocate of his wish to divorce and marriage with Mrs. B. . . . So for me, it was a case of honorable love versus convention; there my interest ended and the situation has not changed since then.
>
> (qtd. in Warner, 1994, p. 142)

What Freud frames as a choice between "honorable love" and the bourgeois "convention" of marriage can (as I shall seek to prove in a subsequent book) be read as a covert apologia for having taken the side of his own "repressed desires" and striven for "sexual gratification" in his affair with Minna Bernays in 1900; and he spurred the lovers on by presenting a photograph of himself inscribed "To Angie *Frink*, in memory of your old friend, Sigmund Freud, September 1922" (p. 143), three months before she had assumed her new name in reality.

Although the sexual side of this story is seamy enough, what is most reprehensible about Freud's conduct, as Angelika Frink came to realize, is that he was after her money. His ulterior motives are laid bare in a letter to Frink on November 17, 1921:

> May I suggest to you that your idea that Mrs. Bijur had lost part of her beauty may be turned into her having lost part of her money. If so I am sure she will recover her attraction. Your complaint that you cannot grasp your homosexuality implies that you are not yet aware of your phantasy of making me a rich man. If matters turn out all right let us

change the imaginary gift into a real contribution to the psychoanalytic fund.

(qtd. in Warner, 1994, p. 149)

Here Freud shows himself to be a veritable scoundrel. He assures Frink that his perception of Angelika's waning beauty will be miraculously reversed when Frink persuades her to make "a real contribution to the psychoanalytic fund," an action which would have the collateral benefit of enabling Frink to recognize his repressed desire to submit homosexually to Freud by gratifying his equally unconscious "fantasy of making me a rich man."

By a twist of fate, Angelika, who, in addition to paying Doris $100,000 to induce her to agree to the divorce from Frink, had subsidized Frink's analysis with Freud, subsequently sought analysis with Ferenczi and is the patient known as "G." in the *Clinical Diary* (Brennan, 2015a). According to Severn's (1952) interview with Eissler, however, this analysis did not go well either. Angelika told Severn that she was "disappointed" in her sessions with Ferenczi, which "made a very bad impression on her," while Ferenczi, being, as usual, "scared of an intelligent woman," had done "all the wrong things" with Angelika "because he was upset and annoyed" (p. 22). The grinding of gears can be heard in Ferenczi's diary entry of August 17, 1932, where he notes her protest against his failure to comprehend the trauma of her divorce and remarriage, "If I don't get any more understanding from *him* (me), what can I expect at all? Even he calls it a happy marriage, that is, something I may have wanted" (Dupont, 1985, pp. 204–5).

But when Angelika Frink (1952) did her own interview with Eissler, which she did not permit him to tape-record but for which we have his notes, it was not Ferenczi but Freud whom she described as "completely selfish" and "ready to sacrifice any human being for the sake of analysis," just as it was Freud who "was interested in Mrs. Frink's money" (pp. 2–3). Her complaint continues, "Mrs. Frink thinks she is a victim of psychoanalysis, that Freud knew to rationalize all the mistakes he made. . . . She trusted him because he was the greatest authority and she did not derive any benefit of Freud's genius" (p. 7). When we compare Freud's crass and self-serving behavior with Horace and Angelika Frink to Ferenczi's altruistically motivated mutual analysis with Elizabeth Severn, it is beyond dispute which of them should be found guilty of "a direct exploitation of the patient." Indeed, not only did Severn affirm her hope for "a *reciprocal* 'honorable' recognition of mutual achievement," but, as she wrote (1952) in a note appended to the text of her interview with Eissler, *The Discovery of the Self* "replaced to some extent the plans Ferenczi and I had had for a more scientific mutual publication," and "he saw the MSS. before I left and approved of it" (p. 24).

In the same valedictory entry to the *Clinical Diary* in which he quoted Severn's tribute to their "mutual achievement," Ferenczi poses the question, "must every case be mutual?—and to what extent?" (Dupont, 1985, p. 213). Under the subheading "Mutuality—*sine qua non*," he ponders: "Once mutuality has been attempted, one-sided analysis then is no longer possible—not productive." As Bass (2015) has commented, an acceptance of the principle of mutuality is "at the heart of what makes psychoanalysis relational and distinguishes its unique approach to listening and engaging" (p. 14). If Bass is correct, as I believe he is, then Ferenczi's mutual analysis becomes the paradigm for the contemporary shift to a two-person conceptualization of clinical work, just as Freud's self-analysis was paradigmatic for the one-person perspective of classical theory. Both of these epochal events are paradoxically at once unique and unrepeatable foundational acts of psychoanalysis and continuous sources of inspiration that must be emulated and revivified by each of us who follows in their footsteps.

If Ferenczi's experiment with Severn is viewed as a limit case of an indispensable dimension of every psychoanalysis, then it becomes possible to vindicate not simply his motives but also his clinical judgment. Consider the following excerpts from Steven Stern's (2017) "nine principles of needed analytic relationships":

1   Every analytic patient and dyad is *unique*; thus the needed relationship(s) that emerge in each treatment are also unique.
2   The *telos* of analytic treatment is *progressive fittedness* . . . between the patient's evolving therapeutic needs and the relationship that emerges to meet those needs.
3   Achieving progressive fittedness . . . means *co-creating the therapeutic conditions* that best enable the patient to work and move toward her mostly implicit therapeutic/developmental aims as these become actualized and articulated within the analytic setting over time. (pp. 11–12)

He writes in later passages:

> Whereas in professions such as medicine and spiritual teaching, and in non-relational psychotherapies, the relationship between the persons

giving and receiving treatment or guidance is usually seen as an important *vehicle* for delivering needed help, in psychoanalysis the analytic relationship itself *is* the primary treatment agent.

(p. 19)

Because developmentally traumatized persons have grown up in situations that were decidedly *unfitted* to their early needs, their relational expectancies (transferences) and character adaptations incline them to be suspicious of, unpracticed in, resistant to, and even destructive of the natural collaborative tendency [inherent in the concept of "progressive fittedness" introduced by the infancy researcher and theorist Lewis Sander].

(p. 28)

My concept of needed relationship, and Sander's concepts of fittedness, and specificity of recognition and connection, all suggest that the "agents of change" are always unique and specific to each analytic dyad, and emerge on an ongoing basis through the collaboration of patient and analyst in the context of their particular analytic field.

(p. 99)

In the broadest terms, the patient's forward-edge participation is synonymous with simply doing her job of being an engaged patient. . . . On the analyst's side, it is *the impulse to heal psychoanalytically* that provides the core motivation to always be reaching for progressively fitted understandings and forms of engagement.

(p. 100)

It is the total lived intersubjective relationship that is transformative.

(p. 172)

In a sense, we could say that it is the patient's "job" to enact. . . . But, as I have emphasized in different contexts throughout the previous chapters, the fate of a given interaction, especially enactments, in relation to the dyad's movement toward greater fittedness and complexity, is hardly automatic, but rather depends on the analyst's capacities to *meet* the patient "in the enactment" in ways that move toward greater specificity of recognition and connection.

(p. 219)

Although Ferenczi figures only incidentally in Stern's book, and Severn is not mentioned at all, everything he says here constitutes a searching commentary on—and implicit justification of—Ferenczi's decision to undertake the mutual analysis. This was the relationship that Severn needed, and it emerged over time as they moved together toward an increasingly calibrated "progressive fittedness." Severn throughout was "doing her job of being an engaged patient," although her severe traumas also made her "destructive of the natural collaborative tendency," and Ferenczi was motivated above all by *"the impulse to heal psychoanalytically"*—though this, as Stern notes, was belittled by Freud as a "*'furor sanandi'*" or "form of 'fanaticism'" (p. 35). It was the "analytic relationship itself" that was "the primary treatment agent" for both Severn *and* Ferenczi, and the "total lived intersubjective relationship" that was "transformative."

Ferenczi's *Clinical Diary* distills his movement away from Freud and articulation of a new psychoanalytic paradigm that has made him the most important influence on contemporary relational theory and practice. He accomplished this breakthrough in the writings of his final period, bracketed by his paper at the 1929 Oxford Congress of the International Psychoanalytical Association, "The Principle of Relaxation and Neocatharsis" (1930), and his paper at the 1932 Wiesbaden Congress, "Confusion of Tongues between Adults and the Child: The Language of Tenderness and of Passion" (1933a). As I shall argue, Severn was his full partner in effecting this paradigm shift, and she set forth its fundamental principles with equal clarity and cogency in *The Discovery of the Self*. Her book thus forms a "mutual publication" with the *Clinical Diary* not simply in giving us her side of the story of her relationship with Ferenczi, culminating in the mutual analysis, but also in the "scientific" sense of expounding their jointly held convictions concerning psychoanalytic theory and therapy.

The essence of Ferenczi and Severn's revolution on the plane of theory was a return to—and incalculable deepening of—Freud's euphemistically named "seduction theory," given its fullest expression in "The Aetiology of Hysteria" (1896), and privately abandoned in his September 21, 1897 letter to Wilhelm Fliess. As Freud himself put it (with chronological precision) on September 3, 1932 in a letter to his daughter Anna, after hearing Ferenczi read aloud the paper he was about to deliver in Wiesbaden: "He has made a complete regression to etiological views that I believed and renounced 35 years ago, that gross sexual traumas of childhood [*grobe sexuelle Traumen der Kindheit*] are the regular cause of neuroses" (qtd. in Schröter, 2004, 2:829).[5] What Ferenczi and Severn proposed, for the first time in a psychoanalytic context, was indeed a fully elaborated *trauma* and not a "seduction" theory; and they went far beyond Freud in focusing, as Gianni Guasto (2013) has pointed out, not "on the sexual nature and contents of the event," but rather on "the mortal anguish, the psychic shock" (p. 44) that afflicts the victims of sexual and other forms of abuse (including genocide and all manner of political or collective trauma).[6] Guasto encapsulates the soul-shattering effects of these horrors in the phrase "the loss of basic trust."

If what impels people to seek analytic therapy are traumatic experiences, and trauma by definition possesses an overwhelming quality, then it follows, to quote the unjustly maligned contention of Franz Alexander (1946), that "the patient, in order to be helped, must undergo a corrective emotional experience suitable to repair the traumatic influence of previous experiences," and "this can be accomplished only through actual experience in the patient's relationship to the therapist; intellectual insight alone is not sufficient" (pp. 66–67). In *The Development of Psycho-Analysis* (1924), coauthored with Rank, Ferenczi foreshadows his later views when they stress that it is "absolutely unavoidable" for the patient to repeat during analysis "just those portions" of his early history "which cannot be really experienced from memory, so that there is no other way open to the patient than that of repeating" (p. 3). As Severn put this corollary to the resuscitation of trauma theory in *The Discovery of the Self* (1933), the "*sine qua non* of successful analysis" is "emotional reproduction and recollection," and an "important measure that was worked out between Ferenczi and me in the course of my own long analysis with him" is that the patient must be enabled "to relive, as though it were *now*, the traumatic events of his past, aided by the dramatic participation of the analyst" (pp. 93–94). With or without the theatrical metaphor, this is as much to say, in Stern's words, that "the analytic relationship itself *is* the primary treatment agent" in Ferenczi and Severn's radically relational conception of psychoanalysis.

Although Ferenczi and Severn are the originators of trauma theory in psychoanalysis, there is a formidable—and extremely sophisticated—body of literature on trauma largely ignored by psychoanalysts which has its roots in the work of Pierre Janet, who, according to Bessel van der Kolk (2014), should be considered "the real hero of this story" (p. 180). As Henri Ellenberger (1970) has written:

> Janet contended that certain hysterical symptoms can be related to the existence of split parts of the personality (subconscious fixed ideas) endowed with autonomous life and development. He showed their

origin in traumatic events of the past and the possibility of a cure of hysterical symptoms through the discovery and subconscious dissolution of these subconscious psychological systems.

(p. 361)

It is impossible to read this summary of Janet's contributions without being reminded of Freud. Indeed, in the 1893 "Preliminary Communication" to *Studies on Hysteria* (1895), jointly authored with Breuer, Freud adhered to the view, derived from Janet, that a "splitting of consciousness . . . is present to a rudimentary degree in every hysteria, and that a tendency to such a dissociation, and with it the emergence of abnormal states of consciousness . . . is the basic phenomenon of this neurosis" (p. 12).

But if Janet has been subjected to collective amnesia by psychoanalysts, that is because, even before *Studies on Hysteria* had been published, Freud had abandoned the framework he and Breuer had set forth two years earlier in the "Preliminary Communication," eventually replacing it with a theory of the mind based on the repression of endogenous instinctual drives. On the few occasions that he mentioned Janet in his subsequent writings, Freud did so in disparaging terms, as when he claimed in *An Autobiographical Study* (1925) that "historically psychoanalysis is completely independent of Janet's discoveries, just as in its content it diverges from them and goes far beyond them" (p. 31).[7] Before Freud had repudiated the trauma theory, therefore, as Onno van der Hart (2016) has observed, he had already repudiated the dissociation theory, and both of these seeming advances have in reality been profound losses for psychoanalysis.

Despite Freud's attempts to banish Janet from psychoanalytic consciousness, there is an illustrious lineage of authors, from Breuer, through Fairbairn and Sullivan, to Donnel Stern and Philip Bromberg, who, with varying degrees of explicitness, have built on and extended Janet's legacy. As Bromberg (1998) has eloquently written, "it is hard not to imagine the ghost of Pierre Janet, banished from the castle a century ago, returning for an overdue haunting of Freud's current descendants" (p. 189); and he adds of Sullivan that his "theory of interpersonal relations, reduced to its bare essentials, is . . . a theory of the dissociative organization of personality in response to trauma" (p. 215). Fairbairn (1949) likewise hits the mark when he declares that "a theory of the personality based upon the conception of the splitting of the ego would appear to be more fundamental than one based upon Freud's conception of the repression of impulses by an unsplit ego" (p. 159). Fairbairn continues:

> The theory which I envisage is, of course, obviously adapted to explain such extreme manifestations as are found in cases of multiple personality; but as Janet has pointed out, these extreme manifestations are only exaggerated examples of the dissociation phenomena characteristic of hysteria. Thus, if we implement the slogan "Back to hysteria," we find ourselves confronted with the very phenomenon of splitting upon which my theory of repression is based.

Fairbairn deserves immense credit not only for recognizing the continuity of dissociative phenomena—from the ordinary panoply of self-states at one end of the spectrum to full-blown multiple personalities on the other—but, perhaps even more, for acknowledging that his object relations theory owes at least as great a debt to Janet as it does to Freud.[8]

Ferenczi is a linchpin of this tradition, but, with a few notable exceptions (Hainer, 2016; Mucci et al., 2019), there has been a paucity of attempts to bring together the cornucopia of scholarship on Ferenczi with that on dissociation. This lacuna can be explained in part by the deficiencies of the current three-volume edition of Ferenczi's writings in English, which has only a handful of scattered references to Janet, whose name does not appear in the index. (The German *Bausteine zur Psychoanalyse*, in four volumes, lacks a name index altogether.) The Italian edition of Ferenczi's *Opere*, by contrast, despite being translated from the French, gives a much more accurate picture inasmuch as it contains as many as twenty-five references to the French psychologist.[9] From his memorial tribute to his mentor and father figure Miksa Schachter, we know that Ferenczi (1917a) had read Janet as a young physician because he recalls that "Janet had already published interesting findings on this phenomenon" of spiritism, which had emboldened him to publish his own "first medical paper" (p. 430) on the same subject in Schachter's journal *Gyógyászat* (*Art of Healing*) in 1899, nearly a decade before his first meeting with Freud in 1908.

Despite the frequency with which Ferenczi alludes to Janet in his writings, however, the crucial point is that he does so only between 1912 and 1924, while he was (at least consciously) unwaveringly loyal to Freud—but not after 1925, the period of his association with Severn, as he moved fitfully but inexorably toward intellectual independence. In "Exploring the

Unconscious" (1912a), for instance, Ferenczi invokes Janet, together with Charcot and Möbius, as eminences who had failed to draw the "general conclusions from the phenomenon of hysteria" (p. 309) that it was left to Freud to uncover. Ever since Freud heard from Breuer about the case of Anna O., Ferenczi continues, which was "the first time that anyone had succeeded with a predetermined method in exploring the content of ideas hidden in unconsciousness," and grasped its significance more deeply than Breuer had himself, the "exploration of the underworld of the mind has been connected solely with the name of Freud" (p. 311).

Ironically, therefore, Ferenczi to the end remained under the sway of the received narrative of the history of psychoanalysis, in which Janet did not have to be excommunicated, but could simply be left behind as a relic of the past whose discoveries were "completely independent" of—and superseded by—the tradition to which Ferenczi continued to belong, even as he increasingly went his own way and not Freud's. When, in his most revealing reference to Breuer in the *Clinical Diary*, Ferenczi contrasts him with Freud, he does so not with respect to Breuer's theory of hypoid states or "splitting of consciousness," which would have aligned Breuer with Janet. Rather, Ferenczi uses him as a bulwark in his disagreements with Freud over trauma theory and the essential elements of psychoanalytic therapy: "Return to trauma (Breuer). *In opposition to Freud* I developed to an exceptional degree a capacity for humility and for appreciating the clearsightedness of the uncorrupted child (patient)" (Dupont, 1985, p. 160). Unlike Fairbairn, with his slogan "Back to hysteria," when Ferenczi says "Return to trauma" he does not make the link to dissociation. This blind spot explains why scholars have failed to realize that, in rehabilitating trauma theory for psychoanalysis, Ferenczi was also reinventing dissociation theory and is thus Janet's heir, even though he himself had "forgotten" that he belongs to this lineage.

Coming from an American tradition, Severn shows a deep understanding of dissociative phenomena not only from own experience as a trauma survivor but also through her reading of Morton Prince, whose *The Dissociation of a Personality* (1906) she cites as early as her own first book, *Psycho-Therapy: Its Doctrine and Practice* (1913). There Severn writes that the "disturbance of the coherence of the mind is called dissociation by psychologists and, although probably present in everyone to some degree, leads in extreme cases to a complete anaesthesia of certain parts or faculties, or to such phenomena as double personality" (pp. 62–63). In her second book, *The Psychology of Behaviour* (1917), she reiterates, "The greatest danger to the personality is that of *dissociation*. In its extreme form we have multiple or alternating personalities, where one phase emerges with such strength and vividness as to temporarily, or perhaps for a long period of time, entirely eclipse the others" (pp. 335–36).

From the outset of her career as a psychotherapist, therefore, it is clear that Severn had reached a remarkably prescient theoretical position, to which Ferenczi would catch up only in his final period, thanks in no small measure to her intellectual as well as personal influence. Then, through their eight-year collaboration, Ferenczi and Severn jointly gave birth to trauma theory in psychoanalysis, and in the process formulated a model of the mind based (in Fairbairn's words) on "the splitting of the ego" and "dissociation phenomena," rather than on "Freud's conception of the repression of impulses by an unsplit ego." This revolution on the plane of theory goes hand in hand with a shift to a fully two-person, intersubjective approach to clinical practice. And since, as David M. Terman (2014) has observed, Kohut and his colleagues came to realize that "the essential task" of mental life "is the development and maintenance of a cohesive, functioning self" (p. 1,017), and "defense in self psychology protects a vulnerable, developing self from trauma" (p. 1,018), Severn and Ferenczi's "mutual achievement" can lay claim to being the fountainhead of self-psychology as well as of relational psychoanalysis. It is not only by virtue of its title that *The Discovery of the Self* forms a "prequel" to Kohut's classics, *The Analysis of the Self* (1971) and *The Restoration of the Self* (1977).

In their introduction to my edition of *The Discovery of the Self*, Adrienne Harris and Lewis Aron (2017) quote from Christopher Fortune's groundbreaking paper on Severn in their volume *The Legacy of Sándor Ferenczi* (1993), which was the first flowering of the Ferenczi renaissance following the publication of the *Clinical Diary*.[10] Quoting Harris and Aron quoting Fortune, "'Severn may have been the first sexually abused analysand whose actual childhood trauma was the focus of psychoanalytic treatment since Freud abandoned his seduction theory in the late 1890s'" (p. xii; see Fortune, 1993, p. 102). Severn's forerunner in this respect is Emma Eckstein, the pivotal patient in both Freud's initial espousal and subsequent repudiation of the "seduction" theory, who, as Carlo Bonomi's (2015a) research has established, shared with Severn a history of gross sexual abuse in childhood. But since Severn was not only sexually, physically, and emotionally abused but as a result suffered from what would today be classified as a dissociative identity disorder (Brenner, 2016), this makes her the avatar also of Bertha Pappenheim, better known as Anna O., the patient with whom, as Freud (1910) declared in his lectures at Clark University, not he but Breuer first "brought psycho-analysis into being" (p. 9). Thus, in rectifying both of Freud's ill-starred wrong turns—his successive abandonments of the dissociation and the trauma theory—Ferenczi's analysis of Severn simultaneously coupled her destiny with these two legendary women in the history of psychoanalysis.

The realization that Severn, in addition to being the foremost patient in the *Clinical Diary*, has turned the tables by including a disguised case history of Ferenczi in *The Discovery of the Self* allows her to emerge as a subject in her own right whose life and work warrant thoroughgoing reappraisal. We can hear in her writing the voice of the patient that has too often been lost in psychoanalysis, as it has been with Bertha Pappenheim, Emma Eckstein, and Ida Bauer—the "Dora" of Freud's (1905a) first full-length case history, whose only recourse to his tragically misguided attempt to blame her for the sexual abuse of which she was in reality a victim was to walk out his door, so all that now remains is *his* side of their story. At the same time, however, because Severn also includes her own case history, and that of her daughter, in *The Discovery of the Self*, her book takes its place in the venerable analytic tradition—extending from Freud and Ferenczi to Horney and Kohut—of covert autobiography, while at the same time employing material from the analyses of both a colleague and a family member.[11] But because we know that Ferenczi "saw" and "approved" the manuscript of *The Discovery of the Self*—as Margaret must have done as well—Severn deserves to be commended for not venturing into print without securing the informed consent of at least these two most directly affected patients.

One frequently encounters references to the relationship between Freud and Ferenczi as a "dialogue," nowhere more influentially than by André E. Haynal and Ernst Falzeder (1991): "It was a *dialogue*, it was friendship; more, it was 'an intimate community of life, feelings, and interest'" (p. 4). Analogously, Lewis A. Kirshner (1993) has opined, with respect to "the familiar distinction between Ferenczi's emphasis on trauma and Freud's on fantasy in the aetiology of neurosis," that "the two colleagues were not so divergent in their views but developed a contrapuntal duet in their correspondence about these two major strands of experience" (p. 221). Most dismayingly, even Balint (1968), widely believed to have been Ferenczi's foremost champion, effectively functions as Freud's apologist in rendering the colossal misjudgment that, in a "very rare" exception to his normal behavior, Freud became "somewhat insensitive" when he saw Ferenczi "slipping away into the same morass from which he (Freud) could escape only by a supreme effort" (p. 150) when he had repudiated the "seduction" theory in 1897. Indeed, in Balint's view, Ferenczi, "because of his own uncertainty, could not make use of Freud's well-meant and well-founded criticisms; he saw in them only lack of understanding" (p. 152). Allegedly, Ferenczi even "accepted that, in a way, he failed" in his "'grand experiment'" (p. 113), a claim made by Balint notwithstanding the fact that he had been entrusted with the manuscript of the *Clinical Diary* and thus would have known that Ferenczi endorsed Severn's wish for a "recognition of mutual achievement" in the final entry.

The problem with this line of argument is shown by a closer look at the quotation embedded by Haynal and Falzeder in their sentence. It comes from Freud's penultimate letter to Ferenczi, dated January 11, 1933, and it is indeed deeply moving. What Haynal and Falzeder neglect to mention, however, is that Freud goes on to declare: "When I have to conjure this up from memory today, then what remains to me as consolation is only *the certainty that I have contributed especially little to this change*" (Falzeder and Brabant, 2000, p. 446; italics added). Not only does Freud cast this "intimate community of life, feeling, and interest" as a thing of the past, but he insists that he has "contributed especially little" to the rift that has arisen between himself and Ferenczi. Even when he waxes nostalgic, Freud one-sidedly blames Ferenczi for their estrangement and is incapable of imagining that he might have benefited from displaying even a pinch of that "capacity for humility," which, as Ferenczi observed of himself in the *Diary*, he had "developed to an exceptional degree" precisely *"in opposition to Freud."*

In assessing the relationship between Freud and Ferenczi, Balint (1968) portrays himself as a judicious mediator between the "fictitious statements" (p. 149) of Erich Fromm, on the one side, and Jones, on the other. The former is said to describe Freud as "a ruthless autocrat, a dictator," while the latter is said to describe Ferenczi as "a mean, cowardly schemer." According to Balint, however, "all the monstrosities alleged are utterly untrue; what they show up is the difference between the greatness of the victims and the pettiness of their calumniators." But this view of things is seriously misguided, and it reveals Balint to be a trimmer when taking a principled stand is necessary.

Jones, to be sure, *is* a "calumniator," who, in the third volume (1957) of his Freud biography, injected into the psychoanalytic bloodstream the absurd libel that, like Rank, Ferenczi "towards the end of his life developed psychotic manifestations that revealed themselves in, among other ways, a turning away from Freud and his doctrines" (p. 45). Nothing, however, could be further from the truth than what Balint says about Fromm, whose *Sigmund Freud's Mission* (1959) was a necessary corrective to Jones's hagiography and offers the most clear-sighted analysis of Freud's authoritarianism that we have on record.[12] Fromm did with courage and lucidity what Balint spectacularly failed to do with his craven capitulations masquerading as evenhandedness. As early as 1935, only two years after Ferenczi's death and while Freud was still alive, Fromm had the perspicacity to discern that they embodied radically divergent alternatives for the future of psychoanalysis: *"The example of Ferenczi shows . . . that the Freudian attitude need not be that of all analysts"* (p. 163; italics added). There is nothing "untrue" in Fromm's (1959) critique that, whereas Freud "was a loving father to submissive sons," he became "a stern, authoritarian one to those who dared to disagree" (p. 71), or "petty" in his recognition that "the most drastic example of Freud's intolerance and authoritarianism can be found in his relationship to Ferenczi" (p. 68).

Just as it is widely believed that Freud and Ferenczi engaged in a "dialogue," it is no less frequently repeated that Ferenczi's mutual analysis with Severn was a deplorable enactment because it constituted, in Gabbard's words, "a direct exploitation of the patient." If, however, we are prepared to heed Donnel Stern's (2010) profound observation that "enactment can be defined as the interruption of true conversation" (p. xvi), then the conventional wisdom must be reversed. Notwithstanding the turbulence, the relationship between Ferenczi and Severn always remained a "true conversation," because (to quote Steven Stern again) even the "enactments" were part of a "movement toward greater fittedness and complexity"—a movement made possible by Ferenczi's capacity "to *meet* the patient 'in the enactment,'" which permitted them to inch their way toward "greater specificity of recognition and connection."

By the same token, what may appear at first glance to have been the "dialogue" between Freud and Ferenczi was in reality a massive enactment. This may not have been obvious at the outset, when, for example, in a letter to Freud on December 26, 1912, Ferenczi lambastes Jung for a sputtering attempt at what he himself would do full-throttle twenty years later:

> Mutual analysis is nonsense, also an impossibility. Everyone must be prepared to tolerate an authority over himself from whom he accepts

analytic correction. . . . I, too, went through a period of rebellion against your "treatment." Now I have become insightful and realize that you were right in everything.

(Brabant et al., 1993, p. 449)

This supremely ironic passage bears out Fromm's thesis that Freud was a "loving father" only to his "submissive sons," since Ferenczi's claim to have "become insightful" because he had recovered from his "period of rebellion" and could now discern that Freud was "right in everything" is in reality proof of his blindness and a pathetic surrender of his intellectual independence. This docility was the precondition of Ferenczi's association with Freud, and once Ferenczi woke up to how much he had suffered by trying to placate Freud's "intolerance and authoritarianism," Freud metamorphosed into the "ruthless autocrat" and "dictator" whose existence Balint denies.

During Ferenczi's final period, when he was able to see the truth about Freud, their relationship evolved to the point where it was no longer what Donnel Stern (2010) terms a "mutual enactment," but rather one in which, "in the face of one person's enactment, the other person in the interaction manages to respond in a way that recognizes the dissociation without responding from within a dissociation of his own. The analyst who is not caught in a reciprocal enactment is instead able to mentalize his own experience" (pp. 15–16). From the beginning, Ferenczi desired nothing more than a "true conversation" with Freud, but for too long he was caught in the "interpersonalization of dissociation" (p. 14) that Freud demanded from his loyal followers. Only toward the end was Ferenczi able to "recognize the dissociation" emanating from Freud and to emancipate himself from it.[13] Because he always tried to listen and not to respond defensively even to Freud's most unjust criticisms, Ferenczi was able to "mentalize his own experience" and, with Severn's help, to bequeath a new paradigm for psychoanalysis.

One statement by Balint (1968) that is unquestionably true, however, is his memorable pronouncement that "the historic event of the disagreement between Freud and Ferenczi acted as a trauma on the psychoanalytic world" (p. 152). Their conflict was traumatic for the two men personally—although Freud, characteristically, denied that he had been wounded at all—and it became a trauma for the "psychoanalytic world" inasmuch as Ferenczi's contributions were marginalized for more than a half-century, while the name of Severn was effaced altogether from the historical record. In the same way that traumatic experience, as Werner Bohleber (2010) has written, "forms a kind of dissociated foreign body in the psychic-associative network" (p. 127) of an individual, so too trauma theory has functioned as a "dissociated foreign body in the psychic-associative network" of psychoanalysis. This analogy is elaborated by Bennett Simon (1992):

> Virtually from the beginning, one can speak of a "split brain," a mental severing of the metaphoric corpus callosum connecting the two hemispheres of psychoanalytic knowledge. Like the defense victims of incest frequently learn to adopt, psychoanalysis has both known and not known, simultaneously or oscillatingly, about the role of actual incest and the trauma inflicted by an adult.
>
> (p. 962)

In daring to promulgate his trauma theory, and to modify his therapeutic technique accordingly, Ferenczi incurred Freud's wrath and became himself the victim of emotional abuse. Freud, of course, did not know of the existence of the *Clinical Diary*, nor did Ferenczi ever inform him about his analytic odyssey with Severn. In seeking to preserve a zone of privacy for his work with Severn and other trauma victims, Ferenczi exemplifies the truth of Judith Lewis Herman's (1992) observation:

> Many therapists treating survivors elect to withdraw rather than to engage in what feels like fruitless debate. Their practice goes underground. Torn, like their patients, between the official orthodoxy of their profession and the reality of their own experience, they choose to honor the reality at the expense of the orthodoxy. They begin, like their patients, to have a secret life.
>
> (p. 152)

Ferenczi, indeed, went "underground" from Freud and chose to "honor the reality" of his experience with patients when that could not be reconciled with the "official orthodoxy" of psychoanalysis. His first entry to the *Clinical Diary*, "Insensitivity of the analyst," opens with an indictment of "unfeeling and indifferent" (Dupont, 1985, p. 1) analysts—of whom Freud was the prototype—before reflecting on Thompson's having made it publicly known that she felt entitled to kiss him during their analytic sessions, and finally turning to how he had "derived much profit" from his participation in a mutual analysis "in one case."

Since Freud had severely reprimanded Ferenczi for his "kissing technique" only one month earlier, and Severn (1952) specified to Eissler that "it was the last year I was there that I did his analysis" (p. 13), Ferenczi's decision to begin keeping his *Clinical Diary* in January 1932 seems clearly to have been prompted by these converging developments with his two principal patients. The *Diary*, in short, as Bonomi (1999) has insightfully remarked, was Ferenczi's response to the "broken dialogue with Freud" (p. 510). It was, by the same token, the repository of his "secret life," but so also, as we now know, was *The Discovery of the Self*, which took the place of the "scientific mutual publication" that he and Severn had planned to write together.

Even before his differences with Freud started to bubble to the surface in his Oxford Congress paper, when he tried to play the part of the "submissive son" by convincing himself that Freud was "right in everything," their relationship took a great toll on Ferenczi. Indeed, it was structured for two decades by the symbiosis between Freud's "traumatic narcissism" (Shaw, 2014) and Ferenczi's "pathological accommodation" (Brandchaft et al., 2010). This oppression left Ferenczi with a "complex post-traumatic stress disorder" from which he sought to recover with the aid initially of Groddeck, who proved unequal to the task, and ultimately of Severn. According to Herman (1992), who introduced the diagnostic category of complex PTSD, this condition results from "a history of subjection to totalitarian control over a prolonged period," and its symptoms include "explosive or extremely inhibited rage," "compulsive or extremely inhibited sexuality," "amnesia or hypermnesia for traumatic events," "transient dissociative episodes," "preoccupation with relationship with perpetrator," "idealization or paradoxical gratitude," "sense of special or supernatural relationship," and "acceptance of belief system or rationalizations of perpetrator" (p. 121), each of which Ferenczi exhibited in spades. Just as Steven Stern has furnished us with a framework to conceptualize Ferenczi's relationship with Severn, Herman gives us the vocabulary we need to understand the relationship with Freud that was its tragic counterpart. But since the origins of the latter lie in the childhood experiences of both men, what they painfully lived through together should more accurately be described as a retraumatization.

In the three parts of the book that follow, I first examine the "Conceptions" of the story by telling as much as I know about the lives of Elizabeth and Margaret Severn. I offer my reading of Elizabeth's three books, with special attention to both their overt and covert autobiographical elements, including the pivotal case histories in *The Discovery of the Self*, and I delve into the intergenerational transmission of trauma from mother to daughter. In becoming acquainted with Severn, we will have occasion to contemplate her fascination with the occult, which she shared with Ferenczi, and is common in people with traumatic histories. Next, in "Contexts," I begin by setting Severn in the midst of Ferenczi's bevy of female patients in the *Clinical Diary*, notably Thompson and Izette de Forest—who became the main conduits of his legacy in the United States—and then follow many of the branching paths that radiate from that nodal point. Finally, in "Consequences," I set forth the contrast between Freud and Ferenczi as both men and thinkers and make it clear why, like Fromm, I believe Ferenczi's example shows that Freud's attitude need not be that of all analysts.

On a personal level, the choice between Freud and Ferenczi comes down to one between authoritarianism and humanism. During their trip to America in 1909, Freud halted Jung's attempt to interpret one of his dreams (having to do with the love triangle with his wife and sister-in-law) with the fateful words, "I could tell you more, but *I cannot risk my authority*" (qtd. in Billinsky, 1969, p. 42; italics added); and after the onset of his cancer of the palate in 1923, he spurned the entreaties by both Groddeck and Ferenczi that they be permitted to aid him analytically. As Ferenczi wrote to Freud on February 26, 1926, "Perhaps this is the occasion on which I can say to you that *I actually find it tragic that you,* who endowed the world with psychoanalysis, find it so difficult to be—indeed, *are not at all—in a position to entrust yourself to anyone*" (Falzeder and Brabant, 2000, p. 160; italics added).

On the plane of theory, the logical consequence of Freud's stance can be seen in the statement by Peter Fonagy and Mary Target (1997), "There can be *only psychic reality* behind the recovered memories—whether there is historical truth and historical reality is *not our business as psychoanalysts and psychotherapists*" (p. 216; italics added). Ferenczi's position, conversely, subtends Daniel Stern's (1985) conviction that "infants from the beginning *mainly experience reality*," which means that "the usual genetic sequence should be reversed" and "*reality experience precedes fantasy distortions in development*" (p. 12; italics added). This is no mere "contrapuntal duet" but an ontological cleavage with far-reaching clinical repercussions; and it is the thesis of this book that we must return to a model of the mind grounded in trauma and dissociation if psychoanalysis itself is to undergo its own renaissance in the twenty-first century. In the words of Elizabeth Severn, quoted by Margaret in Peter Lipskis's award-winning documentary film *Dance Masks: The World of Margaret Severn* (1981),

"Read until the book that you're reading makes you think. At that point, close the book and think."

Notes

1 The first swallow of the Severn summer came to me in the form of the invitation by Matt Ffytch, editor of *Psychoanalysis and History*, to read the manuscript of a paper by John Boyle (2021), who "sets out to explore the idea of trauma acting as a catalyst for anomalous or 'occult' modes of consciousness through the writing of two of the most important representatives of the Budapest School of Psychoanalysis, namely Sándor Ferenczi (1873–1933) and Elizabeth Severn (1879–1959)" (in press). Boyle characterizes Ferenczi and Severn as "the core nexus of a wider group of analysts within the Budapest School whose collective researches into thought-transference . . . prefigured the subsequent rise in interest regarding the role of intersubjectivity in psychoanalysis."
2 For example, Rachman (2018) refers to Charles Kenneth Heywood as Severn's father (p. 89), when he was in fact Severn's husband; he states that "Freud, as a young man, had worked in Breuer's laboratory" (p. 244), when it was, of course, the laboratory of Ernst Brücke; and in attempting to rectify Masson's (1984) incorrect identification of a 1926 painting by Olga Kovács Dormandi— Judith Dupont's mother and the sister of Michael Balint's first wife Alice—as a portrait of Elizabeth Severn, when it was actually one of Margaret at the age of twenty-five, Rachman (2018) himself mislabels a photograph of it as "Portrait of Mrs. Elizabeth Severn" (p. 103).
3 Ferenczi did engage in extensive self-disclosure both with Thompson and with Alice Lowell, known as "B." in the *Diary* (Brennan, 2015a), and he also admits that he "*would have much preferred* to conduct such mutual analysis" (Dupont, 1985, pp. 44–45; italics added) with Harriot Sigray ("S.I."), but it was only with Severn that Ferenczi lay on the couch, suspended fee payments, and allowed her to analyze him in an ongoing fashion. What Ferenczi did with Severn goes far beyond such fleeting role reversals as took place between Jung and Otto Gross as well as Maria Moltzer, or between Ferenczi and Groddeck, or in the analysis of each other's dreams by Freud, Jung, and Ferenczi during their 1909 trip to America. Although a closer analogue, Groddeck's prolonged treatment of Miss G., about whom he writes in *The Book of the It* (1923), "And now I was confronted with the strange fact that I was not treating the patient, but that the patient was treating me" (p. 223; see Rudnytsky, 2002, pp. 177–79), likewise pales by comparison.

Of utmost interest, however, is the precedent of Trigant Burrow, a cofounder of the American Psychoanalytic Association, who in his paper "The Laboratory Method in Psychoanalysis" (1926), presented at the 1925 Bad Homburg Congress of the International Psychoanalytical Association while he was the president of APsaA, set forth how a challenge from his analysand Clarence Shields led him to accede to a mutual analysis, which in turn impelled Burrow to originate the field of group analysis. When pressed by his patient on "the discrepancy between my theoretical statements regarding our socially common basis of consciousness and the individualistic position which, as an analyst, I continued to maintain," Burrow recounts, "I reluctantly agreed to an arrangement whereby the student should become the analyst and I the analysand" (p. 152). Over time, he continues, the limited success of this innovation "led to a further extension of my experiment, which consisted in the gradual development of a technique involving groups of individuals" where "there was abrogated entirely the distinction between analyst and analysand, each individual automatically becoming both" (pp. 152–53).

In their excellent overview of Burrow's groundbreaking contributions, Pertegato and Pertegato (2013) note that, by 1932, Burrow was extruded from APsaA, although in 1949, "in a sort of belated *mea culpa*," he was awarded "a gold medal, the Abraham A. Brill Memorial Medal" (p. cviii; see p. lxxv). They conclude by comparing the fate of his work—and his career in psychoanalysis—to Ferenczi's:

> Its reappraisal in some ways follows the same path as Ferenczi's thought, rediscovered in these latter years after decades of censorship and now of great topicality besides being essential points of reference. After all, the analogy between these two great men of psychoanalysis, beyond their suffering personal vicissitudes in their relationship with Freud and their experiences with reciprocal analysis, may be traced to the urge to question those aspects of the theories and technical modalities which, instead of being in attunement with life, are the antithesis to it, or restrain it, or mortify it.
>
> (p. cx)

4 For fuller accounts of this episode, see Edmunds (1988), Warner (1994), and Zitrin (2012).
5 In what is at once a verbal and a theoretical "Freudian slip," the English edition of the correspondence between Sigmund Freud and Anna Freud (Meyer-Palmedo, 2006), translated by Nick Somers, turns the meaning of the passage on its head by confusing the words *Traumen* and *Träumen* so that it reads "gross sexual *dreams* [*Träumen*] in childhood" instead of "sexual traumas [*Traumen*]" (p. 386).
6 Ferenczi's experience as a physician treating hospitalized soldiers during World War I constitutes a harbinger of the breakthroughs of his final period. But though he movingly describes the "morbid condition" of these patients as "the affective reactions to certain *psychic traumata*" (1916–17, p. 134), in his contribution to the symposium on war neuroses at the 1918 Budapest Congress he falls in line behind Freud by attempting "to bring the traumatic forms of disorder into the category of psychoanalysis," so that his readers "will be much more easily convinced of the correctness of the sexual theories of the neuroses, and agreement about the sexual background of the war neuroses will follow" (1921b, pp. 16, 18). In a paper that Louis Breger (2000) has described as "clearly the best" (p. 259) in the monograph, by contrast, Ernst Simmel (1921) argues that "the war neurosis, like the peace neurosis, is an expression of a splitting of the personality" (p. 33), and he employs "psycho-catharsis" as a therapeutic technique to treat the "terror and dread of death" in traumatized soldiers that "form the primary basis for the dissociation of the psyche and for the attack-like mastery of the conscious by the unconscious" (pp. 39–40).
7 See my Foreword (Rudnytsky, 2019b) to Craparo et al. (2019), the first collection of essays dedicated to recuperating Janet's legacy for psychoanalysis.

8 On Janet and Fairbairn, see the excellent paper by Davies (1998), and, for psychoanalytic perspectives on multiple personality, Berman (1981). Landmark contributions to the literature on dissociation include Davies and Frawley (1994), Stern (1997), and Howell (2005; Howell and Itzkowitz, 2016).
9 I am indebted here to personal communications from Gabriele Cassullo, as well as to his series of seminal contributions (2014, 2018, 2019a, 2019b) on Janet's relations to Freud, Ferenczi, and object relations theory.
10 In the wake of the volume by Aron and Harris came my coedited collection, *Ferenczi's Turn in Psychoanalysis* (Rudnytsky, Bókay, and Giampieri-Deutsch, 1996), and André Haynal's (2002) monograph restoring Ferenczi to his rightful place in the history of psychoanalysis, in which his coauthored paper with Ernst Falzeder, cited below, is also included.
11 See the informative mappings of these overlapping traditions by Harris (1998) and Bromberg and Aron (2019).
12 On Fromm's unsurpassed anatomy of Freud's authoritarian character, and of the politics of the psychoanalytic movement, see chapters 2 and 3 of my *Formulated Experiences* (Rudnytsky, 2019a).
13 See also Berman (2004a): "Ferenczi apparently had given up on his dialogue with Freud as a springboard for creativity and felt forced to progress on his own" (p. 50).

Part 1

Conceptions

Chapter 1

Traces of a Life

Elizabeth Severn, who became "R.N." in Ferenczi's *Clinical Diary*, was not always Elizabeth Severn. Born on November 17, 1879 in Milwaukee, Wisconsin, she began life as Leota Loretta Brown. In her autobiography, her daughter Margaret Severn (1988) states, "my parents came from the Chicago area" (p. 1), and baby and child photographs of Leota taken in a Chicago studio are preserved in the Severn Archives in the Library of Congress. Leota's father, Marcus M. Brown (b. December 31, 1854, Batavia, IL–d. May 12, 1909, Cleveland, OH), was a successful attorney. His marriage to her mother, Harriet ("Mattie") Maria Mann (b. August 26, 1856, Elgin, IL–d. 1956, Batavia, IL), took place in Batavia on April 8, 1876. Although this was Harriet's second marriage, her tombstone, surprisingly, carries the inscription Harriet Mann Armstrong, the surname being that of her first husband, Robert Armstrong, who was born in Scotland on November 15, 1841. Leota was Marcus and Harriet Brown's only child.

At the age of eighteen, Leota Brown married Charles Kenneth Heywood (b. February 14, 1876, Carter, TN–d. February 2, 1945, Johnson City, TN) in Chicago on August 15, 1898. The 1900 census lists Charles Heywood as residing in Chicago with Leota's mother, identified as a "teacher" and "widow," although Marcus Brown did not die until 1909. Presumably, Leota was living there as well. From the evidence, as it emerges from Severn's analysis with Ferenczi, that Marcus Brown perpetrated horrific acts of sexual and physical abuse on his daughter, I would conjecture that this led Harriet to consider him, too, as "dead" to her and eventually to revert to the name of her literally deceased first husband, which she then preserved on her tombstone.

Charles and Leota's only child, Margaret Harvey Heywood, was born in Birmingham, Alabama, on August 14, 1901. In what turns out to have been a tragic irony, her middle name was given in honor of her paternal

DOI: 10.4324/9781315280134-3

grandfather, Harvey S. Heywood. Margaret (1988) recounts that her parents "had been lured south by the promise of a position for my father as an accountant," but "apparently this did not work out well for within a year they returned to Illinois with me and our two cats" (p. 1). She adds, "I adored my mother but had a strong feeling of dislike for my father." When her parents were first married, Margaret believes, "they were very romantically in love, but by the time I was four years old they had decided to separate" (p. 2). During a family meeting in Chicago, Margaret hid under an "ugly maple table" as she heard her mother "arguing violently" with her father and her Uncle Harry and Aunt Rose about who was to have custody of the child. The Heywoods promised Leota that the discussion would be continued on the following day, so she left Harry's home where the meeting was taking place, but early in the morning Margaret's father returned and "whisked me away to the home of his parents in Wayne, Michigan" (p. 3). After this abduction in 1905, Margaret continues, "I did not see my mother for two years," and "I never saw my father again." Charles Heywood became the auditor and assistant manager of the Whiting Manufacturing Company, a lumber business, and subsequently married Hattie Moore, with whom he had four children.

What befell Margaret—who was told that her mother was "very ill" and thought she must be dead, causing her to want "to die myself in order to be with her" (p. 5)—during the time she spent with her grandparents in Wayne will be revealed in Chapter 6. For her part, the desolate Leota remained in Chicago, where she "attended what must have been a very remarkable though short period of study with a certain Dr. Levitt," whose "system was similar to what today might be called 'Positive Thinking' with a Theosophical turn added to it, but at that time it was known as 'New Thought'" (pp. 12–13). New Thought was based on the teachings of the mesmerist and inventor Phineas Quimby, the mentor of Mary Baker Eddy, who founded Christian Science. The "Dr. Levitt" instanced by Margaret was C. Franklin Leavitt, M.D., possessed of a piercing gaze and the author of treatises promoting his own brand of New Thought, including *Leavitt-science: the Power-Path to Mental and Physical Poise and Achievement* (1900) and *Mental and Physical Ease and Supremacy; Being a Practical Adaptation of Leavitt-science to Individual Use* (1914).[1] The experience with Leavitt "seems to have changed the course of her life," and from it Leota "gained the courage and self-confidence" that "enabled her, despite her own ill health" (p. 13), which was, in fact, a severe breakdown following the collapse of her marriage and the kidnapping of her daughter, to begin to believe that she might be of aid and comfort to others. As Leota wrote to her mother in Denver on April 18, 1907, "I am going to work now to become a healer myself. There is no question but that I have the power" (qtd. in Fortune, 1993, p. 104).

Leota's recovery also enabled her, in Margaret's (1988) words, "to rescue me from the Wayne situation and take the daring risk of a long train ride across the continent, where my father would be unlikely to find us" (p. 13). One day, as she was eating a jelly sandwich in the yard of a neighbor near her school, Margaret "heard the most beautiful sound I have ever heard in my whole life. It was the voice of my mother calling, 'Hoo, hoo!'" (p. 9). Fighting fire with fire, Leota, "so thin and pale that she looked more like an apparition than a living person," after embracing her daughter, said, "'Come quickly,'" quelling the protests of Margaret's caretaker with the outcry, "'I am her mother. Tell them they will never get her away from me again!'" (pp. 9–10). In a rescue operation that was also a retaliatory abduction, Leota and her still-very-young daughter boarded a train to Chicago, where they changed for another one that "transported us to a far city—San Antonio, Texas—and a new life" (p. 10).

Upon their arrival in San Antonio, Leota, "down to her last ten dollars, found a job, going from house to house trying to sell encyclopedias" (p. 12). When she realized from her conversations with prospective customers that "the last thing in the world they had need of was an encyclopedia," Leota instead "discussed with them their lives and their problems," selling few books but putting into practice the resolution in her letter to her mother. Every week, Leota scrimped to save fifty cents to have her knee-length hair washed at a beauty parlor. When a favored client became indignant because a masseuse had failed to keep her appointment, the slightly built Leota surprised the assembled company by volunteering to give the heavy-set woman the massage herself. So pleased was the woman that she returned the next day for another massage, bringing her friends. "In addition to having the magic touch of a natural healer," Margaret observes, her mother "had had training in philosophy and psychology at the University of Chicago," though without taking a degree of any kind.

Having mustered the courage to reclaim her daughter and begin life anew in San Antonio, Leota, by going door to door as an encyclopedia saleswoman and then by discovering her gifts as a "natural healer" at the beauty parlor, where she "combined her physical treatments with suggestion and mental affirmations," gained a measure of economic independence, as a consequence of which she "engaged a room in a hotel where she could see her patients" (p. 13), thereby setting herself up in private practice for the first time. Although Margaret had already expressed her emotions through dance while still in her grandparents' custody in Wayne, she "determined immediately" to become a professional dancer in San Antonio after beholding a "skirt dancer" (p. 14) in a vaudeville performance. "Incidentally," Margaret adds, "this decision was fortified by a certain Professor Dahl, a mystic with whom my mother was continuing her music studies, having had to abandon these at the time of her marriage." This "Professor Dahl" turns out to have been a figure of historical importance, since Nikolai Dahl (1860–1939) was a Russian physician and psychologist, as well as a viola player, who is reported not only to have read Charcot's works but to have trained with him in Paris. In 1900, Dahl treated Sergei Rachmaninov using suggestion and hypnotherapy after the composer suffered a breakdown and a creative block due to the disastrous reception of his Symphony No. 1 (1897), in gratitude for which Rachmaninov dedicated his Piano Concerto No. 2 (1901) to Dahl. How this Russian, who emigrated from Moscow to Beirut in 1925, came to be in San Antonio is a mystery, but as Margaret and her mother had the satisfaction of verifying years later, Dahl was not boasting when he told Leota that "he had been instrumental in helping Rachmaninov overcome the extreme depression which had enveloped him when one of his early compositions met with disheartening failure."

Although Margaret describes Dahl as a "mystic," through her musical studies with a follower of Charcot's Leota Brown Heywood had come into contact with the world of European depth psychology, and this period in San Antonio, building on her empowerment by Leavitt in Chicago, marks the second stage in her journey of self-discovery that would take her to Budapest and Ferenczi. It was in San Antonio that Leota "obtained a divorce and a legal change of name, so we could really feel safe and say good-bye to the past forever" (p. 20). Why she chose the name Elizabeth Severn has never been conclusively explained, though Elizabeth has regal connotations and Rachman (2018) has surmised that her surname "was taken from the river Severn" (p. 90), the longest in Britain, running for 220 miles from its source in the mountains of Wales through Shrewsbury, before flowing into the Severn Estuary and the Bristol Channel.[2] Whereas the name of the river is pronounced with an emphasis on the first syllable, *Sev*ern, Elizabeth's surname should be pronounced Sev*ern*, as is confirmed by the fact that it was misspelled "Severne" in the typescript of her interview with Eissler, before Severn (in one of her meticulous handwritten corrections) crossed out the last letter. Whatever its determinants, Margaret's references to feeling safe and saying goodbye to the past make it clear that Severn's act of self-creation was spurred by the desire to render her and her daughter more difficult to track down by her estranged husband should he ever take it into his head to come after them.

By 1911, Severn had grown "tired of the Texas climate and longed for the mountains that she loved. So we again boarded a train and set out for Colorado, where her mother was living" (p. 20). Being unhappy at a Montessori boarding school in Boulder, Margaret moved in with her grandmother Mattie, whom she called "Amma," in Denver, while Elizabeth "occupied a suite at the Brown Palace Hotel in the center of town, where she pursued her work as usual." Both in San Antonio and in Denver, and thereafter in Washington, D.C., where she and Margaret also resided briefly, Severn made herself known by giving public lectures and represented herself variously as a "Metaphysician and Healer," "Metaphysician and Psychologist," and "Teacher and Healer." As Margaret recollects:

> She had a very charismatic personality and was an excellent speaker so there was no difficulty in attracting patients or in keeping them, because she was always able to help and heal them. People found her to be an inspiration and felt better for just coming into her presence. She accepted only a limited number at a time as she preferred to concentrate with great intensity on the particular problems of each individual.

In 1912, while in Washington, she obtained a passport under the name of Elizabeth Severn. Emulating her mother, Severn designated herself a "widow," even though her husband was still living. In another fabrication that might be viewed as a symptom of the problems addressed two years earlier in the Flexner Report, which successfully sought to compel medical schools in the United States to adhere to the norms of natural science in their teaching and research—and to stigmatize as quackery or charlatanism alternative practices that ignored or rejected these evidence-based protocols—Severn's passport listed her occupation as "physician," notwithstanding her lack of medical qualifications or, for that matter, a formal degree of any kind; and she had no compunctions about arrogating to herself the title of "Dr." for the rest of her life. Reflecting the emerging fault lines in the medical profession, Margaret states from her retrospective vantage point in the 1980s, "at that time there were some doctors who probably considered my mother a quack, but fortunately there were also some who did support her methods," and "I have often had to giggle as the years passed by and I read certain pronouncements by the A.M.A. or other medical societies, about their wonderful discoveries regarding the relationship of disease, and, more recently, even organic disease, to the mental and emotional state of the patient" (p. 23), since these insights had been anticipated by her mother in her first book, *Psycho-Therapy: Its Doctrine and Practice*, published in London by William Rider and Son as part of its Christmas list in 1913.

Severn's decision to set sail for England in 1912 was prompted not only by her own professional aspirations but also by the desire to further Margaret's training as a dancer. For a time, the itinerant pair rented "a very old and romantic looking dwelling called Stone Cottage" (p. 30) near the town of Epsom, in Surrey. Their delight in this residence was, however, tempered by the fact that "my mother was always taken ill when she sat in the dining room," a phenomenon that became explicable when they learned that the ancient pile "had once been used as an insane asylum, and this particular room had been the place where the most violently demented persons were confined." As Severn was "always ultra-sensitive to thought waves," she "was apparently overwhelmed by the vibrations of pain, fear, and grief which had clung to the spot," so they decamped and came to London by the end of the year. Severn's susceptibility to being haunted by the sufferings of the previous inmates of Stone Cottage is glossed by the parapsychological researcher and maverick psychoanalyst Nandor Fodor, with whom she would subsequently form an important relationship. As Fodor remarked in an interview he gave shortly before his death in 1964:

> It seems as if emotion, if it has been very deep—anguish, particularly—leaves an impression in the house where it is endured. And if somebody is in a disturbed mental condition, it is possible that somehow an attuning takes place, and as if on a screen—by a kind of etheric television—suddenly a scene from the past becomes visible.[3]
>
> (Spraggett, 1969. p. 133)

Once ensconced in London, Severn began firing on all cylinders. In addition to being elected Honorary Vice President of the Alchemical Society, she came into contact with an array of groups, including the London Psycho-Therapeutic Society, the Higher Thought Centre, the Psycho-Medical Society, and the Society for Psychical Research, which cumulatively had a transformative effect on her intellectual development.[4] The London Psycho-Therapeutic Society (LPTS), founded in 1901 by the journalist

Arthur Hallam, aimed, in Philip Kuhn's words, "to offer free psychotherapeutic treatments to anybody who needed help, and those treatments, which were offered by volunteers, included various aspects or types of psychical and spiritual healing." Hallam was also the founding editor of *The Psychotherapeutic Journal*, subsequently renamed *The Health Record*. There it is documented that Severn lectured at the LPTS first in the spring of 1913 on "Colours and Their Meaning" and then in November on "Mental States in Relation to the Cause and Cure of Disease." The account of the first lecture reports that "Dr. Severn stated at the beginning that this was only one small phase of a very large subject"—one explored at greater length in her book—and that "there are many methods of treating the body through the mind, both directly through the spoken word and indirectly through telepathy in the subconsciousness" (*Health Record*, 1913a, p. 46; see also 1913b). Relying as it does on the "theory of vibration," the unsigned notice in *The Health Record* continues, Severn's "use of colour as a therapeutic agent" blends the findings of "physical scientists" with the occult, and it calls upon "the healer's ability to mentally visualize the patient surrounded by the colour vibration which he, because of illness or some abnormality, lacks."

As Kuhn has pointed out, although there is "no evidence that Severn was anything other than one of the speakers in Hallam's series, it is not inconceivable that she might have volunteered, for a time, as one of their psychotherapists." Also worth noting, given Severn's reference to Hindu philosophy in *Psycho-Therapy* (1913) as one of the sources of "the modern system of Mind-Cure, and much of the New Thought philosophy which goes with it" (p. 135), is that, again according to Kuhn, "Dr. C. Metha of the Mendip Hills Sanatorium lectured on Hindu Medicine around the same time as Severn delivered her lectures."

Founded in 1900 and later run by the American Orlando Edgar Miller, who was briefly imprisoned for manslaughter in 1914, the Higher Thought Centre was another venue of Severn's activities. As early as December 1912, she lectured there on "The Higher Thought in Practice" and again in February 1913 on "The Faults of Women" (*Daily Herald*, 1912, 1913). Reprising her talks at the LPTS, Severn, who is described as "a well-known exponent of psycho-therapeutics," gave three more lectures in August 1913 as part of the Centre's Summer School on "Mental Causes of Disease," "What Mental Healing is—How it is done," and "Colours and their Meaning" (*Mastery*, 1914, p. 46). Kuhn deems it "quite possible" that Miller "was inspired by the work of Hallam and the LPTS," and he highlights the similarities between the two organizations, "not least that both attached journals and lecture series to their work of healing."

In 1912, both Freud and Ferenczi were elected Honorary Members of the Society for Psychical Research (SPR), which had been founded in 1882 by a committee that included Frederic Myers, who became its president in 1900. Another leading figure in the SPR was T. W. Mitchell, who was also president of the Psycho-Medical Society (PMS). The PMS, according to Kuhn, "was founded in 1906 by a group of medical practitioners who were particularly interested in the treatment of disease by hypnotic suggestion," and it was set up "as a direct counter to the (unorthodox) growth of the LPTS, which they saw as a serious threat." Mitchell, "who discovered the works of Freud probably sometime in early 1910," was by 1911 "actively discussing and promoting Freud's work in the SPR journal." In *Psycho-Therapy* (1913), Severn avows that the phenomenon of "mental telepathy, which has been so authoritatively established as a fact and carefully tabulated in the annals of the Psychical Research Society," warrants the conclusion that "suggestion and all forms of mental treatment are based on the great law of the transmission of thought" (p. 34), so we know that she was aware of this distinguished body, which served as a conduit for her first encounter with psychoanalysis.

Since she personified the unorthodox tendencies that the Psycho-Medical Society sought to keep in check, it is not surprising that Severn would not have been invited to hold forth under its auspices, as she was by both the Psycho-Therapeutic Society and the Higher Thought Centre. But, as Kuhn remarks, Mitchell, "as President of the PMS, along with his deputy Douglas Bryan, who subsequently became a staunch right-hand man for Ernest Jones, organised a series of monthly lectures which were open to the public," which, in December 1912, featured a reading of Ferenczi's "The Psychoanalysis of Suggestion and Hypnosis," published in an English translation in *Transactions of the Psycho-Medical Society*, while the ensuing meeting, in January 1913, was devoted to a discussion of Ferenczi's paper.[5] Although there is no proof that Severn attended these meetings, we know that she was in London by December 1912, and the topic was one in which she would have been keenly interested. It is therefore not far-fetched to imagine that Severn first became aware of Ferenczi—who, in one of his earliest scientific papers, "Spiritism" (1899), had urged skeptics not to "shrink from sitting down at the moving table or from visiting spiritistic gatherings of lay people," and affirmed that "the alchemic gold, the hidden treasure of the spiritist may bring us a rich harvest, beyond anticipation in a little cultivated field of science, the psychology of the human mind" (p. 143)—during her initial sojourn in London.

The assassination of Archduke Franz Ferdinand, heir to the Habsburg throne, by the Serbian nationalist Gavrilo Princip on June 28, 1914 led one month later to the outbreak of World War I, which prompted Severn to return to the United States. By combing the nautical records, Kuhn has established that Severn left London for New York on September 26, 1914, aboard the SS Minnetonka, operated by the Atlantic Transport Line, where she appeared on the passenger manifest as "Elizabeth Severn, 34, Doctoress," accompanied by "Margaret Severn, aged 13."

Despite the upward trajectory of her career and the success of her first book, while in New York, as Margaret told Fortune (1993) many decades later, Severn "suffered chronic, often debilitating, psychological and physical symptoms—including confusion, hallucinations, nightmares and severe depression, which often left her suicidal" (p. 104). Nancy Smith (1998) has accounted for Severn's deterioration by the hypothesis that, whereas "she seemed to thrive" in London, the return to America "might have triggered old internal conflicts" (p. 243). Having imbibed psychoanalysis while abroad, it was natural that she should now seek psychoanalytic therapy. In her interview with Eissler, Severn (1952) reveals that she had "attempted analysis with at least three men" in New York, Smith Ely Jelliffe, Joseph Asch, and Otto Rank, the latter two of whom "had been pupils of Freud" (p. 3). Rank was never analyzed by Freud (or anyone else), but Asch, a urologist and member of the New York Psychoanalytic Society, was in analysis with Freud in 1922 (Falzeder, 1998, pp. 86–87). In a letter to Karl Abraham on May 4, 1924, Freud calls Asch's analysis "the most miserable you can imagine" and belittles him personally as "a pathological fool" who is "without any trace of understanding." Freud does, however, "say in his favour" that Asch "is a very kind-hearted helpful person—because of inhibited sexual aggression—and therefore much loved" (Falzeder, 2002, pp. 501–2).

That this analysis was a disappointment also from Asch's perspective is corroborated by Severn's (1952) admission to Eissler that whereas she "got absolutely nowhere" (p. 4) with either Jelliffe or Rank, Asch was "a very nice fellow" who had told her that Freud "was a great man but that he hadn't understood him" (p. 11) and his analysis "was incomplete" (p. 3). Severn does not say when her analyses with Jelliffe and Asch took place, but since she confirms that Jelliffe was her first analyst, and we know that Asch was in analysis with Freud in 1922, she presumably must have seen Asch after that date in order to have learned his opinion of Freud. She can, therefore, only be drawing on her treatment with Jelliffe when she writes about psychoanalysis in her second book, *The Psychology of Behaviour: A Practical Study of Human Personality and Conduct*, which was published by Dodd, Mead and Company in 1917, three years after she arrived in New York.

Just as Severn had found herself immersed in the psychoanalytic ferment of London, she caught the same cresting wave in New York. Although Severn did not mingle with the "movers and shakers" who flocked to the salons at 23 Fifth Avenue over which Mabel Dodge (who in 1923 became Mabel Dodge Luhan) presided from 1913 to 1917, and where, at one historic evening in 1915, as Patricia Everett (2016) has chronicled, "A. A. Brill spoke about Freudian theory, thereby providing her guests with their first glimpse of psychoanalysis" (p. 45), there is a striking synchrony between Dodge's and Severn's forays into this brave new world. Dodge's analysis with Jelliffe began on January 3, 1916 and ended (apart from a valedictory session in October) on June 7, when, while Jelliffe was on vacation, she reached out to Brill, with whom she remained in an intermittent analytic relationship until 1938 (pp. 181–88). Severn arrived in New York on the Minnetonka at the end of September 1914, while her book came out in 1917, from which it follows that her analysis with Jelliffe took place in 1915 or 1916, almost or exactly contemporaneously with that of Dodge.

Even more striking than this simultaneity is the concurrence between the testimonies of these two gifted women concerning their experiences with Jelliffe. In her interview with Eissler, Severn (1952) describes him as "very sadistic," though also an "able man, intellectually" (p. 4), a judgment foreshadowed in *The Psychology of Behaviour* (1917), in which, without mentioning Jelliffe by name, she compares the "operation" performed "by the average present-day Psycho-analyst," who fails to provide a "careful synthesis" of the dissected elements of the mind, to "having a surgical process for the removal of a tumour without any succeeding medical care for the upbuilding of the weakened constitution" (p. 258). For her part, Dodge voiced her discontent directly to Jelliffe in a May 1916 letter:

> I think your dogmatic trend halts me! I don't feel your right to prescribe a philosophy & that is really what it comes to! It seems to me we should work together to remove obstacles which impede a free flow of energy but I *don't* believe it comes within the realm of psychoanalysis to impose a formula for thinking, or a set of symbols which you arbitrarily designate in consistency with your particular constitution.
>
> (Everett, 2021, p. 218)

Both Dodge's desire to "work together to remove obstacles" as well as her objection to Jelliffe's tendency "to impose a formula for thinking" are in Severn's spirit. Although Jelliffe, to his credit, responded with a paradoxical apology, "I am sorry you feel I dogmatize. I myself am dogmatic that I have no right to do so" (p. 219), both Severn and Dodge felt him to lack empathy and evidently discontinued their treatments for that reason.

With respect to Rank, to whom she turned with high hopes when he came to New York "with a flair and a lot of noise, and the publicity that he was *the* most brilliant student of Freud's," Severn (1952) told Eissler that she "had his regular three-month course" of analysis in 1924. To her dismay, however, Rank showed himself to be "completely wrapped up in the one idea of the birth trauma, and incapable of thinking of anything else," promulgating the "extraordinary theory" that, "if you could recall the feelings of being born, every subsequent difficulty in your life would be eliminated" (pp. 4–5). Consequently, Severn judged both Rank and Jelliffe to be "very one-sided" men, from whom she "learned their theories, but their application of them was most unsatisfactory." In a state of desperation after this latest disillusionment, Severn resolved to uproot herself from New York and move to Budapest, with several of her own patients in tow, in order to stake everything on an analysis with Ferenczi.[6]

A persistent confusion about the starting date of Severn's analysis with Ferenczi has been sown by Fortune's (1993) assertions in his first paper that she "stepped off the train" in Budapest "late in the summer of 1924" (p. 101) and commenced the analysis "in the fall of 1924" (p. 105). Although Fortune's error was understandable at a time when the sources that have since become available were unknown, it is harder to explain why he should persist in the misconception that Severn was in treatment with Ferenczi "between the years of 1924 and 1933" (2015, p. 25). To begin with, Severn (1952) declares in her interview with Eissler, "I first went to Budapest in 1925" (p. 1), adding (in another of her handwritten corrections of the typescript) that she had been there "nearly 8 years" when she left "early in'33," which she recalls as having been "two months" (p. 9) before Ferenczi's death. What is more, Ferenczi first mentions Severn in his correspondence with Freud on Easter Sunday 1925, which fell on April 11, and he does so again a week later. Without naming her, he writes in the earlier letter, "Chance had it that for some time I have been treating a patient whom Rank analyzed in America, so that I was now able to catch glimpses of his technique" (Falzeder and Brabant, 2000, p. 211); and he reiterates the same point on April 18. Thus, Ferenczi, who, as Severn (1952) told

Eissler, "was sorry that he had written a book" (p. 4) with Rank—that is, *The Development of Psycho-Analysis*—saw in her arrival an opportunity to prove his fealty to Freud by reporting on the missteps of his erstwhile collaborator.

What Ferenczi meant by telling Freud on April 11, 1925 that he had been treating this ex-patient of Rank's "for some time" would, however, be impossible to determine exactly were it not for a third piece of evidence concerning the debut of Severn's analysis. Among Margaret Severn's (1988) letters to her mother in *Spotlight* is one from Chicago dated April 2, 1925, in which she writes, "I am a trifle worried at having no cable message from you since your arrival in Budapest" (p. 949), which establishes that she must have crossed Ferenczi's threshold by the end of March or, at the latest, the beginning of April 1925.[7]

From the fall of 1926 to the spring of 1927, Ferenczi, who in 1909 had accompanied Freud and Jung on the expedition to Clark University, came for the second time to the United States, primarily to lecture at the New School for Social Research in New York City, but also at other venues in New York, Washington, D.C., and Philadelphia. There is no reason to doubt Severn's (1952) assertion that she "helped to arrange" (p. 8) Ferenczi's trip, and among his American analysands was Joseph Asch (Falzeder, 2002, p. 91), who evidently sought out Ferenczi to address what had been left undone in his analysis with Freud. Severn had herself turned to Ferenczi because of the insufficiency of her three prior analyses, and it compounds the irony of the situation that, as she told Eissler, in the course of her prolonged analysis with Ferenczi she "gradually got the feeling that he was hampered in spite of a very brilliant mind and a very responsive personality . . . by the lack of a complete analysis in his own case" (1952, p. 2)—namely, with Freud—which culminated in his consenting to take the plunge into mutual analysis with her.

Margaret Severn's autobiography (1988) allows us to pinpoint Elizabeth's farewell to Budapest even more precisely than her arrival, since Margaret wrote from Paris on February 24, 1933 that she would meet her mother's train on Wednesday, March 1, at 9:40 a.m. (pp. 2,430–31). According to Fortune (1993), Severn was again in a state of "emotional and physical collapse" (p. 112), but by June 14, the date of Margaret's next letter, she had established herself anew in London, where she resumed her clinical practice and an energetic round of writing and lecturing activities. While in London, as Brennan (2015b) has documented, Severn on July 16, 1934 participated in a séance with Margaret Naumburg, which likely took place under the auspices of the International Institute for Psychical Research, of which Severn had been a member since its founding in that same year (Summerscale, 2020, p. 107). Naumburg was a pioneer of art therapy who in 1915 had opened the Walden School in New York City.[8] In *The Discovery of the Self* (1933), Severn reports that, in doing therapy with a boy of nine, she connected with her young patient by "encouraging him to draw pictures" (p. 100). That she continued to employ this modality with children was movingly attested by the Boston architect James V. Righter, who, at the 2015 conference of the Ferenczi Society in Toronto, showed slides of the drawings he had made during his analysis as a teenager with Severn in New York from August 1951 to January 1953.[9]

The remainder of the 1930s saw Severn shuttle between England and the United States. Two articles from the *Cincinnati Enquirer*, dated April 29 and May 10, 1934, herald and then report on her lecture, "The Psycho-Analysis of Today," attended by more than 500 people. The first article states incorrectly not only that she was born in Chicago but also that she took a Ph.D. in that city. But these errors or confabulations do not invalidate the tribute to Severn in the second article as having enjoyed a "long and distinguished scientific experience as a practitioner of psychoanalysis." Significantly, Severn disclosed in her lecture that she had analyzed her daughter, and that a wrong "pattern" had begun with Margaret's weaning. As is common knowledge today, many far more famous analysts, including Freud, Jung, Abraham, and Klein, also treated their own children (Bromberg and Aron, 2019, pp. 699–700), but only Severn had the courage publicly to disclose what she had done.

Without referring to Ferenczi, Severn in 1937 delivered two lectures to the Practical Psychology Club in London, "What Is a Psychic Injury?" (1937b) and "Mental Catharsis: A Means of Cure" (1937a), in which she summarized in plain language their joint rehabilitation of Freud's pre-1897 "seduction" theory and concomitant modifications of psychoanalytic technique. In the first, Severn (1937b) distinguishes between "psychic injuries in the nature of specific shocks" and those resulting from "a generally disturbing or unfavorable environment," arguing that when there has been an injury "of the 'shock' kind, the only thing that will help it is a deep analytic process," which she compares "to what the medical man would do if he found certain symptoms of serious internal illnesses, we will say something like tumour" (pp. 14–16). In the second, Severn (1937a) contends that "depressed states, morbid anxieties, and fears of illness and incapacities . . . come to us almost entirely from the early impressions received by the child" when "the emotional conflicts of the parents vitiate the atmosphere" (p. 11). Decades before Winnicott (1960) proclaimed that "there is no such thing as an infant" (p. 39*n*1), she grasped this axiom of object relations theory when she said in the question-and-answer period, "analytically one feels that one is working with the environment almost more than with the patient" (1937a, p. 17).

Just as she had left London for New York at the start of World War I, so, as she informed Eissler, Severn (1952) again moved back to New York in 1939 "before the war began" (p. 11). Margaret (1988) reports that she and her mother shared an apartment "on East Eighty-sixth Street close to Park Avenue" (p. 3,098), where Severn lived and worked for her final two decades. In addition to her three published books, her archive contains three unpublished manuscripts, *65 Degrees of Psychological and Mental Healing* (n.d.a), *An Analysis of Love and Sex: A Psychological Study of Love, Sex and Marriage, with some Counsel to Lovers* (n.d.b), and *Crystals* (1921?), an autobiographical novel, which Rachman (2018) asserts is "based on her involvement with Leon Dabo" (p. 92), a French-born American artist (1864–1960), some half-dozen of whose paintings hung in Margaret's apartment in Vancouver.[10] Margaret (1988) was convinced that her mother "became a victim of the 'Strontium 90' which was said to pervade the air as a result of A-Bomb tests" (p. 3,098). Leota Loretta Brown Heywood vanished into the ether long ago, while R.N. has gained a new lease on life as Ferenczi's patient, but Elizabeth Severn died of leukemia on February 11, 1959, at the age of seventy-nine, three years after her centenarian mother.

Notes

1 I am grateful to personal communications from Kathleen Meigs for information concerning Franklin Leavitt and Nikolai Dahl, mentioned below.
2 In a personal communication, Simon Partridge has further enlightened me: "The name 'Severn' is thought to derive from a Celtic original name *sabrinnâ*, of uncertain meaning. That name then developed in different languages to become Sabrina to the Romans, Hafren in Welsh, and Severn in English. A folk etymology later developed, deriving the name from a mythical story of a nymph, Sabrina, who drowned in the river. . . . The story of Sabrina is featured in Milton's *Comus*. There is a statue of 'Sabrina' in the Dingle Gardens at the Quarry, Shrewsbury." This story goes back to Geoffrey of Monmouth's twelfth-century *History of the Kings of Britain*, where the Severn is hailed, alongside the Thames and the Humber, as one of the "three noble rivers" of Britain (1999, p. 3; see p. 25). It is retold by Spenser when Prince Arthur reads *Briton moniments* in Book II, canto x, of *The Faerie Queene*;

and with many other rivers the "stately Severne" also attends the marriage of the Thames and the Medway in Book IV, canto xi. Drawing on Holinshed, Shakespeare refers to the Severn several times in *1 Henry IV*, most notably in Act III, scene i, where it is one of the boundaries demarcating the territory to be divided among the rebels Mortimer, Glendower, and Hotspur, whose hopes are crushed by Prince Hal's victory in the Battle of Shrewsbury.

3 I am indebted to John Boyle for putting me on Fodor's trail and, directly or indirectly, for all my references to Fodor throughout this book.

4 In what follows I rely on the research and scholarship of Philip Kuhn. Kuhn mentions Severn briefly in his book, *Psychoanalysis in Britain, 1893–1913* (2017), but I shall be quoting from a personal communication in which he has generously supplied me with copies of all the primary sources.

5 The paper appears in the current English edition of Ferenczi's works with the title "Suggestion and Psycho-Analysis" (1912b).

6 See Ferenczi's letter reproduced as the frontispiece to this book, which shows that Severn must have written to him sometime before March 6, 1925.

7 As the frontispieces to his book, Rachman (2018) reproduces the handwritten dedication in a copy of *The Psychology of Behaviour*, which Severn gave to Ferenczi, dated July 9, 1925, as well as the inscribed photograph of himself, which Ferenczi gave to Severn, dated December 1925.

8 Ferenczi (1927a) mentions that during his recent trip to America he "had the opportunity of studying the methods" of the Walden School, "which is run by psycho-analytically trained and mostly psycho-analysed teachers" (p. 69), so he would undoubtedly have met Naumburg at that time, as Severn very likely did herself.

9 I am grateful to Olga Umansky for informing me that 144 of Righter's drawings are now deposited in the Severn Archives in the Library of Congress.

10 According to Lipskis (2018), the paintings were originally given by Dabo to Elizabeth Severn about 1916, and "one of them that Margaret had above her piano turns out to be a long-lost major American masterpiece from the 1913 Armoury Show 'Canadian Night'" (p. 116). A biographical sketch of Dabo—and many of his paintings—can be seen on the website of Stillwell House Antiques, Red Bank, New Jersey.

Chapter 2

The Metaphysical Calling

Noting that the Practical Psychology Club has a "Problem Evening on the program," Severn begins her first lecture, "What Is a Psychic Injury" (1937b), by observing that "anybody interested enough in psychology to study it must have a problem" and that she hopes her London audience will be able to follow what she has to say "about a particular point of view in psychology, which arises specifically through psychoanalysis" (p. 1). Although her hearers could have had no idea of the depths of her agonies, Severn evidently means to include herself among those whose professional interest in psychology originates in the need to solve a personal "problem," and she steps forth unabashedly as a champion of psychoanalysis.

In tracing the arc of Severn's development through a reading of her three published books, beginning with *Psycho-Therapy: Its Doctrine and Practice*, my emphasis will be on the interplay of autobiography and theory. I shall argue that the subjective elements of Severn's writing are both manifest and latent, so that along with many explicit self-references there is an undercurrent of even more revealing veiled confessions, culminating in the disguised case histories of Ferenczi, herself, and Margaret in *The Discovery of the Self*. The years spent by Severn in three of the urban centers in which psychoanalysis took root in the first decades of the twentieth century—New York, London, and Budapest—as well as her experience as a patient with four eminent analysts, are enough to call into question the received impression of her work as naive and amateurish. It is, on the contrary, the oeuvre of a self-taught genius who forged a synthesis of mysticism and science the brilliance of which we are only now beginning to appreciate.

The autobiographical dimension of *Psycho-Therapy* (1913) is evident from the outset when Severn writes: "Everything that I shall postulate in this book has grown out of my personal experience as a healer and teacher, and is presented as the best working hypothesis I am able to obtain at the present time for a new and as yet little-known science" (p. 3). Severn addresses the reader with a voice of authority, as someone who (as we have seen) was regarded as "a well-known exponent of psycho-therapeutics," and she does so again in the preface to the 1914 second edition, where she refers to "those who are brought under my care, as patients or as pupils" (p. vii). Severn's renown as a "healer and teacher" is attested both by the "welcome which this record of my work has received at the hands of the general press" (p. v) and by the letters she garnered from admirers as far away as San Francisco and Australia. Lavinia Cole Cook, of Albany, New York, for example, wrote on November 21, 1918 that it "is just the sort of book for which I have been seeking in vain," while Fred Smith, a former mayor of Cape Town, South Africa, concluded on April 14, 1918, "With deep appreciation and a sense of gratitude for the great help you have already given me in your splendid works, and praying that you may continue to be a great blessing to humanity." As Margaret (1988) recalls, "This book was very warmly received and letters from readers continued to arrive throughout the years," though she adds that when she questioned her mother about her first foray into print "a short time before her death, she gave me the impression that she would no longer uphold all of the statements therein. She said, 'It's not so simple'" (p. 24).

In the final chapter of *Psycho-Therapy* (1913), Severn appends for illustrative purposes "a list of cases selected from the last five years of my practice" (p. 150). The book thus looks back to the inception of her self-fashioned career as a clinician in San Antonio in 1908 and distills the profound transformation she had already undergone in this short period of time. But Severn does not conceal that the story she has to tell is also one of herself as a suffering patient. Indeed, she announces that her conviction that "physical disturbances" are "always and entirely the consequence of some impingement upon or deflection of the mind" took hold "as a startling proposition some years ago after a long personal history of apparently hopeless invalidism," from which she was able to recover "with the aid of an able practitioner" (pp. 7–8). This must refer to Severn's breakdown in Chicago in 1905 following the collapse of her marriage and the abduction of her daughter, for which she sought help from Franklin Leavitt—an experience, as Margaret (1988) has documented, that "changed the course of her life" (p. 13) and empowered Severn to rescue her only child from her grandfather's clutches in Wayne, Michigan.

Because Severn's (1913) belief in the psychological causes of physical illness was "a startling proposition" that dawned on her during a period of "apparently hopeless invalidism," she evidently alludes to this same crisis when she later recounts how, "on first getting out of bed after a three or four weeks' serious illness," she was surprised "to find that my expectation of taking a few steps was quite frustrated by my subconscious will," an inhibition that "it required vigorous measures" to overcome (p. 27). Another illuminating glimpse of Severn's inner life is afforded by her account of "an early experience of my own when first experimenting with my own subconsciousness" (p. 51). Severn discloses that she "had for years been unable to eat anything with comfort, and had been obliged to eliminate one food after another until reduced to the most abstemious diet." Her bugbear was the "comparatively unoffending pancake" (p. 52), and, as with her difficulty in walking, she managed to vanquish her aversion by sheer force of will. When she demanded "perfect obedience" from her stomach, the digestive organ at first "rebelled so vigorously that it refused to keep the pancakes at all," but she redoubled her efforts to habituate herself to the dreaded stimulus. After three days, she was able to eat pancakes "in peace and comfort," and, Severn concludes, "from that day to this I have been able to eat what I chose at any time and of whatever nature, in perfect peace" (p. 53).

Although Severn does not affix to herself the diagnostic label of anorexia nervosa, introduced into the medical literature by Sir William Gull in 1873, this was one of the sequelae of her traumatic history. Without making the autobiographical dimension explicit, Severn encapsulates the psychological meanings of her disorder when she comments in *Psycho-Therapy*, "The stomach is the centre through which nourishment is taken, and in those who are starving themselves through an inability to get the good out of life, or who are given to the worry-habit, consuming their mental energies, stomach trouble in some form is almost sure to develop" (p. 91). It is therefore an inside joke when Margaret (1988), on the train from Tarrytown to New York City, writes in a March 16, 1915 letter to her mother, "Your little pancake is now on the way home" (p. 60).

Severn's (1913) resort to what she called "a violent and defiant optimism" (p. 141) to combat the depression of which her eating disorder and motor paralysis were two of the most debilitating symptoms appears to have been what she had in mind when she told Margaret late in life that she "would no longer uphold all of the statements" in *Psycho-Therapy*, and "It's not so simple." After her analysis with Ferenczi, Severn realized that positive thinking alone would not suffice to pull her out of the Slough of Despond, and she abjured the Nietzschean credo she had espoused in her first book that suffering could be alleviated "through the will, until the Superman is no longer a dream" (p. 29).

Based on her experience as both a patient and a practitioner, Severn expands her thesis in the opening sentence that psychotherapy is "the healing of the body through the mind" (p. 1) to claim that "physical disturbances, due to whatever proximate or immediate causes, are always and entirely the consequence of some impingement upon or deflection of the mind itself" (p. 7). She affirms that "such diseases as cancer are attributable to consuming emotions which eat up or destroy the cellular tissue," and "when the eyesight is defective there is usually intellectual confusion of some sort, or a lack of what may be called 'vision'" (p. 93). Severn's belief that "all mental healing consists in 'raising the vibrations' of the patient in some manner through the concentration of the healer" (p. 43) leads her to promote the efficacy of "absent treatment" on the grounds that "since Mind is not bound by space or time, the transfer of all these images and impressions, and even the force and vitality of the healer, may be made with no diminution of power at any distance" (p. 101)—a conviction to which she adhered throughout her career and that, after Ferenczi's death, made her the target of ridicule by Freud and Jones.

The role that both Groddeck and Severn were later to play in Ferenczi's life makes it uncanny that in 1913, the same year in which Severn affirmed in *Psycho-Therapy* that "healing, as opposed to curing, has little to do with symptoms and much with causes" (p. 5), Groddeck published *Nasamecu: The Healthy and Sick Man*, the title of which—an acronym derived from the Latin phrase *natura sanat, medicus curat* ("nature heals, the physician cures")—draws the same distinction between healing and curing. Even Severn's instancing of defective eyesight and cancer as examples of psychogenic illness is echoed by Groddeck. In *The Book of the It* (1923), Groddeck contrasts the man with "protruding eyes," who emblazons on his face "his curiosity and his horror at the remarkable discoveries he has made," with one whose "deep-sunken eyes withdraw themselves when his hatred of mankind grown great; they do not wish to see, and still less to be seen" (p. 171). In one of his final texts, "On the Psychic Conditioning of Cancer Sickness" (1934), the manuscript of which he sent to Freud, who had been stricken for more than a decade with oral cancer, Groddeck posited that there is an "unconscious identification of the growth of a child and cancer," and since the male "does not possess the organs required for actual pregnancy," this equation must be "symbolically expressed," so that cancer most often strikes men in "sites specially connected with intake, nourishment, and expulsion, i.e., the mouth, the stomach, and the rectum" (p. 162).[1]

In the United States, Severn's interest in what has come to be known as psychosomatic medicine was shared by Jelliffe, though there is no evidence that she and Jelliffe influenced each other in this respect. But we do have the testimony of Mabel Dodge Luhan (1936) that, in her analysis with him, "one of the most interesting speculations Jelliffe went in for was apparently a new field never worked much before—the set of symbols that compose all parts of the body" (p. 440). Together with William Alanson White, Jelliffe in 1915 published *Diseases of the Nervous System: A Text-Book of Neurology and Psychiatry*, in the 1917 introduction to the second edition of which the authors declare:

> So long as the unconscious failed to be recognized, just so long was the gap between so-called body and so-called mind too wide to be bridged, and so there arose the two concepts, body and mind, which gave origin to the necessity of defining their relations.
>
> (p. 21)

Similarly, in a paper coauthored with his assistant Elida Evans, Jelliffe (1916) considers "the dynamics of the skin reactions in terms of the hidden psychological factors of the individual life, the patient's thought fossils, to wit" (p. 5).[2]

All this is extremely reminiscent not only of Severn but also of Groddeck, of whom Jelliffe was made aware when he met Freud for the first time in Bad Gastein in August 1921. Freud himself had only met Groddeck the previous year at the congress of the International Psychoanalytical Association in The Hague. As Jelliffe reported to White, Freud "was very much interested in our organic work and told me of one of his pupils in Baden-Baden who was carrying on similar types of analyses and with the same ideas we have been working on" (Burnham, 1983, p. 205). Groddeck immediately wrote to Jelliffe, on August 20, 1921, to tell him that "to hear about your studies on the other seaside is a great satisfaction" (p. 131). The first English translation of *The Book of the It* was published in 1928 in Jelliffe and White's Nervous and Mental Disease monograph series, and this prompted Jelliffe to pay Groddeck his most generous tribute:

> I am amazed at the wealth of suggestive material, and, feeling its great emotional value, am telling you how much the book means to me, as

I now read it again.... I know that you know that my thoughts have been paralleling many of yours now for some years and I wish to say how fruitful for me yours have been.

(p. 131)

Claiming both Groddeck and Jelliffe as his pupils, Freud twice coupled them (once including Felix Deutsch as a third) in his papers as therapists who have attested that "the psycho-analytic treatment of serious organic complaints shows promising results" (1924, p. 209; see also 1923b, p. 250). But where the same furrows are being plowed, there is often rivalry, and the collegiality between Jelliffe and Groddeck gave way to competition. Astonishingly, in a letter to Freud on September 9, 1927, Groddeck was unable to recall Jelliffe's name even as he depreciated both him and Deutsch: "The fact that not one of the members of the Association has dared to follow my suggestion—Deutsch and the American, whose name I can't remember any more, can't be counted seriously—is no basis for thinking that my way is not correct" (Giefer, 2008, pp. 235–36). Jelliffe did not repress Groddeck's name, but he did diminish his contribution in writing to Freud on August 22, 1932, "All of Groddeck is suggestive but it does not get down to the minute steps of the process" (Burnham, 1983, p. 243). He again asserted his independence from—and greater intellectual rigor than—Groddeck in a 1939 introduction to a collection of his papers on psychosomatic medicine: "From an actual historical point of view my earlier papers were written before I knew of Groddeck's work, in which latter the principles here worked out at times in considerable detail are but suggested in Groddeck's intriguing contributions" (p. 137). As I have documented elsewhere (Rudnytsky, 2002, pp. 144–45), a bidirectional anxiety of influence haunted Groddeck's relationship with Freud, especially over their diverging conceptions of the "It" or "id," and, as we shall see in Chapter 11, issues of priority also exacerbated the strains in the friendship between Ferenczi and Groddeck.

Just as Severn's (1913) conviction that every human being possesses "an innate or subconscious intelligence," and "it is the derangement of this intelligence from its natural and harmonious workings that is the ultimate cause of all disease" (pp. 6–7), forms a counterpart to Groddeck's (1926) elevation of the It into "life's unknown ruler," so, too, her belief in telepathy belongs to the Zeitgeist out of which psychoanalysis emerges. As we have seen, among the groups with which Severn interacted while she was in England from 1912 to 1914 was the Society for Psychical Research, to which she appeals in *Psycho-Therapy* (1913) as having "authoritatively established" (p. 34) the existence of telepathy, while in *The Psychology of Behaviour* (1917) she cites Frederic Myers's definition of genius as "a capacity for utilizing powers which lie too deep for the ordinary man's control" (p. 29).

If one is tempted to dismiss out of hand the beliefs of Groddeck, Jelliffe, and Severn, it is salutary to reflect on how difficult it is to distinguish between conceiving of psoriasis as a manifestation of a patient's "thought fossils" and attributing cancer to "consuming emotions which eat up or destroy the cellular tissue." Similarly, the positivist who mocks Severn's (1913) embrace of healing at a distance, which relies on the premise that "all forms of mental treatment are based on the great law of the transmission of thought" (p. 34), would do well to pause when she goes on to invoke the analogy of "wireless telegraphy, which must have instruments attuned to one another before messages can be registered" (p. 36). Where does psychoanalysis end and telepathy begin when Freud (1912) himself uses the telephone as a metaphor to illustrate how "the doctor's unconscious is able, from the derivatives of the unconscious which are transmitted to him, to reconstruct that unconscious, which has determined the patient's free associations" (p. 116)? As Fodor (1951) has put it, "the unconscious has its own channels of awareness. What we call 'telepathy' appears to be one such channel" (p. 15).[3]

Drawing largely on her own experience, Severn in *Psycho-Therapy* formulates a theory about the links between trauma and dissociation that Ferenczi would come to only in his final period, and which synthesizes the essential insights of the tradition that extends from Janet to Bromberg. As Severn (1913) writes:

> when the coherence of the mind is cleft or destroyed by a sudden emotion there is at least a temporary insanity. . . . This disturbance of the coherence of the mind is called dissociation by psychologists and, although probably present in everyone to some degree, leads in extreme cases to a complete anaesthesia of certain parts or faculties, or to such phenomena as double personality.
>
> (pp. 60, 62–63)

Not being familiar with the French school, Severn instances the "most able study of the latter given us by Dr. Morton Prince in his famous case of Sally Beauchamp" (p. 63).[4] Severn then moves from Prince and dissociation to repression and her first mention in the book of Freud, whom she credits with having originated the concept of "thought complexes." She continues:

> Although I am not prepared to go the whole way in his views on the prevalence of sex perversions with Professor Freud, who has given us some valuable and much-needed instruction on this neglected point, I am constantly impressed with its importance as a primary cause in the larger number of cases of mental and nervous disorders.
>
> (p. 64)

By Freud's "views on the prevalence of sex perversions," Severn means his pre-1897 "seduction" theory, which held that the sexual abuse of children by adults was the "primary cause" of later "nervous disorders." With respect to treatment, she writes, "Freud claims that a cure is obtained by raising the dissociated mental complexes to the surface of the consciousness, which is done through a careful analysis of the patient's mind and getting him to express freely in words his repressed thoughts and desires," but she appends a qualification that she will underscore from her mature perspective in *The Discovery of the Self*: "I find this to be only the beginning in most cases" because "such mental states are among the worst, and require a great deal of constructive work and reeducation of the will before they can be said to be cured" (pp. 64–65).

In *Extraordinary Knowing* (2007), her superlative synthesis of the objective and subjective evidence for parapsychology, Elizabeth Lloyd Mayer highlights the frequency with which psychoanalysts have found that "patients with extreme intuitive gifts, extreme enough to register as anomalous, . . . believed that they had developed their gifts in response to trauma, in order to survive circumstances that required knowing more than people can possibly know" (p. 101). Almost a century earlier, Severn intimated the traumatic origins of "extraordinary knowing" in *Psycho-Therapy* (1913):

> The psychic quality is merely an extension of mental perceptions to traverse realms not ordinarily covered. It means the opening up to consciousness of another, a deeper, phase of mind, and its possessors are usually people of fine and delicate organisms whose very sensitiveness to vibrations not registered in the usual manner renders them the recipients of both mental and physical influences which may be detrimental.
>
> (pp. 71–72)

Based on his analysis of Severn and other deeply traumatized patients, but also on his own history, Ferenczi develops this theme in his *Clinical Diary*: "Presumably, therefore, all mediums are such overanxious people, who are attuned to the slightest vibrations, those accompanying cognitive and affective processes too, even from a distance" (Dupont, 1985, p. 140). Both Ferenczi and Severn speak of "sensitiveness to vibrations" or "being attuned to the slightest vibrations . . . even from a distance," and Severn's reference to the frequently "detrimental" nature of such influences accords with Mayer's (2007) observation that "many of those patients also reported that their apparently anomalous capabilities terrified them" (p. 101).

Severn's (1913) ostensibly objective but in reality heartrendingly personal disquisition on the propensity of trauma victims for telepathy continues:

> Having once experienced a shock of grief or any strong emotion, they are never able to forget it. Their memories are extraordinarily keen, which tends to make them introspective and even morbid. . . . Their minds are as photographic plates reproducing all sorts and kinds of conditions. They become as waste-baskets, collecting even the subconscious thoughts and feelings from all those about them. They are in a chronic state of susceptibility. . . . These people are also liable to many "splits" in the mind, as heretofore mentioned in the exposition of Psychosis. . . . It is the type of mind suggesting great scope and possibilities, but also subject to the greatest mutilation and failure. In it one finds an extensive field for interesting mental research.
>
> (pp. 72–73)

The full extent of the "shock of grief" undergone by Severn will become clear in the ensuing chapters, but there can be no doubt that it is first and foremost her own shattered mind of which she speaks as a "photographic plate" on which layers of traumatic memory have been engraved, as well as a "waste-basket, collecting even the subconscious thoughts and feelings of those around them." Notwithstanding her determination to carry on with her life, Severn was inwardly an emotional wreck in search of a savior. There is again a thinly veiled self-portrait in her description of "those who have been wandering aimlessly from one 'cure' to another with a vague and perhaps half-hearted hope of final recovery" as people "who have lost lost all control of the subconscious will and have become incapacitated for any genuine and persistent effort without assistance"

(p. 16). It foreshadows what she will obtain from Ferenczi when she pays tribute to the healer of lost souls who "reaches down into the abyss into which they have fallen, offering the right hand of helpfulness and strength, lifting the fallen one into a position of erect power and instructing him how he may stand."

Averring that Mayer's book "could well hold the future of psychoanalysis between its covers" (p. 137), Bromberg (2011) affirms his belief in "the existence of people . . . who retain or develop the seemingly *uncanny* ability to make mutual contact with the 'other' in ways that cannot be understood within what we call a rational frame of mind" (p. 8). Although Mayer (2007) cautions against drawing "absolute or literal" analogies between the behavior of subatomic particles and "ESP or telepathy in human beings," she points out that experiments in quantum physics have conclusively demonstrated that

> *particles that have been in close association with each other as a two-particle system will defy familiar constraints of time and space in relation to each other.* They'll each instantly compensate for a change in the state of the other, no matter how distant they happen to be and without any identifiable channel of communication between them.
> (pp. 257–58)

Instead of "ordinary thinking" that takes for granted "the experiences of separation we consider most basic, such as those imposed by the familiar boundaries of space and time" (p. 147), Mayer upholds "the idea of things existing not as separate entities but as a single, indivisible system" (p. 255), so that "connectedness, not separateness, becomes the new continent" (p. 147).[5]

No one has possessed "the seemingly *uncanny* ability to make mutual contact with the 'other'" in mysterious ways to a greater degree than Severn, and her argument for "the great law of the transmission of thought" is based, like Mayer's, on a theory of the interconnectedness of all things. Comparing "the objective part of the mind" to "islands of the sea" and "the individual subconsciousness" to "their submerged bases," Severn (1913) develops her metaphor in a most compelling fashion:

> At the very bottom these mountain chains will be found to be united, and in some such way as this the minds of all human beings are bound together. . . . Thus we are in direct relation, however subconscious it

may be, to the thoughts of all living beings, and in all probability to all the thoughts of those who have been before us. . . . We live in a sea of thought and are tinged with the nature and quality of every particle in it.

(p. 77)

Once again, what may at first glance seem to be implausible shades imperceptibly into the irrefutable. In saying that "we live in a sea of thought," Severn takes field theory, which sees the analytic dyad as comprising "a single, indivisible system," to its logical conclusion.[6] To affirm that our minds are connected "to the thoughts of all living beings" is a psychoanalytic version of the "butterfly effect," which holds that a minute change in one part of a complex system can have vast effects at a far remove in the same system. As Severn makes the case for action at a distance, so, too, she crosses the threshold of time when she describes those who are living as being "in direct relation . . . to all the thoughts of those who have been before us," a concept familiar to psychoanalysts as the intergenerational transmission of trauma.

Setting the controversies over parapsychology in a historical context, Herman (1992) observes that, after Freud's recantation of his "seduction" theory in 1897, "the study of trauma came to a halt" and "hypnosis and altered states of consciousness were once more relegated to the realm of the occult" (p. 15), whence they had previously been thought to arise. As one whose propensity for collecting the "subconscious thoughts and feelings from all those about them" was exponentially magnified by the "many 'splits' in the mind" to which she was liable because of her own history of trauma, Severn exemplifies how psychoanalysis nestles cheek by jowl with the occult. Her praise of intuition leads her to declare that "it is in diagnosis that this psychic faculty is especially valuable, and if the thought radiations known as the human aura can be sensed it is of great assistance" (1913, p. 84).

But while Severn believes that "purely clairvoyant diagnosis" can be "remarkably successful," she concedes that "equally often it is uncertain and unsuccessful," and it may therefore be necessary to fall back on something less ethereal. This is where psychoanalysis comes in:

Failing such methods as these, several very careful systems have been worked out by scientific psychologists with a view to tapping the lower levels of the mind and exposing its hidden operations.

Probably the most notable and successful of these is Professor Freud's Psycho-Analysis.

(p. 84)

In view of the eight years she would spend with Ferenczi, it is ironic that Severn should go on to describe psychoanalysis as "an elaborate process extending over some weeks or months of time," and even to hold out the possibility of a more accelerated timetable: "However, even two or three experiments with his word-association tests with a patient often bring to light points that the healer who is quick to read may find most helpful" (p. 84).

As I have noted, Severn credited Freud with the concept of "thought complexes," and here she speaks of "*his* word association tests." In reality, however, it was Jung who, beginning in 1904, published a series of studies on word association experiments conducted at the Psychiatric Clinic of the University of Zurich in the first successful effort to lend empirical support to Freud's theories, just as it was Jung who coined the term "complex" to designate the nexus of associations aroused by the presentation of a stimulus word that caused a delay in a subject's reaction-time during the test.[7] Thus, despite her allusions to "Professor Freud's Psycho-Analysis" and her awareness that "the analysis of dreams . . . has been dealt with very extensively by Freud" (p. 86), it would seem that Severn's exposure to psychoanalysis in London did not extend to the reading of Freud, just as she did not undertake any psychoanalytic therapy until she set up shop in New York. Indeed, none of Freud's works is cited in *Psycho-Therapy*, in which he is synecdochically equated by Severn with the school of which he was the head.

Like Mabel Dodge, who sought treatment from her friend Nina Bull, a practitioner of Divine Science, at the same time that she was in analysis with Jelliffe, Severn (1913) forged an amalgam of psychoanalysis with the "modern system of Mind-Cure, and much of the New Thought Philosophy which goes with it" (p. 135). Another of Dodge's friends, the writer and political contrarian Max Eastman, likewise saw no incompatibility between consulting both Brill and Jelliffe for psychoanalysis in 1915 and being open to New Thought, which he later characterized (1948) as "a kind of practical-minded first cousin to Christian Science, a mixture of suggestive therapeutics, psychic phenomena, non-church religion, and a business of conquering the world through sheer sentiments of optimism" (p. 240).

Eastman's listing of the ingredients of New Thought might have served as a recipe for Severn, with the addition of some exotic spices. While not a Christian Scientist, she affirms in *Psycho-Therapy* (1913) that "there have been some authentic cases of healing a broken leg without mechanical aid of any kind, notably by Christian Science" (p. 55). Severn's primary allegiance, however, is to the "New England School of Transcendentalism," and she wagers that Emerson "will prove to be among the world's greatest philosophers," while also praising "the extensive and convincing studies in psychology" by William James, together with Walt Whitman, "the poet, pouring forth in his *Song of Myself* the very essence of this religion of optimism and accomplishment" (pp. 136–37). Among the foreign tributaries feeding into this American river are "a certain strain of Hindu philosophy" and the "idealism of Berkeley" (p. 135), as well as Swedenborg (p. 88), Ruskin (p. 123), and "the great German philosophers of the last century" (p. 38), especially Nietzsche. A forerunner of the Independent tradition in psychoanalysis, Severn summarizes her syncretistic credo, "I feel very strongly the need of adaptability in those who profess the metaphysical calling, so that each patient and student may be dealt with as an individual and all theories and aims fitted in in the most subtle manner possible to his temperament and type" (p. 79).

The final chapter of *Psycho-Therapy*, "Cases," picks up the interwoven strands of overt and covert autobiography that run through Severn's book. There is no difficulty in identifying the former, as when Severn calls attention to "two cases of accident to myself, which were handled without material assistance," to wit, "a spraining of the ankle, due to a hard fall," and "being thrown from a bucking horse," which rendered her "unconscious for a few moments" (pp. 176–77). But these are inconsequential, and it is where Severn is most thoroughly concealed that she reveals herself most nakedly. Utilizing Margaret Naumburg's notes of her 1934 séance with Severn, Brennan (2015b) has detected a disguised autobiographical case history in *Psycho-Therapy* that provides a template for the triptych of herself, Ferenczi, and Margaret in *The Discovery of the Self*.[8]

In the séance, Severn recalled a dream about eggs and broken eggshells and associated it to an operation in which her ovaries were extirpated without her knowledge or consent: "They did not tell me they were going to do it. It was done against my will. I was victimized. I was indignant" (qtd. in Brennan, 2015b, p. 3). Armed with the knowledge of this horror to which Severn was subjected, Brennan convincingly argues that Severn tells her own story in case number 22 of *Psycho-Therapy* (1913), which concerns a woman who had undergone a "severe *ovariotomy* . . . two years previously" for the removal of a "cystic tumour" (p. 173). The surgery was "'successful,'" but the patient grew "steadily worse until she was physically incapable of any effort, never free from pain, and her mind so affected as to develop suicidal tendencies." Severn's narrative continues:

> She was of a sensitive, high-strung nature, susceptible to many impressions, and the operation had been a serious factor in disturbing her psychic poise. She had had great difficulties in her married life for years, and had fallen into the way of brooding upon them without any expression in words of her very intense and unhappy feelings. This had resulted in various subconscious dissociations expressed in severe hysterical symptoms, such as nervous convulsions. A great deal of analysis was necessary to eradicate the real cause of these disturbances. . . . The abdominal pains disappeared in the first few weeks of the treatment and also the convulsive attacks, but a year was required to put in order the tangled threads of a complex mind. During this time there were many set-backs and discouragements, but in the end the patient said she was "all made over."
>
> (pp. 173–74)

Since Severn's breakdown, which undoubtedly included "subconscious dissociations," "severe hysterical symptoms," and "suicidal tendencies," occurred in 1905, following Margaret's abduction by her father, it follows that her "severe *ovariotomy* . . . two years previously" can be dated to 1903, five years into her marriage to Charles Heywood, upon the miseries of which she had been brooding. The in-laws who kidnapped her daughter would surely have been capable of duping Leota (as she was then still known) into submitting to an operation, and this involuntary surgery, which compounded her woes and became "a serious factor in disturbing her psychic poise," was in all likelihood arranged by her husband and his family in an effort to cure Leota's "hysteria" by eliminating its supposed anatomical cause.

As Bonomi (2015a, p. 18) has documented, the removal of the ovaries as a treatment for hysteria in women was introduced in Europe by Alfred Hegar in 1872, and three years later by Robert Battey in America, where the procedure became widespread after 1885. Ovariotomy (or ovariectomy), moreover, was considered medically to be the female version of *castration*, just as the excision of any portion of the external genitalia—the labia and clitoris—constituted *circumcision*. Bonomi's research into the history of gynecology is in the service of his thesis that Emma Eckstein—Freud's most important female patient during his formative years as a psychoanalyst, when he still believed early sexual trauma to be the crucial factor in the etiology of hysteria—on whose nose Fliess performed his infamous botched surgery in February 1895, had had one of her inner labia "circumcised" in childhood. To this we can now add that Severn, Ferenczi's most important patient in the final years of *his* career, was the victim of "castration," thereby making these two women—both of whom became colleagues of their male analysts—mirror images in the history of psychoanalysis and bringing the theme of trauma in the Freud-Ferenczi relationship full circle.

Just as she will do two decades later in *The Discovery of the Self*, Severn presents the disguised case history of her ovariotomy in *Psycho-Therapy*, which adds a crucial stone to the mosaic we are assembling of her life, as though she were one of her own patients.[9] In reality, however, Severn was far from having been able "to put in order the tangled threads of a complex mind" by her own unaided efforts; but, thanks to the therapy she obtained in Chicago with Leavitt following her breakdown in 1905, Leota—as we have learned from Margaret's (1988) autobiography—"gained the courage and self-confidence" that "enabled her, despite her own ill health" (p. 13), to rescue her daughter from her father-in-law in 1907.

I think it is safe to say that Leavitt never became Leota Brown Heywood's patient, and so there is no case history of him encrypted in *Psycho-Therapy*. But having been alerted by Brennan to the hidden subjective significance of case number 22, I am led to see case number 40 in an altered light. Severn's (1913) recitation begins:

> A young girl on the verge of a mental breakdown was brought to me by her father in desperation. She seemed perfectly well physically, and there seemed no way of accounting for her distressing mental state which gave every sign of a *paranoia*. She was very intelligent and able to discuss her case in part, but was thoroughly hopeless and depressed, and entirely sceptical of Psycho-therapeutic methods of treatment, of which she knew nothing.
>
> (pp. 197–98)

If, as I believe, this "young girl" is Margaret, then Severn's statement that she was "brought to me by her father" reverses the true state of affairs, in which Severn stole her back from her husband's family, whose members had kidnapped her. But everything else corroborates the hypothesis that Severn is describing her newly rescued daughter, with whom would she had the greatest incentive imaginable to practice "the metaphysical calling," concomitantly with her discovery of her gifts as a "natural healer" in San Antonio.

The highlights of the saga are as follows:

> There was a long history of religious difficulties and sex perversion arising primarily out of a wrong conception of life due to a lack of the proper training. The patient continued to come for her treatment, however, and followed the various mental exercises I prescribed only because of the liking she had conceived of me and her dislike of disappointing me. . . . One by one the subconscious phantoms which had pursued her were dissolved. Even the constant and persistent washing of her hands, which was one of her many dominating delusions, was conquered, and she realised she could really be like other people. Along with many another poor sick soul, she believed she had committed the unpardonable sin, though what this was she had not the least idea. The washing of the hands was a symbol of the overwhelming desire to rid herself of supposed impurities.
>
> (p. 198)

Despite being "entirely sceptical of Psycho-therapeutic methods," this girl "continued to come for her treatment" and adhered to the "prescribed mental exercises" due to a "dislike of disappointing" her therapist, which comports with what one would expect of the relationship between a mother and daughter. Unlike Severn's ovariotomy, the detail of the "constant and persistent" hand-washing is not mentioned in any extant documentation of Margaret's life, but it stands to reason that she, like Lady Macbeth, would have sought to "rid herself of supposed impurities" in this symbolic fashion.

As we have seen, although Severn had earlier declined "to go the whole way in his views on the prevalence of sex perversions with Professor Freud," she did acknowledge that she was "impressed with its importance as a primary cause in the larger number of cases of mental and nervous disorders." Since "sex perversions" is Severn's shorthand for Freud's original theory that hysteria could always be traced back to sexual abuse in childhood, her use of the phrase again here warrants the inference that the "young girl on the verge of a mental breakdown" had been subjected to sexual abuse in a household that also left her with "religious difficulties," and it is this devastating trauma that lies beneath the patient's compulsive hand-washing and the "subconscious phantoms" by which she is haunted. Severn does not specify "the unpardonable sin" that, without having "the least idea" of what it was, the girl "believed she had committed," but it requires no preternatural powers to divine that she means incest.

As Severn tells it, case number 40, like case number 22, has a happy ending:

> The entire length of treatment was only seven months, and more than half of it had to be absent treatment with frequent correspondence to assist. The patient now writes "only those who have been in the blackness of such a night can know its horrors. I can hardly realise even yet how completely I am released."
>
> (p. 199)

Exactly when this seven-month treatment took place cannot be definitively proven, but it was probably while Margaret attended the boarding school in Boulder, where, as she wrote to her mother on March 9, 1929, "the principal said I was a wicked child to cry for my mama" (1988, p. 1,514). It was very premature for Margaret to think she had been "released" at this early stage, just as Severn herself was far from "all made over" by the time she wrote *Psycho-Therapy*. But the title of Margaret's autobiography, *Spotlight: Letters to My Mother*, leaves no doubt that she and her mother engaged in "frequent correspondence" during their periods of separation; and, as we shall see in Chapter 6, Elizabeth's analysis of her daughter indeed included liberal doses of "absent treatment."

Notes

1 This paper is published in an amalgamated chapter together with *Man as a Symbol* in *The World of Man* (1951).
2 I am indebted to Patricia Everett (2021) for these citations from Jelliffe and Luhan, as well as for those following from Nina Bull and Max Eastman. See also Nolan D. C. Lewis's (1966) chapter on Jelliffe in *Psychoanalytic Pioneers*, "Psychosomatic Medicine in America," and John Burnham's superb volume *Jelliffe: American Psychoanalyst and Physician* (1983).
3 For a valuable study of "how Ferenczi's thoughts on telepathy illuminate both the relevance of psychical research to psychoanalysis and the relevance of psychoanalysis to psychical research" (p. 145), with commentary on the

contributions to this hybrid tradition of a wide range of analysts linked to the Budapest School, including Balint, Fodor, Hollós, Rickman, and Severn, see Gyimesi (2012).
4 Prince presented his classic case of multiple personality in *The Dissociation of a Personality* (1906). Saul Rosenzweig (1969), who uncovered Sally Beauchamp's real identity as Clara N. Fowler and has masterfully reconstructed the facts of her life, hypothesizes that, in addition to repeated experiences of sibling loss, the phenomenon of "physical and sexual abuse of teenage daughters living with a recent widower" (p. 28) may have led Clara to run away from home at the age of sixteen and been one of the factors contributing to her dissociation.
5 Compare the appreciation of the work of Trigant Burrow by Herbert Read, who wrote in 1958 that his main thesis "points to the anciently recognized truth that *man is not a detached particle of life, pursuing a separate orbit, but that we are part of one another. From that fact it follows that the analysis of the individual can never be completed without an analysis of the group of which he is an organic part*" (qtd. in Pertegato and Partegato, 2013, p. cvii).
6 In their Afterword to Thierry Bokanowski's *The Modernity of Sándor Ferenczi* (2011), Bartlett et al. (2018) assert that "the reach of Ferenczi's ideas may be seen . . . in the articulation of field theory by Madelon and Willy Baranger" (p. 118). Ferenczi, however, is conspicuously *not* cited either in the 2008 paper to which they appeal or in the Barangers' 1983 paper with Jorge Mom, also included in *The Pioneers of Psychoanalysis in South America* (Lisman-Pieczanski and Pieczanski, 2015).
7 See the series of papers in Part 1 of Volume 2 of Jung's *Collected Works* (Adler, 1973).
8 Brennan found the notes, which appear to have been taken down as Severn was speaking, among Naumburg's papers in the Kislak Center for Special Collections at the University of Pennsylvania.
9 Smith (1998) is thus mistaken when she asserts that Severn's "first two books are full of cases of other people experiencing trauma, never Severn" (p. 243).

Chapter 3

Much Farther Than Freudianism

During the four-year interval between her first and second books, psychoanalysis comes to occupy an increasingly prominent place in Severn's thought. "Taking its origin in pathological studies made by Dr. Breuer, in Vienna, in 1881, and later by his brilliant successor Dr. Freud," she declares in the opening chapter of *The Psychology of Behaviour* (1917), "Psycho-analysis today presents us with a large mass of scientific observation and theories concerning human emotions and experiences" (p. 12). Both her growing allegiance and continued skepticism are on display when Severn elaborates:

> In my personal work with students I have at times used psychoanalytic methods with excellent results, though I do not say that the application of these methods has always, or even often, led me to the same conclusions as those of its originators. Like every independent worker in this field, I have developed methods of my own, which for my purposes and intentions yield far better results, especially when working with the individual for the alleviation of various mental and physical disorders.
>
> (p. 13)

Severn concludes this initial staking out of her position with the exhortation, "But we have the inspiration of their theories, which depart boldly from old established canons; *only*, we must go much farther than Freudianism if we are to understand man's deepest yearnings and spiritual capacities."

Despite these signs of Severn's intellectual growth, *The Psychology of Behaviour*, whose long-winded subtitle *A Practical Study of Human Personality and Conduct with Special Reference to Methods of Development*

DOI: 10.4324/9781315280134-5

gives fair warning of what is to come, is today of almost exclusively antiquarian interest. The book, essentially an exercise in "life coaching" organized as a treatise on faculty psychology, lacks the case histories that enliven both *Psycho-Therapy* and *The Discovery of the Self*, and the autobiographical undertones are far more muted than in either of these works. While not gainsaying her interest in telepathy or New Thought, Severn keeps herself on a leash that gives her writing, as Smith (1998) has observed, "a much more insistent and defensive tone than her 1913 book" (p. 243). Indeed, *The Psychology of Behaviour* constitutes what Ferenczi would call a "colossal superperformance" (Dupont, 1985, p. 89), by means of which Severn attempted to keep at bay the childhood agony she had not yet been able to confront, let alone begin to recover from, in a therapeutic relationship.

Severn, as we know, had already had her first experience of personal analysis with Jelliffe, whom she found to be "very sadistic," and this debacle helps to explain the problems with *The Psychology of Behaviour* (1917). She describes her ordeal on his couch:

> To perform this operation as it is done by the average present-day Psycho-Analyst is like having a surgical process for the removal of a tumour without any succeeding medical care for the upbuilding of the weakened constitution. The mind is a delicate instrument and the application to it of the analytic process is more than likely to produce a mental shock of some kind, a reaction simple or violent according to the extent of the original damage.
>
> (p. 258)

Severn's comparison of the technique of the "average present-day Psycho-Analyst" to that of a surgeon who removes a tumor without adequate post-operative care echoes Freud's dictum in "Recommendations to Physicians Practising Psycho-Analysis" (1912) that his followers should "model themselves during psycho-analytic treatment on the surgeon, who puts aside all his feelings, even his human sympathy," although she does not appear to have read this paper, in which Freud in the ensuing paragraph proceeds to liken the analyst's unconscious—much as she had used the analogy of "wireless telegraphy" in *Psycho-Therapy*—to a "telephone receiver" that should be adjusted to "the transmitting unconscious of the patient" (p. 115).

Despite the dearth of autobiographical material in the book, Severn's analogy between the "operation" of an insensitively conducted analysis and the "removal of a tumour" does seem to be a veiled allusion to her own operation for the excision of a "cystic tumour" into which she had been duped by her husband's family in 1903, a heinous act that cost her her ovaries. As we have seen, in "What Is a Psychic Injury?" (1937b) Severn again reverts to "what the medical man would do if he found certain symptoms of serious internal illnesses, we will say something like tumour," to make the point that in cases "of the 'shock' kind, the only thing that will help it is a deep analytic process" (pp. 15–16). By the time of this lecture, however, Severn was able to speak from the perspective of the "deep analytic process" she had undergone with Ferenczi, whereas her encounter with Jelliffe had succeeded only in producing a "mental shock" and "violent reaction" that corresponded "to the extent of the original damage." Severn's use of the tumor metaphor, moreover, undoubtedly influenced Ferenczi's (1930) comparison of the cleft mind of a traumatized person to "the so-called *teratoma* which harbours in a hidden part of its body fragments of a twin-being which has never developed," and that "no reasonable person would refuse . . . to surrender to the surgeon's knife, if the existence of the whole individual were threatened" (p. 123).

Thus, like many another "independent worker in this field," Severn had to struggle to maintain her faith in the promise of psychoanalysis despite being repeatedly disillusioned and retraumatized by its orthodox practitioners. This revisionist perspective is exemplified in *The Psychology of Behaviour* by her conviction that "for the best results . . . the work of a Psycho-analyst is indispensable" (p. 43), even as she criticizes "the somewhat limited and arbitrary methods of Psycho-analysis and also some of its sweeping but unproved conclusions" (p. 12), not to mention its undue "emphasis upon the analytical process with a corresponding weakness on the constructive side" (p. 257). Just as she did in *Psycho-Therapy*, Severn remarks that "it has remained for Dr. Freud and his disciples to properly emphasize the importance of dreams in the psychic life" (p. 34), but her skeptical voice comes to the fore when she goes on to question "whether the elaborate symbolisms worked out by the Psycho-analysts are to be depended upon as throwing much light upon the real nature of the unconscious thought-life or not" (p. 35). Severn's critique of the Freudian penchant for "elaborate symbolisms" and "arbitrary methods" parallels that of Mabel Dodge, who, as we have seen, chastised Jelliffe for imposing "a formula for thinking, or a set of symbols which you arbitrarily designate in consistency with your particular constitution" (Everett, 2021, p. 202).

When Severn locates the origins of psychoanalysis "in pathological studies made by Dr. Breuer, in Vienna, in 1881," she is harking back to the case of Anna O., whose "*'absences'*" and "alternating states of consciousness" (Breuer and Freud, 1895, pp. 24, 32) make her the prototype of a dissociated patient in psychoanalysis, and therefore, like Emma Eckstein with her surgical "circumcision," a forerunner of Severn. Although Severn shows a greater awareness of psychoanalytic history in *The Psychology of Behaviour* than she did in *Psycho-Therapy*, most of it still seems to be secondhand and nebulous. Indeed, the only direct quotation from a psychoanalytic author in *The Psychology of Behaviour* is the definition of psychoanalysis by the Harvard neurologist James Jackson Putnam, a philosophical idealist and first president of the American Psychoanalytic Association, as "'an attempt to make the facts and principles discovered through the analysis of individual lives, of service in the study of race history and of life in general'" (p. 11).[1]

Insofar as Severn is conversant with psychoanalytic theory, she takes her stand—from which she will never waver—on Breuer and Freud's intertwined concepts of trauma as a "psychic injury" and catharsis as "a means of cure." She writes in *The Psychology of Behaviour* (1917):

> The fundamental theory of Psycho-analysis is that the symptoms of hysterical patients (of which there is a much wider class than is generally supposed) depend upon impressive but forgotten scenes in their lives. The treatment consists in causing the patients to recall and reproduce these experiences in consciousness, a process very properly designated as *catharsis*, because the whole idea is to *eliminate* the *source* of the trouble. The symptoms themselves represent undischarged centres of excitement and only require conversion into normal channels for relief to ensue—hence the necessity of this "clearing out" process.
> (p. 252)

Without giving the slightest hint, as she had done in her disguised autobiographical case history in *Psycho-Therapy* (1913), that she herself had suffered "various subconscious dissociations expressed in severe hysterical symptoms" (p. 173), Severn is at her best in *The Psychology of*

Behaviour (1917) when she draws from the wellsprings of psychoanalysis and expounds its core tenets:

> The greatest danger to the personality is that of *dissociation*. In its extreme form we have multiple or alternating personalities, where one phase emerges with such strength and vividness as to temporarily, or perhaps for a long period of time, entirely eclipse the others.
> (pp. 335–36)

To this she adds, again with a subtext of personal reference that no reader of this book alone could possibly divine: "*Disintegration* is the logical outcome of *dissociation* and other negative disturbances of the personality. In its most serious and final form it results in insanity or suicide" (pp. 336–37). In light of her fidelity to Breuer and Freud's foundational theory of trauma and dissociation, it is striking that Severn twice refers to "'fixed ideas'" to describe the "unwanted and disagreeable thoughts and feelings which have had their origin in the past, and over which we seem powerless'" (pp. 117–18; see also p. 120), but does so without any acknowledgment of Janet, even though Putnam (1909) had ranged Janet alongside Freud as "one of the great pioneer leaders . . . in the investigation of a series of phenomena of the highest importance alike for medicine and psychology" (p. 2).

The limitations in Severn's knowledge of psychoanalytic terms and concepts are shown when she states that the psychoanalyst "acts as an *agent* or substitute, upon which the patient can transfer his unconscious psychic forces," but then continues, "the doctor overcomes by his skilful *suggestions* the unconscious conflicts and disquietudes of his subject" (p. 43). She is right about the analyst's function as a transference figure, but overlooks that analysis differs from other modes of therapy precisely in its *avoidance* of direct suggestion. Equally dubious is Severn's definition of the will as "simply the *life-force in action*; the same as Bergson's *élan vital*, and Freud's *Libido*" (p. 149), because it was Freud's insistence that the libido should *not* be construed as a generalized "life-force," but rather as a sexual drive, that was the key point of theoretical disagreement in his recent break with Jung.

But it is not these minor infelicities that make *The Psychology of Behaviour*, unlike both *Psycho-Therapy* and *The Discovery of the Self*, a largely moribund work. It is, rather, Severn's valiant but doomed attempt to speak exclusively with the voice of impersonal authority, which stems from her denial of the pain that fuels her creativity. She quotes Nietzsche to the effect that "courage is man's greatest virtue" (p. 334), but tries in vain to convince the reader—and herself—that it is possible to "develop the 'philosophical' mind, whatever our temperaments or tendencies, thus learning to erase the scars and marks of injury as we go along, turning evil, failure, pain, and ignorance into knowledge, power, and harmony" (p. 79). Equally lame is her assertion, "There is a psychic process by which thoughts can be completely annihilated—and if not successful in this we can at least relegate them to the closet shelf in such a manner that they will no longer hurt or trouble us" (p. 118). She gets closer to the truth when she says of this "closet" that "sometimes the objects collected therein are more like jacks-in-the-box, possessing concealed springs that cause them to jump out at us in the least expected moments; . . . hence the 'family skeleton' to be found in some closet in every house" (pp. 111–12). But Severn's leitmotif is her "conception of the Superman" whose "foremost attribute will be an understanding of the law of Freedom, thus making his Will paramount" (p. 154; see also p. 7), bolstered by the platitude that "there is no such thing as failure *except to those who believe in it*" (p. 205), both of which protestations ring hollow and are belied by Severn's suicidal depressions and inability to escape the skeletons in the family closet that kept jumping out at her at unexpected moments.

This book, however, is only a way station on Severn's journey. After Jelliffe, she sought analysis first from Asch and then from Rank, finding the former well meaning but ineffectual and the latter self-absorbed and monomaniacal, before risking everything on a last-ditch bid to get what she desperately needed from Ferenczi. Beautifully extending her meditation in *Psycho-Therapy* on how healing takes place through vibrations and the creation of what might today be called the "analytic third," Severn writes in *The Psychology of Behaviour* (1917), "when two people come together who are in any sense mated, there is not only an exchange of their respective qualities, there is also the creation of something new, a power, a third element which represents the sum total and combination of all their energies and attributes" (p. 297). Severn makes clear, moreover, that such a "mating" can be not simply one of bodies but a marriage of true minds as well:

> When it is a physical union *only* that takes place, the natural outcome is a physical conception, the production of another human being; when the contact is on one of the higher planes also, there may be in

addition, or instead of, the usual physical outcome, a conception and birth of new powers, new visions—an *im-material* fruition it is true, but who shall say that it is not of at least equal import, if not greater?

(pp. 297–98)

Just such an "*im-material* fruition," "a conception and birth of new powers, new visions," is what she would gain from her communion on a "higher plane" with Ferenczi, culminating in their "love child" of mutual analysis, the vibrations of which reach us across oceans of space and time to this day.[2]

Notes

1 I have not been able to find Severn's quotation from Putnam in either his *Human Motives* (1915) or any of the papers in *Addresses on Psycho-Analysis* (1921). But Severn's reference to "Dr. Breuer, in Vienna, in 1881," seems to be cribbed from "Personal Impressions of Sigmund Freud and His Work" (1909), written in the afterglow of the conference at Clark University, where Putnam begins his "history of Freud's investigations and opinions" by recounting how, "in 1881, an older colleague, Dr. J. Breuer, of Vienna, had occasion to treat a young woman suffering from hysteria in a serious form" (p. 3); and I suspect that Severn is relying heavily on Putnam for intellectual ballast.
2 Compare Ferenczi's meditation on August 4, 1931, "The love relation apparently comes about—neither in Subject A nor in Subject B—but between the two. Love therefore is neither egoism nor altruism, but mutualism, an exchange of feelings" (1920 and 1930–1932, p. 248).

Chapter 4

The Psychoanalytic Severn

As Severn (1952) informed Eissler at the outset of her interview, when she resolved to move to Europe to seek further analysis in 1925, she approached Ferenczi rather than Freud because she "thought he was more of a physician than Freud was. In other words, that he was more interested in the patient," whereas "Freud was primarily interested in the science that he was formulating." This, she added, was "a fundamental difference between the two men," and "I was not sorry that I had chosen to work with Ferenczi" (p. 2). She had, moreover, already been "practicing psychoanalysis for a number of years at that time" (p. 1), and it must have been at least in part on the basis of what she heard from Asch, who had complained that Freud had not understood him and left his analysis incomplete, as well as her disenchantment with Rank, that Severn made the decision to cast her lot with the Hungarian Grand Vizier rather than with the Sultan in Vienna.

What Severn accurately perceived to be the "fundamental difference" between Freud and Ferenczi, which has shaped the entire history of psychoanalysis no less than it did her personal destiny, is comprehensively presented in *The Discovery of the Self: A Study in Psychological Cure* (1933). Once again, Severn's theoretical arguments and insights, in addition to being intrinsically compelling, can simultaneously be read as outgrowths of—and reflections on—her personal experience. The subjective dimension, as we might expect, is sometimes overt but more often covert. As she writes in the opening pages, "this psyche, or self, is . . . only now in the process of being 'discovered,'" in the sense that it has begun to be "subjected to the microscope" of psychoanalysis; but (like Oedipus) she also means "to follow the quest personally, seeking answers to such questions as 'What am I?,' 'How did I come to be the way I am?,' and 'How can I become other than what I am?'" (p. 22). It is, ultimately, her own "discovery of the self" that Severn records, and the "psychological cure" made

DOI: 10.4324/9781315280134-6

possible by her eight-year analysis with Ferenczi of which she furnishes an enduring monument. Knowing that Severn became literally a "wandering soul" when she transplanted herself from New York to Budapest in her quest for psychic healing, we cannot fail to be moved when we read:

> Nearly every victim of a severe neurosis displays eventually the disposition to be "adopted." . . . An ideal arrangement would be something like a huge home for "homeless children"; probably such an idea is quite fantastic, but at least its equivalent must be provided in a psychic sense, by a feeling on the part of the analyst that provides in the immaterial but powerful realm of the mind succor and support for a "homeless" psyche. "Wandering souls" they are, all suffering internally from a lack of the sense of security, and very often from a lack of the sense of reality as well—people whose personalities have been "split," or at least injured, by some events and conditions beyond their control and usually forgotten.[1]
>
> (p. 68)

Not only did *The Discovery of the Self* disappear virtually without a trace after its publication in 1933, until it received a new lease on life in my edition of 2017, but even those who have led the way in rehabilitating Severn's reputation have spoken of it in condescending terms. According to Masson (1984), who first brought to light Severn's identity as R.N., it is "a curious work, written in a pious, mystical manner, unprofessional and unscholarly" (p. 164), while Fortune (1993) deems it to be "stylistically dated" (p. 113). In my view, however, far from being "dated" or "unprofessional," the book is brilliantly original and astonishingly prescient, worthy of being compared to Groddeck's *Book of the It* as what Severn (1952) termed in her addendum to the interview with Eissler an "explanation to the lay public of the real meaning and value of Psycho-analysis" (p. 24). As long as Severn was a psychoanalytic nobody, it was impossible to take the full measure of her achievement in what she also described as her "best work," but now that we know that she was not only Ferenczi's most important patient but also his analyst and intellectual partner, we can begin to read *The Discovery of the Self* with the same expectation of being in the presence of a master spirit that we bring to the *Clinical Diary*.

As a psychoanalytic revisionist, Severn (1933) strikes the keynote of her book by paying generous tribute to Freud while offering an incisive critique of his shortcomings. Invoking in the first sentence Socrates' dictum,

"Know thyself," as the watchword of psychoanalysis, she notes that the Greek philosopher not only "turned the light of unflinching reason on human motives and behavior" but also "had his 'daemon,' a personification of what we now regard as the inner voice of the self and that may be likened to intuition or gnosis, i.e., direct or unconscious knowledge" (p. 21). The Socrates possessed of "unflinching reason" is the precursor of Freud, while the one who harkens to "intuition and gnosis" foreshadows Severn and Ferenczi. Within a few pages, Severn moves from Socrates to Freud and makes clear the immense debt he is owed by everyone who travels the psychoanalytic path:

> The truth is that there is a very large part of the mind, actively functioning, that is completely unknown to the conscious self. . . . This lifting of the invisible into visibility was a prodigious work and has entitled Freud to a distinguished place among the scientists and benefactors of mankind.
>
> (p. 24)

Without utilizing any direct quotations, Severn in *The Discovery of the Self* refers to four works by Freud, beginning with *The Psychopathology of Everyday Life*, in which she says one "learns to recognize the 'hinterland' of the mind" (p. 26). She also singles out *The Problem of Lay-Analysis* (as it was known in the English translation of the time), in connection with which she incisively observes that when psychoanalysis is "utilized in a superficial and even deleterious way" by physicians, these supposed experts may be said to be " 'lay analysts' in the psychological sense," whereas "the nonmedical practitioner, if possessed of adequate training, may be as well or even better equipped to do the necessary delicate work" (p. 44). Finally, she moves from *The Interpretation of Dreams*, where Freud showed that an "analysis and understanding of the patient's dream-life" is "the royal road into his unconscious," to *Beyond the Pleasure Principle*, in which he modified his original wish-fulfillment theory by recognizing that "dreams also contained the repressed or forgotten painful parts of one's life, historically reproduced in vivid, though often distorted form," a phenomenon he called the "repetition compulsion" (p. 47).

These references attest to Severn's esteem for Freud, as do her lauding of the technique of free association as a "triumph of psychoanalysis" (p. 45) and her definition of transference as Freud's way of describing how the analyst may become for the patient "a sort of figurehead (or even 'punching bag') for various persons or events of his past" (p. 46). But embedded in Severn's words of praise are the seeds of her critique. When, for example, Severn again locates the origins of psychoanalysis, as she did in *The Psychology of Behaviour*, in "the treatment of a hysterical patient by Dr. Breuer of Vienna, some fifty years ago," it is significant in light of her experience as Ferenczi's partner in mutual analysis that she now characterizes psychoanalysis as "the outcome of *mutual* talks between him and his patient" (p. 43; italics added). Similarly, when she decries as "the greatest limitation of psychoanalysis . . . its exclusive—one might also say fanatic—devotion to the analytic process *per se*" (p. 62), and argues that a therapeutic "synthesis" must complement and complete the preliminary work of "analysis," she again appeals to Breuer and Anna O. while giving an innovative twist to the latter's celebrated metaphor of "chimney sweeping":

> The first step is iconoclastic, the second is creative. The tearing down, or clearing out, process may be likened to that of a chimney sweep—it was, indeed, called so by the first analytic patient, Dr. Breuer's famous case—but to sweep out the soot of the soul does not *cure* any more than sweeping a chimney provides a fire.[2]
>
> (p. 64)

The increasing confidence with which Severn advocates her views in *The Discovery of the Self* is further exemplified by her remarks on Prince and Putnam, both of whom, as we have seen, she mentioned favorably in her earlier books. With respect to Prince, whereas in *Psycho-Therapy* (1913) she had hailed his "most able study" of double or multiple personality "in his famous case of Sally Beauchamp" (p. 63), now, in setting forth how "in nearly every case of deep analysis one becomes aware of separated parts of the person, as though each part had an existence of its own," and in "severe cases of double or split personality each of these portions is like a separate entity, well organized, sometimes with a name of its own, and capable of independent action," Severn (1933) observes that "no outstanding work on the subject exists, except the comparatively slight contribution made by Morton Prince some twenty years ago in America," adding that "neither the explanation nor the therapy in this case was, however, very convincing" (p. 106).

Clearly, in her analysis with Ferenczi Severn had succeeded in exploring the "separated parts" of her own psyche at a depth that far exceeded what

Prince had been able to capture in his text, and she had no compunctions about taking him to task on the basis of her personal experience. When it comes to Putnam, the evolution in Severn's thinking did not result in any diminution of her admiration, but led her rather to use him as a stalking horse to shoot an arrow at Freud. Commending Putnam for being "one of the first persons of note in America to espouse the cause of psychoanalysis," Severn again points out, as she had in *The Psychology of Behaviour*, that he "argued and pleaded for the addition to it of some sort of idealism or philosophical point of view" (p. 56). Now, however, she underscores the cleavage between Putnam's belief in the need for "synthesis"—to which she also subscribes—and Freud's purely "iconoclastic" orientation. She writes that Putnam's "efforts were called 'obstinate' and entirely rejected by Freud, who jealously guarded his method as a thing in itself and refused to have anything to do with philosophical concepts."

With these statements in mind, it is not surprising that Severn should devote a considerable portion of her chapter, "Psychoanalysis," to what she regards as "some of the *limitations* of psychoanalysis" (p. 51), before turning in "Psychosynthesis" to her exposition of its missing "creative" counterpart. As she would also later tell Eissler, the nub of the matter for Severn is that the "therapeutic value" of psychoanalysis was "not . . . the most important one to Freud, his interest being rather that of the observer who desires to tabulate the facts he finds in a new and important field" (p. 50). Although Freud's interest in "research," in and of itself, is by no means a bad thing, it leads Severn to mount a critique of his sensibility that is no less just than it is trenchant. Reiterating that Freud's attitude caused him to devise "a method that is largely observational in character," and consequently "does not . . . fill the purpose fully when it comes to a therapeutic application," she drives home her point by observing that "he presented for the first time the strange doctrine that a man might become cured of his neurosis merely by becoming aware of it" (p. 51). Severn recognizes the importance of "making *conscious* that which was previously unconscious," which entails "excavating lost or dissociated parts of the memory or personality" (p. 46), but she insists that this is not merely an intellectual process. It is instead one that calls on all the emotional resources of the analyst to minister to the "damaged psyche" of the patient, for whom "the feeling of helplessness at the very source of one's being is a kind of torture for which there is no comparison" (p. 44).

In contrasting those "*limitations* of psychoanalysis" that are "inherent in the nature of the treatment," and thus unavoidable, such as its "length of time" and the need on the part of the analyst to charge a "commensurate fee" for the number of hours spent with each patient, with the defects that "should and could be remedied," Severn begins:

> The greatest objection to be made against psychoanalysis as such is, in my opinion, its *rigidity*. Being devised as a systemic and observational method, it lacks in flexibility and humanness in its personal application to sick people. It requires them to be put through a certain regime in a certain way, and if they refuse or object, they are dismissed as "unsuitable for treatment."
> (pp. 51–52)

In setting aside what are still commonly known as criteria of "analyzability," Severn—who was herself the furthest thing imaginable from a typical "neurotic" patient—censures the tendency of psychoanalysts to place their patients on a Procrustean couch and insist that they conform to a prescribed "regime," or else risk being turned away as "'unsuitable for treatment.'" The onus, in her view, should rather be on the analyst to summon the "flexibility and humanness" necessary to meet the needs of each patient, many of whom are likely to be suffering from extreme forms of mental "torture."

Recognizing that patients are always "full of resistances" because change requires giving up deeply engrained survival strategies, Severn stresses that the analyst "has to be very tactful in this process," which entails being aware that the patient "needs a very friendly understanding of and entering into his difficulties. He needs also an opportunity to say when he thinks the analyst is wrong, since the person of the analyst represents of necessity an authority to him" (p. 52). But it is not enough for the patient to be allowed simply to voice his opinions, for "unless the patient's objections are encouraged and treated seriously, and unless the analyst is prepared to admit that he may sometimes be in the wrong, even to the relinquishment of his most pet theories, no progress can be made and, indeed, great harm may be done."

Having just championed the principles of tact and elasticity, as well as friendliness and humility, Severn makes her first reference to Ferenczi—his name appears a total of eight times in in *The Discovery of the Self*—in the following sentence, where she writes with disarming casualness: "I think it was Ferenczi who first said, 'The patient is always right'" (p. 52). Indeed, Ferenczi throughout his final period stressed the importance of acknowledging one's mistakes, as when he declares in the *Clinical Diary*: "The analyst must be an authority that for the first time admits its faults, especially hypocrisy" (Dupont, 1985, p. 120); and in her interview with Eissler, Thompson (1952a) summarizes Ferenczi's "favorite theme" in the apothegm, "there are no bad patients, there are only bad analysts" (p. 13).

Severn's (1933) critique of Freud's "largely observational" method, which is bound to fall short in its "therapeutic application," leads her to maintain that the analytic relationship "should be anything but a pedagogical one, of a teacher and pupil nature" (p. 61). Based on his own experience as Freud's patient, Ferenczi writes even more pointedly in the *Clinical Diary* that Freud had "a narcissistic nature" and, because of "his antipathy toward any weaknesses or abnormalities, could not follow me down into those depths, and introduced the 'educational' stage too soon" (Dupont, 1985, p. 62). Ferenczi, however, refrained from taking Freud to task so directly in his writings for publication, whereas Severn did not hesitate to do so in her book.

Not only did Severn set forth the "fundamental difference" between Ferenczi and Freud in *The Discovery of the Self*, but what is still more remarkable is that she dared to voice her objections to Freud's face. It is a little-known fact, revealed in her interview with Eissler, that Severn met Freud on three occasions.[3] Severn's first interview with Freud took place in Vienna in 1925, within a few months of her arrival in Budapest. It had been arranged by Ferenczi at her request, and she likewise had a letter of introduction from Asch. She describes Freud as having been at that time "a very cordial, friendly person, and impressive but very reserved," who asked her about her analysis and "complimented me on coming to Ferenczi" (1952, p. 1). She makes it clear to Eissler that she sought out Freud not to ask what he thought about Ferenczi or for any therapeutic reason, but rather because she "wanted to see the great man" who "was the head of the whole system I was so absorbed in" in order to gain a sense of "what his personality was like" (p. 14).

Severn's final encounter with Freud occurred "in London late in '38, a few months before he died" (p. 9), more than five years after she had left Budapest and the death of Ferenczi. This valedictory meeting was an elaborate shadowboxing match. Freud concealed his anger toward Ferenczi, as well as his antipathy toward Severn herself, while Severn concealed not only what she knew of Ferenczi's true feelings about Freud but also the fact of their mutual analysis. In what appears to be a conflated memory of what she had heard from Ferenczi about three different visits of his own to Freud—the first in June 1929, the second in December 1931, and the last in September 1932 on his way to the Wiesbaden Congress—Severn tells Eissler how "just crushed" and "very hurt" Ferenczi was by Freud's response when he put forward the idea that the analyst must have "a sensitiveness to the patient's need that you could perhaps use the word love for," and also that it was essential for the analyst "to have been thoroughly analyzed himself so that he didn't have any hidden pockets in his mind or emotions that might affect his attitude toward his patients" (pp. 6–7).[4] As Severn was aware, Freud was "very annoyed" especially by the first of these proposals, and had gone so far as to accuse Ferenczi of being "adolescent or senile."

Against this backdrop, it is impossible to see Freud's "very friendly" reception of Severn in 1938—and his "expressed admiration for Ferenczi"—as anything other than a pretense, since, as Severn knew, such praise "was a little different from what he had said to Ferenczi himself a few years before" (p. 10). She quotes Freud as having said, "'Oh, I'm sure Ferenczi did the right thing'" in his analysis of her, by which he meant dissecting the Oedipus complex as well as "the usual resistances." A worthy sparring partner, Severn replied drily, "'Oh, certainly, exhaustively. But there was still something lacking,'" adding to Eissler that Freud "had no answer for that."

But the most significant of Severn's three encounters with Freud is the second, which she believes took place in 1929, when she had begun to discern that Ferenczi "hated intelligent women," which "naturally . . . made it a little difficult for my analysis to proceed" (p. 2). Without "criticizing Ferenczi in any way," Severn told Freud that "the trouble was" that his "early students . . . had not been thoroughly analyzed. They had been analyzed in an intellectual manner, and I don't think the transferences had been worked out very fully," though, she went on to observe to Eissler, "this limitation did not appear to Freud to be a limitation" (p. 3). Because Freud had not adequately analyzed Ferenczi's transference toward him, Severn was insinuating, Ferenczi's "hidden pockets" of emotion gave rise to a negative countertransference that became a stumbling block in his analysis of her. But what she was saying openly was unpalatable enough—namely, that Freud's "intellectual manner" of analysis was insufficient. He had let down not only Ferenczi but also Asch and his other "early students" who had been in analysis with him, to the detriment of their ability to treat their own analysands, and thereby hindered the "therapeutic application" of psychoanalysis.

Freud's enmity toward Severn becomes fully comprehensible once it is realized that, in addition to blaming her for having caused Ferenczi to stray from the path of orthodoxy, she had impugned his clinical skills as a psychoanalyst. Expatiating on the virtues of elasticity, tact, friendliness, and humility, as well as on her insistence that the analytic relationship "should be anything but a pedagogical one, of a teacher and pupil nature," Severn writes in *The Discovery of the Self* (1933) that "the patient is a human palpitating being, needing endless understanding and *Einfühlung*, as the Germans say it, a kind of 'feeling in' or identification with him and his problem" (p. 53). To do this, she adds, "requires not only great liberality of thought but great humanness of feeling," which is "not sentimentalism . . . but the kind of *pity* that unifies itself with its object—in short, in its highest sense—love."

As Severn acknowledges, "to speak this word to an orthodox analyst in regard to his patient is a sort of blasphemy from his point of view," but she reiterates that "any mechanized method of dealing with sick people, especially sick souls, is not only harsh but also dangerous" (p. 53). Lest there be any doubt, she clarifies that by "love" she does not mean erotic desire, but rather "the love that is tolerant, all-merciful, and warm, such as a wise mother gives her children, especially the sick ones, as a spontaneous and natural gift. Only this can bring about a real healing, but the need of it is unfortunately decried by psychoanalysis as a dangerous and weak indulgence." To round out her exposition of the betrayals—beginning with Freud—of the potential of psychoanalysis as a therapeutic endeavor, Severn concludes:

> Because every neurotic patient is in some sense still a child, not having completed his emotional maturity, he needs in a special sense to be treated as a child when ill and, especially in analysis, when reliving the throes of his childhood. The analyst must be a *better* parent—either father or mother—who was the cause of, or failed to understand, the emotions of the child.

Decades before Kohut, Severn recognized the indispensability of empathy in the analyst, while her claim that "the analyst must be a *better* parent" to the patient who is "reliving the throes of his childhood" prefigures Alexander's concept of the corrective emotional experience. Finally, in asserting that the analyst must feel love for his patients, which finds its prototype in the "spontaneous and natural gift" of a devoted mother to her child, Severn lays the groundwork for the argument of Daniel Shaw (2014) that, "given the specific ways in which many of our most important theorists have emphasized the crucial role of love in their theories of development, it should follow that our clinical theories call for and make use of the analyst's emotional responsiveness—in particular, the analyst's capacity to love authentically and use his love therapeutically" (p. 120). In a profound variation on this theme, Steven Stern (2017) has proposed that "it is the love of healing rather than the love of our patients per se that is our deepest, most fundamental motivation," though "the fullest psychoanalytic healing tends to occur in analytic dyads where analytic love does develop in a deep and unique way" (p. 33). As Severn (1952) told Eissler, she and Ferenczi "made many notes" both about analytic love and about the need for the analyst to have been "thoroughly analyzed," and they did so "with a view to possibly writing a book together about it" (p. 7). Although Severn was unaware of the *Clinical Diary*, Ferenczi had read her *magnum opus*, and the many points of convergence between their texts can therefore be ascribed not only to their eight-year analytic dialogue, or to Ferenczi's influence on her, but also to Severn's intellectual influence on Ferenczi, a number of whose later writings, she discloses, "were dictated to me or rearranged by talking to me, and I typed many of them for him" (p. 8).

Everything Severn had to say to Freud in their 1929 meeting about the impossibility of adequately analyzing the transference in an exclusively "intellectual manner" is spelled out at length in *The Discovery of the Self* (1933). If the negative transference is not resolved, she cautions, so that the "aggressive elements in the unconscious of the patient have been merely *transferred* and not *transformed*," the resulting "fiasco is, of course, very unfortunate and, having not infrequently occurred, has been the occasion of much just criticism against the practice of psychoanalysis" (p. 55).

Although Ferenczi's reproaches of Freud on this score, which elicited Freud's embittered apologia in "Analysis Terminable and Interminable," are well known, it has not been sufficiently appreciated that Abram Kardiner (1977) reached an identical verdict on his analysis with Freud, which appears to have commenced on October 3, 1921 and been terminated six months later, against Kardiner's wishes, on April 1, 1922. Exactly as Ferenczi did to his infinitely greater psychological cost, Kardiner writes that he made a "silent pact with Freud," which stipulated, "'I will continue to be compliant provided that you will let me enjoy your protection'" (p. 59). As a man of thirty, Kardiner knew that his hopes for a career in psychoanalysis depended on Freud's patronage, and "if he rejected me, I would lose my chance to enter this magical profession"; but, as he retrospectively came to recognize, "this tacit acceptance on my part sealed off an important part of my character from scrutiny." As a consequence of this unspoken bargain with Freud, Kardiner elaborates, "I surrendered my aggressive drive and masked my self-assertion under a cloak of submission" (p. 99).

Only in hindsight did Kardiner grasp the irony that, although Freud had no difficulty informing him "of my fear of uncovering a repressed hostility to my father," Freud "failed to point out that this was a pattern that was now operative in the present" with himself in the analysis, as well as with "other male authority figures" (p. 100). In other words, "the central fact of the transference situation was overlooked by the man who had discovered the very process of transference itself." The upshot of this unhealthy situation was that Kardiner left Vienna feeling his own version of the elation aroused in Ferenczi when he was told by Freud, as he recalled in the *Clinical Diary*, that he was "the most perfect heir of his ideas" (Dupont, 1985, p. 184). As Kardiner (1977) puts it, "I was puffed up with pride, arrogant as a peacock with having been one of the elect, molded fresh by the hand of the master himself" (pp. 93–94). Inevitably, however, as Severn would not have been surprised to learn, Kardiner's sense of election "did not last long, for I soon discovered that my training was inadequate to the practice of psychoanalysis, and that I had embarked on an odyssey without map or compass."

After her critique of the "*limitations* of psychoanalysis" as it had been promulgated by Freud, Severn (1933) turns in "Psychosynthesis" to the radically different conception of theory and practice she had elaborated together with Ferenczi. As an exordium, she shares an autobiographical anecdote about the analyst–patient relationship:

> *Response* is needed and a kind of pre-vision, if one may say so, of what this hampered person is trying to tell. I know a well-known analyst who sat and *looked out of his window* with a vacant, bored expression, without a single word of response, while listening to the tragic tale that a distressed and anxious person was struggling to tell him.
>
> (p. 67; italics added)

Since, as we have seen, Severn had covertly described her traumatic experience with Jelliffe in *The Psychology of Behaviour*, but had her brief analysis with Rank in 1924, it follows that it must be the latter whom she here has in her sights. Rank was, indubitably, "a well-known analyst" who, as she told Eissler, had advertised himself to his American clientele at that time as "*the* most brilliant student of Freud's."

Just as Severn's critique of Jelliffe is echoed by Mabel Dodge, so, too, her portrait of Rank gains credence when set alongside that of Anaïs Nin, who, in her exquisite short story "The Voice" (1945), gives a fictionalized rendering of her relationship with Rank as both her analyst and her lover. As Nin's narrator says of her alter ego Djuna, who is sitting with the Voice in his consulting room: "The little man no one ever saw, he was *standing by the window*" (p. 100; italics added), looking out at the skaters in the park. He then engages in a self-pitying lament, "'My body is cramped. I want to do the things they do. At most I am allowed to watch. I am condemned to see through a perpetual keyhole every intimate scene of their life. But I am left out.'" Nin first met Rank in Paris in 1933, and subsequently joined him in New York, amid the skyscrapers of which "The Voice" is set and where Severn had likewise had his "regular three-month course" of treatment nine years earlier. The reference to the window in both women's accounts is an uncanny parallel. But whereas Rank was sexually obsessed with Nin, who gratified his transgressive longing "'to be taken in . . . to be desired, possessed, tortured too,'" he could muster no interest in Severn even as a "human palpitating being." On the contrary, he listened to her "tragic tale" with a "vacant, bored expression," about which Ferenczi undoubtedly heard an earful when she commenced her analysis with him the following year.

The two prongs of Severn's (1933) answer to Freud are her revival of trauma theory and the modification of therapeutic technique that this alternative conceptual framework entails. She throws down the gauntlet in her chapter "Nightmares Are Real":

> The importance of *trauma* as a specific and almost universal cause of neurosis was first impressed upon me by Ferenczi, who, probing deeply, found it in nearly all his cases. He thus resurrected and gave new value to an idea that had once, much earlier, been entertained by Freud, but that was discarded by him in favor of "fantasy" as the explanation of the strange tales or manifestations given by his patients.
> (p. 91)

She goes on to point out the insufficiency of Freud's explanation of the "seemingly lurid ideas" frequently voiced by patients in psychoanalysis:

> It was supposed by Freud to be an exaggeration of some comparatively slight early mishaps, aided and abetted by the child's alleged

"perversities" that Freud believed were an inherent part of his early development and due to the severe conflict between his instincts and society. Experience has convinced me, however, that the patient does not "invent" but *always tells the truth*, even though in a distorted form; and, further, that what he tells is mostly of a severe and specific injury, inflicted on him when he was young and helpless.

Everything that is at stake in the quarrel between Ferenczi and Freud is here spelled out by Severn with exemplary lucidity. She gives credit to Ferenczi for having convinced her that trauma is the "specific and almost universal cause of neurosis," and the "experience" to which she refers surely includes the excavation of her own memories of childhood abuse, in addition to what she had learned as an analyst from her work with patients, including Ferenczi and her daughter Margaret. Then, having said so many fundamental things on the subject of trauma, Severn proceeds to cite for the first time in the history of psychoanalysis Ferenczi's final paper:

That the patient, when a child, might have been the innocent victim of unrestrained passion of various sorts from certain adults in his immediate environment was never considered seriously, and has only very recently been stated by Ferenczi as his opinion in a published paper. I believe, however, as he does, that it will be found to be the *chief* if not the *only* cause of severe neurosis and also of psychosis.

(p. 91)

Although she speaks of Ferenczi's "published paper," in a footnote Severn refers to it not as "Confusion of Tongues between Adults and the Child (The Language of Tenderness and of Passion [*Leidenschaft*])," the now-famous title under which it appeared (in German) in 1933 in the *Internationale Zeitschrift für Psychoanalyse*. Rather, she cites it by the more prosaic title it bore when Ferenczi presented it as a lecture the previous year at the Wiesbaden Congress, "The Emotions [*Leidenschaften*] of Adults and Their Influence on the Development of the Sexual Life and Character of Children." Severn's book, which, she told Eissler, "contains the fruit of my long and intensive analysis" with Ferenczi (1952, p. 24), must therefore have gone to print before the publication of Ferenczi's paper, and a substantial portion of it been written between September 1932 and her departure from Budapest in February 1933, while Severn was going through the excruciating termination of her analysis, but before she had learned of Ferenczi's death on May 22, of which her text contains no hint.

Having posited trauma as the "almost universal cause of neurosis" and rejected Freud's fantasy theory, Severn then describes what happens to a child who becomes "the innocent victim of unrestrained passion" of his or her adult caretakers. When "some piece of sexual knowledge or experience" is "abruptly or inconsiderately thrust upon the child's attention," she writes:

> It is really the same kind of "shock" or impact which one sees quite plainly if an automobile runs at full speed into a moving train. The psyche *breaks*, is fragmented into bits too small for any one of them to retain anything more than its own tiny portion of the total catastrophe. There is no *memory* of the event because the shock is too great and the connecting threads between what existed before and what exists after are quite out of commission. Fortunately, we psychologists—or some of us at least—do not believe that the material is *destroyed*, but that it exists still in its fragmented form and can, by dint of much labor and skill, be re-collected and put together again. This means recovering the memory, bringing it back into *time*, and thus establishing a unity in the psyche where previously only chaos existed.
>
> (p. 93)

Severn's focus on trauma, especially the sexual abuse of children, leads her ineluctably to the intertwined topics of dissociation and the workings of memory. The depth of her reflections shows why Severn can now dismiss Prince's work on "split personality" as a "comparatively slight contribution." It is impossible to tell whether Severn is channeling Ferenczi, or whether she is his medium, when he addresses (1933a) his largely uncomprehending audience of Freudian loyalists in Wiesbaden:

> If the shocks increase in number during the development of the child, the number and various kinds of splits in the personality increase too, and soon it becomes extremely difficult to maintain contact without confusion with all the fragments, each of which behaves as a separate entity yet does not know of even the existence of the others. Eventually it may arrive at a state which—continuing the picture of *fragmentation*—one would be justified in calling *atomization*. One must possess a good

deal of courage when facing such a state, though I hope even here to be able to find threads that can link up the various parts.

(p. 165)

These passages from Ferenczi and Severn encapsulate all the issues in the forefront of contemporary thinking about trauma, while they simultaneously take us back to Janet, whose ghost continues to knock at the doors of the psychoanalytic castle. As Van der Kolk (2014) has observed, just as it was Janet who "coined the term 'dissociation' to describe the splitting off and isolation of memory imprints" in traumatized patients, so, too, did he point out that "dissociation prevents the trauma from being integrated within the conglomerated, ever-shifting stores of autobiographical memory, in essence creating a dual memory system" (p. 182). From this standpoint, as Severn argued, it is the task of therapy to transform traumatic memory into autobiographical memory by restoring the "connecting threads" between the atomized fragments of the "total catastrophe," thereby "recovering the memory, bringing it back into *time*, and thus establishing a unity in the psyche where previously only chaos existed."

Severn's (1933) axiom that what made traumatic events "harmful in the first place was, in every case, the *shock*, the psychic reaction to them," so that the emotion that was aroused "was incapable of assimilation by the person suffering it," has as its corollary that it is precisely "this feeling-tone that has to be recovered and experienced again in order to bring, first, conviction and, second, release through reconstruction" (p. 72). This insistence that "emotional recollection and reproduction" are "the *sine qua non* of successful analysis," which Severn says "might more properly be classed as a *synthesis*," prompts her to reiterate her critique of the "intellectual methodology" of psychoanalysis that "has never encouraged such scenes ('reenactment,' etc.) or believed in them when they spontaneously occurred as anything more than fantasies" (p. 71). Once again, she makes it clear that the ideas she is presenting are not hers alone:

> It is an important measure that was worked out between Ferenczi and myself in the course of my long analysis with him—a development that enables the patient to relive, as though it were *now*, the traumatic events of his past, aided by the dramatic participation of the analyst.
>
> (pp. 71–72)

Severn explains that she was led by these jointly achieved breakthroughs to devise "a 'direct method' for entrance into the unconscious, inducing a trance state, etc., to foster recollection" (p. 72), observing in a footnote that "this addition to, or alteration in, psychoanalytic technique has since been adopted by Ferenczi and is the basis of his so-called 'relaxation principle.'"

Severn gives no hint in her book that her "long analysis" with Ferenczi turned into a mutual affair, presenting herself to public view as having been solely his patient. On the other hand, she has no compunctions about casting herself, at least on occasion, as the majority shareholder in their partnership, since she asserts that her use of trance states to access the unconscious was "adopted" and renamed by Ferenczi. That Ferenczi would not have disputed this claim is supported by the fact that, whereas the names of Thompson and de Forest, his other two leading American disciples, are nowhere to be found in his published writings, he pays tribute to Severn on two separate occasions.

He does so first in "The Principle of Relaxation and Neocatharsis" (1930), the paper he gave at the 1929 Oxford Congress that inaugurates Ferenczi's final period, and in which he employs the teratoma metaphor to describe the effects of trauma.[5] Hs says there that he is "partly indebted to discoveries made by our colleague, Elizabeth Severn," for the notion that "in every case of neurotic amnesia . . . it seems likely that a *psychotic splitting off* of a part of the personality occurs under the influence of shock," but that the "dissociated part" survives "hidden, ceaselessly endeavouring to make itself felt, without finding any outlet except in neurotic symptoms" (pp. 121–22). Ferenczi's reference to Severn as "our colleague" at a meeting of the International Psychoanalytical Association must have been especially gratifying to her, a lifelong outsider, because it signaled his public approbation of her as a psychoanalyst. Similarly, in "Child-Analysis in the Analysis of Adults" (1931) Ferenczi again credits "our colleague, Elizabeth Severn, who is doing a training analysis with me," with pointing out how "I sometimes disturbed the spontaneity of the fantasy-productions" with extended interventions, and urging him to confine himself instead to "very simple questions instead of statements, which should compel the patient to continue the work by his own exertions." With exemplary humility, Ferenczi does not fail to "confess" to his readers this "error in tactics, the remedying of which taught me a great deal on an important matter of principle" (p. 133).

No aspect of Ferenczi and Severn's recalibration of psychoanalysis has proven more controversial than the proposal that the patient's "emotional recollection and reproduction" of traumatic memories should be "aided by the dramatic participation of the analyst." Notwithstanding her insistence on the limitations of "the accepted psychoanalytic mode of treatment, which is purely dissecting in nature and that places its reliance instead on the mental grasp or 'reconstruction' the patient can gain of the past," as well as her defense of a method that, "having found the trauma or specific cause of the illness, does not scorn to 'play mother' or be Good Samaritan to the injured one and that encourages the full reproduction of the feeling-tone of the traumatic period or events *under new and better circumstances*" (1933, p. 73), however, Severn is far from being opposed to reconstruction or recollection. Her point is that this process, rather than being purely cerebral or cognitive, is above all emotional and visceral, because it is the hitherto unprocessed "feeling-tone that has to be recovered and experienced again" in order to build "a bridge" in the analysis from the present back to the past, so that "the broken pieces of the psyche" can "return to their original places and the patient is helped to endure the catastrophe again, this time without 'bursting,' losing consciousness, or going insane, which is what shock consists of" (p. 94).

As Severn makes clear in "Nightmares Are Real," dreams occupy a central role in both her theoretical and her personal projects. Not only, as she informs the reader, has she "made a collection of dreams of my patients running into the thousands," but she has compiled a parallel archive of her own dreams "over a long period of years, numbering also several thousand" (p. 86). Like Ferenczi in his posthumously published *Notes and Fragments* (1920, 1930–1932), Severn goes beyond Freud's wish-fulfillment model to accentuate the "traumatolytic function of the dream" (p. 240). In Severn's (1933) words:

> Now dreams have, as Freud pointed out, a special function of compensating for the deficiencies and pains of actual life; but, as I would like to show, dreams are also *the magazine and repository of forgotten facts*, and the theater wherein these facts are dramatically reenacted.
> (p. 88)

From the perspective of trauma theory, dreams, rather than being primarily pleasurable hallucinations, and only in exceptional cases manifestations of the repetition compulsion, are better understood as "a collection of disturbing or disastrous incidents that one is trying, by fantastic means, to ameliorate and render harmless" (p. 89). Even a wish-fulfilling dream can be regarded as a rudimentary instance of a problem-solving activity. To be sure, dreams are psychic productions, with admixtures of "fantastic" distortion, but at their root are the "deficiencies and pains" that have become the *"forgotten facts"* of the dreamer's life. Since these anxiety-inducing episodes are "dramatically reenacted" in the "theater" of the dream, this makes the dream for Severn the prototype of the analytic situation, in which the patient is invited "to relive, as though it were *now*, the traumatic events of his past, aided by the dramatic participation of the analyst."

Unlike the legion of fashionable theorists in the tradition of Klein and Bion who, like Fonagy and Target (1997), focus exclusively on "psychic reality" and dismiss the quest for "historical truth and historical reality" as "not our business as psychoanalysts and psychotherapists" (p. 216), for Severn the "other scene" of both the dream and the analytic situation is a place where the truth of the patient's experience going back to infancy can be revealed. As she writes of nightmares, "they are *historical* and tell always of some *decisive and destructive event in the past*. They are records of personal catastrophes, the consequence of which was the destruction of the whole mental machinery" (1933, p. 90). Indeed, while not denying the constructive aspects of memory, Severn's commitment to mitigating the impact of traumatic shocks on the psyche leads her to bring out the enduring truth of Freud's archeological metaphor for the psychoanalytic project. According to Severn:

> It is my belief that no nightmare can exist except a severe trauma has taken place of which it is the repetition and sign and symbol. . . . This is the puzzle that the analyst has to solve, like the putting together of mosaics, the key to whose pattern has been lost. When the old pattern can be successfully reconstructed and come into consciousness as a piece of emotional reality, the mind can be mended and the energy that was previously contained in it, only "shot to pieces," can be salvaged and turned to new uses in the present life. This is the "cure."
>
> (p. 94)

Or, in an epigrammatic formulation that might have served as Severn's motto for *The Discovery of the Self*: "'Hallucination,' they say—*Memory*, I say, a memory that had been kept alive in the unconscious and that was now, perhaps for the first time, projected outward into the objective world where we could see it" (p. 74).[6]

Notes

1 For an account of a forty-year treatment exemplifying these themes, see Steven Stern, "Analytic Adoption of the Psychically Homeless." Citing the justly admired work of Aron (1991), Stern (2021) cautions that what he terms "mutual adoption" must not "violate the fundamental frame and asymmetry of the analytic relationship" (p. 29). Discussing his paper in an online forum of the International Association of Psychoanalytic Self Psychology, however, Stern (March 14, 2021) offers the nuanced elaboration that, although no arrangement should be countenanced "in which meeting the therapist's needs became a major factor," if during this primal experiment in mutual analysis "there was still a sense that this was happening within Ferenczi's analytic frame, and that its primary purpose was that Severn (not Ferenczi) seemed to need that 'equality,'" then he could see how "their mutual work could still fit within an analytically viable needed relationship where a 'complex asymmetry' was retained." As I have argued in the Prelude, while Ferenczi unquestionably benefited from his analysis by Severn, he was chiefly motivated by the desire to give her the analysis she needed—even if that meant becoming her patient—and the irresolvable paradox in this exception that (in every sense) proves the rule about the importance of preserving the analytic frame is captured by Stern's concept of "complex asymmetry."
2 In a footnote, Severn acknowledges that Jung "is associated with 'synthesis'" and espouses a "'prospective' view of psychoanalysis," but she criticizes him for minimizing "the analytic procedure too much, especially in relation to childhood, thus weakening the value of his conception as a whole" (p. 63n2).
3 Masson (1984) asserts incorrectly that "Freud never met Mrs. Severn" (p. 183), while Eissler, despite having done his analytic training in Vienna in the 1930s and his subsequent career as "Freud's bulldog," had to admit to Severn (1952) that he "never saw him" (p. 1).
4 In "Confusion of Tongues" (1933a), Ferenczi addresses the issue of "the analysis of the analyst" in order to make the point that "the average training analysis lasts only a few months, or at most, one to one and a half years," with the result that frequently "our patients gradually become better analyzed than we are" (p. 158).
5 Just as Ferenczi changed the title of his Wiesbaden Congress paper for publication, so, too, his Oxford Congress paper was initially called "Advances in Psychoanalytic Technique" before he retitled it more memorably "The Principle of Relaxation and Neocatharsis."
6 Compare Van der Kolk's (2014) searching question, "But if the stories I'd heard [from patients] in the wee hours were true, could it be that these 'hallucinations' were in fact fragmented memories of real experiences?" (p. 25).

Chapter 5

The Case of Ferenczi

On December 14, 1932, Margaret Severn (1988) wrote to her mother from Paris that "the cat is out of the bag" because she had "told Neder that you are no longer being analyzed by Fer but that he is being analysed by you" (p. 2,372). In a superlative feat of research, Brennan (2015a) has established the identities of the eight principal analysands designated by code names in the *Clinical Diary*, one of them being the Australian-born Roberta Morphet Nederhoed—abbreviated by Ferenczi to "N.D."or "N.H.D."—who came to the United States in 1916, where she became (among other things) head of the advertising department for Cunard Ship Lines in New York. Margaret (1988) justifies her disclosure not only by pointing out that "there are other people there, like Lowel and Clara, who know it"—"Lowel" being Alice Lowell, or "B." in the *Diary*, of the "Boston Brahmin" family of Lowells, while Clara is, of course, Clara Thompson, or "Dm."—but also by reminding her mother that neither she nor Ferenczi had "told me that his analysis with you was to be regarded as a secret" (p. 2,373).

Margaret's testimony contradicts Fortune's (1993) assertion that Severn had informed her daughter in a December 1932 letter that "Ferenczi insisted that she keep his analysis by her a secret" (p. 112). But it remains true that Ferenczi would not have wanted this extremely sensitive information to leak out as it did. Indeed, in one of her handwritten interpolations to the interview with Eissler, Severn (1952) stated that when Ferenczi "at last" went to Vienna to put before Freud his ideas about analytic love, he did so "without telling him that he had been analyzed by me" (p. 6). Since the mutual analysis took place in 1932, and was evidently still ongoing as late as December of that year, this can only refer to Ferenczi's final meeting with Freud before the Wiesbaden Congress. But though Severn was willing, twenty years after the fact, to disclose to Eissler that she and

Ferenczi had engaged in a mutual analysis, in *The Discovery of the Self* she protected his reputation by portraying herself before the public as having been solely his patient. Thus, until my edition of Severn's book, the sole published source of knowledge concerning their experiment had been the *Clinical Diary*. But since Severn informed Eissler not only that *The Discovery of the Self* "replaced to some extent the plans Ferenczi and I had had for a more scientific mutual publication," but also that "he saw the MSS. before I left and approved of it" (p. 24), we know for a fact that he was aware that she had preserved for posterity—albeit in camouflaged form—the "other side of the story" of their experiment in mutual analysis.

The case history of Ferenczi is the third of six extended narratives in "Nightmares Are Real," which forms the clinical heart of Severn's book, even as her exposition of their views on trauma and technique in "Psychosynthesis" is its theoretical soul. Severn (1933) introduces her patient as "a man of especially high moral and intellectual standing, with a very balanced outlook on life and marked serenity of manner," who "suffered from various physical symptoms, which he ascribed mostly to bodily causes," and was "in a state of constant depression in regard to his health" (p. 96). Contending that the analysis uncovered not only a "definite psychological clinical picture quite sufficient to account for his state of physical deterioration," but also, "after considerable work, a clearly outlined psychosis," Severn affirms, "the patient was not the balanced, well-adjusted person that he, and others, had imagined."

Ferenczi had for decades been worried about his health, and by October of 1932 he was in a "state of physical deterioration," which he attributed in the *Clinical Diary* to his toxic relationship with Freud—a "definite psychological clinical picture." Severn's initial perception of her "patient" as being "very balanced" and possessing a "marked serenity of manner" comports with Ferenczi's account in the *Diary* of how he had been taught by Freud to exhibit a "calm, unemotional reserve" and "unruffled assurance that one knew better" (Dupont, 1985, p. 185). In describing the "antipathy" and "apprehension" aroused in him by Severn, he acknowledges, "I appear to have assumed, perhaps unconsciously, the attitude of superiority of my intrepid masculinity, which the patient took to be genuine, whereas this was a conscious professional pose, partly adopted as a defensive measure against anxiety" (p. 97). Severn (1933) adds that "this condition was naturally perceived by me in advance of the patient and was only recognized by him after it had been involuntarily enacted" (p. 96).

Although Severn's account makes it seem that she is the analyst, while her patient could be anyone, what she is describing is how she recognized, long before Ferenczi did himself, that his negative countertransference was the root cause of the impasse that had arisen in his analysis of her. In her interview with Eissler, Severn (1952) adds that she came to this realization through her dreams:

> As we got further on in my analysis, we began some mutual research work, and he discussed all the various technical points with me. This was very valuable but I gradually got the feeling that he was hampered in spite of a very brilliant mind and a very responsive personality . . . by the lack of a complete analysis in his own case; that there were certain feelings that he had applied to patients in spite of himself that were unsuitable and a block to the work. He theoretically knew that he shouldn't have any personal reactions and he didn't for a long time admit that he had any, but through my own dream life they were revealed and they were largely of an aggressive and critical nature against me.
>
> (p. 2)

Pressed to elaborate, Severn explains that it became evident from her dreams "that Ferenczi had these feelings against me, and he finally admitted, with my prodding, that, among other things, he hated intelligent women, and this naturally made it a little difficult for my analysis to proceed."

Without mentioning the part played by Severn's dreams in the process, Ferenczi tells the story from his point of view in the *Clinical Diary*. In his account, he and Severn each insisted on the unconscious hatred they detected in the other, and the logjam was not broken until he relented and acceded to her demands that she be allowed to analyze him:

> There was one point over which we came to be at loggerheads. I maintained firmly that she ought to hate me, because of my wickedness toward her; she resolutely denied this, yet these denials were at times so ferocious that they always betrayed feelings of hatred. For her part she maintained that she sensed feelings of hate in me, and began saying her analysis would never make any progress until I allowed her to analyze those hidden feelings in me. I resisted this for approximately a year, but then I decided to make this sacrifice.
>
> (Dupont, 1985, p. 99)

By his "wickedness" toward Severn, Ferenczi means his having informed her that he could not fulfill her fantasy of being the "perfect lover" (p. 98). When she had asked whether he "was in love with her," he responded "quite frankly" that analysis "was a purely intellectual process" and "the genital processes of which we were speaking had nothing to do with my wishes."

This brusque reminder of the impossibility of sexual relations between them produced in Severn an "indescribable" shock, which in turn impelled Ferenczi to curtail the "medical superperformances" to which she had grown accustomed: "After a hard inner struggle I left the patient by herself during vacations, reduced the number of sessions, etc." (p. 98). Severn's "ferocious" reaction to these successive rejections formed the basis of Ferenczi's insistence that she harbored "feelings of hatred" for him, which she countered with an insistence on his "hidden feelings" of hatred toward her. Only after a year-long stalemate, when Ferenczi had the grace and courage to concede, to his own "enormous surprise," that Severn was "right in many respects" (p. 99) in what she had been saying about him, did he agree to make the ultimate sacrifice by capitulating to the role reversal for which she had vociferously clamored.

Although Severn's imputing of "a clearly outlined psychosis" to Ferenczi might seem to lend credence to Jones's (1957) accusation that Ferenczi, like Rank, "towards the end of his life, developed psychotic manifestations that revealed themselves in, among other ways, a turning away from Freud and his doctrines" (p. 45), she does not mean that he suffered any loss in his sense of reality. Rather, Severn (1933) takes her stand on the principle that "the *chief* if not the *only* cause of severe neurosis and also of psychosis" (p. 91) is what, in "Confusion of Tongues" (1933a), Ferenczi calls the "*introjection of the menacing person or aggressor*" (p. 163). As Severn (1933) expounds their jointly held trauma theory, "the damage or evil one finds hidden in the unconscious" should not be understood as the expression of endogenous "emotions that were aroused in the unfortunate subject," but is rather the result of the "angry and insane emotions" of the adult abuser, "which were projected directly into the defenseless psyche of the child and left there as a perpetually destructive force or 'alter ego'—a sort of parasite on his own personality" (p. 76), which, following Severn's lead, Ferenczi (1930) called a "teratoma" (p. 123). Severn (1933) continues, "nearly all patients suffering from severe trauma complain of feeling 'something foreign' in their make-up. This something finally proves to be the influence of another personality which was forcibly imposed upon the patient some time during his tender years" (p. 77).

Thus, what Severn is arguing, in an apothegm occurring twice in her book, is that "*all insanity is the result of cruelty*" (pp. 81, 91), and that if one is to "solve the problem of the neurotic," it is frequently necessary "to push the analysis far enough to come upon the hidden psychosis" (p. 90) that even "a very balanced outlook on life and marked serenity of manner" may conceal. This formulation prefigures Winnicott's (1969) definition of a "borderline" case as one "in which the core of the patient's disturbance is psychotic, but the patient has enough psychoneurotic organization always to be able to present psychoneurosis or psychosomatic disorder when the central psychotic anxiety threatens to break through in crude form" (p. 87), so that the analysis will remain incomplete as long as the psychotic core has not been penetrated. That Severn was correct in her assessment of Ferenczi as a "borderline" case is corroborated by his own avowal in the *Clinical Diary* that "psychoanalytical insight into my own emotional emptiness, which was shrouded by overcompensation (repressed—unconscious—psychosis) led to a self-diagnosis of schizophrenia" (Dupont, 1985, p. 160).

Exactly how Ferenczi's façade of "intrepid masculinity" crumbled, and his psychosis was "involuntarily enacted" during their mutual analysis, is recounted by Severn (1933) in a literally dramatic fashion: "He spoke to me suddenly one day about Strindberg's play *The Father*, and became himself almost immediately the insane son. He broke down and asked with tears in his eyes, if I would sometimes think of him kindly after he had been put away in the asylum" (pp. 96–97). Severn says that Ferenczi "evidently expected to be thus sent away at that moment," and that he added, "with terrible pathos, 'And we like, when the straitjacket must be put on us, that it shall be done by our mother.'" She interprets, "I immediately saw by this that the patient was reexperiencing a severe trauma in which he expected his mother to send him away as insane" (p. 97).

The title of Strindberg's 1887 masterpiece is ironic, since the Captain, a military officer and freethinker who initially seems to dominate his household full of women, becomes obsessed with doubts that he is the father of his daughter, Bertha. The conflicts with his wife, Laura, lead to a regression in which she takes on a maternal role: "Weep then, my child, and you will have your mother with you again. Do you remember that it was as your mother I first came into your life? . . . You were a giant of a child and had either come into the world ahead of your time—or perhaps you were unwanted" (p. 39). The Captain confirms, "My father and mother did not want a child; and so I was born without a will of my own."

Strindberg here encapsulates the syndrome delineated by Ferenczi in "The Unwelcome Child and His Death Instinct" (1929b), a paper that (notwithstanding its title) actually *dispenses* with the concept of a death instinct in favor of "conscious or unconscious signs of aversion or impatience on the part of the mother" to explain the "unconscious self-destructive trends" (pp. 103–4) so often seen in analytic patients. The Captain likewise displays the "*precocious maturity*" that, as Ferenczi sets forth in "Confusion of Tongues" (1933a, p. 165), is a common response to childhood traumas. Laura's plan to have her husband declared insane and committed to an asylum is termed by her brother, the Pastor, "an innocent murder that cannot be reached by the law" (Strindberg, 1887, p. 45). As the straitjacket is placed on the unsuspecting Captain by his erstwhile nursemaid, Margaret, she reminds him, "Do you remember when you were my darling little child and I used to tuck you in at night and read 'God loves the little children dearly' to you?" (p. 51). Once pinioned, the Captain rages against every woman he has ever known as his "deadly enemy" (p. 53), but soon collapses on Margaret's breast: "Let me put my head in your lap. There! It's so nice and warm! Lean over me so that I can feel your breast!—Oh, how wonderful to fall asleep at a mother's breast—whether mother or mistress... but most wonderful at a mother's!" (p. 55; ellipses in original). As the play ends, the Captain wails, "A man has no children, it is only women who bear children," before falling victim to a stroke. Feeling his pulse, the Doctor pronounces, "he may still come back to life: ... but to what kind of awakening—that we cannot tell" (p. 56; ellipses in original).

In disclosing Ferenczi's identification with the character of Strindberg's Captain, Severn opens a window into his psyche. It is striking that she should write, "He spoke to me suddenly one day about Strindberg's play *The Father*, and became himself almost immediately the insane son," since the crux of the play is that the father *is* "the insane son" and psychically not a father at all. Ferenczi himself, of course, who allowed himself to be "adopted ... almost like a son" (Dupont, 1985, p. 184) by Freud, had only stepchildren, thus embodying the Captain's plight. It is equally striking that Ferenczi should have said to Severn, "And we like, when the straitjacket must be put on us, that it shall be done by our *mother*," since in the play the straitjacket is put on the Captain not by his mother but by his nursemaid.

But just as Margaret is conflated by the Captain with his mother, so, too, the "traumatic events of his past" relived by Ferenczi "as though it were *now*," thanks to Severn's "dramatic participation" as his analyst, were perpetrated by both his mother and his caretakers. Severn (1933) first recounts "a severe trauma" with his mother that he had reenacted with her:

> We already knew something of the story, of his mother as an angry, hysterical woman, often scolding and threatening her child, and especially for a certain event that she had treated with such harshness and vituperation as to make him feel completely crazy and branded as a felon. He had already gained much insight into himself, and the unexpected reproduction in the analysis of a part of this painful scene enabled him to acknowledge this traumatically-caused insanity for the first time in himself, which was the beginning of its dissolution.
> (p. 97)

Although it is less important to try to ascertain exactly what happened to Ferenczi as a child than it is to recognize how he was able "to acknowledge this traumatically-caused insanity for the first time in himself," not just by managing "to recollect these events mentally" but above all by reactivating in his analysis with Severn the "feeling-quality that has to be recovered and experienced again in order to bring, first, conviction and, second, release through reconstruction" (p. 72), we can nonetheless establish with a considerable degree of confidence the cascade of events by which he was traumatized. In his sublime self-analytic letter to Freud on December 26, 1912, written in the throes of his love triangle with Gizella and Elma Pálos, Ferenczi confessed to Freud that, "at the age of about three," he was "caught by the cook in mutual touching" with his one-year-elder sister Gisela, "and (after having been reported to my mother?) threatened with a kitchen knife (obviously a threat of castration)" (Brabant et al., 1993, p. 452).[1] This appears to be the earliest "painful scene" in Ferenczi's life of which Severn witnessed the "unexpected reproduction" when he became her patient during the mutual analysis.

Whatever Severn (1933) may have meant by a "certain event," she proceeds to narrate "still another serious trauma, allied to that caused by the mother," in which household servants were also involved, namely, "an unscrupulous attack by an adult person on the child's sensibilities, which was ruinous to his mental integrity and subsequent health" (p. 97). Sándor is now six years old, and rather than engaging in mutual masturbation with his sister, he is the victim of sexual abuse by an adult, with all the sequelae that one would expect:

> He was a boy of six, his nurse the offender. She was a comely young woman of voluptuous type who, for the satisfaction of her own urgencies, seduced the child, i.e. used him forcibly as best she could in lieu of an adult partner. The effect on the child was twofold: he was, on the one hand, horrified, frightened, and emotionally shocked by coming in contact with such emotional violence. On the other hand, he was in a real sense "seduced" in that he was made suddenly and unduly precocious, a *desire* was aroused in him that was beyond his years and his capacity, but which remained, nevertheless, to act as a constant excitation, with an inclination to a repetition of the experience.
>
> (p. 98)

As in the episode with his sister and the cook, where we are aided by Ferenczi's letter to Freud, he augments Severn's disguised case history by providing in the *Clinical Diary* his own version of what happened to him with the nurse. There he reports how, during mutual analysis, "I submerged myself deeply in the reproduction of infantile experiences" involving "passionate scenes" with a housemaid, who "probably allowed me to play with her breasts, but then pressed my head between her legs, so that I became frightened and felt as if I was suffocating" (Dupont, 1985, p. 61). Severn's (1933) narrative of Ferenczi's later traumatic experience continues:

> Another servant, having been a partial witness of the affair, told it at once to the boy's mother, after having threatened him with violent punishment herself. His mother's reaction was even more severe and was aimed chiefly at the boy, as though he were the culprit, and of an unspeakable sort. By her violent condemnation she made him feel the worst of sinners and completely alienated from her love and understanding. He bowed before the inevitable, but was broken. He became bitter and sullen and obliged to "forget" an experience that in a psychic sense ruined his whole existence.
>
> (pp. 98–99)

In both instances, household servants engage in reprehensible acts, including threats of "violent punishment," but then report the boy to his mother, whose "even more severe" reaction makes him feel "the worst of sinners," "completely crazy," and "a felon." As if this were not enough, Ferenczi in the *Diary* also recalls having received "terrifyingly rough treatment from a nurse in my early childhood after an incident of anal soiling" (Dupont, 1985, p. 36). Ferenczi's mother perpetrates the most extreme forms of "emotional violence," while the servants are chiefly associated with physical and sexual trauma. This polarity returns in Ferenczi's triangle with Gizella and Elma Pálos, in which Gizella (whose name makes her simultaneously a reincarnation of his sister) occupies the maternal role, while Elma is the "seductive" nurse. But the roles are reversed when Severn enters the picture. As she informs Eissler, it emerged from her analysis of Ferenczi that his wife "represented a nurse of his early childhood," who aroused "probably the strongest feeling he had" toward a woman, whereas she herself "figured in the mother category," toward whom Ferenczi's feeling "was one of more or less resentment" (1952, p. 13). Ferenczi confirms that he identified Severn with his mother when he writes in the *Clinical Diary*, "in R.N. I find my mother again, namely the real one, who was hard and energetic and of whom I was afraid" (Dupont, 1985, p. 45).

But just as mother and nursemaid are conflated by Strindberg's Captain, and confused by Ferenczi in his reference to the straitjacket in the play, so these split images of women are two sides of the same coin. Ferenczi connects his memory of feeling suffocated between the legs of his housemaid as a boy with the way he continues to be haunted by "the image of a corpse, whose abdomen I was opening up, presumably in the dissecting room," linked to which was "the mad fantasy that I was being pressed into this wound in the corpse" (Dupont, 1985, p. 61). He concludes his autobiographical narrative as follows:

> This is the source of my hatred of females: I want to dissect them for it, that is, to kill them. That is why my mother's accusation "You are my murderer" cut to the heart and led to (1) a compulsive desire to help anyone who is suffering, especially women; and (2) a flight from situations where I would have to be aggressive. Thus inwardly the feeling that in fact I am a good chap, also exaggerated reactions of rage, and finally exaggerated reactions of guilt at the slightest lapse.

In most courageous fashion, Ferenczi comes to grips with the unconscious roots of his misogyny as well as with his "compulsive" rescue fantasies and "exaggerated reactions" of both rage and guilt.[2] The image of the dissected abdomen of the corpse condenses the sexual abuse by the housemaid and his murderous fantasies toward his mother. Corroborating what Ferenczi wrote of himself in the *Clinical Diary*, Severn (1933) sums up her conclusions from his analysis:

> The analysis of this patient's character revealed, first, bitterness and anger and strong aggressive impulses, hidden under a smooth and kindly exterior; second, it revealed a man terrified of all women, fearing equally their anger and their passion; and, third, it revealed the shock or psychosis in which was contained the acute suffering, the lost sexual confidence, and the hate at the injustice he had endured, in equal portions. All this was fragmented into small bits, much of it converted into physical symptoms, and none of it recognized for what it was, a repressed insanity of a virulent sort.
>
> (p. 99)

There is no more compelling case history in the psychoanalytic literature than this one authored jointly yet separately by Severn and Ferenczi. Having been made aware of Severn's disguised case history of Ferenczi in Chapter 5 of *The Discovery of the Self*, moreover, we can on closer inspection see "small bits" of her longer narrative embedded elsewhere in the book. Arguing in the first chapter that "one of the chief necessities of psychological therapeutic procedure is to uncover the forgotten life of childhood and bring it back, so far as possible, to consciousness," Severn (1933) then offers what appears to be a random illustration:

> If there was, for example, a doting grandfather in the family always giving sweets to the child, the same child, when an adult, will be looking for another substitute grandfather to supply him with the equivalent "sweet" in some form or another. Or, if there was an angry and hysterical mother, her boy, when grown, will be unconsciously drawn to other women of the same type or possibly driven to the opposite extreme, seeking relief from his internal picture with a woman of great docility, or even one weakly dependent on him.
>
> (pp. 27–28)

The clue here is Severn's description of this boy's mother as "angry and hysterical," which echoes that of Ferenczi's mother as "an angry, hysterical woman" in "Nightmares Are Real." There is no mention there of his grandfather, but in her interview with Eissler Severn (1952) recollects that "the most important man in Ferenczi's life was his grandfather, who made a pet of this child when he was little" (p. 16), just as in this vignette the "doting grandfather" is "always giving sweets to the child." Severn is under the impression that he died when Ferenczi "was still very young" and affirms that it was because Ferenczi associated Freud with his grandfather that "he expected a great deal of love from him," so when he "didn't feel that he got that from Freud," it "made him very unhappy" (pp. 16–17).

In this embellishment of Severn's portrait, Ferenczi emerges as his grandfather's favored progeny, who sought in vain for the same "sweets" from Freud, now cast as his grandfather in the transference. Although Severn depicts Ferenczi's grandfather as a benevolent figure, a more complex picture emerges from Ferenczi's "psychoanalytical insight into my own emotional emptiness" in the *Clinical Diary*:

> Hatred of the woman, veneration of man (with a compulsion to promiscuity as a superstructure) made possible the rationalization of *traumatic impotence*. Fundamental cause: father's father = God, king, patriarch. (It was impossible to be right against God.) Yet obstinate claim to be right in all other areas.
>
> (Dupont, 1985, p. 160)

This passage confirms that it is Ferenczi's paternal grandfather, Wulf Aron Frenkel (b. April 28, 1804–d.?), who is the primordial "God, king, patriarch" against whom he found it no less "impossible to be right" than he did against Freud.

Following the thread of the grandfather in Ferenczi's psychic life leads us to his short paper, "The 'Grandfather Complex'" (1913b):

> Where the grandfather is the master in the house, actually the Patriarch, there the child in his phantasy goes beyond the powerless father and hopes to inherit the whole of the grandfather's power directly; in a case of this kind that I was able to examine analytically the child could never submit, after the death of the powerful grandfather, to the father who had come to power; he treated him simply as an usurper who had robbed him of his rightful possession.
>
> (p. 324)

In yet another instance of disguised autobiography, the "case" that Ferenczi says he was "able to examine analytically" is unquestionably his own. The grandfather is again called "the Patriarch," and it is "the whole of the grandfather's power" that he hopes to inherit. Beneath Ferenczi's rebellion against his "powerless father," a mere "usurper" to whom he "could never submit," it is to his grandfather's simultaneously worshiped and dreaded ghost that he remains in thrall, and which looms as a "fundamental cause" of the *traumatic impotence* that he suffered with Freud, the "most important man" in his adult life.[3]

Severn (1933) fittingly concludes her extended case history of Ferenczi by invoking Ferenczi himself to reflect theoretically on how, as a child, he "had preserved his sanity as a whole, reestablishing a seemingly normal life after the trauma" of his molestation by the nurse:

> He did it, presumably in the moment of its occurrence, by what Freud would call repression and what Ferenczi would call fragmentation. He eliminated the entire affair with its (for him) mysterious inexplicable elements, and his own fury, from his consciousness. Not only this: I have every reason to believe that he eliminated it from his psyche as a whole and that the exploded bits continued to exist, spatially speaking, outside of him—where we had to "catch" it, so to speak, before it could be restored. By this strange phenomenon his ego preserved itself; it was disabled, minus an important part of its energy system, and obliged to maintain some kind of hidden and complicated connection with its lost portions, causing a definite warping of character.
>
> (p. 99)

Just as in *Psycho-Therapy* (1913), where Severn had refused to distinguish between dissociation and repression, she again equates Freud's concept of repression with Ferenczi's concept of fragmentation. The latter is, however, more radical, envisioning not simply a banishment of discrete ideas from consciousness but a shattering of the mind itself into "exploded bits" that continue to exist "outside" the individual. To recall the most salient passage from Ferenczi's "Confusion of Tongues" (1933a):

> If the shocks increase in number during the development of the child, the number and various kinds of splits in the personality increase too, and soon it becomes extremely difficult to maintain contact without

confusion with all the fragments, each of which behaves as a separate entity yet does not know of even the existence of the others. Eventually it may arrive at a state which—continuing the picture of fragmentation—one would be justified in calling atomization.

(p. 165)

Yet once more, Severn takes us back to the Janetian origins of psychoanalysis and thereby anticipates recent work in trauma theory. Like Van der Hart and his colleagues (2006), who contrast the Apparently Normal Personality, which attempts "to hold and integrate most of an individual's autobiographical memory to the extent possible," with the Emotional Personality that "holds the traumatic memory" (p. 38), Severn delineates how Ferenczi adopted a version of her own survival strategy by "reestablishing a seemingly normal life" in the aftermath of the "emotional violence" to which he had been subjected, even while the "lost portions" of his Emotional Personality wandered in space. By such a "remarkable compensatory mechanism," Severn (1933) writes, her patient "grew to be a person of unusual intelligence, balance, and helpfulness, though not without certain dangers to others" and at a cost that "the reader can well imagine. He was deprived of both happiness and health for most of a lifetime, for it was fifty years after its occurrence that this trauma came under observation and treatment" (p. 99).

Notes

1 In both my introduction to *The Discovery of the Self* and *Formulated Experiences*, I erroneously stated that it was Ferenczi's mother who had threatened him with the kitchen knife, whereas it is clear from the German original of the letter that it must have been the cook. I am grateful to Gianni Guasto for clarifying this point.
2 As I have argued in *Reading Psychoanalysis* (Rudnytsky, 2002, pp. 130–32), the impact of Ferenczi's memory of having his head pressed between the legs of his nurse, which he equated with being pressed into the abdomen of a corpse, can be seen in his response to the death of his pregnant analysand, Erzsebét Radó-Révész, and of her unborn child, following a Caesarian section in 1923. Uncannily, Radó-Révész died of pernicious anemia, to which Ferenczi himself later succumbed as well.
3 Providing no documentation, Bokanowski (2011) claims that "family testimonies suggest that Sándor was his father's favourite child" (p. 7). Among the outright errors in his book are the categorical assertion that Ferenczi "had begun an affair" (p. 12) with Elma after taking her into analysis in 1911, as well as the notion that the *Clinical Diary* "was published in 1969, 37 years after his death" (p. 23). Not only did the *Diary* remain unpublished until 1985, but Ferenczi died in 1933, not 1932, so the math is also off by one year.

Chapter 6

Mother and Daughter

1

The sixth and last of the case histories in "Nightmares Are Real" concerns someone on whom Severn (1933) says she "worked a long time" (p. 107). The patient in question is "a highly intelligent, mentally active woman of middle age, who, though giving little visible sign to the ordinary observer of her internal disintegration, had suffered her whole life from severe illnesses and prostrations." She had been "diagnosed, operated, and treated" by doctors, but it had all been "in vain," and she remained "a very sick woman, carrying on the necessary activities of her life by means of a superhuman will."

The immediately preceding case, used to illustrate the point that it is "more difficult to make 'real' something that *never was conscious* than it is to bring back something that was once known and has since been forgotten," happens to be that of "a young actress who had always been in good health and spirits until a disappointing love affair suddenly broke her down," about whom Severn had come "to suspect that she had chosen a man who would disappoint and treat her badly because of unknown, unconscious urges" (pp. 102–3). It is in a transitional paragraph between these two narratives that Severn dismisses Prince's "comparatively slight contribution" on the topic of dissociation with the observation:

> In nearly every case of deep analysis one becomes aware of separated parts of the person, as though each part had an existence of its own. In severe cases of double or split personality each of these portions is like a separate entity, well organized, sometimes with a name of its own, and capable of independent action.
>
> (p. 102)

Although there was "no external corroboration" for Severn's hypothesis that both women had undergone "psychic cataclysms" in childhood, she employed with the older one her "'direct method' of reaching the unconscious"—Ferenczi's "relaxation principle"—thanks to which the patient "developed the capacity for very complete trance manifestations and what had previously been confined to terrible nightmares finally became visible and convincing through its direct dramatization under analysis" (p. 107). To view this process, in which the patient reenacted "in an almost unconscious state" how, as "a helpless child," she had been "the victim of an erotically insane and sadistic father," was, Severn says, "an unforgettable experience," which "had to be repeated many times and each time laboriously explained to the patient afterwards before she could begin to grasp the reality of it." Thus, in keeping with the guiding theme of her chapter, Severn concludes: "We went through the phase of considering it as a fantasy only, but the amount and terrific intensity of the emotions that accompanied each and every manifestation finally convinced both of us beyond any question that it was a historical reality" (p. 108).

Even taken at face value, these case histories are valuable contributions to the literature on trauma and dissociation. But they acquire far greater significance once we realize that one is Severn's disguised account of her analysis with Ferenczi, presented as though she were one of her own patients, while the other is about the analysis she conducted of her daughter Margaret. Viewed from this standpoint, these narratives become a continuation of cases 22 and 40 in *Psycho-Therapy*, which, as I have argued, are likewise about herself and Margaret.[1] They form a triptych with Severn's case history of Ferenczi in *The Discovery of the Self*. In the *Diary*—a work not intended for publication—Ferenczi uses a pseudonym for Severn while admitting that they had engaged in a mutual analysis. Severn, conversely, admits in her book that she had been Ferenczi's patient, but conceals the mutuality and the fact that she had been his analyst. By putting these two texts together, we get a fourfold perspective, in which each says what it was like to be both the patient and analyst of the other. A fifth dimension is added by juxtaposing the case histories of Elizabeth and Margaret to uncover a story of the intergenerational transmission of trauma, which is no less instructive theoretically than it is a tragic chronicle of both women's childhood experiences of physical, sexual, and emotional abuse.

Whereas Severn's case histories of herself and Ferenczi require us to read *The Discovery of the Self* in conjunction with the *Clinical Diary*, to understand the saga of her family the indispensable companion text is Margaret Severn's unpublished autobiography, *Spotlight: Letters to My Mother* (1988), which, as Rachman (2018) was informed by Peter Lipskis, she "wrote at his suggestion after she attempted suicide in April 1983"

(p. 88). This buried treasure is all we have to make up for the loss of Severn's letters from Budapest, which, again according to what Rachman learned from Lipskis, who witnessed the event, Margaret destroyed in 1986 because she was angry at the "psychoanalytic detectives" (p. 108) who were hounding her for information in order to cast both her mother and Ferenczi in a negative light. Rachman appropriates the term "psychoanalytic detectives" from Fortune (2015), who revealed that Eissler, after the debacle of his appointment of Masson as Research Director of the Freud Archives, had become obsessed with Severn's case in an attempt to refute Masson's "assault on Freud" for his abandonment of the "seduction theory."[2] Eissler was so crass as to woo Margaret "with regular phone calls" from New York, as well as "cards, flowers and chocolates to enlist her trust"; most shamelessly, he even tried to entice the eighty-five-year-old woman "to come to New York to enter analysis with him" (p. 25).

In her presentation of the case of the "young actress," Severn (1933) indicates that one of the patient's symptoms was "an inability to wait even a minute for her accustomed meals" (p. 103), the roots of which could be traced to her "infancy and the fact that she had been forcibly weaned at the unfortunately early age of two months" (p. 105). This detail furnished me with the clue that Severn was speaking of her own daughter. In the interview with Eissler, Severn (1952) states, "I have analyzed her, incidentally" (p. 8); but only when I read the May 10, 1934 article in the *Cincinnati Enquirer* about Severn's lecture, "The Psycho-Analysis of Today," which reports that she told her audience not only about having analyzed her daughter but also that a wrong "pattern" had begun with Margaret's weaning, was I able to fit the pieces of the puzzle together.

As Severn (1933) recounts in her book, she "began to suspect" that the actress's unhappy love affair, which left her "quite prostrated and unable to work," even though she was otherwise "a very intelligent and well-balanced person, successful in her profession and not given to foolish and wasteful experiences," must have been due to the young woman's choice of "a man who would disappoint and treat her badly because of unknown, unconscious urges" (p. 103), which it became the task of the analysis to uncover. A probing of the patient's childhood led her to recall that she had "had quite frequent nightmare dreams as early as her eighth year," which gradually "took the form of a definite attack on her of a sexual nature."

This leads Severn to recapitulate the actress's early history. In an uncanny mirroring of Ferenczi's "grandfather complex," Margaret's fate, too, was indelibly marked by her "father's father," who played the role of

"God, king, patriarch" in her life. "The child," Severn writes, "had made frequent and lengthy visits between the ages of four and seven to the house of her grandparents who lived in another city" (p. 104). There she found "many pleasures that were denied her at home," including "a barn and horse, and best of all, an adoring grandfather." But what emerged from their joint excavations was almost too painful to contemplate:

> It was very shocking to this young woman to entertain the idea that her beloved grandfather, now dead, could have ever done her any harm, but the evidence gathered with increasing volume until it could no longer be doubted. He was a man of intelligence and good standing in his community, but was known to be a person of violent temper at times, as well as disappointed in his career and probably in his family. It appeared only too plainly that he had made love to his little granddaughter, and had lost all control and restraint, giving vent to an attraction that was disastrous in its intensity and consequences. His intentions were probably only self-indulgent ones, and not sadistic or malign, but that they were totally without regard for the child, and sly and unscrupulous, extending over a period of several years, became only too certain as we progressed in the analysis.

Severn's extenuation of the grandfather's sexual abuse as "only self-indulgent," as opposed to "sadistic or malign," becomes comprehensible when it is seen as a contrast to the cruelty to which she had been subjected by her own "erotically insane and sadistic father," who occupies an even deeper circle of hell. A "typical nightmare" of the adult actress was, "'Now I am going back to the house at W. . . ,'" where she "'cannot bear to look'" at an approaching streetcar that "'is full of mutilated children, there are dozens of little girls with their bodies and legs all cut, they are bleeding, they are smashed to pieces. I cannot bear it'" (p. 104). After she awakens and falls back to sleep, the nightmare resumes in the barn, where the girl feels the hay beneath her and then sees "'a man coming toward me. I know what is going to happen, and I try to scream "Mama" but cannot speak, it is terrible.'" The actress awakens for a second time "in a cold sweat, trying to scream, but frozen with terror," scarcely able to believe that she is "safe in her own room and bed with no intruder to harm her," unable for hours to shake off the spell of the dream, which was "usually followed by a severe headache."

In her previous chapter "Psychosynthesis," Severn describes how she employed her "direct method of revealing the origin of the neurosis" by "encouraging the lost emotional state to which the mind seemed attracted," so that "the patient gradually fell into a kind of trance, in which *another* reality emerged and was produced with startling vividness and genuineness" (p. 73). She had hitherto been speaking of her "patients" in the plural, but the switch to the singular is followed by a paragraph containing a clinical vignette:

> I reacted to these manifestations in the same manner that I would act had I been present at the time they originally occurred—that is, I entered fully into the situation and became not only an onlooker but a participant. The patient who was a few moments before a sufficiently calm and reasonable adult had become a child; she was pointing excitedly to my door and crying: "See, there he comes," with many signs of terror. Often my encouragement had to take the form of keeping her quiet on the couch where she was lying, the inclination being so strong to run away. She had to feel morally supported to endure the apparition that was now advancing toward her.

In the same way that Severn includes in her opening chapter a detached portion of Ferenczi's analysis having to do with his relationship to his grandfather, so, here again, I am convinced that we have an additional fragment of her analysis of Margaret, separated from the main case history in "Nightmares Are Real."

The patient's terrified cry, "See, there he comes," is a clear link to Margaret's nightmare of being molested in the barn by her grandfather. Exactly as Severn relived with Ferenczi, "as though it were now, the traumatic events of his past" through her "dramatic participation" in the scene from Strindberg, so, too, with Margaret her consulting room door becomes the door of the barn, and she reacted to the emergence of Margaret's traumatic memories exactly as if she had been "present at the time they originally occurred—that is, I entered fully into the situation and became not only an onlooker but a participant." The fact that what Margaret had wanted to scream—but could not at the time—was "Mama" makes the conflation of the past and present in the analysis especially poignant. As Ferenczi puts it in "Confusion of Tongues" (1933a), when the patient cries, "'Help! Quick! Don't let me perish helplessly!'" (p. 157), the analyst must do more than encourage the drowning person from the shore. Only by extending a lifeline, or even plunging into the water, can one hope to effect a rescue, though there is always the danger of being pulled under in the process. This is what Ferenczi means when he observes in the *Diary*, "no analysis can succeed if we do not succeed in really loving the patient" (Dupont, 1985, p. 130).

Severn emphasizes that she and her patient "had no external corroboration of these psychic cataclysms," and this for two very common reasons in such cases—first, the events are "carefully shrouded in secrecy by the person responsible for them," and, second, "the child who is the victim of such a shock becomes totally incapable of remembering and therefore of revealing it" (pp. 104–5). In the catastrophic moment, the "child who has been sacrificed to the selfish brutality of a beloved adult usually makes . . . a dream of something beautiful and pleasant, and thus escapes a certain portion of the overwhelming shock and all memory of it. It is only later," Severn continues, that "the 'repressed' or, as I think, 'exploded' knowledge makes itself felt" (p. 105).

In addition to her "urgent necessity for food," the patient—who is, of course, Margaret—suffered "fainting attacks," the analysis of which led back to her premature weaning, a traumatic loss of her mother that was all the more severe because "the mother was really ill and unable to give the child what it needed, even psychically" (p. 105). During the attacks by the grandfather, the "acute distress" of this early abandonment was reexperienced when the girl "naturally called for her mother, but had to live again the feeling that the mother did not come, was not there, and that there was no help to be had." The young woman's masochistic choice of a lover came to be understood as having been "conditioned by the original one that had been forced upon her, but which a certain part of her had enjoyed and craved again in spite of the pain and terror attached to it." As a result of the "deep psychological dredging" Severn and her patient did together, not only did they begin to free her from her compulsion to become "unconsciously enslaved in every love relation," but they also realized that "in her profession as an emotional actress she had been living out the experiences that had hitherto been enwrapped in the darkness of her unconscious," especially in the "tragic roles" that were her forte, following every performance of which she would come off the stage "in a state of exhaustion and collapse—a result due, we were forced to conclude, to the *tragic reality* she was experiencing while acting" (p. 106).

Although Masson (1984) disparaged Severn's case histories as "badly presented" (p. 166), I think it is now incontestable that, like her veiled portrait of Ferenczi, this is a masterful account of early sexual trauma, its long-term effects, and psychoanalytic treatment. Just as Ferenczi presented to the world "a very balanced outlook on life and marked serenity of manner" (p. 96), so, too, Severn (1933) characterizes Margaret as outwardly "a very intelligent and well-balanced person." But the Apparently Normal Personality of both patients, which brought them professional success, concealed the shell-shocked Emotional Personality that rendered them "insane" or "psychotic" as a result of the cruelty to which they had been subjected. The same dynamic obtains in Severn's narrative of her own case, which, as we have seen, she introduces as that of "a highly intelligent, mentally active woman of middle age, who, though giving little visible sign to the ordinary observer of her internal disintegration, had suffered her whole life from severe illnesses and prostrations." All three sought to cope with their traumas by means of dissociation, or what Severn and Ferenczi interchangeably term fragmentation, atomization, and exploding into pieces.

Severn's recounting of Margaret's story hews with remarkable fidelity to the historical truth, and—like her revelation concerning Ferenczi's enactment of the scene from *The Father*—it preserves crucial details about which we would otherwise have never known. The reference to "the house at W. . . ," to which Margaret returns in her nightmares, is to the home of her paternal grandparents in Wayne; and Severn's use of the letter "W" attests to the trustworthiness of her narrative. Apart from her transformation of Margaret from a dancer into an actress, the only liberty Severn has taken is to say that Margaret had "made frequent and lengthy visits" to her grandparents between the ages of four and seven, when we know that she had been kidnapped. This airbrushing of the prolonged separation from her daughter in *The Discovery of the Self* is of a piece with the way that, in case number 40 in *Psycho-Therapy* (1913), Severn had turned the situation into its opposite by making it seem that the "young girl on the verge of a nervous breakdown" had been "brought to me by her father in desperation" (p. 197), when in fact Charles Heywood had conspired with his family to kidnap Margaret from Leota during the family meeting in Chicago, and to transport their captured pawn across state lines to Wayne, in what was then a rural area west of Detroit, and which even today has fewer than 20,000 inhabitants.

2

In her massive autobiography, Margaret Severn provides an invaluable perspective on her mother's life and work, as well as a "third side" to the story of Elizabeth Severn's relationship with Ferenczi. Margaret's gifts as a writer make her narrative eminently readable, and the depth of her insight into psychoanalysis is remarkable. Writing to her mother on March 23, 1927, for instance, asking what she thought of a series of five dreams, including one in which she dreamed of having sexual intercourse with her father (*not* her grandfather) as a five-year-old, Margaret (1988) muses, "Old unkie certainly handed it out straight. I wonder if the material was historical, fantasy historical, or identification with mama?" (p. 1,142). "Old unkie" is Margaret's moniker for the unconscious, and the three possible explanations she proposes concerning the material in her dream, in which she "was weeping hurt and frightened, and there was blood around. There was also a certain sense of satisfaction and a terrible guilt" (p. 1,140), delineate the range of hypotheses that must be considered whenever one seeks to ascertain the veridicality of traumatic memories from childhood. While not being sure whether the dream is "historical" or "fantasy historical," the one explanation that Margaret excludes is that it is purely a fantasy; and the likelihood that "identification with mama" may be involved is increased by the fact that Margaret never saw her father again after being abducted to Wayne, where she was sexually abused by her grandfather, whereas Elizabeth's abuse was perpetrated by her father.

The sophistication of Margaret's understanding of psychoanalysis is shown by her letter of July 13, 1928, in which she continues a discussion of Freud's *The Question of Lay Analysis* (1926b) she had evidently been having with her mother. Margaret (1988) writes:

> What I had to say about the "Problems of Lay Analysis," by the way, chiefly concerned the fact that Freud seems to stress the point that P.A. is for nervous cases ONLY and not for those where medical attention is generally employed. Does he do this merely for policy's sake or does he by any chance believe that? I cannot see why analysis should be limited to this, as an organic state is merely a further development of the illness . . . and in your own practice you have certainly had proof enough of how it may actually change physical conditions. So I cannot see why he should make this statement unless to protect himself against medical onslaught and I should think he would be used

to that by now. The other point was that I do not agree with you that the explanation contained therein would be entirely clear to a person unacquainted with the subject. I myself had to read certain sentences concerning the "id" many times before I was sure of their meaning and I think that the mind which did not understand from experience the process of analysis would be completely baffled. Of course I admired the general clarity and wit and logic and greatness immensely.

(pp. 1,399–400)

The Question of Lay Analysis is one of the five works by Freud cited by Elizabeth Severn in *The Discovery of the Self*, and Margaret's question about Freud's views on the applicability of psychoanalysis to cases of organic illness goes to the heart of her mother's radical vision of its healing power. Her surmise that Freud's caution in this respect may have been a strategic maneuver "to protect himself against medical onslaught" is by no means farfetched. In disputing the notion that Freud's exposition would be "entirely clear" to the uninitiated reader, moreover, Margaret speaks as one who is herself in a position to "understand from experience the process of analysis," and thus with more than a bookish familiarity with the subject.

The extent to which Margaret was acquainted with psychoanalysis from personal experience is one of the most surprising revelations of *Spotlight*. As she informs the reader, once her mother decided to relocate to Budapest in 1925, Margaret made it a custom at the end of her season of vaudeville road tours to join her in the Hungarian capital: "I invariably took the first boat to Europe to visit my mother in Budapest where I could recuperate in an atmosphere of psychoanalysis and art" (p. 585). It is to be expected that Margaret would have met Ferenczi as well as many of his patients who formed an analytic colony on the Danube. But who would have guessed that Margaret not only knew Ferenczi but also had analysis with him, as well as with her mother, who was, of course, in her own long-term analysis with Ferenczi? Yet, among other evidence for this, there is Margaret's letter from Boston on February 22, 1927, which begins, "My dear Dr. Ferenczi: I am awfully happy that I can at last commence to pay you what I owe and only too sorry that I couldn't do it sooner." She continues:

> I really am forced to admit that you and mother seem to have done a pretty good job on me. I was a little afraid I was too much in need of further analysis to get along comfortably, but, really, nothing seems

to be the matter. I do not suffer from undue fatigue, I don't seem to be hungry, and I don't seem to be hot, and I don't seem to be lonely or unhappy. Instead of being a weakling without a mind of my own (which I still feel like if mother is around), I find that, compared to all the people I meet, or the members of the company, I am a perfect Amazon of strong-mindedness and independence. So, if I continue like this, I trust that all yet may be well.

(p. 1,121)

Given our knowledge of Margaret's eating disorder, her declaration, "I don't seem to be hungry," indicates an abatement of one of her chief complaints, while the equivocal assurance, "I don't seem to be lonely or unhappy," means that she believed herself to be on the road to recovery from her love affair with a man who, as her mother had written, "would disappoint and treat her badly because of unknown, unconscious urges." The man in question was Ota Gygi, a Hungarian-born violinist and vaudeville entertainer to whom Margaret lost her virginity at the age of twenty-three, and with whom she had a "glimpse of infinity" and thought she would be "bound together throughout eternity," until she realized, after "two or three unhappy years," that he was not going to leave his wife, as a consequence of which she was "devastated with grief" and "mourned deeply for the next five years" (p. 1,109). In the letter to Ferenczi, Margaret oscillates between her sense of being "a weakling without a mind of my own" in her mother's presence and "a perfect Amazon of strong-mindedness and independence" in her absence. She concludes with a heartfelt expression of affection for both Ferenczi and his wife, whom she had met as well: "I was awfully sorry not to see you and Mrs. Ferenczi before I left, but hope it won't be frightfully long before we meet again. Do give her my love and keep lots for yourself" (pp. 1,121–22).

Among Ferenczi's patients whom Margaret knew in Budapest was the Englishman John Rickman, but most were the American women who appear under pseudonyms in the *Clinical Diary*. These included Roberta Nederhoed (N.D.), Alice Lowell (B.), and Clara Thompson (Dm), as well as Natalie Rogers (O.S.), Harriot Sigray (S.I.), and Izette de Forest (Ett.), the last of whom, in a letter to her mother on January 9, 1929, Margaret disparaged as someone she would be averse to seeing for further analysis:

Well, the difficulties in the way of my having analysis are manifold. I need every inch of time for my work, and I would suffer terribly at the idea of putting myself more into debt. Besides, I cannot imagine effecting a transference to either Gaites or de Forrest. They are both imbeciles.

(p. 1,470)

Margaret misspells the name of de Forest, and "Gaites" refers to Ruth Gates, identified by Brennan (2009) as having, together with de Forest and Caroline Newton (the translator of Rank and Ferenczi's *The Development of Psycho-Analysis*), "helped behind the scenes with Ferenczi's trip to the New School of Social Research in 1926" (p. 432), and who would have known—and likely been in analysis with—Ferenczi while he was in New York.[3]

Despite her reluctance, Margaret, who was languishing in bed in New York while her mother was prostrate in Budapest, did entertain the overtures of both Gates and de Forest to see them for analytic treatment. Lambasting Gates because she "plays her radio while conversation is going on," which "shows a complete lack of intelligence," and finding fault with de Forest for being "too motherly and sympathetic, which I loathe," Margaret (1988) nonetheless concedes on January 14, 1929 that she is in a precarious state:

Both of them show, however, a sweet and touchingly earnest desire to help the daughter of their colleague. I find this so touching that I may be laughing and feeling quite sane, but if one of them calls up or comes in I go immediately into torrents of tears for their benefit.

(p. 1,476)

One of the principal reasons Margaret was hesitant to see Gates was, as she wrote to her mother on January 10, "because she is not sufficiently loyal to you, and I wouldn't like to give her a dose of family history that might increase her understanding" (p. 1,473). She reiterates this concern in her letter of January 14, after she had accepted Gates's offer of appointments: "I regret greatly that I shall have to talk about your situation as that is a thing which worries me frightfully, the agony of your past, I mean. Not to mention the agony of your present" (p. 1,476).

Unavoidably, in undertaking analytic therapy with a colleague of her mother's Margaret would be constrained to reveal intimate details not only of her own history of childhood abuse but also of her mother's, which she did not want to do with someone who was not "sufficiently loyal." Such a therapist would also have to be apprised of Margaret's experience of analysis with her mother, and this indeed came up in her preliminary consultations with Gates. Margaret's letter of January 14 continues:

> Gaites summarized my difficulties as being my struggle to become independent of you and expressed her belief that a mother could not solve this problem in analysis with her own daughter. I pointed out that Ferenczi was not in agreement with this opinion and that she would have to expect a great deal of abuse from me. She does, but she doesn't know how much yet!
>
> (p. 1,476)

Since Elizabeth Severn's analysis of her daughter was known to Gates, it was undoubtedly also disclosed to de Forest, who shuttled between New York and Budapest, where she would likely have shared this information with the other Americans in Ferenczi's entourage. Strikingly, Margaret was able to parry Gates's objections by invoking the approbation of Ferenczi himself for this dubious venture, just as he was prepared to take Margaret at least intermittently into analysis himself alongside her mother.[4] When Margaret forewarned Gates that "she would have to expect a great deal of abuse" from her, she was alerting her to the negative maternal transference, of which a prodrome was Margaret's objection to Gates's playing of the radio during their conversation.

Notwithstanding her doubts, Margaret did commence a twice-weekly analysis with Gates, about which she reported on January 21, 1929 in a letter with the salutation "Dear old Freud Ferenczi Mama":

> My analysis with Gaites seems to be doing alright, but of course at the start with a new analyst, there is so much excess material to be waded through and so many explanations to make. But my resistances to her are apparently not so great as I had anticipated. I must say she seems pretty good—I'm really surprised. Of course, twice a week is too little, and I have complained about that, but she says we'll just try it and see. I feel that we cannot handle the material in so little time, but as I am not in a position to pay right now, and she has said nothing about my paying her anything anyhow, I don't like to ask for more. If you feel any jolt it may be because in my dreams I am busy smashing up statues of Madonnas.
>
> (p. 1,484)

Counting her mother and Ferenczi, Gates was at least Margaret's third analyst, and the work began auspiciously enough. The issue of the fee reverberated across the dyads, however, since, as Margaret wrote to her mother on March 9, 1929, when she informed Gates that Ferenczi had told Elizabeth that "he could wait for payment" from her, Gates, who had neglected to spell out the financial arrangements of her treatment of Margaret, became "jealous . . . and proceeded to preach" that Margaret "could reduce expenses by not riding in taxis," while "Ferenczi, by relieving you of immediate payment, was being made to suffer for my extravagance" (p. 1,513).

When Margaret objected to being accused of "exploiting Ferenczi" and threatened to quit the analysis, Gates made matters worse by saying she "never expected to be paid for it anyhow." In high dudgeon, Margaret rejoined that "this was an insult and I certainly wouldn't continue," upon which Gates prolonged the session for an hour and "tried to imitate Ferenczi and be very humble" (pp. 1,513–14). This, in turn, prompted Margaret—who admitted to her mother that "all of this may be one grand 'resistance' on my part"—to tell her that "she is too dumb to help me," while Gates tried to make her feel guilty by reminding her, "in a sad voice," that "Ferenczi used to live in a dark little apartment in Budapest because he couldn't afford to get a nice bright house," which Margaret said "was none of my business" (p. 1,514).

3

Although Margaret had limited analysis with both Gates and Ferenczi, with her mother she had a lifelong relationship that from early on included a therapeutic or analytic component, of which her autobiography is the enduring testament. In starting at the beginning of her story with her birth on August 14, 1901, an unbearably hot day in Birmingham, Alabama, Margaret (1988) fills in the details of what Elizabeth had revealed about her having been "forcibly weaned" at the age of two months: "Because of my mother's prostration, a black wet-nurse was procured, but I refused to suckle at her breast and also refused the bottle formula prescribed by the doctor. Thus began, I suspect, the frustrating sensation of insatiable hunger which has pursued me for the whole of my life" (p. 1). It would appear from this that Leota, whose "prostration" was likely a postpartum depression exacerbated by her unhappy marriage to Charles Heywood, was never able to nurse her daughter, and it must have been from the "black wet-nurse" that Margaret suffered a second loss in the form of a premature weaning, if indeed she was ever fed at the breast at all.

Thus, even before her abduction as a four-year-old, Margaret had lost her mother both physically and psychically, and when she was told by her grandparents in Michigan that her mother was "very ill" or perhaps dead, it caused her to wish "to die myself in order to be with her" (p. 5). Margaret describes her new residence, including "the barn, which housed two horses and a white wagon with the insignia 'U.S. Mail' emblazoned in gold on its sides," and then masterfully limns her grandfather's character:

> He had been a captain in the cavalry and later became a builder of bridges; but his career was cut short, apparently by some catastrophe in which he was seriously involved, and he eventually retired to the village of Wayne where he delivered the rural mail and lived with his wife, daughter and two sons, indulging in a kind of bitter seclusion. He was a man of violent temper and was feared by most of those who knew him, but not by me. I was the apple of his eye and he was my devoted slave though actually, in a larger sense, a tyrant.
>
> (p. 3)

Margaret's account lines up exactly with that of her mother in *The Discovery of the Self*, down to the details of the barn and the portrayal of the grandfather as a man of "violent temper" who was "disappointed in his career and probably in his family." Severn's revelation that the "beloved grandfather" had "made love to his little granddaughter and had lost all control and restraint, giving vent to an attraction that was disastrous in its intensity and consequence," prepares us for the sickening continuation of Margaret's story:

> What I now know is so devastating that I can hardly bear to think of it, but the conviction stands like a pillar of steel brutally shining in my mind—that the pent up passion of my grandfather vented itself on the body of his small granddaughter. I became the object and the satisfaction of his desire, the very center of his life. That drugs were used seems certain, and although I have no conscious memory of such, I do recall frequent headaches, dopiness, sensations of confusion, and a dull terror, a feeling of impending disaster. It can happen that a shock or threat of death to the abused child, if she should tell, may cause a complete blackout of the mind.
>
> (p. 8)

Although Margaret does not give her grandfather's first name, she does state that he had been "a captain in the cavalry." Photographs of the tombstones in Glenwood Cemetery in Wayne, Michigan, however, include one, adorned with an American flag, for "Harvey S. Heywood, Lieut. Col. Mich. Cav.," with no dates, and another for "Harriet D., Wife of Harvey Heywood, Jan. 30, 1842–Aug. 18, 1920." Other records indicate that Harvey was born "about 1836" in New York State, and died in April 1909 in Wayne County. During the Civil War, he enlisted on July 28, 1862 as a corporal in Company D of the Michigan 4th Cavalry Regiment, and he mustered out as a Brevet Captain on September 1, 1865. His service pension was transferred to his widow, Harriet ("Hattie") Heywood, after his death.[5]

If Harvey Heywood was born in 1836, he would have turned sixty-nine when his granddaughter and namesake, Margaret Harvey Heywood, came to live with him and his family in 1905. The Civil War cavalryman and disgraced engineer had been reduced to driving a wagon for the U.S. mail, and he compensated for his failures by imposing his patriarchal will on his captive brood and becoming at once the "tyrant" and "devoted slave" of the four-year-old he sacrificed on the altar of his "pent up passion." His death in 1909 means that he survived Leota's counter-abduction of his prized possession by only two years; and, as Margaret (1988) recalls, while she and her mother were living in San Antonio she woke up one night "to see a vision of my grandfather," who was "standing framed in the doorway of the room wearing his blue overalls and looking just as he always had. I cried out to him as he approached the bed, but when I leaned forward to embrace him, he instantly vanished" (p. 14). Her mother subsequently learned that Harvey "had actually died at about that time with the words 'Little Wolf' on his lips." Writing to Elizabeth from Paris on April 2, 1932, Margaret shared an epiphany: "By the way, NO WONDER I hate Easter. I have always loathed it but never knew why before: that was the day on which I was stolen" (p. 2,128).

While under her grandfather's spell, Margaret would go outside in her grandmother's red calico petticoat to dance for the spectators in a passing tram car, or surrender to the thunder and lightning of a raging storm:

> From it I had learned the passion of the elements; from my grandfather I had learned the passion of man—strange, overpowering, both beautiful and terrifying, emotions much too shattering for the psyche of a young child and therefore a threat to the very core of her existence. In later years, to many audiences in many cities, I continued to tell this story in disguised form through the medium of dance; but only much

later, through intensive work in psychoanalysis, was I able to divine its true origin and meaning.

(pp. 7–8)

Repeatedly, Margaret stresses the "shock" and "shattering" effects of the sexual abuse by her grandfather, in the course of which she was given drugs and menaced with the "threat of death" should she tell anyone what happened, causing her to have a "complete blackout of the mind." In agreement with her mother's explanation of how "in her profession as an emotional actress she had been living out the experiences that had hitherto been enwrapped in the darkness of her unconscious," Margaret recognizes that she "continued to tell this story in disguised form through the medium of dance," but only through the "intensive work in psychoanalysis" they did together was she "able to divine its true origin and meaning."

As Margaret elucidates with unflinching honesty, the effect of her abuse, which she had dissociated, is that she could not help continuing to love and revere her grandfather at the same time that she hated and dreaded him:

> So, despite the bewildering disquiet in my heart (fear of the thing I sensed but did not know about consciously), I continued to regard my grandfather as a hero, and thus an unending dichotomy was planted in the center of my being: fear and desire confronted one another in a battle that left part of my mind in shreds. Even in my adult life no other man could equal the image of great stature, power, and passion left in my unconscious by my grandfather. Thereafter I inevitably longed for the unattainable; to ride a dangerously wild horse or to tangle with an immense ocean wave was an irresistible temptation to me.
>
> (pp. 8–9)

Because of the "unending dichotomy" between "fear and desire" in her mind, the grandfather whose abuse was "a threat to the very core of her existence" was also an "image of great stature, power, and passion" whom "no other man could equal." Thus, even though Margaret was in one sense saved when she was reclaimed by her mother to start their new life together in San Antonio, she simultaneously suffered yet another incalculable loss in being wrenched from the "hero" she loved:

> Nevertheless, in the hidden recesses of my heart the storm still raged: the fear, the joy, the terror inspired by my grandfather burned like a

hidden flame about to start a great conflagration. Near to these scarlet emotions lay a pool of indigo water wherein drowned the grief, the pain and the sorrow of parting from the man who had meant all of life to me. Again, a searing conflict: supreme relief at finally being safe in the arms of the mother whom I adored, versus a devastating sense of loss, a terrible emptiness where my grandfather had been. Throughout most of my adult life, the seeds thus planted in my unconscious resulted in the conviction that my mother and whatever man I might imagine myself to be in love with, stood necessarily at opposite poles. In the back of my mind, to have my mother meant losing my man or, having my man meant losing my mother, and I could not bear the schism. Hence the dynamo: I had to explode, and I exploded into dance.[6]

(p. 10)

Margaret renders in exquisite prose how the combustible mixture of emotions toward her grandfather was compounded by the pain of being torn "from the man who had meant all of life" to her, which gave rise to a "searing conflict" between "mother" and "man," because to have one meant losing the other. Consequently, Margaret felt an ineradicable ambivalence also toward her mother, who occupied one of the two "opposite poles" in her mind, and who had not only robbed her of her grandfather but had also abandoned her first by being "unable to give the child what it needed, even psychically," following Margaret's birth, and then by her absence, involuntary though it may again have been, when the girl "naturally called for her mother" while she was being violated.

The lasting effects of Margaret's "grandfather complex," displayed most conspicuously in her masochistic love affair with Gygi, constitute a recurring theme in *Spotlight*. On September 12, 1925, she writes to her mother that she has "a large rotten spot in my personality" (p. 1,098), while on April 19, 1928 she confesses "this terrible fear of sex in my unc.," which she tries to overcome by performing "a little scientific experiment." Margaret resolves to take a lover to discover whether she "can be attracted only by cruelty and the bad papa motive," and "if this fails and I still find myself in the same stupid condition, then I will admit that you and F[erenczi] are right and we should be worried" (pp. 1,356–57). On April 19, 1929, she reports a dream in which she is "fighting the Civil War"—evoking her grandfather's service in the Union army—and despite having a "lover or husband" who might disapprove, she lies down on the floor of a "country farmhouse" and shows her "patriotic spirit" by telling a soldier who looked as though he "needed intercourse. . . . 'Take me now if you wish!'" (p. 1,551). As Margaret comments, "the associations are endless but practically all tie up with my grandfather and the Wayne 'farmhouse,'" although "my husband in the dream had hair like my father," while the soldier "was dark," like a man she had just met who "showed a too thinly veiled desire to become my lover immediately" (pp. 1,151–52).

A further aftershock of Margaret's sexual abuse by Harvey Heywood is her infatuation with Otto Hermann Kahn, a banker and patron of the arts thirty-four years her senior, who she hoped would subsidize her dance academy in New York during the Great Depression. As Margaret wrote to her mother on November 20, 1930: "This passion I've got for Grandfather Kahn is something fierce. It isn't even funny any more. . . . I've even lost my appetite—food simply nauseates me—and I can't sleep, and I can't sleep or think of anything else" (pp. 1,881–82). The eating disorder that constituted one of the severest symptoms of her abuse was revived by this lovesickness. Describing herself as "in a fever most of the time" and having "all kinds of fantasies," Margaret continues:

> The whole thing certainly tends to confirm your theory that my grandfather excited me sexually in some way because many of my associations do concern Kahn—and I don't think I ever felt a stronger sexual desire in my life. It is simply devastating, and so unaccountable; after all he is so old and I only saw him for 20 minutes. However, his eyes had a look in 'em that—well, gave one the feeling that one gets in dreams sometimes, when you suddenly find yourself walking down 5th Ave. in your nightgown and you try in vain to conceal the fact.
> (p. 1,882)

As Margaret acknowledges, her "unaccountable" passion for "Grandfather Kahn" makes sense as a compulsive manifestation of her longing for the figure of "great stature, power, and passion" by whom she was involuntarily aroused when he forced himself on her as a little girl. But the saga of Margaret's love life has a happy last chapter in her relationship with Peter Lipskis, the Vancouver video artist who became her literary executor, and in 2003 sold the Severn papers to Arnold Rachman. In his book, Rachman (2018) calls Lipskis Margaret's "personal friend and companion" (p. 105), but he was in reality far more than that. My first inkling of the true state of affairs came from a handwritten letter from Margaret to her fellow dancer

Agnes de Mille on June 2, 1992, "I love Canada and for the last ten years or more I have a very compatible companion, a man (only about 53 years younger than I am) and we have a very jolly happy time together."[7]

But the proverbial "smoking gun" is an article by Lipskis himself, "Why Margaret Severn Was the Most Fascinating Person I Ever Met" (2018), published in the inaugural issue of the Italian journal *Il Poppante Saggio* (The Wise Baby). As Lipskis recounts, he first met Margaret in 1978, and then contacted her again in 1980, when he was "twenty-six and heartbroken because a woman I had slept with no longer wanted to" (p. 113). This led to their first collaborative film project, *Dance Masks*, and weekly visits to Margaret's apartment. On one of these, in September 1982, Lipskis confessed to Margaret that he "loved her 'totally,'" to which the eighty-one-year-old woman of the world replied, "'The bedroom is over there'" (p. 114)! Lipskis comments, "Our 53-year age difference felt a bit strange at first, but intimacy grew and continued for almost a decade."

In this final twist of the oedipal drama, Margaret shifts from being (literally or figuratively) the granddaughter to being the grandmother, now in a mutually fulfilling consensual relationship, but the unconscious determinants of her desire remain unchanged. It was fortunate not only for Margaret but also for posterity that fate led her to Lipskis, since it was at a screening of *Dance Masks* that she met Patty Burn, who from 1985 to 1987 accomplished the "Herculean task" (p. 115) of typing the manuscript of *Spotlight*. In his memoir Lipskis confirms that it was after a "failed suicide attempt" by Margaret in 1983 that the two of them developed "the idea of selecting and editing excerpts from Margaret's hundreds of old letters stored in a large trunk." Lipskis subsequently recorded a video of Margaret reading the opening chapters of her autobiography; and, in 1991, when Margaret turned ninety, he produced a final film, *Portrait of an Artist as a Young Woman (1914–1919)*, released in 1992, "focusing on her artwork and letters from age 13 to 18" (p. 116). All of Lipskis's films about Margaret Severn are available on YouTube, and especially *Dance Masks* (1981) and *Spotlight* (1991) should be viewed by every serious student of Ferenczi and Elizabeth Severn.

4

Whereas Margaret had a series of passionate attachments to men, this was only one pole in her "unending dichotomy," and the most important relationship in the lives of both Severns was that with each other. *Spotlight* constitutes a mammoth love letter to Elizabeth in her twofold capacity as not only Margaret's mother but also her analyst. We have seen the negative vector to this force field when Margaret (1988) tells her mother that, if she feels a "jolt" in Budapest, it is because she herself has been "busy smashing up statues of Madonnas" in her dreams during her analysis with Ruth Gates in New York. The belief in telepathy Margaret shared with her mother forms a refrain in her letters. Twelve days earlier, on January 9, 1929, while laid up with the flu, she expostulates: "Don't worry about asking your patients to come to Budapest. Start long distance analysis. You can do it perfectly and nearly kill a person nine million miles away just as easily as if they lay in the same room" (p. 1,468).

Although there is a lighthearted tone to these jests, their underlying seriousness comes through in Margaret's outburst on December 10, 1927, in response to a letter from her mother reporting an eerily accurate dream about her:

> Well, but I guess I am in a rage, the result of your telepathic perceptions. The fact of the spying in of your damned unconscious has put my unconscious into such a fit that it has half a mind to flit right over to Budapest and tear your unconscious into seventy-nine strips. . . . How the Hell CAN I become independent when our uncs are so closely united? The idea of you knowing what I am doing when I don't tell you! I would like to kick and scream and throw the radiator out of the window. Every thought leads in some undisguised manner to a vision of your death, after which I immediately get married. It is as though I could look right down into the pit of my unc. and see smoke and flame there, a furnace of fury which has been neatly sealed for so long with my sweet little daughterly ways.
>
> (p. 1,291)

Even as an adult woman on another continent, Margaret is unable to escape the "spying in" of her mother's "damned unconscious," and this symbiosis making it impossible for her to "become independent" stokes the "furnace of fury" smoldering beneath Margaret's "sweet little daughterly ways." Indeed, Margaret's "every thought leads in some undisguised manner to a vision" of her mother's death, and her fantasy of getting married "immediately" thereafter shows her enduring "schism" between "mother" and "man," such that it is only possible for her to have the one by psychically killing off the other.

The counterpart to Margaret's wish to kill her mother was her conviction that life would be unendurable without her. As she wrote on April 14, 1929, "I am the only thing that means anything to you, and vice versa. If you died, I am sure I'd kill myself. I'm damned if I would be such a fool as to keep up this awful striving for a living if it weren't for you. And you've done it just for me for years" (p. 1,550). Yet again, Margaret confesses on December 6, 1929, "I hate you and wish you would die," but so consumed is she with guilt for her matricidal impulses "that I hate myself and nearly kill myself instead" (p. 1,694). Ultimately triumphing over her murderous hate, however, is the surpassing love that made Leota's cry of "Hoo, hoo!" when, a wraithlike Demeter, she came to rescue her Proserpina from Pluto's realm the "most beautiful sound" that Margaret had ever heard in her life. The most moving expression in *Spotlight* of Margaret's love for her mother is the following retrospective passage:

> On my long tours I seldom found much compatibility among my traveling companions, although we were always on friendly terms around the theater. I never really felt lonely, but I admit to having been aware sometimes of the sharp contrast between a warmly applauding audience and, after the last show, sitting alone at a dreary drugstore counter for my milk and doughnuts. I was sustained, however, by always being able to feel the presence of my mother and her love. It did not matter that there might actually be an ocean between us; even since her death our closeness has remained immutable. From my earliest memories I thought of her as my best and very true friend. When I was a child it was unthinkable that she should ever raise a hand or even her voice against me, and the result was my complete confidence in her, and therefore obedience to her. She was never a "theater mother" hovering around the dressing room, washing tights and gathering gossip, but when I needed her she was always available spiritually if not physically. If she had asked me to jump off a cliff into the ocean I would have done so without a second thought because I knew that she would never demand anything not based on reason or necessity, no matter how bizarre it might appear; and, furthermore, she was always right. Our relationship was candid and honest; subterfuge could not exist between us. Her utterly unselfish love has been the greatest boon and the most heartening and enlightening experience of my life.
>
> (pp. 585–86)

Because Elizabeth's love was at its core "utterly unselfish," her relationship with Margaret was always fundamentally healthy notwithstanding the traumas endured by both of them in their childhoods. Despite the mixed blessing of their "immutable closeness," which outlasted death, Margaret's choice of dancing as a vocation was her own, and the unconditional support she received from her "best and very true friend" meant that she enjoyed a considerable measure of independence and autonomy despite her frequent protests to the contrary.

That Elizabeth's love for Margaret was truly for her as a separate person and not as a narcissistic extension of herself applies also to their analytic relationship. We have seen that Elizabeth had begun to treat her daughter when she was still a child, and the modality of their therapy evolved in tandem with Elizabeth's intellectual evolution, so that by the time she arrived in Budapest it was unquestionably an analytic process. As Margaret wrote on April 23, 1926, "I am continuing to think along the lines of the analysis I did with you and looking forward to when it may be continued" (p. 1,098). Indeed, when Severn published *The Discovery of the Self* in 1933, her analytic therapy of Margaret had lasted far longer than her own eight years with Ferenczi.

But to know that Severn intermittently analyzed her daughter for a quarter-century is not to be prepared for Margaret's revelation in the concluding chapter of her autobiography. As the Second World War erupted in Europe, she was reunited in 1939 with her mother in New York, where they lived together in an apartment on East Eighty-Sixth Street. Margaret counts it among the advantages of this arrangement that "it gave me the opportunity to undertake a serious analysis with her, which had previously been impossible, owing to the fact that we were both engaged in our respective professional endeavors, usually at different points of the globe" (p. 3,097). Thus, in Margaret's estimation, all the work they had done previously did not amount to "a serious analysis," but "now, for a period of six years, I had sessions of fifty minutes each, six times a week, rain or shine, summer and winter."

A six-days-a-week analysis lasting for six years would be impressive under any circumstances, but for it to have been between a daughter and her mother is truly extraordinary. In 1929, Margaret had cited Ferenczi's defense of their earlier work together to Gates, and as she brings her search for lost time to a close, she reaffirms the benefit she derived from her mother's clinical acumen:

> It is generally considered that psychoanalysis by the mother of the patient cannot be successful, but in my case I feel it most certainly

was. My mother had so much experience in analysis herself and was capable of such an impersonal and complete detachment, plus an invincible determination to attain her goal, that, with my willingness to work hard, ultimate success was inevitable. From then on, I became not just a victim of the buffets of fate, but, to a large measure, the captain of my ship. It was not always easy, but the beneficial results of the intensive analytic work continued to blossom and to fill my life with mastery and comparative ease long after the cessation of the daily probing of the mind, plus the eventual cultivation of its potential resources.

(pp. 3,097–98)

Although Freud, Jung, Abraham, and Klein all analyzed their own children, only Severn publicly acknowledged that she had done so. The pact of silence between Sigmund and Anna Freud about his analysis of her—which also took place six days a week, first from 1918 to 1922 and then from 1924 to 1925 (Bromberg and Aron, 2019, p. 700)—was tied to what Esther Menaker (2001) has called the "assault on the self" inherent in Freud's desire to seal his daughter's loyalty not only to him personally but also "to his theories and to the 'cause,' the movement" (p. 93). In contrast, the courage and honesty exhibited by both Severns attests to the altruism on Elizabeth's part that made this unorthodox venture a genuinely therapeutic experience for Margaret.

5

After Elizabeth's death in 1959, Margaret (1988) remained in New York for three years, then "moved to a village in Maine where I was able to subsist on the very small income which remained to me" (p. 3,099). She lived there for a decade before one day "looking at a picture of Vancouver," of which she had fond memories from her days in vaudeville, and resolved to have herself "transported bag and baggage to Canada," where she died on July 7, 1997, at the age of ninety-five, having lived sixteen years longer than her mother but five fewer than her maternal grandmother. The closing words of her autobiography capture eloquently what it means to have discovered the self:

I have lived here for some fifteen years. I revel in the beauty and tranquility, and I feel that the spirit of my mother is always close. The quality of my life has now changed from the ceaseless struggle of earlier days to a state in keeping with the harmony of nature which surrounds me: the mountains, the sea, the sky, and a personal love which fills me with joy and contentment. I no longer need to wander or to achieve. I just sit still and I *am*.

Although the sexual abuse of Margaret Heywood, as she was then still named, was perpetrated by her *father's* father, Harvey Heywood, not by Marcus Brown, one can imagine the guilt and horror with which Leota must have learned that the curse of her terrifying experience with her father had been transmitted to her daughter. As Severn, cloaked in anonymity, recalls her own nightmare of a childhood in *The Discovery of the Self* (1933):

The analysis revealed, first, an astonishing story of almost complete amnesia prior to her twelfth year and, second, a history of incredible abuse that had filled her life during that time, leaving not a single trace in her conscious memory. It was the story of a diabolically clever and secretly criminal father who had used his child unmercifully throughout this period for his own selfish purposes and of a stupid enslaved mother who completely closed her eyes to all that took place. The man kept up a semblance of respectability before society and even before his wife, who, however, had sufficiently numerous evidences of his misdoings that she chose to ignore. He had left the family after a final and violent crisis in connection with his daughter, evidently being satisfied that the culminating shock to which he subjected her had deprived her of all memory. Thus it came about that the patient grew to adulthood with no knowledge whatever of her tragic past and no one to tell her even a suspicion of what it might have been.

(p. 107)

In her interview with Eissler, Severn (1952) describes her father as "a gentleman crook" who "had practiced all sorts of malpractice on me as a little child" (p. 5), but the crucial details corroborating Severn's "history of incredible abuse" by her "diabolically clever and secretly criminal father" are provided by Ferenczi in the *Clinical Diary*. In keeping with Severn's (1933) observation that "in nearly every case of deep analysis one becomes aware of separated parts of the person, as though each part had an existence of its own," and in "severe cases of 'double' or split personality each of these portions is like a separate entity, well organized, sometimes with a name of its own, and capable of independent action" (p. 106), Ferenczi chronicles a sequence of traumas, which exceeded his own, that led to an increasing atomization of Leota Brown's personality.

As Ferenczi outlines, "the first shock occurred at the age of one and a half years (a promise by an adult to give her 'something good,' instead of which, drugged and sexually abused)," leading Leota to "wish not to be alive," although outwardly "a normal schoolgirl's existence prevails: in other words, an artificial double life, together with complete repression of her own inclinations and feelings" (Dupont, 1985, p. 8). Then, "at the age of five, renewed, brutal attack; genitals artificially dilated, insistent suggestion to be compliant with men; stimulating intoxicants administered." As a "consequence of the second shock," Leota's psyche now fractured into not two but three "separate entities":

> (1) A being suffering purely psychically in his unconsciousness, the actual child, of whom the awakened ego knows nothing. . . . (2) A singular being, for whom the preservation of life is of "coûte que coûte" significance. (Orpha.) This fragment plays the role of the guardian angel. . . . In the case of the second shock, this maternal part could not help in any other way than by squeezing the entire psychic life out of the inhumanly suffering body. (3) After the second shock, we therefore have to deal with a third, soulless part of the personality, that is to say, with a body progressively divested of its soul, whose disintegration is not perceived at all or is regarded as an event happening to another person, being watched from the outside.
>
> (pp. 8–9)

Thus, beneath the Apparently Normal Personality of her "schoolgirl's existence," Leota's Emotional Personality had three components: the "actual child" suffering unbearable agony, a protective "guardian angel," and a "soulless" corpse. As Severn (1933) corroborates, because of "the shock of repeated misuse," she underwent a "fragmentation" out of which "there gradually appeared at least three persons with distinctness and clarity" (p. 108). Concerning "the last great shock . . . at the age of eleven and a half," when Leota "was already split into three parts," Ferenczi records that the "sudden desertion by the tormentor" struck her "like a bolt of lightning" (Dupont, 1985, pp. 9–10). What is more, "the situation was made worse by the fact that the father, before the separation, as a kind of farewell, had cursed the child, and thus had used his influence to the end to make the child indelibly aware of her own filthiness, uselessness, and contemptibility" (p. 10). As we have just seen, Severn confirms that her father "left the family after a final and violent crisis" in which she was involved. He did so believing that this "culminating shock . . . had deprived her of all memory," and indeed she so completely dissociated everything that had happened that she "grew to adulthood with no knowledge whatever of her tragic past," until she began to reassemble the shards in her analysis with Ferenczi.

What precipitated Marcus Brown's "sudden desertion" is indicated by Ferenczi's reference to "R.N.'s extraordinary, incessant protestations that she is no murderer, although she admits to having fired the shots" (Dupont, 1985, p. 17). This seems to mean that the "culminating shock" came when Leota's father forced her to participate in a homicide and then fled the area.[8] But as early as the age of five, in Severn's (1933) words, "as part of the abuse heaped upon the child we found to have been the constant use of narcotic drugs" (p. 107), which links up with Ferenczi's comment that Severn "considers the effect of anesthetics a monstrous act of violence. . . . To be anesthetized is thus to be temporarily split off from one's own body: the operation is not carried out on me, but on a body to which I used to belong" (Dupont, 1985, p. 17).

That Leota was given drugs while being sexually exploited by her father forms a red thread in her traumatic history as well as in the legacy she transmitted to her daughter. As Brennan (2015b, p. 5) has suggested, Ferenczi's use of the word "operation" (also in German) brings out how the dissociated memory of being anesthetized during her molestation as a girl must have been revived when Leota was once again subjected to a "monstrous act of violence" when her ovaries were involuntarily removed during surgery as an adult woman. As Severn was "deprived of all memory" by the abuse involving "the constant use of narcotic drugs," moreover, Margaret (1988) affirms of the molestation by her grandfather "that drugs were used seems certain . . . although I have no conscious memory of such," and she indeed experienced "a complete blackout of the mind" (p. 8) as a result of the same lethal combination. Because of her postpartum depression, Leota was unable to breastfeed Margaret in infancy, and she was then absent physically when Margaret was being assaulted by her grandfather in Wayne. Unlike her own "stupid enslaved mother," Harriet Mann Brown, however, who "completely closed her eyes" to the torture inflicted by her father, Leota was devastated by the kidnapping of her daughter, and came to rescue her at the earliest opportunity. But it comes as no surprise that Margaret acquired her mother's eating disorder, and when Ferenczi writes in the *Clinical Diary* that "the most frightful of frights is when the threat from the father is coupled with simultaneous desertion by the mother" (Dupont, 1985, p. 18), the truth of this statement is borne out by the cases of both Elizabeth and Margaret Severn.

Although Severn does not disclose in *The Discovery of the Self* (1933) that she had taken part in a violent crime, the theme of "soul murder" is conspicuous in her dream life.[9] She reports that her "very sick" patient, who was a "highly intelligent, mentally active woman of middle age," had "a dream entitled 'This is how it feels to be murdered,'" in which she reenacted, "in an almost unconscious state, . . . a helpless child being the victim of an erotically insane and sadistic father" (pp. 107–8). As Severn comments, "we went through the phase of considering it as a fantasy only, but the amount and terrific intensity of the emotions that accompanied each and every manifestation finally convinced both of us beyond any question that it was a historical reality" (p. 108). Her disguised account of how, through "trance manifestations," what "had previously been confined to terrible nightmares finally became visible and convincing through its direct dramatization" in her analysis with Ferenczi is echoed by his insistence in the *Diary* that "patients cannot believe that an event really took place, or cannot fully believe it, if the analyst, as the sole witness of the events, persists in his cool, unemotional, and, as patients are fond of saying, purely intellectual attitude" (Dupont, 1985, p. 24). As an analyst, he continues, one must be prepared "actually to transport oneself with the patient into that period of the past (a practice Freud reproached me for, as being not permissible), with the result that we ourselves and the patient believe in its reality." Thus, just as Severn accompanied Ferenczi in his return to the past when he acted out the scene from Strindberg's *The Father*, he did the same for her when she dramatized the realities behind her "terrible nightmares," and in the process they jointly devised a radical challenge to Freud's "purely intellectual" mode of psychoanalytic therapy that was the complement to their rehabilitation and transformation of trauma theory.

In the course of recounting how the parts of herself that existed in "fragmented form" could, with Ferenczi's help, "by dint of much labor and skill, be re-collected and put together again" (p. 93), Severn (1933) reports a "typical dream" in which she either performed or danced to music "played by another girl, her double, at a nearby piano." Although "both girls were thus active, they were also both *dead*, and the patient felt dead while dreaming it and also while living it (if one may say so) in its trance reenactment" (p. 108). Thanks to the analysis, Severn continues, "the patient finally came to recognize herself as both these girls *at the same time*," an "achievement" that resulted in "the successful welding together of these two separated parts of her person." This culminating feat of "psychosynthesis," to borrow Severn's term, managed to undo "the completeness of the separation" that "was due not only to the final and critical shock that has obliterated eleven years of her life, but was also greatly augmented by the long artificial drugging to which she had been subjected and that had permanently dissociated her personality."

In addition to her piano dream, Severn had another "double" dream, " 'I attend my own funeral' " (p. 108). Against Freud's claim that "no one ever really dreams of his own death" Severn counters that it is "perfectly possible for a person to be psychically 'killed,' or some part of him killed, while he still continues to live in the flesh" (pp. 108–9). Ferenczi concurs in the *Clinical Diary:*

> Trauma is a process of dissolution that moves toward total dissolution, that is to say, death. . . . Neurotics and psychotics, even if they are still halfway capable of fulfilling their functions as body and also partly as mind, should be considered to be unconsciously in a chronic death-agony.
>
> (Dupont, 1985, pp. 130–31)

For both Ferenczi and Severn, therefore, "nightmares are real," and in this dream of observing her own funeral Severn (1933) "was not so much looking back upon an earlier psychic catastrophe as she was expressing, exactly as it was registered in her mind, what had actually occurred at the time" (p. 109), namely, the dissociation with which she responded to her father's abuse so that it was "not carried out on me, but on a body to which I used to belong." Thus, what Severn relived in her dream "was nothing less than a recognition of the destruction or loss of an integral part of her being, while another part was sufficiently removed from the immediate psychic environment to look at what was occurring and suffer accordingly."

Severn concludes by drawing attention to "another illuminating type of dream" that showed "the remarkable resources of her psyche for preserving itself when thus attacked" (p. 109). She cites as an illustration, " 'The child's life is insured by magic.' " In this dream, the part of her that she termed her "Intelligence," which, as in Ferenczi's case, "had developed to unusual proportions as compensation for the damages done, came to her rescue like a ministering angel and took over the care of the child while she was physically and psychically exposed to the evils of her father." As if to compensate for her mother's willful blindness, Severn reports that the "Intelligence" which came to the aid of her supposed patient was "'magical,' had appeared very early in the child's life, and continued to watch over her like a mother, giving her a kind of psychic sustenance by means of which she managed to withstand the cruelties both moral and physical that fate had placed upon her."

Severn's comparison of this protective part of her psyche to a "ministering angel" that never ceased to "watch over her like a mother" echoes Ferenczi's description in the *Diary* of the "maternal part" of Leota's psyche that was dedicated to the "preservation of life" at all costs and played "the role of the guardian angel," even if it meant "squeezing the entire psychic life out of the inhumanly suffering body." Severn never reveals the name of her angelic "Intelligence" in *The Discovery of the Self*, but Ferenczi identifies this "singular being" as "Orpha." Although Dupont (1985) states in an editorial note to the *Clinical Diary* that "it was in connection" with the patient whom we know to be Severn that "Ferenczi developed the theme of 'Orpha'" (p. 95*n*1), the passage in question uses the name to refer to Severn herself: "Immense resistance within myself, when, yielding to Orpha's proposal, I tried to allow myself to be analyzed by the patient" (p. 92).

Rather than being a concept primarily associated with Ferenczi, however, or even, as Rachman (2018) supposes, "a co-created term with Severn" (p. 265), Judith E. Vida (2015) is undoubtedly correct in asserting that "'Orpha' ought to be regarded more as Severn's construct than Ferenczi's: it belonged to *her* experience, and the quotation marks accompanying it in the diary are suggestive that the *name itself* came from Severn" (p. 8).[10] Indeed, the evidence indicates that Severn came up with the name Orpha initially to designate the "guardian angel" portion of her psyche and then adopted it as yet another name for herself in her capacity as a protective analyst-mother of others. In a letter dated May 23, 1941, the Brooklyn pediatrician Manning C. Field addressed Severn as "Dear Orpha" and thanked her for being "a great and good friend and wise counsellor to Dot and me thru our long struggle to grow up and get going under our own steam," while his wife Dorothy greets Severn from the Grand Canyon on July 8, 1941 as "Orpha dear": "I think of you as I sit on the rim of all this majesty. It's like your soul, you know." The original meaning is preserved by Margaret in a letter of June 16, 1937, written when she was ill and feared her mother might be ill as well: "I appealed to Orpha but she seemed weak and far away and this frightened me as I felt you must surely be ill. . . . So I told Orpha that only *part* of you was sick and part of me, that my well part was full of strength to help you and vice-versa" (qtd. in Rachman, 2018, p. 269).

Although we don't know when Severn began using the name, Ferenczi discloses that she was convinced that this emanation of "the organizing life instincts" (Dupont, 1985, p. 8) is what led her to seek him out in the first place:

> Patient R.N. even imagines that at the time of the principal trauma, with the aid of an omnipotent Intelligence (Orpha), she so to speak scoured the universe in search of help. . . . Thus her Orpha is supposed to have tracked me down, even at that time, as the only person in the world who owing to his special personal fate could and would make amends for the injury that had been done to her.
>
> (p. 121)

If Leota "scoured the universe in search of help" as an abused child of eleven and a half, she must have redoubled her efforts during her depression following Margaret's birth in 1901. Ferenczi specifies very precisely in his *Diary* of 1932 that "the patient believes that she discovered me, through mystical thought-transference (N.B. thirty-one years ago), as the only person who would be able to help patients in great distress" (p. 43).

And just as it was Ferenczi's "special personal fate" that made him the "only person in the world" with the power to "make amends" to Severn for her psychic injuries, so, too, was it Severn's fate to be and do the same for him. In a note on March 23, 1931, Ferenczi describes how "the man abandoned by all gods escapes completely from reality" and "splits off from himself a part which in the form of a helpful, loving, often motherly, minder" becomes a "guardian angel" that is "intelligence and kindness itself" (1920, 1930–1932, p. 237). He brilliantly explicates that the trauma victim's "self-splitting" is a form of self-soothing in which the dissociated "omnipotent Intelligence" is a response to the transformation of "the object-relation that had become intolerable into narcissism." Ferenczi continues:

> This angel sees the suffering or murdered child from the outside (consequently he must have, as it were, escaped out of the person in the

process of "bursting"), he wanders through the whole Universe seeking help, invents fantasies for the child that cannot be saved in any other way, etc.

Without naming Orpha, Ferenczi again clearly refers to Severn's "motherly minder" that led her to find him, but "the man abandoned by all gods" is also himself. The prognosis in such cases is by no means certain. In the event of "a very strong, repeated trauma even the guardian angel must confess his own helplessness . . . and then nothing else remains but suicide, unless at the last minute some favorable change in the reality occurs" (pp. 237–38). Although it may never be possible fully to heal the wounds of the past, it is above all simply through being there for the patient that change can occur in psychoanalysis, as Ferenczi and Severn became companions and witnesses to "the suffering or murdered child" in one another:

> This favourable change to which we can point against the suicidal impulse is the fact that in this new traumatic struggle the patient is no longer alone. Although we cannot offer him everything which he as a child should have had, the mere fact that we can or may be helpful to him gives the necessary impetus to a new life in which the pages of the irretrievable are closed and where the first step will be made towards acquiescence in what life yet can offer instead of throwing away what may still be put to good use.
>
> (p. 238)

Notes

1 According to Rachman (2018), Severn's analysis of Margaret began "as early as 1916" (p. 98), but we know from *Psycho-Therapy* that she had started trying to help her daughter recover from the consequences of her "unpardonable sin" long before that, in all likelihood when Margaret was attending a boarding school in Boulder in 1911, while Elizabeth was living and practicing in Denver.
2 In addition to her anger at Eissler, Margaret told Fortune (2015) when they first met that "her mother had made her promise to destroy all her letters after her death" (p. 25).
3 As I remarked in Chapter 1, Severn (1952) told Eissler that she, too, "helped to arrange" (p. 8) Ferenczi's trip to the United States in 1926, while Margaret (1988) reveals that her mother returned to Europe on the same boat as Sándor and Gizella the following May, which meant that she would be "poring over unksyunk complexes and not mind the ripples of the deep at all" (p. 1,166).
4 As Ferenczi's triangle with Gizella and Elma Pálos attests, he had a proclivity for inserting himself into mother/daughter pairs.

5 As I noted in Chapter 1, after his divorce from Leota, Charles Heywood married and had four children with Hattie Moore, a woman with the same first name as his mother.
6 Margaret's reference to "the dynamo" alludes to a review in a New Orleans newspaper that had hailed the intensity of her dance performances by calling her "'Pavlova Plus a Dynamo!'" (p. 9).
7 I found this letter in the collection of Margaret Severn's papers, photographs, and newspaper clippings donated by Lipskis, together with the typescript of *Spotlight*, to the Library of the Performing Arts in New York City.
8 In an uncanny parallel, Ferenczi writes of Harriot Sigray (S.I.), who was also a patient of Severn's, that "the most abominable cruelty" to which she had been subjected was that "she was forced to swallow the genitals of a repugnant black man who had just been killed" (p. 140). In both my introduction to *The Discovery of the Self* and *Formulated Experiences*, I erroneously ascribed this horror, which may have been a lynching, to Severn. It is likewise in connection with Sigray that Ferenczi describes mediums as "overanxious people, who are attuned to the slightest vibrations . . . even from a distance" (Dupont, 1985, p. 140).
9 On the concept of "soul murder," psychoanalysts almost invariably cite the later book by Leonard Shengold (1989), while overlooking Morton Schatzman's (1973) study of the impact of Moritz Schreber's childrearing practices on his son Daniel Paul Schreber, whose memoirs formed the basis of Freud's theory of paranoia. Schatzman (1990) attempted to set the record straight in a letter to the *New York Review of Books*.
10 Smith (1998, 1999) explores the precursors of Orpha in Severn's first two books, while Hayuta Gurevich (2016) links Orpha to Winnicott's concept of "regression to dependence" in the analytic relationship.

Part 2
Contexts

Chapter 7

Polygamous Analysis

1

Although Severn as "R.N." stands first among equals, the *Clinical Diary* contains Ferenczi's meditations on a cluster of patients, predominantly American women, most of whom were still in analysis with him in Budapest in 1932. Thanks to Brennan (2015a), we know the cast of characters, which includes Clara Thompson ("Dm."), Izette de Forest ("Ett."), Roberta Nederhoed ("N.D."), and Alice Lowell ("B."), as well as Angelika Frink ("G."), whom, as we have seen in the Prelude, Freud had sought to exploit financially and encouraged to divorce her first husband, Abraham Bijur, in order to marry her analyst and Freud's own favored patient, Horace Frink, with disastrous results.

Of these women, the three who went on to transmit Ferenczi's legacy—Thompson, de Forest, and Severn—were all marginal from the perspective of the ego psychologists who exercised hegemony over American psychoanalysis for decades following the Second World War. Although ego psychology has today largely been eclipsed and Ferenczi rehabilitated as the progenitor of relational analysis, it is indicative of the slighting of the Ferenczian tradition that the names of de Forest and Severn are absent from both Nathan Hale's (1971, 1995) two volumes on psychoanalysis in America and Nellie Thompson's (1987, 2001) papers on early women psychoanalysts, while Clara Thompson garners only cursory mention. As well as being "outsiders" to varying degrees, each represented Ferenczi in a different way, not only due to their individual temperaments but also because of the effects of what Emanuel Berman (2015; see Dupont, 1985, p. 34) has termed the "polygamous analysis" Ferenczi conducted with this band of émigrées—some with their own patients in tow—who had sought out the "analyst of last resort" during what proved to be his final years in Budapest.[1]

DOI: 10.4324/9781315280134-10

In the hothouse atmosphere suffusing the expatriate communities that gathered around Ferenczi and Freud, all of its members would have known—and had opinions about—one another. With respect to Vienna, Smiley Blanton, who was there initially from September 1929 to June 1930, reports in his *Diary* (1971) that "the whole of the foreign colony," which included musicians, journalists, and medical students, "seemed to revolve around Freud" (p. 49). Thompson (1952a) recalls that "there were thirty-five Americans in all Budapest" (p. 11), of whom eight were her own patients. When Severn arrived in Budapest on or about April 1, 1925, she would have met de Forest, to whom, as we have seen, Margaret Severn considered turning for analysis in 1929. As Brennan (2009) chronicles, de Forest "first went to Budapest in February 1925 and spent a year in analysis with Ferenczi, leaving in February 1926," and she and Severn "dined together on several occasions at the Ritz" (p. 437). For five months of that time (some of which was spent in Baden-Baden), de Forest's husband Alfred, a distinguished metallurgist and cousin of Dorothy Tiffany Burlingham, was also in analysis with Ferenczi.

Whereas Severn was on cordial terms with de Forest, she and Thompson never hit it off. According to Thompson (1952a), when she arrived on the scene in 1928, Ferenczi suggested to her that Severn "had rented a villa and she wanted somebody to live with her," but when Thompson went to look at it Severn told her, "I mustn't make a noise at such hours and I must use this room and I must not use that room, and that when she had certain people I must go out of the house" (p. 7), which was the end of it as far as Thompson was concerned. When she relayed what had happened to Ferenczi, he responded, "'Why, you had courage,'" which caused Thompson to realize that this was "an emotionally tinged situation" and to infer that Ferenczi "would have been afraid to say no" to Severn.

Not only was de Forest sufficiently well-liked by Severn that Margaret nearly became her patient, but she was on even friendlier terms with Thompson, with whom she remained in contact and who became the analyst of de Forest's daughter Judith as an adult woman.[2] After her year in Budapest from February 1925 to February 1926, de Forest continued her analysis with Ferenczi from the fall of 1926 to the spring of 1927, when he was in New York to lecture at the New School for Social Research, and she returned to Budapest during the summers from 1929 to 1931. Thus, "Ett." was no longer in treatment with Ferenczi by 1932 when he wrote the *Clinical Diary*. For her part, Thompson met Ferenczi for the first time when he came to New York in 1926. Due to financial constraints, she could not afford to travel to Budapest until 1928 and was able to stay for only two months. She did so again in 1929, and then stayed for three months in 1930, before returning on a firmer footing in 1931 and remaining until after Ferenczi's death in May 1933. From Brennan's (2009, 2015c) meticulously documented papers it emerges that, like Angelika Frink, who had not only had an affair with but married her analyst, de Forest had previously had an affair with Frederick Pierce, with whom she was in analysis from 1923 to 1925, while Thompson during the same years had her first analysis with Joseph Cheesman Thompson (no relation), about whom she had to rebut the rumor that she was his mistress. This prehistory of alleged or actual sexual boundary violations among several of Ferenczi's patients raised the temperature in the Hungarian hothouse. After their respective analyses with Ferenczi, both de Forest and Thompson went for a third analysis to Fromm.

To de Forest belongs the distinction of having published the first article on Ferenczi in the *International Journal of Psycho-Analysis*, "The Therapeutic Technique of Sándor Ferenczi" (1942), which preceded by seven years the Ferenczi issue of the *International Journal* that featured the long-suppressed English translation of "Confusion of Tongues," as well as of being the author of the first book on Ferenczi in any language, *The Leaven of Love: A Development of the Psychoanalytic Theory and Technique of Sándor Ferenczi* (1954). De Forest's titles proclaim her allegiance to Ferenczi, and she dedicates herself to a lucid and faithful exposition of his ideas. In her article, de Forest (1942) lays it down as the starting point of Ferenczi's conception of neurosis that "there must have actually occurred in the childhood of the individual" one of the following circumstances: (1) "a traumatic experience of great intensity"; (2) "a sequence of less intense traumatic experiences"; or (3) "a constant exposure to the highly emotional reactions, either sadistic or masochistic, of one or more adults" (p. 121). In keeping with trauma theory, neurosis is understood to be the result of acute or chronic failures in the interpersonal world rather than arising from endogenous factors within the individual. With respect to technique, de Forest emphasizes that for Ferenczi the therapeutic process "should centre dynamically around the *mutual relationship* of analyst and patient" (italics added), a statement that hints at her awareness of his mutual analysis with Severn, though without betraying the secret to the reader of her paper. Crucially, she adds that "the analyst's aim is to assist the patient to penetrate through the repressed and distorted experience of his life to *the traumatic occurrence or sequence of occurrences which are at the root of the neurosis*; then to aid him to *face dramatically* the trauma or traumatic series by *re-living it emotionally*, not in its original setting but as *an actual part of the analytic situation*" (italics added).

The following year, Thompson (1943) published a brief rejoinder to de Forest's paper, which spells out her own "somewhat different" (p. 64) conclusions about Ferenczi's technique. While praising his recognition that "the analytic situation is a human situation involving the interaction of two human personalities," and that "no therapeutic results are possible unless the patient feels and is accepted by the analyst," Thompson parts company with Ferenczi in several respects. First, she faults his "tendency to take ideas to extremes," as when "the idea of admitting one's fallibility to the patient" is construed "as an invitation to mutual analysis" (p. 65), at once an echo of de Forest's reference to "the mutual relationship of analyst and patient" and a covert rebuke of Ferenczi's experiment with Severn. Second, she takes Ferenczi to task for having been "not entirely clear" about the meaning of analytic love because he "tended to confuse the idea that the patient must be given all the love he needs with the idea he must be given all the love he demands." In Thompson's view, Ferenczi failed to recognize that the neurotically deprived individual "may develop an insatiable need of love," which it is "not only humanly impossible" but also "not therapeutically valuable" to attempt to gratify. Finally, Thompson expresses "serious doubts about the entire validity" of "the idea of making the analytic situation very dramatic" by encouraging the analyst to enter into the patient's emotional reliving of past traumatic experiences. She insists instead that "one of the most important functions of the analyst is to keep the patient in contact with reality," which means helping the person who feels that the analyst has failed him "to know with some remnant of rationality in himself that his accusations are not true, and that the analyst really wishes him well" (p. 66).

Of his three American conduits, therefore, Thompson is the most skeptical in her attitude toward Ferenczi, whereas de Forest and Severn concur with him on the need for a reenactment of early traumas as part of the therapeutic process and on the power of the analyst's love as a healing agent. In the opening sentence of *The Leaven of Love*, de Forest (1954) implicitly counters Thompson's assertion that Ferenczi had misunderstood the kind of love needed by deprived patients by quoting his own words in a personal communication: "'Psychoanalytic "cure" is in direct proportion to the cherishing love given by the psychoanalyst to the patient; the love which the psychoanalytic patient *needs*, not necessarily the love which he thinks he needs and therefore demands'" (p. 15). In Ferenczi's defense, de Forest maintains that he is aware of the challenges posed by the patient's "neurotic character structure," but holds that these can best be overcome by a "determination to offer to the conscious and unconscious areas of the patient's personality the degree and kind of loving care for which he is in fact starving."

In American psychoanalysis, de Forest's commitment to maintaining an empathic stance is carried forward by Kohut and self psychologists, whereas Thompson belongs to the tradition of defense analysis stemming from Wilhelm Reich. According to Helen Swick Perry (1982), it was Harry Stack Sullivan who had persuaded Thompson to obtain an analysis with Ferenczi, "so that she could come back and teach him what she had learned" (p. 201). In recompense, Thompson took Sullivan into analysis, from probably December 1934 to February 1936, but this treatment, as Kathleen Meigs (2017) has convincingly argued, ended when Sullivan quit "in a rage" because Thompson attempted what he experienced as a Reichian "aggressive attack" (p. 325) on his character, rather than practicing "Ferenczian trauma-oriented 'relaxation' and 'neocathartic' therapy" (p. 313).

Notwithstanding this fiasco, Sullivan outdid Thompson in his penchant for confrontation. Indeed, as Thompson (1952b) observes, "Sullivan's therapeutic technique . . . has in its general theory much in common with the more active character analysis technique described by Wilhelm Reich and practiced pretty generally by analysts today" (p. 87; see Conci, 2012, pp. 400–1). In *Psychoanalysis: Evolution and Development* (1950), her sole authored book, Thompson underscores her critique of Ferenczi's indulgence: "No matter how much genuine warmth the analyst is capable of giving, the childhood lack in the patient cannot be repaired except through insight-provoking analysis of the character defenses which thwart and block him at every turn" (p. 187). Thompson (1952a) told Eissler that she joined a study group on Reich's work when she returned to the United States from Hungary, and again wonders why Ferenczi was not "influenced by the growing trend of character analysis more than he was" (p. 23). Strikingly, as Esther Menaker (1989) recounts in her memoir, this study group was organized by de Forest, and, in addition to herself and her husband William, its participants included Alice Lowell, a younger woman whom Menaker describes as de Forest's "cousin" but with whom de Forest had in actuality fallen in love (Brennan, 2009, pp. 444–45). According to Menaker, "we met once a month to discuss Wilhelm Reich's *Character*

Analysis, which had not yet been translated into English and from which Bill read aloud at our meetings, translating as he went" (p. 170).

Despite her own reading of Reich and having a closer friendship with Thompson than she did with Severn, however, de Forest remained aligned with Severn in her defense of Ferenczi's belief in the healing power of analytic love and the efficacy of the patient's emotional reliving of past traumas accompanied by the analyst. Yet de Forest never acknowledges Severn nor does she cite *The Discovery of the Self*. Perhaps because she had left Budapest by 1931, and thus was not present when Ferenczi and Severn embarked on their mutual analysis, or simply because of her irenic temperament, de Forest did not take a side in any of these conflicts and contented herself with being Ferenczi's advocate. From a privileged background and raised as an Episcopalian, de Forest in later life became a member of the Society of Friends. She concludes *The Leaven of Love* (1954) by grounding her advocacy of a "redemption by love" (p. 179) in Christian teaching and her "faith in God's loving presence" (p. 181).

Of the three women, Thompson alone had an institutional base in psychoanalysis, having been a member of the New York Psychoanalytic Institute and then of Karen Horney's American Institute of Psychoanalysis before becoming director of the William Alanson White Institute from its founding in 1943 until her death in 1958. Even though she resigned from the New York Institute and became a "maverick," Thompson was a leading figure in the "neo-Freudian" group that left a lasting mark on subsequent generations of interpersonal analysts. Both Anthony Bass (2015) and Sue A. Shapiro (2000) have recounted their experiences of analysis with Benjamin Wolstein, who had been in analysis with Thomson and was himself one of the principal channels of Ferenczi's legacy. Although de Forest received a handwritten "Certificate" from Ferenczi in June 1929 attesting that she "went through her personal analysis, which lasted 15 months, did controlled analysis with 3 patients, and is sufficiently instructed in theory and literature of Psycho-Analysis" (reproduced in Brennan, 2009, p. 438), she did not attempt to join any analytic institute, choosing instead to define her professional identity as a pastoral counselor. As a member of this community, she had the satisfaction of seeing *The Leaven of Love* chosen as a book of the month by the Pastoral Psychology Book Club (p. 433).

Despite remaining an outsider, de Forest appeared on the radar of organized psychoanalysis through her article published in the *International Journal of Psycho-Analysis*. Her book even garnered a review by Jones (1956), who, discomfited by de Forest's revisionist perspective one year before the appearance of the final volume of his Freud biography, derided her "ardently expressed gospel of love and charity" and (like Balint) repudiated "her extraordinary view of Freud's imagined hostility" (p. 488) toward Ferenczi. *The Leaven of Love* was no less roundly disparaged in an omnibus review in the *Journal of the American Psychoanalytic Association* by Helen Tartakoff (1956), who alleged that "no serious attempt is made by de Forest to place her method on a comprehensive theoretical foundation" (p. 332). Fromm (1955), on the other hand, hailed the book in the *New York Times* as "a significant contribution to psychoanalytic literature, but beyond that, of significance to anyone concerned with the power of love in human relations" (p. 2).

2

At the opposite end of the spectrum from Thompson and lacking institutional support of any kind, Severn, in the words of her daughter, was "a one-woman show" with "no friends or colleagues, only patients" (qtd. in Fortune, 1993, p. 105). The only person to my knowledge to have acknowledged a debt to Severn is Nandor Fodor. As we have seen in Chapter 1, Fodor (1959) first met Severn, whom he describes as "a well known practicing psychoanalyst in London and a former pupil of Sandor Ferenczi," in 1934 through the International Institute for Psychical Research, of which Fodor became Director of Research, and he credits this contact with "having renewed my interest in psychoanalysis" (p. 78). Fodor, after his emigration from Hungary in 1921, had worked as a journalist in New York until 1929, in the course of which he "interviewed [Ferenczi] in the United States in 1926," so one can readily imagine the excitement with which Severn and Fodor must have recognized their elective affinity when their paths crossed in London.

What Fodor deemed "a turning point in my life" (p. 79) came in 1938, when he was summoned to investigate the case of Thornton Heath Poltergeist, so-called from the London suburb in which the house in question was located. Without discounting the possibility that the phenomena of flying crockery and the like were genuine, Fodor understood them as emanations of unconscious conflicts in the mind of the protagonist, "an attractive married woman of thirty-five" (p. 5) to whom he gave the pseudonym "Mrs. Forbes" in his full-length study, *On the Trail of the Poltergeist* (1958), and other publications, but who was in reality named Alma Fielding. As Fodor (1968) recounts, it was from Severn that he "learned the elementaries of a psychoanalytic approach to mediums," and she "took part in the beginnings of my investigation," but, "unfortunately, as soon as her profession was revealed, Mrs. Forbes refused to tolerate her presence" (p. 105). Notwithstanding this rebuff, however, Kate Summerscale, who had access to Fodor's papers at the International Institute for her book *The Haunting of Alma Fielding* (2020), attests that "privately, Fodor continued to discuss Alma's case with Elizabeth Severn" (p. 107).[3] Under Severn's influence, Fodor (1958) arrived at the reconstruction that Alma Fielding had been the victim of "an unforgivable injury before the age of five" (p. 211), specifically of a rape, adding that "the devastating effects of such an experience on children are well known to all practising psychoanalysts" (p. 222). Citing the analogous ideas of F. W. H. Myers, but also inscribing himself in the tradition extending from Janet to Bromberg, Fodor maintained that the disturbances arose "from a severe traumatisation and consequent dissociation," and what he called "Poltergeist Psychosis" (p. 7) was due to

> a profound cleavage of personality—to the explosive loosening of an infantile part of the psyche in which severe conflicts are kept repressed. This torn-off part of the mind would be strictly conditioned in its development by the conflict-material which the main personality (in a therapeutic reaction to a disintegrating shock) had expelled and is preventing from returning to consciousness.
>
> (p. 222)

Not surprisingly, Fodor's (1959) interest in investigating the traumatic histories of his subjects incurred the wrath of "the prim, elderly ladies who supported the International Institute for Psychical Research," for whom "the mention and investigation of any sexual factors in a case of psychical phenomena was an inexcusable, shocking development" (p. 6). His manuscript of *On the Trail of the Poltergeist* was temporarily confiscated—and did not appear in print until twenty years later, after having been repeatedly rejected by publishers—and he was dismissed from his position at the International Institute. But this setback led to Fodor's supreme triumph when his wife "conceived the idea of appealing to Freud" and carried "a bunch of beautiful tiger lilies" (p. 7) to his residence at 20 Maresfield Gardens. As it happened, "on that day Freud was feeling lonely and bored" and as a consequence "had her stay for tea," during which Mrs. Fodor told him of "the impasse that had developed" because of her husband's "lone championing of the psychoanalytical approach" to the study of purportedly paranormal phenomena. Intrigued, Freud asked to see the "controversial manuscript," which Fodor hastened to send him "in fear and trepidation."

On November 22, 1938, Fodor (1959) was elated to receive a letter from Freud, who commended his efforts in resounding fashion:

> "The way you deflect your interest from the question of whether the phenomena observed are real or have been falsified and turn it to the psychological study of the medium, including the investigation of her previous history, seems to me to be the right step to take in the planning of research which will lead to some explanation of the occurrences in question."
>
> (p. 8)

Freud proceeded to deplore the unwillingness of the International Institute to follow Fodor's lead and to assure Fodor that he regarded as "'very probable the result you come to with the particular case,'" adding that "'naturally it would be desirable to confirm it through a real analysis of the person, but that evidently is not feasible.'" Freud invited Fodor to call on him to retrieve his manuscript. During their conversation, Freud encouraged Fodor "to stick to my guns and fight for the truth as I saw it" (p. 9), and granted Fodor permission to use his letter as a frontispiece to his book (although Fodor ended up including it in *The Haunted Mind* rather than in *On the Trail of the Poltergeist*). Fodor, then in the middle of libel case against the spiritualist newspaper *Psychic News*, felt that "it would have been inexcusable to drag [Freud's] name into our quarrel," but was vindicated when he prevailed in his lawsuit and was awarded admittedly modest damages in the amount of £105.

Like Severn, who returned to New York before the outbreak of World War II, Fodor (1968) left London and again took up residence in the American metropolis "in the spring of 1939" (p. 111). Fodor (1958) reports that, among the reasons he was subjected to criticism for his research on the Thornton Heath case, in the course of which he administered free association tests to Alma Fielding (as Severn had done early on with her patients), was that he "was not a psychoanalyst" (p. 8), and thus was not qualified to interpret their results. Fodor concedes that this reproach "was true at the time" since he "had no training in it" and was "relying on insight and enthusiasm" for his "semi-psychoanalytical" approach to the investigation. In addition, as he writes elsewhere, it was Freud's "magnanimous" praise of the manuscript of *On the Trail of the Poltergeist* that confirmed him in his "decision to forsake parapsychology for psychoanalysis as a professional pursuit" (1963, p. 119).

From these statements, it is evident that Fodor did not practice as a psychoanalyst during his period in London, and Summerscale (2020) is accordingly correct that he must have "trained as a psychoanalyst" in "New York City in the 1940s" (p. 304). According to his obituary in the *New York Times* (1964), which bore the caption "A Psychoanalyst; Author of Theory to Explain Poltergeists," Fodor earned a Ph.D. and a law degree in Hungary but had "no formal medical education," but where and with whom he trained is surprisingly difficult to determine. A key figure turns out to have been Theodor Reik, on whose behalf Freud had written *The Question of Lay Analysis* and who in 1948 founded the National Psychological Association for Psychoanalysis (NPAP) to offer training to qualified professionals whose lack of a medical degree barred them from applying to institutes of the American Psychoanalytic Association.

Fodor's (1944) first analytic paper appeared in *The Psychoanalytic Review*, then still under the editorship of Jelliffe, while Freud's letter to Fodor was published, in a translation by Reik, in the Winter 1955 issue (Fodor, 1955; see Fodor, 1963, p. 127n2) of *Psychoanalysis*, the journal of NPAP from 1952 to 1958, when it merged with *The Psychoanalytic Review* to become *Psychoanalysis and The Psychoanalytic Review*, until the name reverted to *The Psychoanalytic Review* in 1963.[4] Two issues later, in Summer 1955, Fodor's name appears for the first time as a member of the editorial board of *Psychoanalysis*. Following the merger, when Marie Coleman (later Marie Coleman Nelson) became editor of *Psychoanalysis and The Psychoanalytic Review*, Fodor published an article in the inaugural issue accompanied by the following note: "Nandor Fodor is a member of the Editorial Board of this journal. He is a practicing psychoanalyst and a member of NPAP and the American Psychological Association" (Contributors, 1958, p. 160). On Fodor's death, Nelson (1964), who shared his interest in parapsychology, wrote an obituary in which she hailed "the courage that fortified Dr. Fodor's interest in psi research" as well as his appreciation for "originality of thought and his liberal viewpoint" (p. 157).

Fodor's membership in NPAP and position on the editorial board of its journals gave him an institutional affiliation that legitimated his claim to call himself a "practicing psychoanalyst." One wonders how he became a member of the American Psychological Association when he did not have a degree in psychology any more than he did in medicine. But what is even more curious is that Fodor nowhere reveals where he received his analytic training. During this period at NPAP, however, it was possible for the president or a board member to nominate someone for membership, and if that person was deemed to have a sufficient background in psychoanalysis to warrant the bypassing of training, he would be accepted as a member.[5] What therefore seems to have happened is that Reik saw in Fodor another cultivated and prolific European who had likewise had personal contact with Freud, and in keeping with his conviction that "psychoanalysts are born—not made" (Gargiulo, 2020, p. 3), sponsored Fodor for membership in NPAP in this fashion. Having received Reik's blessing and found a group of congenial colleagues, Fodor then made this freestanding institute his home for the last decade of his professional life.

In the course of paying tribute to Severn for teaching him "the elementaries of a psychoanalytic approach to mediums," Fodor (1968) offhandedly remarks that "it was a standard joke between us that I was her illegitimate son, until one day she told me, now you can consider yourself legitimate" (p. 105). I interpret this "joke" to mean that Severn pronounced Fodor to be her "legitimate" son when he terminated an analysis with her in New York during the 1940s, so that he became her protégé not simply as a psychical researcher but also as a psychoanalyst. If this is indeed what happened, Fodor would naturally have shared with Reik that he had been in analysis with a pupil of Ferenczi's, and this experience would have helped to open the door to NPAP. Of course, Fodor continued to enjoy the charisma bestowed by his letter from Freud—a tangible proof of his consecration much like de Forest's "Certificate" from Ferenczi—which, according to Summerscale (2020), he "framed and hung on his wall," and with the help of which he "built up a successful psychoanalytic practice" (p. 305) in New York.

As John Boyle (2021) observes, the fact "that both Severn and Fodor acquired general recognition as 'psychoanalysts' during their lifetimes," despite the lack of any formal training by either, "hints at the possibility of a psychoanalytic 'transmission of knowledge' outside of accredited institutional frameworks." Indeed, if Fodor, after having "privately" discussed the case of Alma Fielding with Severn in London, staked his claim to being a psychoanalyst in large measure on his equally private experience of analysis with her in New York, then this "underground" laying on of hands exemplifies the "secret life" that Herman (1992, p. 152) has argued is characteristic not only of victims but also of therapists of trauma, who after Freud's repudiation of the "seduction" theory continued the study of the "profound cleavages of personality" resulting from "disintegrating shocks," which were otherwise relegated to the realm of the supernatural whence they had previously been thought to arise.

In view of Fodor's visit to Freud on or about November 22, 1938, only two months after Freud had moved in to 20 Maresfield Gardens, it becomes ironic that Severn's (1952) final interview with Freud, during which Freud seemed "very friendly" and "expressed admiration for Ferenczi," likewise took place "late in '38, a few months [actually, closer to a year] before he died" (pp. 9–10). When Freud praised Fodor's manuscript so fulsomely, it was because he saw Fodor as an ally in his "championing of the psychoanalytical approach" to parapsychology, but the version of psychoanalysis espoused by Fodor in *On the Trail of the Poltergeist* was none other than the theory of the "devastating effects" of "unforgivable injuries," frequently of a sexual nature, inflicted on children's "tender" psyches by the "passions" of adults, against which Freud had fulminated when he heard Ferenczi read aloud his Wiesbaden Congress paper, and in which Fodor had been schooled by Severn herself.

Like Ferenczi, therefore, Fodor charted his course as a psychoanalyst by the lodestars of Freud and Severn, but whereas for Ferenczi they were polar opposites whose conflicting pulls caused him immense anguish, Fodor received the blessing of them both. But if Fodor (1958) can be seen as Ferenczi's fortunate double, there is also, as he himself recognized, a "strange parallel" between his position and that of "the great founder of Psychoanalysis" (p. 8). As Fodor gleaned from reading the third volume of Jones's biography, "it is clear that just as I tried to bring Psychoanalysis into Psychical Research, so did Freud try to incorporate the occult into Psychoanalysis" (pp. 8–9). Freud's letter to Fodor is one piece of evidence for Freud's openness to the occult, but the crucial document is a 1921 letter to Hereward Carrington, "one of the most indefatigable of all psychical researchers" (p. 2), whom Fodor (1959) befriended after he had interviewed Carrington during his stint as a reporter for a Hungarian newspaper in New York in the 1920s. Carrington had written to Freud to invite him to join the advisory council of the American Psychical Institute. Although Freud declined Carrington's invitation and asked him "'to forgo the use of my name in connection with your undertaking,'" he did confess, when he still had eighteen years to live, "'If I were at the beginning of a scientific career, instead of as now, at its end, I would perhaps choose no other field of work, in spite of all difficulties'" (p. 12).

What is even more surprising than this confession, however, is the fact that Freud subsequently denied that he had ever made it. As Jones (1957) recounts, when George Lawton, whom Carrington had told about Freud's letter to him, wrote to Freud to express his doubts that Freud could ever have said what Carrington said he did, Freud responded on December 20, 1929, "'I deplore the fact that you yourself did not read my letter to Carrington. You would have easily convinced yourself that I said nothing to justify his assertion'" (p. 392). It was only, Jones adds, when Fodor "kindly procured from Mr. Carrington a photostat of Freud's letter" that the truth emerged. Not only was Freud "wrong in his denial," but "in the eight years that had passed he had blotted out the memory of that very astonishing and unexpected passage."

If we set this episode of Freud's letter to Carrington in the broader context of the history of psychoanalysis, Fodor takes on the role of Severn's avenging angel who brings to light the proof of Freud's fascination with the occult that he had sought to repress—or, rather, dissociate—and which even the implacably hard-headed Jones had to concede could no longer be doubted, although he regarded it as "unexpected." Fodor (1963) struck a further blow on behalf of the compatibility of psychoanalysis with parapsychology when he was the first to publish, in *The Psychoanalytic Review*, Freud's letter to Jung of April 16, 1909 attempting to explain away the incident during Jung's recent visit to Vienna when he had correctly predicted that a loud noise he and Freud had heard coming from a bookcase in Freud's study would be repeated, which Freud dismissed as "'sheer bosh'" (p. 121) before it happened.

This incident—and the letter in which Freud blamed Jung for having "'divested me of my paternal dignity'" on the same evening that he "'formally adopted'" Jung as his "'eldest son, anointing you as my successor and crown prince'"—have since become notorious. But it was Fodor who brought to light this letter, in which Freud gave his views on "'poltergeist phenomena'" (p. 122), and Fodor went on to raise the "fantastic query" whether Jung's "frightening powers" of telekinesis may likewise have been "responsible for the two instances in which Freud fainted" (p. 126) in his presence, the first in Bremen in 1909 and the second in Munich in 1912. In 1963, furthermore, the same year in which he published Freud's letter to Jung on "poltergeist phenomena," Fodor also published in *The Psychoanalytic Review* the first English translation of Ferenczi's 1899 paper on spiritism, where, as we have seen, before his encounters with either Freud or Severn, Ferenczi affirmed that "the hidden treasure of the spiritist may bring us a rich harvest, beyond anticipation in a little cultivated field of science, the psychology of the human mind" (p. 143).[6]

Apart from Fodor, however, Severn had no heirs in the psychoanalytic world; and by comparison with *The Leaven of Love*, *The Discovery of the Self* sunk like a stone. It sold a total of fifty-six copies in the United States in its first two years (Fortune, 1993, p. 114) and garnered a lone review—not in the *International Journal of Psycho-Analysis* but in *The Psychoanalytic Review*. In view of the subsequent hospitality of *The Psychoanalytic Review* to Fodor and "psi research," it is another irony that the anonymous author (1938) eviscerated the book as "Santa Claus to the populace with Christmas tree pop-corn masquerading under the guise of a . . . treatise on psychoanalysis" (p. 135). Although the review is unsigned, Jelliffe had become sole editor of *The Psychoanalytic Review* in 1937 upon the death of White and would have had final say over the publication of the piece even if he were not the author, a possibility that cannot be excluded. That Jelliffe retained an interest in Severn is evidenced by his correspondence with Jung, whose wife Emma wrote to him on January 16, 1928: "I am finding among Dr. Jung's letters one of yours . . . where you ask about a Mrs. Elizabeth Severn. Now, Dr. Jung cannot remember her at all, neither under the name of Brown or Haywood" (Burnham, 1983, pp. 226–27). In addition to documenting that Jelliffe has asked Jung about Severn, Emma Jung's letter reveals that his inquiry was sufficiently detailed as to give both her maiden and her married names, although "Heywood" is misspelled.[7]

The reasons for Jelliffe's curiosity about Severn more than a decade after she had been his patient remain obscure, but it can be posited that he would have read *The Psychology of Behaviour* and been none too happy about her portrait of him in that book. Indeed, Severn's (1933) critique in *The Discovery of the Self* of "the very superficial and even deleterious way" that the "profound principles" of psychoanalysis are applied by "certain members of the medical profession" whose deficiencies make them "'lay analysts' in the psychological sense" (p. 44) might well again have been aimed specifically at Jelliffe, just as her plea that the metaphorical "broken bones" of the traumatized patient "require not only to be broken again but to be 'set' and to be bound or held in position until the natural healing forces can do their work" (p. 63) reprises her earlier comparison of his technique to that of a surgeon who excises a tumor "without any succeeding medical care for the upbuilding of the weakened constitution" (1917, p. 258). The vituperative dismissal of *The Discovery of the Self* that Jelliffe countenanced—and may even have penned himself—in *The Psychoanalytic Review* constitutes a deferred expression of his countertransference as well as an act of retaliation on Jelliffe's part.

3

Although Thompson took issue with de Forest's endorsement of Ferenczi's ideas on theory and therapy, she did so respectfully and with an absence of rancor. Not so with Severn, whom Thompson viscerally loathed. Indeed, so obsessive is Thompson's (1952a) preoccupation with her nemesis that she said almost immediately to Eissler that one of Ferenczi's innovations which "disturbed Freud a lot" was "telling the patients your faults," but "not in the sense . . . of letting him analyze you—*though he did have a patient who did that, too*" (p. 2; italics added). Later, in making the point that Ferenczi "had never really believed in the deprivation idea" and "he thought that some devil in him had forced him to carry it to such extremes that it would prove it was absurd," Thompson adds, "And of course his shift to the relaxation therapy was largely due to Elisabeth La Verne [*sic*], who was his patient. I would say she was a paranoid bitch" (p. 6).[8]

This testimony to Severn's impact on Ferenczi's development carries added weight because it comes from a hostile witness, but Thompson's bile seeps out as she proceeds to describe Severn as "one of these very controlling, hypochondriacal women" who "ruled from her bed" and "had her daughter under her thumb," where she "presently had Ferenczi." Once again, however, Thompson pays tribute to Severn by observing that "the last two years I was there, there was quite a change in him," and much of what Ferenczi did during that period "was his attempt to solve the problem of this woman" who "demanded the endless hours." After serving up, among other morsels, the anecdote about calling on Severn to inquire about living with her in her rented villa, Thompson discloses, "I used to call her 'Bird of Prey,'" before stopping short and asking herself, "why did I get off on her?" (p. 7).

Thompson's description of Severn as a "controlling" and "hypochondriacal" woman who "ruled from her bed" depicts her as a malingerer who used a factitious disorder to manipulate other people, above all Ferenczi. Ferenczi gives an account of the situation from his point of view in the *Clinical Diary* that allows us to see how it could have appeared as it did to an unsympathetic observer such as Thompson. "Right from the beginning," he writes, Severn "had claimed to be more important than the other patients," and "when the case did not show any progress" he resolved "not to be frightened off by any difficulty," to the point where he "gave in more and more to the patient's wishes, doubled the number of sessions, going to her house instead of forcing her to come to me; I took her with me on my vacation trips and provided sessions even on Sundays" (Dupont, 1985, p. 97). For Ferenczi to say he "gave in" does imply an element of submission on his part to Severn's demands, and he adds that he "resisted" for "approximately one year" Severn's pleas that "her analysis would never make any progress" unless he allowed her to analyze the "feelings of hate" (p. 99) she sensed in him.

When we turn to Severn's (1952) narrative of these same events, however, the picture comes into focus from an altogether different perspective. Far from being "hypochondriacal" and "controlling," Severn portrays herself to Eissler as having grown increasingly desperate and suicidal in the course of her long analysis with Ferenczi. As she recapitulates, "it took about two years to discover that there was a very serious amnesia in my life in my childhood. . . . But there was no other way of accounting for various feelings and symptoms I had, particularly a desire for suicide" (p. 1). The threat of suicide thus loomed from the beginning, and this initial phase lasted from 1925 to approximately 1927. After continuing "for a few years more" because she wanted the analysis "to be as complete as it could," Severn felt herself to be worse off than she had been before: "I was in a desperate state by that time, being much worse than when I came, because I didn't feel that I could live unless I got rid of this thing that was still troubling my unconscious, causing me violent headaches and deep depressions" (p. 5). Externally, Severn's "affairs were all right" and there was "very little in my conscious life to be worried about," but "the feeling that I couldn't live, that I would have to kill myself, was overwhelming and I was getting weaker all the time."

The middle phase of malignant regression spans the years from roughly 1927 to 1930. Eventually, Severn's amnesia was lifted and she recovered her memories of being abused by her father, but the analysis with Ferenczi remained stymied:

> Now, then, we reached the point of uncovering what had caused the trouble, which was my father, who was a gentleman crook and who practiced all sorts of malpractice on me as a little child—when we uncovered that, I was convinced that that was the cause of my suffering and that I ought to be relieved of it. But I wasn't. I was completely broken down.
>
> (p. 5)

Endorsing this timeline, Ferenczi recollects in the *Clinical Diary*, "About three years ago discovery of the amnesia, two years ago reproduction of the trauma" (Dupont, 1985, p. 193). In her autobiography, Margaret (1988) records that "by the end of 1931," when the finances of the dancing school she had founded in New York were in dire straits as a result of the Great Depression, "a cable arrived from Dr. Ferenczi in Budapest" in which he announced that "my mother was critically ill and asked me to come at once," impelling her to leave everything behind and sail to Europe "on the first boat available" (p. 1,695). Far from being a hypochondriac, Severn (1952) was by this juncture "completely broken down" and "critically ill," to the point where Ferenczi feared for her life. She attempted to carry on analytic work with her own transplanted patients, but when, "in spite of all our efforts," she "did not get any better" in her analysis with Ferenczi, the questions arose, "What is the trouble? What has gone wrong, or what needs to be done?" (p. 5).

After exhausting every other explanation, the emotionally shattered, physically ill, and financially destitute Severn came to the realization that "the trouble lay in him" (p. 5) and that her analysis was blocked because Ferenczi "did not have the sympathetic feeling that he theoretically advocated" (p. 8). This interpretation is repeatedly corroborated by Ferenczi in the *Clinical Diary*, as when he documents that he had to confess that "in actual fact and inwardly" he "did hate the patient, in spite of all the friendliness I displayed," which paradoxically "had a tranquilizing effect" on Severn, who "even began to reduce her demands," causing Ferenczi "to find her less disagreeable" (Dupont, 1985, p. 99). Elsewhere he links "the start of 'mutual analysis'" to his having "admitted to almost everything I held back with regard to antipathy and resistance in the face of excessive suffering and this was recognized and traced back to infantile elements in myself" (p. 193). As we have seen, it was above all by heeding her dreams that Severn (1952) arrived at this insight, which, when she succeeded in convincing Ferenczi of its validity, led him to assent to her radical proposal:

> So my dreams finally placed the blame on him, that is if you call it blame. He was not consciously aware of the difficulty, until at long last he saw it, and it resulted in a rearrangement of our relationship—that I became the analyst. He submitted to that, and I certainly admired him for his courage in doing so. Naturally it was very painful to him, but it was equally painful to me. I was sore and wounded, of course. And when I found that my analyst hated me, it was hard to take, because I knew or felt that that was the reason I was not getting free. I finally got free on my own steam.
>
> (p. 6)

Severn says that Ferenczi "submitted" to the "rearrangement" in their relationship, but she depicts it as an act of "courage" that was no less "painful" to her than it was to him because it required her to face the fact that she was "hated" by the analyst on whom she had grown precariously dependent for her survival.

Heralding the final stage of Severn's analysis, Thompson recalls that she observed "quite a change" in Ferenczi during her "last two years" in Budapest, while Ferenczi acknowledges that he "resisted" for "approximately one year" Severn's pleas that "her analysis would never make any progress" unless he permitted her to analyze his disavowed "feelings of hate." These statements dovetail with the evidence that Severn and Ferenczi had by 1930 succeeded in recovering the repressed memories of her childhood abuse by her father, but to no avail. Having already "completely broken down," Severn deteriorated further in 1931 as she battled to get Ferenczi, who was himself under ever-increasing strain not only from carrying a full load of deeply disturbed patients but also from fighting on a second front with Freud, to admit that the main problem no longer lay in her past but in the dynamics of their relationship in the present. (This is what Kardiner was never able to get Freud to realize.) Only at the end of 1931, however, when he cabled to Margaret, did Ferenczi run up the white flag or earn his red badge of courage—depending on how one looks at it—by consenting to the mutual analysis. Severn could not be clearer on the timing, saying to Eissler that she analyzed him "at least a year or more. For about a year I gave him daily sessions" (p. 13). This accords with my deduction that the mutual analysis began shortly before Ferenczi's first entry in the *Clinical Diary*, on January 7, 1932, and, as we know from *Spotlight*, it was still ongoing on December 14. When Eissler obtusely asks if she had analyzed Ferenczi during their summer trip to Spain, which took place in 1928, Severn reiterates: "No, it was the last year I was there that I did his analysis, and that was what really helped me to get on my feet, you see—to disconnect from him" (p. 13).

Wondering about the precise nature of their arrangements, Eissler inquires whether Ferenczi's analysis "was conducted in such a way that he was on the couch and you were on the chair," to which Severn replies in the affirmative, adding, "I was unable to get out of bed by that time, so most of it was done in my place" (p. 9). Even after the mutual analysis began Severn remained housebound and obliged Ferenczi to visit her for their sessions, which explains Thompson's scathing comment that she "ruled from her bed." Ferenczi recounts in the *Diary* how the two of them haggled over the allocation of the hours, with Severn prevailing in her insistence on "the precise division of the time into two equal parts," with "every session" beginning "with the analysis of the analyst" (Dupont, 1985, p. 71). For "two days in a row," he went so far as to surrender to "only being analyzed" by Severn so that "the customary superiority of the analyst" was reversed into "total subordination," which induced in him an array of psychosomatic symptoms before "the patient's two-day abstinence made it impossible to delay her analysis any longer, and mutuality was again restored" (p. 73).[9]

Not to be overlooked in any stocktaking are the financial accommodations Ferenczi made for Severn, the effects of which reverberated throughout his network of patients. Severn (1952) informs Eissler that she initially paid Ferenczi $15.00 a session, though at some point he increased his fee to $20.00. Once they began the mutual analysis, Ferenczi did not pay her, but he "stopped accepting money from me" (p. 15) and also forgave a debt of several hundred dollars she had accumulated. As Ferenczi confirms, "financial difficulties nearly led to a break in the analysis, but my stubborn faith made me carry on, even without being paid" (Dupont, 1985, p. 193). What is more, Severn (1952) reveals that Ferenczi "did something that he meant to help me and I was not too pleased with" (p. 15). One of the other women he had in analysis at that time was an American who "very wealthy in her own right" as well as being "married to an Hungarian count." This patient had previously been in treatment with Severn, and what Ferenczi did was to ask her either to give or to lend Severn "a couple of hundred dollars," which Severn "really hated to accept" because it was "very humiliating to me" (pp. 15–16), although she did take the money.

This intervention by a third party appears to be what Ferenczi is referring to when he writes, "Greater financial demands on me and increasing demands on my time and interest exhausted my patience, and we had almost reached the point of breaking off the analysis, when help arrived from an unexpected source" (Dupont, 1985, p. 193). Severn (1952) subsequently learned from Ferenczi that he was not charging the wealthy woman anything for her analysis, probably because he felt "very guilty" for inducing the latter to help her, while "at the same time he was charging a young woman who was an analyst and earning her own living," which Severn believed was "quite unfair" because "the countess could pay, and it was hard for the other lady to pay" (p. 16). Ferenczi, she concludes, "thought so, too, but he didn't do anything about it. That was when he was getting shaky, uncertain. It was really pitiful, his breakdown."

Again thanks to Brennan (2015a), we know that the wealthy American woman married to a Hungarian count is Harriot Sigray, while the financially struggling analyst is Thompson. As Thompson (1952a) told Eissler, she "had no background of money at all" and "no money except what I earned" (p. 10). It was for financial reasons that Thompson had been forced to postpone for two years her analysis with Ferenczi—and then could come to Budapest only during the summer for several more years—before finally making a continuous go of it beginning in 1931. Given that Ferenczi not only forgave Severn's debt to him and did not charge her any fee during their year of mutual analysis but also stopped charging the wealthy Sigray for her analysis because she had aided Severn, while Thompson was paying for her own treatment, Thompson had grounds for resentment against both Ferenczi and Severn, which helps to explain her loathing of Severn and increasingly critical attitude toward Ferenczi in later years.

Severn, on the other hand, evinces impressive discretion by not divulging the identities of either Thompson or Sigray—even during what she was assured would be a confidential interview—and equally impressive magnanimity by her indignation at the "quite unfair" way Thompson had been treated by Ferenczi, notwithstanding the fact that she herself was the principal beneficiary of his actions. Ironically, Ferenczi's largesse was experienced by Severn as "very humiliating" as it caused her to incur a debt of gratitude not only to him but also to her former patient. In the *Clinical Diary*, Ferenczi includes among the risks of mutual analysis that "the patient could start to demand financial assistance as recompense for *my* analysis by her," but "providing financial help would . . . involve the analysis too much with reality and make separation more difficult" (Dupont, 1985, p. 46). Although Ferenczi recognized these pitfalls, he was unable to escape them, with an adverse impact not only on Thompson but also on Severn and probably Sigray, toward whom Margaret Severn developed a pronounced antipathy. On April 2, 1932, she wrote to her mother from Paris:

> I suppose I am an ungrateful wretch, but really, I am used to having help given me by the thousands and so I suppose Harriot's offer seems a bit niggardly, not what I'm accustomed to. Still, small contributions—shall I write to thank her, or is the gift really to you and are my thanks superfluous? When I am the star of the Russian Ballet she'll no doubt say, "Oh, I supported Margaret in Paris, the dear little thing!"
>
> (1988, pp. 2,128–29)

Margaret is even more acerbic in her letter of June 14, 1933, after her mother had established herself again in London, "Give Harriot a bit of poison as a memento from me when she comes" (p. 2,471). Margaret might well be accused of being an "ungrateful wretch" with respect to Sigray's "small contribution," but everyone involved had to cope with the fallout from Ferenczi's willingness to play favorites in money matters with his patients.

Beyond Ferenczi's financial dealings and his yielding to Severn's exorbitant demands on his time and attention, Thompson had additional grounds for resenting them both. Even before she tells Eissler that Ferenczi was analyzed by one of his patients and launches into her diatribe against Severn, Thompson (1952a) voices another grievance:

> When I first went to Budapest in 1928, I expected to visit Freud also on my way there or going home, and Ferenczi didn't want me to go and meet Freud. . . . He told me that Freud did not like to meet women any more because of his mouth; but since then I knew many women who did meet him, so I think maybe that was not quite the fact.
> (p. 1)

Later in the interview she states that not only was Ferenczi "uncomfortable to have his pupils meet Freud," he also "didn't want me to go to see" Helene Deutsch in Vienna, though the reason he gave in this instance was that "he didn't like her" because Deutsch was "a hypocrite" who "didn't tell the truth in her papers" (p. 10). As Thompson must have known, Severn was one of the "many women who did meet" Freud, so this was another instance of Severn being accorded preferential treatment by Ferenczi while she herself was relegated to second-class status.

From Severn's (1952) interview, we learn that, along with Sigray and Ferenczi's Hungarian analysand and friend Wilma Kovács, Thompson was one of the people "present at the very end" (p. 16) of his life. Thompson (1952a) specifies that she saw Ferenczi "about three days before he died" (p. 7), and she was afterwards assured by his wife "that he had often told her I would be his best pupil" (p. 9). But this praise from beyond the grave did not assuage Thompson's sense of not having been close to Ferenczi's heart. She confesses her belief that Ferenczi "was rather ashamed of me," citing as evidence the fact that she "was a person whom he almost never invited to his house," although she wonders whether "this may be a patient's projection" (p. 9) on her part. In feeling herself kept at a distance,

Thompson identifies with Teddie Miller, another of Ferenczi's patients, known as "U." in the *Diary*, with whom she became romantically involved (Brennan, 2015a, p. 12). She describes Miller to Eissler in disparaging terms as "just an ordinary [L]ower East Side Jew, a Polish Jew . . . with no education at all, but plenty of money," and discloses that Ferenczi once told her "he was ashamed to have him in his house" (1952a, p. 9).

Just as a sense of social stigma comes through in Thompson's reference to her paramour as a "Polish Jew" from the mean streets of New York, she clearly felt "ashamed" of her own plebeian origins by comparison with someone such as Alice Lowell, by whom Ferenczi was "very much impressed . . . because of her American aristocratic background" (p. 9). She emphasizes her conviction that Ferenczi, being a Hungarian, was "impressed with status" (p. 9) and "impressed by pomp and ceremony" (p. 18), criteria according to which she would always be found wanting because she "didn't have enough polish to make him comfortable" (p. 9). Severn's background was far more hardscrabble than Thompson's, but she was free of the latter's anxiety about class and status. Although Thompson is widely regarded as having been Ferenczi's "best pupil" in the United States—the editors of the Freud/Ferenczi correspondence describe her as "the most influential pupil of and successor to Ferenczi in North America" (Falzeder and Brabant, 2000, p. 423)—while Severn has been consigned to the limbo of psychoanalytic history, the truth is rather the reverse: Severn was Ferenczi's most important patient and intellectual collaborator, whereas Thompson harbored an inferiority complex not only toward Severn, whom she had manifold reasons to envy as a rival for Ferenczi's attention and love, but also toward more peripheral members of his "harem" such as Sigray and Lowell.

When Ferenczi employs the metaphor of "'polygamous' analysis" in the *Diary*, he does so in the context of imagining how he might "avoid being excessively influenced by any one patient" (Dupont, 1985, p. 34), as he was by Severn in their mutual analysis. If he were to be analyzed by more than one person, or only to a limited extent by a single individual, he contemplates, this would correspond to "the group analysis of American colleagues" and provide "a certain control over the various analyses" (p. 34). But the term applies equally well to the "confused situation" in which Ferenczi actually found himself when "two analysands know each other, particularly when the one I let myself be analyzed by has neurotic traits and weaknesses of character that make him seem inferior in the eyes of the world (although I must acknowledge his ability to uncover things in me analytically, in spite of his greater or lesser failings otherwise)" (p. 34). Notwithstanding Ferenczi's use of masculine pronouns, Severn and Thompson fit the description of "two analysands" who "know each other," in which "the one" with "neurotic traits and weaknesses of character" by whom he permits himself to be analyzed is, of course, Severn, while Thompson represents "the eyes of the world" that condemn Severn for being "inferior" not simply in her lack of formal education and arrogation of a spurious doctoral degree, but above all for her apparently histrionic and self-serving panoply of symptoms.

As Thompson (1952a) confirms to Eissler, she saw Severn "quite often" in Budapest (p. 21). When asked what Ferenczi might have told her about Severn, she responds by speaking of the "uncanny experience" that all three of her own analysts had "been involved with women who had a great deal of hypochondriasis." Affirming that Ferenczi "did tell me quite a bit about her," Thompson elaborates:

> I had an analyst before Ferenczi, a totally unknown American—a man named Joe Thompson. He's dead now. He married a patient who also had the same kind of weird childhood memories. Mrs. Severn and this other woman also reconstructed the most sadistic sexual accomplishments having been perpetrated on them as children. Now they were almost identical, those stories, so there must be something that goes on in that type of person. . . . All kinds of tortures, of having been tied to their beds and beaten and so forth. . . . I put Eric [*sic*] Fromm in here now because of his wife's having been ill for so long. But maybe she was more ill than we realized.
>
> (p. 21)

Henny Gurland, Fromm's second wife, died in Mexico in June 1952, in all likelihood by suicide (Friedman, 2013, p. 141), the same month as Thompson's interview with Eissler, though the news had evidently not reached her as yet. We have no way of knowing what Clara may have heard from Joseph Thompson about the patient who became his wife, and it is unclear whether Ferenczi breached confidentiality and disclosed to her the "tortures" visited on Severn as a child, or whether Severn may have spoken of these herself to her. In either case, what Thompson dismisses as Severn's "weird childhood memories" of being tied to the bed and beaten are, in fact, credible recollections of the "sadistic sexual accomplishments" that Leota Brown had had to endure at the hands of her father.

By the unconscious logic of Clara Thompson's repetition compulsion, because Severn shared a hypochondriacal tendency with the wives of her other two analysts, Joseph Thompson and Fromm, one of whom had also been her husband's patient, for Severn to have been Ferenczi's patient was also to make her symbolically his wife, while she herself was left to play a handmaid's role in the collective psychodrama of a polygamous analysis.

Notes

1 On the affinities between Ferenczi's approach to psychoanalysis, which "implies a constant interchange and mutual influence between individual and collective processes, inner and outer, psychological and social," and "the basic tenets of group analysis," see Tubert-Oklander (2018, p. 25).
2 As a fourteen-year-old, Judith had lived with Dorothy Burlingham in Vienna while being analyzed by Anna Freud; and, as Thompson (1952a) told Eissler, "one of [Judith's] grievances was that there was always the dog there, as if she never had Anna all to herself" (p. 19).
3 Although her book is engaging, Summerscale (2020) makes many blunders. Inexplicably, she states that "Fodor omitted any mention of Elizabeth Severn" (p. 308) in *On the Trail of the Poltergeist*, even though Fodor (1958) expressly informs his readers that Mrs. Forbes "met Elizabeth Severn, the psychoanalyst" and "overheard her remark that the forces of Mrs. Forbes's unconscious mind might be responsible for the phenomena," as a result of which "Mrs. Forbes conceived a violent hatred against Mrs. Severn and refused to sit if 'that woman' were present" (p. 71). Summerscale (2020) likewise appears to be unaware of the mutual analysis, instead mistakenly asserting that Severn "had been treated" by Ferenczi "in the 1920s" (p. 207) and then "adopted" (p. 245) his theory of trauma. I am indebted to John Boyle for drawing my attention to Summerscale's book.
4 For the history of *The Psychoanalytic Review*, see the article on the occasion of its centennial by Barnett (2013). I am grateful to John Leonard for sending me a photocopy of the issue of *Psychoanalysis* in which Fodor's name first appears on the masthead and to Alan Barnett, himself the editor of *The Psychoanalytic Review* from 2008 to 2016, for confirming Jelliffe's undoubted awareness of the anonymous review of *The Discovery of the Self*, discussed below.
5 I am indebted to a personal communication from Gerald Gargiulo, who was a student in Reik's last class on technique, for enlightening me concerning admission practices at NPAP in its early years.
6 Fodor's continuing devotion to Freud is exemplified by his *Freud: A Dictionary of Psychoanalysis* (Fodor and Gaynor, 1958), to which Reik contributed a Preface. While insisting that Rank's approach to the birth trauma "was philosophical," whereas his own "is clinical and independent of his claims" (Foreword), Fodor opens further lines of analytic and parapsychological inquiry in *The Search for the Beloved* (1949): "We all have lived in another world— before we were born. All utopian visions reveal a nostalgia for the bliss which we lost on leaving the maternal womb. The intensity of the ordeal of birth may have a determining influence on the fear and fascination of another plane of life" (p. 77).

7 In his note to Emma Jung's letter, Burnham, who evidently had not heard of Severn, goes completely off track by proposing that the sentence "referring to 'Brown' and 'Haywood' suggests a connection to the American writer Heywood Broun, who may have consulted Jelliffe" (p. 226*n*2).
8 The transcriber of the interview, Maxine L. Rippner, misspells both Severn's first and last names. Eissler's response, "I know nothing about that" (p. 6), shows that neither he nor Rippner had previously heard of Severn, and Eissler's decision to seek Severn out for an interview must have been prompted by what he had gleaned from Thompson. As I have noted in Chapter 1, Severn corrected the misspelling "Severne" in the typescript of her own interview, which, like "La Verne," confirms that her name, unlike that of the river Severn, is pronounced with an emphasis on the second syllable.
9 It was because his own experiment in mutual analysis with Clarence Shields led to a similar role reversal that "served only to prove that the patient's opposition to the inconsistency of my personal method was actuated by an equally personal and inconsistent method on his part" that Burrow (1926) was inspired to take the further step of inventing group analysis, in which "the distinction between analyst and analysand" is "abrogated entirely" (pp. 152–53). Burrow's willingness to go beyond "individual analysis" prompted him to espouse the radical idea that "man is not an individual. . . . He is part of a societal continuum that is the outgrowth of a primary or racial [that is, phylogenetic] continuum" (p. 148). See the Prelude, note 3, above.

Chapter 8

The End of the Affair

On no score do the testimonies of Thompson and Severn to Eissler diverge more sharply than they do on the circumstances of Severn's departure from Budapest. According to Severn (1952), "I finally got free on my own steam. It was a most terrific experience" (p. 6). As she tells it, both she and Ferenczi were exhausted by the ordeal of mutual analysis, and she made the painful but necessary decision to leave: "I saw that he wouldn't be able to stand the analysis for long, and I didn't feel I could either. It would mean giving up some more years of my life, and I was at the end of my strength and my money and everything else, and so I finally managed to get away from Budapest by sheer will force, a complete wreck" (p. 7). She reiterates later in the interview that "it was the last year I was there that I did his analysis, and that was really what helped me to get on my feet, you see—to disconnect from him" (p. 13).

In Thompson's (1952a) version, however, it was Ferenczi who put a stop to what had become an intolerable situation, giving Severn an ultimatum to which she responded with grief and rage: "She left Ferenczi about three months before he died. He finally got the strength to dismiss her, and the day he did, he went into a kind of elation. Her parting words to him were that he would die, that she would see that he died, and that he would be a little man and completely forgotten by the world. This was her parting curse" (p. 7). She adds that Wilma Kovács, another patient who "served as a kind of analyst to him from time to time," should be given credit "for his getting rid of Mrs. Severn" (p. 17). Several years after her interview with Eissler, when Fromm was gathering testimonials for his rebuttal (1958) of Jones's maligning of the sanity of Ferenczi and Rank in the final volume of his Freud biography, Thompson wrote to him along the same lines on November 5, 1957, though without the transfixing detail of Severn's "parting curse": "In February [1933] he had the courage to dismiss a patient who had bullied him for years, Elizabeth Severn. She is one of the most destructive people I know, and there is no doubt Ferenczi was afraid of her." She added that "Severn "practices here in New York and could probably give you a juicy account of her last days with him."

Despite the seeming incompatibility of these accounts, I think we must give both women the benefit of the doubt and presume that each is telling the truth according to her lights. This means that Severn must really have anathematized Ferenczi more or less as Thompson alleges—though presumably Thompson would have heard about what happened from him afterwards rather than witnessed it directly—and there is likewise a factual kernel to Thompson's (1952a) recollection that Severn had boasted to her that "she was the greatest analyst in the world because she had no hate" (p. 7). Even when allowance is made for Thompson's antipathy toward that "Bird of Prey" and "paranoid bitch," which furnished her with a motive to depict Severn as unflatteringly as possible, there is no basis to impeach Thompson's integrity or to conclude that she would be capable of putting on the historical record something that she knew to be false.

What, then, are we to make of the apparent contradiction between Thompson's repeated assertions that it was Ferenczi, prodded by Kovács, who "dismissed" Severn, on the one hand, and Severn's equally emphatic declarations that she "disconnected" from Ferenczi voluntarily and "managed to get away from Budapest by sheer will force," on the other? There is no doubt that Ferenczi's other patients and family would have perceived Severn as a vampire, draining him of life with her incessant demands, especially in the final months when he was acutely ill. Indeed, according to Thompson, Gizella Ferenczi expressed the opinion that Severn had "bled him to death" (p. 15), a poignant metaphor given that he perished from pernicious anemia. This group of people would have wanted Ferenczi to "get rid" of Severn, and, once the deed was done, he would undoubtedly have shared with them a sense of relief that could readily be construed as "elation."

That Thompson and other observers would have interpreted the situation in this way, however, does not negate the likelihood that, within the analytic dyad, Ferenczi and Severn would have discussed the issue of termination at length and eventually set a date by mutual agreement. Indeed, in Margaret Severn's (1988) autobiography, there is confirmation that she and her mother anticipated Severn's move from Budapest to Paris. Margaret writes on February 15, 1933, "Could you stand as many stairs as you have now, if the apt. were irresistable [*sic*] in other respects?" The letter concludes: "Reflecting on why I was glad you were coming to live with me, I was a thinking that you're the most INTELLIGENT person I ever met, and what an honor and an instruction to live with such a bright person. I ought to become bright myself from association" (pp. 2,423–24). From Severn's perspective, therefore, it is clear that she made the decision to cut the cord with Ferenczi herself and was not forced to leave Budapest against her will.

Once it is understood how the end of Severn's nearly eight-year analysis could have been experienced one way by her from the inside and perceived entirely otherwise by Thompson on the outside there is no longer an irreconcilable contradiction between their accounts. Both witnesses have given a faithful report of what they believed to be true from their respective vantage points. Similarly, Thompson's quotation of Gizella Ferenczi's remark about Severn's having bled Ferenczi to death needs to be balanced against Severn's (1952) statement that "Mrs. Ferenczi made me gifts and invited me to their house and was always very friendly," especially since Severn concedes that when her severe illness caused Ferenczi to bring her on a trip to Spain he took with his wife in 1928, she supposes that Gizella "was very annoyed" by her presence because "she preferred, no doubt, to be entirely alone with him" (p. 13).[1]

Even Thompson's allegation concerning the "parting curse" unleashed by Severn against Ferenczi becomes intelligible when set against the backdrop of the crisis in the mutual analysis that came to a head in March 1932. On February 24, Ferenczi reports in the *Clinical Diary* that he took the "dangerous step" of telling Severn that he "would treat her only until she was able to support herself," thereby dashing her fantasy that he "would provide for all her needs," as a consequence of which "she gesticulated like a lunatic, hinted at suicide," although Ferenczi says he "remained firm" (Dupont, 1985, p. 44). Then, on March 3, when he tried to persuade Severn to rest content with only his "fragmentary" participation in mutual analysis and to accept his "resolve to let matters rest there," he says that she responded by referring "to the serious endangering of my work, which would collapse without the patient's help," a "warning" that "felt a bit like a threat" (pp. 46–47). Given that Severn reacted to Ferenczi's attempts to pull back with intimations of suicide and by informing him that his work would founder unless he gave himself over wholly to the mutual analysis, one can readily imagine that she would have greeted the irrevocable end of her analysis—even if she had assented to it consciously—by uttering an imprecation of the sort described by Thompson.

An insight into Severn's state of mind during the preliminary upheaval is afforded by Margaret's long letter from Paris on March 12, 1932. Margaret (1988) balances a critique of Ferenczi for leaving her mother in the lurch with a recognition of how nearly impossible a patient she must have been for him to put up with:

> You ask me again what I think but it's really difficult to form an intelligent opinion with, as I said before, your own viewpoint seeming to fluctuate in every letter. But it is surely very difficult to have Ferenczi remind you that you are only doctor and patient, and further proves what I have said, that he fears you are too big for him. It's quite true that in your demand for love and help you are inclined to devour every scrap of affection in your sight, so to speak, and he is probably afraid that you will divest him of family ties and everything else if given time.
> (p. 2,096)

When even Margaret can acknowledge her mother's tendency "to devour every scrap of affection in your sight," it is easy to sympathize with those who wanted to protect Ferenczi from this woman who would "divest him of family ties and everything else if given time." Margaret throws out the idea that perhaps her mother would be better off coming to live either with her or in London with her friend (and likely also former patient) Mary Wilshire—a Jungian therapist and scion of the family that gave its name to Wilshire Boulevard in Los Angeles (Rachman, 2018, pp. 93–94)—"who would never have to put a limit on the amount of love we could give you," but she then returns to her reflections on Ferenczi:

> I hate to be unjust to Ferenczi, but I must say, after his protestations of friendship and assurances that he would finish your analysis in any case, I find this apparent change of attitude just at a time when money is very low, a little dismaying. This may be in his unconscious only, but I remember another occasion when you had to pay less or something, and he suddenly reduced the number of hours he gave you. I believe he rectified this but that was his first reaction. Granted that he has done everything in his power for you, I still think that you are pretty much his responsibility and for him to sort of turn you loose, so to speak—well, all I can say is that I know that YOU would NEVER do that to a patient.
> (pp. 2,096–97)

Throughout the letter, the tension is evident between Ferenczi's desire to confine his relationship with Severn to that between "doctor and patient" and his impulse to devote himself to her without boundaries or limits, no matter the cost to himself. As frequently happens in psychoanalysis, money became a battleground for the emotional conflicts, as Ferenczi evidently felt inclined on more than one occasion to reduce the number of sessions when Severn could no longer afford his fees, which precipitated a volcanic eruption including threats of suicide, a danger he had to take seriously especially after he had cabled Margaret to come to Budapest on an emergency basis at the end of 1931. It must have been at this point that "help arrived from an unexpected source" (Dupont, 1985, p. 193) in the form of a subvention from Sigray to cover Severn's accumulated debts, which, combined with Ferenczi's decision to stop charging her altogether during the mutual analysis, made it possible for the process to continue without further ruptures until the finale in February 1933.

Margaret (1988) concludes her meditation with the following judicious assessment of Ferenczi's motives and her mother's share of responsibility for their jointly created crisis:

> Could it be possible that he thinks this would be good for you and that you might regain your equilibrium if forced to? I wonder. It has struck me all along that the idea of analysing him was entirely yours and that he seemed most reluctant to it. It has often occurred to me that he submitted to this only to humor you and if so, it's just because he plain doesn't know what to do with you. I think he has got himself so deeply entangled with all this odd psychic phenomena that he ain't used to considering, and whatnot, that he just doesn't know where he's at and he is tired. That's what *I* think. You have so often spoken of a "ray of hope" in these last seven years that I must confess that when I come across a similar phrase in your letters now I find it more pathetic than hopeful. And I don't forget what he said to me when he was about to leave for his vacation last spring. Something to the effect that you THOUGHT you would be very sick when he left. I rather got the impression that he thought that you were a little bit crazy to think you were so sick, or something like that. Perhaps he has a similar idea now; it would be his only excuse to himself. We must, of course, realize that your case is a terribly difficult one and that to give so much time to it as he has done for the past years would of necessity be very exhausting. On the other hand, as I said before, he undertook it and

it's his responsibility. If Mary really would give you a home for a year it's very worth considering of course, plus the fact that you might have patients there.

(pp. 2,097–98)

Margaret charitably raises the possibility that Ferenczi's "apparent change of attitude" might, in the manner of his earlier "active technique," have been something he was doing for Severn's benefit as a way of forcing her to "regain [her] equilibrium," though she adds that this justification of his actions "would be his only excuse to himself." That he might have had a legitimate reason for trying to push her out of the nest, as it were, is shown by his March 8 entry to the *Diary*, where Ferenczi notes that Severn "foresees that even after a further eight years she will still be in the same spot, unless she succeeds in tearing herself loose from the analysis, her family, perhaps the entire human race, and organizing her life independently" (Dupont, 1985, p. 52). Included in Margaret's speculations is the hypothesis that Ferenczi might even have "thought that you were a little bit crazy to think you were so sick," in other words, that Severn's mental illness—as Thompson suspected—was somehow histrionic or factitious, as though she were putting on a show to prevent him from abandoning her. Since Ferenczi admits in the *Diary* that he was participating in his own analysis "only with considerable *reservatio mentalis*" (p. 46), Margaret's intuition that "the idea of analysing him was entirely" Severn's and that the "most reluctant" Ferenczi initially went along with it "only to humor" her is unquestionably correct, though his attitude must have shifted in the ensuing months in order for Severn to have been able to arrive at the depth of insight into his character that she displays in her case history in *The Discovery of the Self*.

Given the severity of Severn's condition, it is not surprising that she should have responded to the prospect of being abandoned by Ferenczi with what we would label today as "borderline" symptomatology, including the cursing and manic boasting alleged by Thompson. Indeed, when she finally arrived in Paris she was in such a shattered state that Margaret wrote what she described to Fortune (1994) as a "'terrible letter' of protest" (p. 221) to Ferenczi on her mother's behalf. The intensity of Severn's reaction can be understood when the termination of her analysis is seen to be a repetition of her climactic childhood trauma. As Ferenczi chronicles, "the last great shock" (Dupont, 1985, p. 9) that struck the already fragmented Severn "like a bolt of lightning" (p. 10) took place at the age of eleven and a half when the father who had been her tormentor suddenly deserted the family. "The situation was made worse," Ferenczi continues, "by the fact that the father, before the separation, as a kind of farewell, had cursed the child, and thus had used his influence to make the child indelibly aware of her own filthiness, uselessness, and contemptibility," so that even the "indefatigable Orpha" was rendered powerless and "sought to encourage suicide." In a final act of revenge against her abuser, when faced once again with abandonment by a father figure, Severn unleashed the full blast of her fury against the cruelty of a fate that was being visited on her not only in the transference but also in reality.

But Severn's season in purgatory was not the end of her journey. The separation from Ferenczi proved in the long run to be a trauma of *re*birth that was the prelude to being able to live her own life. Despite having written Ferenczi a "terrible letter" in the heat of the moment, on looking back on the whole experience more than a half-century later Margaret assured Fortune (1994) that she "had no doubt" that Ferenczi "'ultimately saved my mother's life'" (p. 222). Just as Ferenczi's *Diary* helps us to comprehend why Severn cursed him at parting, so, too, does it explain how what he terms "the pain associated with the analytical weaning process" (Dupont, 1985, p. 49) was integral to her psychic regeneration. He captures the transformative nature of their analytic journey together—and how much he owed Severn—with utmost grace and delicacy in the final entry of the *Clinical Diary*:

> From *my* analysis she expects insight into the *personal* (quite independent of her), historical determinants of my behavior toward patients—and thus definitive detachment. What will remain, she hopes, is a *reciprocal* "honorable" recognition of mutual achievement, of having coped *with such a case.*
> R.N. Mutuality   F. Acceptance of mutuality
>   Perseverance   Insight into own weaknesses—admission
> I released R.N. from her torments by repeating the sins of her father, which then I confessed and for which I obtained forgiveness.
>
> (p. 214)

This passage was written on October 2, 1932, nearly five months before Severn's departure from Budapest, so he had as yet by no means definitively "released R.N. from her torments." But these are his last words on Severn, and they express proleptically the "'honorable' recognition of mutual achievement" that is the enduring legacy of their "having coped *with such a case.*" Severn made this recognition truly *"reciprocal"*—and proved that she had forgiven Ferenczi for "repeating the sins of her father"—by publishing *The Discovery of the Self* and, above all, by living and working productively until her death in 1959.

Although Thompson and Severn present diametrically opposed accounts of the end of Severn's analytic affair with Ferenczi, their descriptions of Ferenczi are strikingly congruent. Severn (1952), as we know, explains that she sought him out as her analyst because "he was more interested in the patient," whereas "Freud was primarily interested in the science he was formulating" (p. 2). Thompson (1952a) concurs, "you can't read his work without realizing that immediately he talks about patients, whereas Freud talks about theory" (p. 6). According to Thompson, Ferenczi translated portions of Freud's correspondence for her benefit, including the letter in which Freud "told him that he was in his second childhood" and "trying to get from patients the love he needed" (p. 2). She adds that "there probably was some truth to that, except that it wasn't useful to Ferenczi to be told that as a scolding parent being horrified at what the child was doing" (pp. 2–3). This almost certainly refers to Freud's letter of December 13, 1931, in which he employed the phrase "new puberty" to castigate Ferenczi "from the brutal fatherly side" for the "technique of maternal tenderness" (Falzeder and Brabant, 2000, pp. 422–23) that he had practiced with Thompson herself when he permitted her to kiss him during their sessions. Severn (1952), for her part, recounts how Ferenczi went to visit Freud in Vienna and laid before him the idea of analytic love, as well as his conviction of "the necessity for the analyst to have been thoroughly analyzed himself so that he didn't have any hidden pockets in his mind or emotions that might affect his attitude toward his patients," both of which came out of their joint work. In response, Freud "told Ferenczi that he was adolescent or senile. . . . He was very harsh. And poor Ferenczi couldn't take it. He came back just crushed, and he talked about it to me, and I saw how hurt he was. He had not succeeded to make any impression on Freud with what he believed was an important contribution to the practice of analysis" (pp. 6–7).

Since Severn had been in Budapest considerably longer than Thompson, she is likely to be alluding not only to the visit with Freud that led to the "kissing technique" letter but also to an earlier one in June 1929, following which Ferenczi described the "shocking impression" that Freud's comment about his appearance of *"premature senility"* (Falzeder and Brabant,

2000, p. 372) had made on him. Severn's account brings home with painful vividness Ferenczi's sense of despair at the impossibility of any genuine dialogue with Freud.

But Thompson's revelations are no less astonishing in their intimacy. When she declares (1952a) that Ferenczi "felt that Freud despised people," citing how Freud talked about "these 'swine of patients'" and "spit on the ground" (p. 4) as he spoke one day to Ferenczi about a homosexual, her veracity is corroborated by passages in the *Clinical Diary* where Ferenczi quotes Freud as having said that "neurotics are a rabble, good only to support us financially and to allow us to learn from their cases" (Dupont, 1985, p. 186). Thompson (1952a) likewise recalls that Ferenczi "always fantasied himself as Freud's favorite son" (p. 5) and "had a great problem with masturbation, and used to practice it to see if he could hit the ceiling with his semen in ejaculating," adding that "he had gonorrhea when he was 16, which he got from a peasant girl" (p. 16). In the *Diary*, Ferenczi refers in the third person to how Freud "adopted Dr. F almost like his son" and "regarded him as the most perfect heir of his ideas" (Dupont, 1985, p. 184), confirming Thompson's account, while he twice alludes to his masturbatory exploits, shrouded beneath the diaphanous veil of a Latin phrase, "ejaculation up to the sky [*Ejakulatio usque ad coelum*]" (p. 15) and "*ejaculatio usque ad tegmen camerae* [ejaculation up to the ceiling]" (p. 134). In a reverberation of Ferenczi's memory of "terrifyingly rough treatment" by his nurse after an "incident of anal soiling" (Dupont, 1985, p. 36), Thompson (1952a) recollects having been told that "he was put on a chamber and the chamber broke and cut him, and he remembered that as a very traumatic experience" (p. 16).

Of all Thompson's disclosures, however, none is more startling than that, when Gizella was still married to Géza Pálos, she and Ferenczi "had a child—she had a pregnancy which she had to get rid of" (p. 16). Ferenczi's mourning over the child he might have had with Elma, who was fourteen years his junior, had he married her instead of Gizella, eight years his senior and with whom he had been conducting an affair since 1900, is well known. In his Christmas-day 1921 letter to Groddeck, which contains the only extant account of how he had felt oppressed by Freud's treatment of him in 1910 during their attempted collaboration on the Schreber case in Palermo, Ferenczi confides that Elma "should have been my wife" but for "a somewhat disparaging remark of Freud's," and "my 'It' isn't interested in analytical interpretations, but wants something real, a young wife, a child" (Fortune, 2002, pp. 9, 11).[2] But in no other source of which I am aware is there any hint that Gizella had to abort a pregnancy caused by Ferenczi and that the grief over his childlessness would have been compounded in this way.

With respect to Ferenczi's love triangle, Thompson (1952a) states that "he was in love with Elmo [sic]" and "no longer loved" Gizella when he married her in 1919, but he went through with it because she "was so unhappy" (p. 17) about his love for her daughter.[3] If Ferenczi's hopes of having a child with Gizella had been dashed by an abortion, this would further explain his lack of passion for her by the time they were married. In a letter written from Groddeck's sanatorium in Baden-Baden on January 8, 1927, moreover, Frédéric Kovács informs his wife Wilma that "Gizella's dearest wish, at present, and her plan, is that Sándor should divorce her and marry Elma—she would not give him up for any other woman, only for Elma—and she would content herself with playing the role of mother" (Fortune, 2002, p. 120). Again, I know of no other source that attests to any incipient realignment of Ferenczi's domestic arrangements at such a late date—Elma had separated from John Laurvik and returned to Budapest in 1924—but Kovács's trustworthy testimony shows that, at the age of fifty-three, Ferenczi continued to be haunted by his dissatisfaction with his marriage and to long to gratify his "It" with "something real, a young wife, a child."

In comparing the two interviews, Brennan (2015c) concludes that Thompson would appear to have been "much more privy to intimacies about Ferenczi's life than Severn" (p. 79). Although this seems counterintuitive, given that it was Severn who had served as his analyst, Severn (1952) does miss the mark in stating that Elma "probably fell in love with her step-father," and Ferenczi, wanting to be "a highly moral man" and not knowing "what to do about it," inadvertently led her to think "that he cared for her more than he did" (p. 18). Not only was Ferenczi not yet Elma's stepfather during the period in question, but he unquestionably fell at least as hard for her as she did for him and made sexual advances toward her. On the other hand, Severn comments perceptively on how the death of Géza Pálos, on the very day when Gizella and Ferenczi were finally married, "created a tremendous guilt feeling in Ferenczi" because he felt "he'd killed his rival" (p. 18).

A possible clue to Severn's lack of clarity regarding Ferenczi's relationship with Elma Pálos lies in the fact that the *Clinical Diary*, although it shows Ferenczi to have been deeply wounded by Freud, makes no mention of Elma or his conflicts over whether to marry her or Gizella. It may be that, by the time he embarked on his mutual analysis with Severn, five years after Frédéric Kovács's letter, he had more fully come to terms with his decision and was at greater peace about his romantic history. As Severn (1952) told Eissler, although Ferenczi believed he had "made some terrible mistakes" in his practice and "suffered from guilt about it," he "had no complaints about his life particularly" (p. 8), which suggests that the embers of his love for Elma had indeed been largely, if not completely, extinguished.

Conversely, in seeking to explain how Thompson came to know the details of Ferenczi's life as well as she did, it is important to bear in mind that, while Severn departed Budapest at the end of February 1933, Thompson remained and saw Ferenczi regularly until three days before his death on May 22. It seems likely that almost everything of an intimate nature that Thompson (1952a) later imparted to Eissler she learned during this final phase when Severn was no longer around. "After Ferenczi was ill," she recalls, "all of a sudden he talked much more in the last few months of his life. I suppose you could hardly say I had analysis" (p. 18). In his "last illness," she confirms, "he told me a great deal about his early life and his unhappiness, about his sexual escapades and things like that. I think by that time he was already mentally quite disturbed" (p. 3). It would appear that Ferenczi at the end had shed most of his remaining inhibitions and therefore had no compunctions about giving Thompson a fuller version of the Elma episode than he had shared while he was in analysis with Severn. Still, even Thompson's picture is by no means complete, as she is only able to "suppose" (p. 16) that Elma had met Freud and is thus unaware of the fact that she had been in analysis with Freud, to say nothing of her analysis with Ferenczi himself.

Taken together, Thompson and Severn's interviews with Eissler create an invaluable "composite portrait" of Ferenczi that highlights many of his most prominent features while they also complement each other with distinctive touches. They both call attention to what Severn (1952) calls the "double tie in the family" due to the fact that Gizella's younger daughter Magda "had already married" Ferenczi's younger brother Lajos "at the time she married Ferenczi" (p. 18), which Thompson (1952a) sums up as a "very mixed-up family situation" whereby Ferenczi became "the father-in-law of his brother" (p. 17). One of the most extravagant flourishes is a collaborative production since Thompson informs Eissler that she had heard from Severn that Ferenczi "used to tie his tongue with a string every night so he wouldn't swallow it. Tie it to his bed, or something like that" (p. 8). Although Thompson immediately adds the disclaimer that "it sounds too fantastic" to be believed, Ferenczi reported in a letter to Groddeck on February 27, 1922 that he had resorted to "keeping my nostrils open with wire" (Fortune, 2002, p. 20) to combat his nocturnal apnea. If Ferenczi could open his nose with wire, why should he not have tied his tongue with string? In psychoanalysis, the seemingly "fantastic" often turns out to be true, while what may appear to be plausible ought to be regarded with skepticism.

Notes

1 The fact that Severn was a guest in Ferenczi's home must likewise have rankled Thompson (1952a), who perceived herself to be, like Teddie Miller, "a person whom he almost never invited to his house" (p. 9).
2 Ferenczi complained to Groddeck that Freud had sought to turn him into his amanuensis and, when Ferenczi refused to take dictation, retorted, "'You obviously want to do *the whole* thing yourself,'" following which he "spent every evening working on his own" (Fortune, 2002, p. 9). Equally pertinent to the Schreber case is Thompson (1952a) statement that Ferenczi "felt also that Freud had stolen his ideas about homosexuality" (p. 12).
3 Maxine Rippner, in addition to misspelling Severn's name in both interviews, repeatedly writes "Elmo" rather than "Elma."

Chapter 9

Ferenczi's Sanity and the "Blood-Crisis"

Apart from what she says about Severn, the most disquieting feature of Thompson's (1952a) interview with Eissler is the picture she paints of Ferenczi at the end of his life. In addition to making mention of an occasion when he "fell in the railway station" and a longstanding "awkwardness of his hands," she testifies that Ferenczi was "mentally quite disturbed," about which she became convinced when "one morning he didn't come in" to summon her from his waiting room, and when someone informed him after a half an hour that Thompson was there, "he didn't seem to be at all concerned that he had overlooked it" (p. 3). Thompson, furthermore, was told by Ferenczi's wife that "during his last illness he was often reading the paper up-side down, just sitting holding it."

Thompson's comments seem at first glance to lend credence to Jones's (1957) allegation that Ferenczi, like Rank, "towards the end of his life, developed psychotic manifestations that revealed themselves in, among other ways, a turning away from Freud and his doctrines" (p. 45)—as though loyalty to Freud were a criterion of mental health! Jones's aspersions were endorsed by Lionel Trilling (1957), who wrote even more intemperately in reviewing the third volume of the Freud biography for the *New York Times* that Ferenczi and Rank "both fell prey to extreme mental illness and died insane" (p. 36). The requisite riposte was delivered by Fromm (1958), who gathered eyewitness testimony from people who had known both Rank and Ferenczi in their final years, and the Jones-Trilling warped view of psychoanalytic history has more recently been contextualized and conclusively refuted by Bonomi (1999).[1]

With respect to Thompson (1952a), the crucial point is that she is speaking only of the terminal phase of Ferenczi's pernicious anemia—the "last winter" when "he had a red count of about a million and a half" (p. 3)—and she otherwise repudiates Jones's imputation of a severe

DOI: 10.4324/9781315280134-12

mental illness. This can be clearly seen in her letter to Fromm on November 5, 1957:

> What I believe is that in the last two months of his life there was some organic mental deterioration. That is, he showed memory defects and forgetfulness characteristic of organic brain disease, but I think it was minimal and a part of the death picture. To try to push it back into preceding years and explain his thinking by this is—to say the least—criminal. . . . To call his belief that Freud was treating him badly, paranoid, is obviously to deny the facts.

Although Brennan (2015c) suggests that, in speaking to Eissler, Thompson "wasn't under any particular pressure to defend Ferenczi, making her narration of events more forthright and candid" (p. 79) than in her letter to Fromm, Ferenczi's sanity had not been publicly called into question when she gave the interview in 1952. In all probability, therefore, it simply did not occur to Thompson at that time to make explicit her conviction that his seemingly psychological symptoms were actually organic in nature and limited to "the last two months of his life," whereas she was at pains to be more precise in traversing the same ground with Fromm after the waters had been muddied by Jones.[2] According to Thompson (1952a) in the interview, Ferenczi closed his practice "about the first of May" (p. 7); and her account is corroborated by Gizella Ferenczi's letter to Georg and Emmy Groddeck on November 2, 1933, describing Ferenczi's condition at the end: "He had to be put to bed because his feet wouldn't carry him any more—his mind began to give and he spent four weeks in bed. On the twenty-second of May, the day he died, he was still speaking to us, read the newspaper (which kept on dropping out of his hands) and was contemplating revisions on his paper from the Wiesbaden Congress" (Fortune, 2002, p. 108).

Just as Thompson distinguishes Ferenczi's "organic mental deterioration" in his last illness from Jones's "criminal" accusation of a severe psychopathology that extends "back into preceding years," so it is imperative not to equate Jones's reference to "psychotic manifestations" with the allusions by Severn in *The Discovery of the Self* and by Ferenczi himself in the *Clinical Diary* to his hidden "psychosis" uncovered in the course of the mutual analysis. That Severn did not believe Ferenczi was "psychotic" in Jones's sense of the word is confirmed by a brief letter she wrote to

Fromm on November 29, 1957 after learning of his planned article. Severn affirmed that when she last saw Ferenczi "he was in full possession of his faculties with no signs whatever of mental imbalance."[3] It is one thing to say that Ferenczi had a traumatized core that rendered him "borderline" in Winnicott's sense and quite another to insinuate that he lacked a capacity for reality-testing. Indeed, Ferenczi perceived the Nazi menace far more lucidly than did Freud, and in a letter of March 29, 1933, less than two months before his death, he urged Freud "to go to a more secure country, perhaps England" (Falzeder and Brabant, 2000, p. 447).

Thompson's letter to Fromm illuminates how Ferenczi himself understood his pernicious anemia. It transpires that she must have accompanied Sándor and Gizella on their train journey from Budapest to the Wiesbaden Congress and waited for him in Vienna while the two of them went to his fateful last meeting with Freud, on September 2, 1932.[4] There, as is well known, he read aloud—partly in the presence of Brill—the paper that we now know as "Confusion of Tongues." As Thompson recalled at Fromm's behest, Ferenczi "apparently had a very rough time. When he came on the train that night, he told me it was terrible, that Freud said he could give the paper in Wiesbaden, but he must never publish it." Ferenczi, she continues, "was very shaken by the Freud interview," and "when he gave the paper he looked like death. I noticed as he sat on the platform that he looked much whiter than the others," although "during this time, nobody I know of thought he was physically ill," and even Ferenczi himself, despite having "dizzy spells," attributed them to "anxiety." Subsequently, he "went away for a month's vacation," and Thompson specifies that it was in a railway station in Paris that he sustained the fall she had mentioned to Eissler, following which he was taken to the hospital, "where it was found that his red blood count was 50% below normal and he had pernicious anemia."

A key point that emerges from Thompson's testimony is that, even at the Wiesbaden Congress, neither Ferenczi nor anyone else "thought he was physically ill." As she had earlier (1952a) said to Eissler: "he became ill while he was on that vacation, and he was brought home and was quite ill all that winter" (p. 14). This chronology is confirmed by multiple sources. In his first communication to Freud since their encounter, Ferenczi wrote from southwest France on September 27, 1932 that the "length of the reaction time" was a measure of the "depth of the shock" left by their conversation, and that because "such things are always connected with bodily ailments in me," his holiday trip by way of Baden-Baden, where he and Gizella stayed for the last time with the Groddecks at their sanatorium of Marienhöhe, "was and is, actually, a 'voyage de lit-à-lit'" (Falzeder and Brabant, 2000, p. 443). Consequently, they had decided to return to Budapest earlier than planned, on October 1. With the benefit of hindsight, Ferenczi informed Georg and Emmy on March 20, 1933, "My indisposition in Baden-Baden was the beginning of an extremely dangerous anemia which almost struck me down in France, so that I only just managed to drag myself home—prematurely" (Fortune, 2002, p. 105).

Further evidence of Ferenczi's state of mind regarding his health is furnished by the *Clinical Diary*, which contains no sign of any worries on this score from the first entry, on January 7, to August 24, 1932, the last before his departure for Vienna and Wiesbaden. Only in the final entry, recorded on October 2—one day after returning to Budapest and exactly one month after seeing Freud—does Ferenczi allude to his "blood-crisis" and his urgent need to "build new red corpuscles" (Dupont, 1985, p. 212). In a crucial addendum to our understanding, Balint (1956) said of Ferenczi's "scientific diary" in his interview with Eissler that, "at the end of each working day, he got a secretary and dictated to her his impressions" (p. 10).

The hitherto overlooked fact that the *Diary* was dictated to a secretary explains the hiatus during Ferenczi's absence from Budapest. He did, however, continue to jot down his thoughts during his travels on pieces of paper that have been collected as his *Notes and Fragments* (1920, 1930–1932), and the theme of health and illness crops up more than once. In Biarritz, he writes on September 19, 1932:

> Case: inability to walk. Fatigue with pains, exhaustion. Someone takes us by the arm (without helping physically)—we lean (depend) on this person who directs each of our steps. . . . Incapacity to decide (weakness) may make the simplest movement difficult and exhausting. Surrendering the will (decision) to someone else makes the *same* action easy.
>
> (p. 254)

Even more unmistakably, on September 26, 1932—one day before his letter to Freud, as well as one week after the foregoing note and a week before his final diary entry—Ferenczi, now in Bagnères-de-Luchon in the Pyrenees, discourses on illness in a manner that demands to be interpreted autobiographically:

> Organic illness: when the chemistry of the body expresses ucs thoughts and emotions instead of caring for its own integrity. Perhaps

still stronger, more destructive emotions and impulses (murderous intentions) which change into self-destruction. Paralysis in place of aggression (revenge).[5]

(p. 256)

In the first note, Ferenczi connects the physical symptom of an "inability to walk" to a psychological "incapacity to decide," while in the second he implicitly attributes his own "organic illness" to a turning inward of his "murderous intentions," which, as he will confirm in the final entry of his *Diary*, are directed at Freud. But not until Ferenczi leaves Wiesbaden for Baden-Baden and his ensuing "voyage de lit-à-lit" through France do we have any indication that he regarded his "bodily ailments" as the warning signs of what would presently be diagnosed as an "extremely dangerous anemia."

Given the centrality of Ferenczi's relationship with Freud to his understanding of his "blood-crisis," the details of their last encounter take on a heightened significance. On February 18, 1957, de Forest wrote for Fromm a detailed narrative in the first person, as she must have heard it from Ferenczi, of what had taken place when he previewed for Freud (and Brill) his paper setting forth the guiding principles of his "search for the beneficent treatment, so deeply needed by his patient." This, as de Forest ventriloquized Ferenczi, had to be "pursued by the analyst with all skill and tact and loving-kindness, and fearlessly. It must be absolutely honest and genuine." After having "listened with increasing impatience," de Forest continued, Freud expressed his displeasure by warning Ferenczi that he was "treading on dangerous ground and was departing fundamentally from the traditional customs and techniques of psychoanalysis," and that his innovations "might easily lead to sexual indulgence rather than be an expression of parental devotion." Despite being stung by yet another rebuke on the topic of sexual boundary violations, which "ended the interview," Ferenczi recalled, "I held out my hand in affectionate adieu. The Professor turned his back on me and walked out of the room. I shall never see him again."

Joining Thompson, Severn, and de Forest, the last witness to take the stand on the question of Ferenczi's mental and physical health during his final years is Lajos Lévy, his friend and personal physician, who, after the Soviet invasion of Hungary in 1956, immigrated with his wife Kata to London. Although Lévy had declined to collaborate with Fromm, deflecting his inquiry by responding (in German) on November 30, 1957 that Jones was very sick and he "could not and did not want to enter into a polemic with a candidate for death," Lévy was much more forthcoming in a October 18, 1958 letter to Robert Waelder. Lévy informed Waelder that he had known Ferenczi since 1899, and in the course of giving a detailed medical history he shared what Ferenczi had told him about his final visit to Freud:

> He recounted to me that he had been stricken with a walking paralysis at the moment of leaving Freud's summer residence: his feet refused to move forward. Whether this reaction had a psychic explanation or whether it constituted a prodromal sign of a spinal myelopathy that only appeared later—even today I would be unable to say with certainty.[6]
> (1998, p. 25)

Although in his letter to Waelder Lévy (1998) mistakenly supposes that Ferenczi visited Freud during "his summer holidays in the south of France," rather than on his way to Wiesbaden, he is emphatic that "I myself discovered the malady of Ferenczi at the end of September or the beginning of October 33 [sic] on his return from the south of France," elaborating that "the blood count and the spinal tap established conclusively the diagnosis of a pernicious anemia" (pp. 25–26). Given Lévy's involvement in Ferenczi's medical care, the diagnosis that Thompson told Fromm he received after his fall in the Paris railway station must have been a provisional one that was confirmed only after he returned to Budapest. Axel Hoffer and Peter Hoffer (1999) substantiate this version of events by quoting Ferenczi's letter to John Rickman, dated October 5, 1932: "In France I contracted a severe stomach and intestinal catarrh with ensuing severe anemia. Dr. Lévy intends to treat the matter aggressively" (p. 1,261). As Hoffer and Hoffer note, the evidence for "Lévy's account of the timing of his diagnosis" means it "clearly could not have been the case" (p. 1,259n2), as Jones (1957) claimed, that Ferenczi had informed him at the Wiesbaden Congress that "he was suffering from pernicious anemia, but hoped to benefit from liver therapy" (p. 173). No such conversation could have taken place since Ferenczi did not know the nature of his malady until he fell in the Paris railway station, and then received a definitive diagnosis from Lévy.

Even more important than sorting out the chronology of events, however, is taking stock of key features of the story furnished independently by de Forest and Lévy—the fact that Freud turned his back as he refused Ferenczi's proffered handshake at the conclusion of their meeting, and that this insult marked the onset of Ferenczi's "walking paralysis." As Bonomi (1999) has observed, Freud's rebuff of Ferenczi cannot fail to remind us that "Ferenczi himself refused to shake hands with Rank, after Rank's turning away from Freud, when they met casually in New York in 1926" (p. 512), at Pennsylvania Station. With poetic justice, whereas Ferenczi had formerly identified with Freud as the aggressor in repudiating Rank, he now had to suffer the humiliation of being himself rejected by the master.

By the same token, even if his motor inhibition was, in Lévy's words, a "prodromal sign" of his spinal affliction, it may also be given a "psychic explanation," as Ferenczi himself did in interpreting the "inability to walk" as a symptom of a lack of willpower. As Bonomi (1999) has proposed, Ferenczi continued to hope "for a new type of emotional response" from Freud, in which he would be able to acknowledge the justice of Ferenczi's reproaches and admit his own mistakes both as Ferenczi's analyst and "as leader of the psychoanalytic movement," but "Freud's symbolic abandonment was pushing him into the role either of dissident or of faithful follower," and Ferenczi "was neither sufficiently insincere to simulate the faith that was lacking, nor sufficiently courageous to think of himself as outside the psychoanalytic movement" (p. 512). Hence, Bonomi continues, Ferenczi's "walking paralysis at the moment of leaving" was a somatic expression of the dilemma in which he had to choose between the equally impossible alternatives "of keeping one's previous identity or changing it."

By piecing together the evidence that Ferenczi did not know he was ill until after the Wiesbaden Congress with the details of Freud's turning his back and refusal to shake Ferenczi's hand at parting, followed by the immediate onset of Ferenczi's "walking paralysis," we can now appreciate what he is saying in the final entry of his *Clinical Diary*: "In my case the blood-crisis arose when I realized that not only can I not rely on the protection of a 'higher power' but *on the contrary* I shall be trampled under foot by this indifferent power as soon as I go my own way and not his" (Dupont, 1985, p. 212). Ferenczi affirms that the pernicious anemia with which he had just been diagnosed was triggered by the tragic realization that he literally could not live either with or without the reincarnation of his grandfather, the "God, king, patriarch" against whom "it was impossible to be right."[7] His difficulty in moving his feet thus becomes a transformation into "self-destruction" of his "destructive emotions and impulses" in response to being "trampled under foot" by Freud.

In existential terms, the double bind faced by Ferenczi was that rebelling against Freud might doom him to physical death, but surrendering to Freud would mean his psychic death, a still more dire fate:

> Is the only possibility for my continued existence the renunciation of the largest part of one's own self, in order to carry out the will of that higher power to the end (as though it were my own)? . . . On the other hand, is it worth it always to live the life (will) of another person—is such a life not almost death? Do I lose too much if I risk this life? *Chi lo sa?*
> (p. 212)

Caught in Freud's authoritarian vise, Ferenczi sought refuge in his clinical work, and he pays tribute to how much he has profited from his collaboration with Severn: "My pupils' confidence in me could give me a certain self-assurance; in particular, the confidence of one person who is both a pupil and a teacher." Ferenczi concludes by choosing autonomy over submission, so that his physical illness—the price exacted for incurring Freud's wrath by going his own way—becomes paradoxically proof of his courage and a sign of his mental health: "A certain strength of my psychological makeup seems to persist, so that instead of falling ill psychically I can only destroy—or be destroyed—in my organic depths" (p. 213).

Having been schooled by both Groddeck and Severn, Ferenczi not only imputes a psychological meaning to his pernicious anemia but accepts the premise that it is psychogenic in nature. Severn concurs that Ferenczi's death resulted from psychological anguish, though her interpretation to Eissler centers on his guilt over "terrible mistakes" with patients, rather than on his battle with Freud. As Bonomi (1999) points out, it follows that Ferenczi "would not have rejected" out of hand the view of his demise put forward by Freud in his letter to Jones on May 29, 1933, although he "would have enriched it with further meanings . . . in conformity with the principle of *mutuality*, as opposed to one-sided analysis" (p. 518). In Freud's words:

> It is now easier to comprehend the slow process of destruction to which he fell victim. During the last two years it expressed itself as pernicious anemia, which soon led to severe motor disturbances. . . . In the last weeks he could no longer walk or stand at all. Simultaneously

a mental degeneration in the form of paranoia developed with uncanny logical consistency. Central to this was the conviction that I did not love him enough, did not want to acknowledge his work, and also that I had analyzed him badly.

(Paskauskas, 1993, p. 721)

This was the privately circulated version of events that Jones (1957) then publicly disseminated and succeeded in establishing as canonical, complete with asseverations concerning Ferenczi's "delusions about Freud's supposed hostility" and "violent paranoiac and even homicidal outbursts," building to a concluding elegy: "The lurking demons within, against whom Ferenczi had for years struggled with great distress and much success, conquered him at the end, and we learned from this painful experience once more how terrible their power can be" (p. 378).[8]

Compounding the tendentiousness of this narrative—as though Ferenczi's sense of Freud's hostility were delusional rather than justified—the insuperable problem with the Freud-Jones version is that, in defiance of all the evidence, it pushes back Ferenczi's illness "for years" into the past and thereby equates his "psychotic manifestations" with "a turning away from Freud and his doctrines." In his obituary for Ferenczi, Freud (1933b) echoed his letter to Jones in referring to "a grave organic destructive process which had probably overshadowed his life for many years already" (p. 229). However, since Ferenczi's pernicious anemia did not become manifest until after the Wiesbaden Congress, and the reason for saying he had been ill "for many years" was to discredit his revolutionary ideas, it is not only false but malicious to claim that "a grave organic destructive process" had afflicted him throughout his final period.

Despite their divergences, Freud and Jones, on the one hand, and Severn and Ferenczi himself, on the other, agree in giving his organic disease a psychological interpretation. The lone holdout is Thompson. When asked by Eissler, "And did he have an explanation for his sickness? Did he look on it psychologically?," Thompson (1952a) seizes the opportunity once more to vent her spleen at Severn:

Yes, I think he felt—well, also he was rather bitter toward Mrs. Severn, because apparently she had been analyzing him. He had been having dizzy spells for a long time, and they had been analyzing them as anxiety, and when they found what was really wrong, he was rather bitter . . . that he hadn't had any medical check-up on it. That's the trouble with analysts. Everything is psychic.

(p. 15)

Despite her refusal to ascribe any psychological meanings to Ferenczi's "blood-crisis," however, Thompson defends the acuity of his mind until the onset of what she rightly understood to be his "organic brain disease," and she stands united with Severn, de Forest, and Fromm in repelling Jones's baseless and indeed "criminal" vendetta against his former analyst.[9]

Notes

1 The Fromm Archives contain letters from, among many others, Harry Bone, who wrote to Fromm on November 19, 1957, "Jones is a skunk for saying what he did" about Rank, and Jessie Taft, Rank's first biographer, who wrote to Izette de Forest on November 22, 1957, "Few men were ever so sane."
2 See also Dupont (1988), who observes that the "ready acceptance of Jones' thesis can be seen as a sign of resistance by the psychoanalytic world to something Ferenczi would have wanted to introduce into psychoanalysis. . . . There must have been something in Ferenczi's message which was threatening to his colleagues, and apparently, to Freud himself" (pp. 250–51).
3 Evidently, Fromm did not follow up Thompson's suggestion that Severn could give him a "juicy account of her last days" with Ferenczi, and Severn must have heard through the grapevine about Fromm's exculpatory project. In his response on December 12, he informed Severn that he had received her letter on the day after he had sent his manuscript to the *Saturday Review*.
4 That Gizella accompanied Sándor on this last visit is confirmed by Freud's letter to Anna on the following day, "So the Ferenczis came before 4 o'clock. She as kind as ever, from him an icy coldness" (Meyer-Palmedo, 2006, p. 386).
5 In the English edition of Ferenczi's *Final Contributions*, this entry is misdated 26.11.1932, instead of 26.9.1932, while an earlier entry from Biarritz, "On Shock," is misdated 19.11.1932, instead of 19.9.1932.
6 The complete text of Lévy's letter to Waelder, also originally in German, appears in a French translation in *Le Coq-Héron*, from which I have translated it into English.
7 According to Hoffer and Hoffer (1999), "It is characteristic of Ferenczi's transference to Freud . . . that he regarded intellectual difference in terms of complete separation—as an either/or situation," and they object that Freud was "certainly not 'indifferent'" (p. 1,265) toward Ferenczi. But this has it backwards. As Fromm (1959) has argued—and all the evidence shows—it was Freud who forced the choice between subservience or rebellion on his followers; and he was indeed "indifferent" toward Ferenczi inasmuch as he regarded him ultimately as a tool to be used in the service of the psychoanalytic movement whose strivings for independence could not be tolerated.
8 Concerning Jones's claim of "homicidal outbursts," as Bonomi (1999, p. 533) notes, Lévy (1998), on whom Jones likely relied as an informant, does refer in

his letter to Waelder to "relational difficulties and delusions of persecution" in Ferenczi's last illness, "which also manifested themselves in aggression against his wife," though Lévy is adamant that before his pernicious anemia, with its attendant dementia, Ferenczi did not display "any trace of paranoid manifestations" (p. 24). This "aggression" against Gizella may represent the extinction burst of Ferenczi's never wholly dissipated resentment at having had to renounce his love for Elma two decades earlier.

9 Hoffer and Hoffer (1999), too, conclude their "reconstruction of the events surrounding Ferenczi's fatal illness" by affirming that "the psychotic episode two months before his death was not a consequence of a gradual descent into mental illness" (p. 1,266).

Chapter 10

Kissing Papa Ferenczi

Thompson's attitude toward Ferenczi undergoes a pronounced evolution from unqualified approbation in the 1930s, when she was in treatment with him in Budapest, to more equivocal and even adverse judgments in the 1940s and 1950s. A starting point for mapping this trajectory is furnished by her paper, "'Dutiful Child' Resistance" (1931), which shows her endorsement of Ferenczi's mature ideas at this early stage of her own intellectual development. By "'dutiful child' resistance," Thompson means a compliant attitude on the part of the patient that masks a protest against the perceived hypocrisy of the analyst. She traces the roots of the syndrome back to the child's relationship with the mother, whose "great crime was not so much that she did not love him, but that she pretended she did" (p. 108). This "pseudo love" creates "a state of doubt and insecurity" in the mind of the child, who can never be certain of the mother's true feelings, which leads to the domination of his fantasy life by "repressed aggressiveness and sadism" that "must be permitted no expression in reality," since "when even an unkind word slips out there is excessive anxiety and guilt" (p. 109). Thompson explains how this resistance played itself out in one of her patients in the analytic situation:

> The repressed criticism of the analytic method related chiefly to its insincerity. This we find symbolized in the "dutiful child" attitude in true unconscious terms. His behavior was announcing, "You have no real feelings for me—you are acting the part of a mother—I also will act a part." So he pretends cooperation; he pretends belief; his whole behavior is a pretense. By it he really says, "I see through you, but do not be afraid or angry; I will not betray you; in fact, I will play the same game. You pretend your feelings; I will pretend mine." . . . Thus it seems apparent that the "dutiful child" attitude is essentially

a reaction to unadmitted insincerity in the individual upon whom the patient is completely dependent for security; that is, it is essentially an imitation of that individual's insincerity and hides the real attitude of the patient.

(pp. 108–9)

Thompson's entire argument is steeped in Ferenczian themes. On the opening page of the *Clinical Diary*, Ferenczi inveighs against the "insensitivity of the analyst," citing the example of a patient "who never tired of telling me of a teacher she found insufferable, who was always very nice to her and yet always maintained a pedantic attitude" (Dupont, 1985, p. 1). As Ferenczi explains, "had I understood her unspoken reproaches and accusations and altered my behavior accordingly, the patient would not have been compelled to reenact unconsciously, in her conduct toward me, the defiant attitudes of her childhood" (p. 2). The displaced nature of the patient's "reproaches and accusations" renders her outwardly docile but inwardly "defiant" toward her "pedantic" analyst. Recognizing that "the prototype of all confusion is being misled about the reliability of a person or situation," Ferenczi expatiates on how imitation can be the insincerest form of protest later in his text:

Now, in situations where protest and negative reaction, that is, all criticism and expression of discontent, are forbidden, criticism can find expression only in indirect form. For example, the opinion "You are all liars, idiots, lunatics, who can't be trusted," is illustrated indirectly on oneself through exaggerated, crazy behavior and nonsensical productions, rather like the child who in grimacing distorts himself but only to show the other how he looks.

(p. 50)

Such behavior, he explains, is a way of testing the analyst to see whether he can help the patient change ingrained patterns of behavior: "The patient makes use of our sensitivity to repeat a past injury. They try for this reason to put us to the test. As long as we keep failing the test, we will get no further than the continued repetition of the infantile repression: apparent obedience, inner defiance" (p. 120). As he does in the *Clinical Diary*, Ferenczi dwells in "Confusion of Tongues" (1933a) on the consequences of "*professional hypocrisy*," pinpointing the analyst's semblance of devotion in the absence of genuine compassion as the source of "a great part of the repressed criticism felt by our patients" (p. 158). In its imitative mockery, therefore, what Thompson calls "'dutiful child' resistance" is a particular form of the "*anxiety-ridden identification*" and "*introjection of the menacing person or aggressor*" (p. 163) analyzed by Ferenczi with such profundity in his last paper.

Nor was Ferenczi's interest in hypocrisy confined to his final period. In a pivotal paper of his middle period, "Belief, Disbelief, and Conviction" (1913a), he draws attention to patients who "start the treatment with an exaggerated ecstasy of belief" and "accept all our explanations without distinction," though deeper analysis shows that this seeming acquiescence is actually an expression of resistance in which "they successfully repressed all their suspicions and objections only in order to keep secure the filial love they had transferred to the doctor" (pp. 437–38). Ironically, Ferenczi's paper has a latent autobiographical dimension since it perfectly describes the dynamics of his own relationship to Freud, although he appears to have been unable to see this at the time. He came to recognize his plight as a "dutiful child" reacting to the "unadmitted insincerity in the individual upon whom the patient is completely dependent for security" only through the protracted ordeal of his disillusionment with Freud, to which he first gave voice in his Christmas-day 1921 letter to Groddeck, and which pervades the *Clinical Diary*.[1] As a sign of his emotional growth, he was able to acknowledge the validity of Thompson's insight that he re-created with his adherents the same double bind in which he had been placed by Freud: "Dm. now has the courage to reproach me for abandoning pupils at the first signs of incomplete adaptation or submission. I have to admit to it, but excuse myself with the argument that pupils do steal my ideas without quoting me" (Dupont, 1985, p. 122). The fact that Ferenczi can hear and accept such criticism from his analysands radically sets him apart from Freud.

In "'Dutiful Child' Resistance," however, Thompson cannot be accused of stealing Ferenczi's ideas since she acknowledges being influenced by "The Principle of Relaxation and Neocatharsis," presented at the Oxford Congress, which, as she told Eissler, she had attended. In agreement at this stage with Severn's (1933) thesis that "nearly every victim of a severe neurosis displays eventually the disposition to be 'adopted'" (p. 68), Thompson (1931) explains that the aim of Ferenczi's "relaxation principle" is to produce recollection in place of repetition: "His theory, which is especially applicable here, is that in cases where the patient suffered great love deprivation in childhood, it is necessary for the analyst to undertake a kind of adoption, that is, it is necessary to give the patient some experience in childhood love before he can realize that he has missed it" (p. 107). Only if the analyst is prepared to "adopt" the patient can the latter begin to recognize for the first time what has been lost by not having been genuinely loved as a child. In contrast to her commentary a decade later on de Forest, where Thompson (1943) contends that it is "not therapeutically valuable" to seek to gratify the deprived patient's "insatiable need of love" (p. 65), Thompson in this paper endorses Ferenczi's belief in the healing power of analytic love. She goes on to recommend that the patient should be encouraged "in a feeling of natural friendliness, with no patient—doctor attitude," by "spontaneous, natural responses from the analyst" (1931, p. 107). On the same opening page of the *Diary* where he takes aim at "insensitivity of the analyst," Ferenczi writes, "*Natural and sincere behavior* (Groddeck—Thompson) constitutes the most appropriate and favorable atmosphere in the analytic situation" (Dupont, 1985, p. 1). In coupling Thompson with Groddeck, Ferenczi may well be paying tribute to the "'Dutiful Child'" paper, which builds on his own work and it is safe to assume he would have read in *The Psychoanalytic Review*.

Even more revealing for understanding Thompson's early attitude toward Ferenczi is a manuscript, "Evaluation of Ferenczi's Relaxation Therapy," a fragment of which was included under the title "Ferenczi's Relaxation Method" (1933) in her posthumous volume of selected papers, *Interpersonal Psychoanalysis*, edited by Maurice R. Green.[2] Noting that "Thompson credits Izette de Forest and Alice Lowell, who were both patients of Ferenczi's, for help with its preparation," Brennan (2011) hypothesizes that the paper was written "just six months after Thompson returned from Budapest" (p. 5) and presented at the meeting of the American Psychoanalytic Association in Washington, D.C., on December 26, 1933. The experience with Ferenczi, who had died that year, was obviously still fresh in her mind, and Thompson's decision to leave the paper unpublished was in all likelihood due to its highly personal nature.

Echoing the melodies of Ferenczi's "Child Analysis in the Analysis of Adults" (1931), Thompson (1933) begins the extant portion of the paper by observing that "with Ferenczi's relaxation method, one says in effect, 'I am interested in you not only as an adult patient, but I am interested in and have sympathy for the child part of you also'" (p. 67). She gives examples of "the way in which the analyst cooperates in the reliving" experienced by the patient in the course of the treatment. Since Thompson later objected even more strenuously to Ferenczi's advocacy of the analyst's participating fully in the drama being enacted by the patient than she did to his concept of analytic love, one can see how far her outlook here diverges from the one she would adopt in subsequent decades after becoming enamored of Reich.

The first case presented by Thompson in "Ferenczi's Relaxation Method" is that of "a woman who had grown up in an intolerant small-town community where childhood sexual activities with boys in her neighborhood brought her open disgrace and ostracism" (p. 67). During her analysis, "it was apparent that she wished to make her body unattractive and avoided, to an extreme degree, all physical contact," and there came a point "when not only did it seem important to talk of whether her body was repulsive to the analyst, but to test it." Accordingly, "she was encouraged to try a natural expression of her feelings," which prompted the patient "to kiss the analyst not only once but many times and to receive from her not simply passivity but an evidence of warm friendliness and a caress in return before she could even become conscious of the degree of degradation she had felt" (pp. 67–68).

In her report, Thompson gives the impression that she is describing one of her own patients, and she imagines how the physical contact might have been limited to "a friendly touch" (p. 68) on the shoulder had the analyst been a man. But gender reversal, as Chaim E. Bromberg and Lewis Aron (2019) have pointed out, is "a common form of case disguise" (p. 702) in psychoanalytic writings; and multiple clues leave no doubt that this vignette is, in Brennan's (2011) words, "autobiographical and disguised" (p. 8), so that Thompson, like Severn in *The Discovery of the Self*, is giving a thinly veiled glimpse of her own experience in analysis with Ferenczi.[3] Thompson, according to Green (1964a), grew up "on the outskirts of Providence," Rhode Island, where her mother, "a rigidly righteous woman, was the disciplinarian of the family" who favored the "strict religious observances" of the Baptist church, although her mother's zeal was the cause of "considerable friction" with her in-laws (pp. 348–49). This fits with Thompson's reference to being raised in "an intolerant small-town community."

But even more striking is the parallel between the statement that her supposed patient "wished to make her body unattractive" and Ferenczi's declaration in the *Clinical Diary* that Thompson "does really have a very unpleasant odor, and people with a fairly acute sense of smell are repelled by her" (Dupont, 1985, p. 87). He reiterates in a later entry, "Specific odor of the mentally ill," that she "perspires quite conspicuously and with a marked odor," and "feels that she herself exudes sexual odors," symptoms that could be traced back to how "'mother always found something wrong with her body' (even in her earliest childhood)" (Dupont, 1985, pp. 131–32). Ferenczi adds that when Thompson made "acquaintance with the analyst," this led to her "behaving improperly at a dance," and "after she was not accepted as a patient at that time, she went straight to the apartment of a young man and lost her virginity" (p. 132). Since Thompson, who was born in 1893, was "not accepted as a patient" when she first met Ferenczi in 1926, this means that she remained a virgin until the age of thirty-three, which comports with the portrait of her supposed patient as someone who "avoided, to an extreme degree, all physical contact."

The clinching evidence for the autobiographical nature of Thompson's vignette is her description of how the patient responded to the invitation "to try a natural expression of her feelings" by kissing the analyst "not only once but many times." This mirrors what Freud, in his letter of December 13, 1931—quoted at length but incompletely by Jones (1957, pp. 164–65)—notoriously castigated as Ferenczi's "kissing technique," on which Ferenczi meditated in his initial entry in the *Clinical Diary*, where Thompson is quoted as having "remarked quite casually in the company of other patients, who were undergoing analysis elsewhere, 'I am allowed to kiss Papa Ferenczi, as often as I like'" (Dupont, 1985, p. 2). Although Freud professed that he was "certainly not one to condemn such little erotic gratifications out of prudishness or consideration for bourgeois convention," he thereby accused Ferenczi of doing that very thing with his patients, and proceeded to warn him of the slippery slope that leads from kissing through "'pawing,'" "peeping and showing," and "petting parties" to genital intercourse (Falzeder and Brabant, 2000, p. 422). But this impugning of Ferenczi's motives in indulging Thompson's behavior is refuted by Thompson's own disguised account of her analysis, where she makes it clear that she initiated the kissing after having been encouraged to give "natural expression" to her feelings, and that any "caress in return" she received from Ferenczi was offered in a spirit of "warm friendliness" to assuage her importunate demands.

From Thompson's interview with Eissler, we learn that the conduit by which Freud learned of Ferenczi's allowing her to kiss him was Edith Banfield Jackson, a wealthy Colorado-born graduate of the Johns Hopkins Medical School who was Freud's patient from 1930 to 1936. When, in a session on September 3, 1929, Blanton (1971) told Freud that his wife Margaret's analysis had "been started by Clara Thompson," Freud asked him "to repeat the name, saying he did not know of her," though he responded "'Ah' . . . in a tone of satisfaction" upon learning that "Clara had been analyzed by Ferenczi" (p. 26). But by December 1931, it is safe to say that Freud had heard plenty about Thompson from Jackson. As David J. Lynn (2003) documents, not only did Jackson meet many members of Freud's family and likely have an affair with his son Martin, but "there were at least two instances where Freud gave Edith Jackson information about his analysands" (p. 615), most notably when he asked for her help in interpreting a dream of Dorothy Burlingham's. In addition, it "made her feel special" when Freud in 1930 invited Jackson, along with two other patients, to accompany him to Berlin "to continue analysis there," and she was "Freud's only patient at Grundlsee" the same year. Lynn's recitation of Freud's signs of favor continues, "he gave her the gift of an antique stone, which she had set in a ring," as well as "a puppy, Fo, a daughter of Jofi, Freud's chow" (p. 614). Finally, while paying a fee of $25.00 per hour, Jackson "began using some of her sessions with Freud to translate his publications from German to English"; even more dismayingly, while still in analysis she "also made donations to several enterprises closely related to Freud," including $3,000 in 1932 to the publishing house run by Martin Freud and an annual gift of $5,000 to "the psychoanalytically influenced nursery school operated by Anna Freud" (p. 618).

Freud's profiteering from Jackson's generosity, which is of a piece with his attempt to exploit Angelika Bijur Frink, renders his censure of Ferenczi for his indulgence with Thompson hypocritical, to say the least. As Brennan (2011) has wittily remarked, "Jackson may not have gotten a kiss from Freud, but she settled for puppy love" (p. 10), something of which Thompson (1952a) was aware since she let it fall to Eissler that Jackson "has one of Freud dogs" (p. 19). Brennan (2015c) surmises that the motive for Thompson's boast about kissing Ferenczi may have been her "rivalry with Jackson around who was getting the better treatment" (p. 84).

But an even more compelling explanation for Thompson's acting out is her rivalry with Severn and her anger against Ferenczi for granting Severn the time and attention which she, too, craved but was never vouchsafed. Thompson writes in "Ferenczi's Relaxation Method" (1933) that whereas not only "the admission of erotic feelings" on the part of the analyst but also "the admission of mistakes in treatment and the admission of negative affect" are important, "the aim is not a mutual analysis" (pp. 69–70). As in her response to de Forest ten years later, Thompson's only conceivable reason for saying this is that she knew about Ferenczi's mutual analysis with Severn but could not speak of it directly. In a lost portion of the manuscript, she cautions that "it is unsafe for the analyst to permit a free expression of tenderness until the analysis is far advanced and the patient's destructive impulses are fairly well understood," adding that "there are certain patients with a compulsive need to get other people into trouble by fair means or foul" (qtd. in Brennan, 2015c, p. 93*n*27). Like her case history of the patient who needed to kiss her analyst to test whether "she" found the patient's body to be repulsive, this warning is autobiographical and conveys Thompson's conviction that Ferenczi had acted rashly in permitting "a free expression of tenderness" before her analysis was sufficiently "far advanced," and it constitutes a confession that she retaliated by giving way to her "compulsive need" to "get [him] into trouble" with Freud "by fair means or foul."

As is shown by both "'Dutiful Child' Resistance" and "Ferenczi's Relaxation Method," Thompson at first aligned herself with Ferenczi's stance on analytic love and the value of the patient's emotionally charged reliving of past traumas during analysis, but unlike both de Forest and Severn she came to view these ideas far more critically in later years. During Ferenczi's lifetime and in the immediate aftermath of his death, Thompson idealized him and kept her resentments mostly in check, but with the passage of time she became increasingly dissatisfied with what she had gotten from him and consumed with envy of Severn.[4] This shift is enacted in her interview with Eissler, where Thompson (1952a) at first says that her analysis with Ferenczi "was almost 100% positive," and then hesitates, "Oh, I mean I can tell you what's wrong with it, but—" (p. 11), but does not explain right away what she means by this qualification. Instead, Thompson's thoughts turn to the way that "Freud figured greatly as the bad mother in my analysis" because her mother "was the harsh one in my family," whereas "my father was very like Ferenczi, and so Freud was the bad mother, and I became partisan in the whole fight." Thompson describes her mother as "really a frightened person" who "covered it up with this controlling rigidity," and she notes that "there was something in Freud's thinking that fit into this, which I immediately fastened on to," whereas "Ferenczi's attitude was like my father's" (p. 20). Ferenczi, that is, especially "in the early part of the analysis," kept telling Thompson she should try to understand Freud and "see him in this setting" rather "than to be hostile to him, so that we worked out the drama very well, except that it wasn't my family." Because of his loving and compassionate nature, therefore, Thompson started out "very much on Ferenczi's side, very much involved emotionally in his fight with Freud, which I think I've gotten over."

According to the picture that Thompson draws of her family, the "bad mother" was poised against the benevolent father, and her allegiance to Ferenczi "in his fight with Freud" was a manifestation of her equation in the transference of him with her father and of Freud with her mother, though she asserts that she had "gotten over" this polarization by the time of her interview with Eissler. As her antipathy toward Severn intensified in the course of her time in Budapest, however, reinforced by Ferenczi's inequity in the matter of fees and Thompson's resentment over the mutual analysis, "Mrs. Severn became a much better bad mother than Freud" (p. 20) in her mind, though the underlying configuration of the "good father" and "bad mother" remained unchanged. Thompson's tendency to polarize her parental imagos is highlighted by Green (1964a), who not only, as we have seen, described her mother as "rigidly righteous" and "the disciplinarian of the family," but also affirmed that Thompson "adored her father" (p. 349).

In the *Clinical Diary*, however, there is a revelation that calls this scenario into question. For in the same initial entry where Ferenczi records Thompson's having divulged to "patients who were undergoing analysis elsewhere" that she had kissed him in analysis, Ferenczi notes that this behavior "was a case of repetition of the father-child situation" because, "as a child, Dm. had been grossly abused sexually by her father, who was out of control," while "later, obviously because of the father's bad conscience and social anxiety, he reviled her," and "the daughter had to take revenge on her father indirectly, by failing in her own life" (Dupont, 1985, p. 3).

The first commentator to draw attention to Thompson's sexual abuse by her father was Sue A. Shapiro (1993), who observed that although Thompson's analysis with Ferenczi should have equipped her "to spread the word when she returned to America about the reality of abuse and its impact on children's lives," she "did nothing of the sort," and indeed "does not mention the reality of sexual abuse and sexual harassment as a causal factor in women's discomfort with their bodies and their sexuality" (p. 162). Thompson's sexual inhibition as well as the belief that she "exudes sexual odor" become explicable in light of her history of sexual abuse. Along these same lines, Brennan (2015c, p. 92*n*17) connects Thompson's paper, "Development of Awareness of Transference in a Markedly Detached Personality" (1938), with her avowal to Eissler that she was "a very detached person" before coming to Budapest, and that she still had "difficulties with intimacy, although not too much" (1952a, p. 11).

Although Thompson's sexual abuse by her father must have come up in her analysis with Ferenczi for him to have recorded it in his *Diary*, her silence on this topic in her writings suggests that it was not worked through, rendering the therapeutic process incomplete. With Ferenczi's help, Thompson confronted her struggle with the emotionally and physically abusive "bad mother," whom she found reincarnated in Freud and Severn. Ferenczi's report of "an infantile trauma" that occurred when "her mother grabbed her so hard by the wrist that she broke her arm" (Dupont, 1985, p. 87) is corroborated by Shapiro's (1993) evidence that Thompson urged a friend to use this experience of hers to warn a disobedient child, "When I was young my mother punished me by breaking my arms" (p. 171). But the analysis was not able to probe beneath Thompson's casting Ferenczi in the role of the "good father" to unmask his identity as her sexually abusive "bad father" in the transference. Instead, much as Severn did with her parting curse, Thompson "had to take revenge on her father indirectly" by bragging about kissing Ferenczi to Jackson, who she had to know would pass this juicy bit of gossip on to Freud, and, masochistically, by causing her analysis with Ferenczi to fail.

Only at the end of the interview does Thompson (1952a) revert to the topic of what went wrong in this analysis. She tells Eissler:

> He never actually had a conception of my character structure. Certainly he dealt plenty with my traumatic experiences and with my relationships to people, but the ways in which my hostility was expressed I don't think he ever saw. The ways in which I manipulated people, I am sure he never saw.
>
> (pp. 23–24)

These comments occur in the context of Thompson's praise of Reich and distill the critique of Ferenczi in her later writings. As Thompson elaborates, this is where Ferenczi's "whole relaxation theory missed out, in that he really thought you could give an adult the love he never had, which you can't, because it's shut off," and "the character has developed a rigidity" by the time people have grown up, so that "no matter how much you feed them, it's just like diabetes; the sugar isn't digested" (p. 24).

Thompson, however, is mistaken in believing that Ferenczi was blind to her hostility or the ways she manipulated people. On the contrary, he recognized the aggressive component in her poor personal hygiene and understood that by telling Jackson about the liberties he allowed her to take with him she was carrying out an act of vengeance against him as a father figure. Thus, as Brennan (2015c) argues, it was not that Ferenczi did not see Thompson's character structure, but rather that "Thompson didn't see that Ferenczi saw her hostility, and that he was choosing to respond to it in a different way" (p. 86). But even though Ferenczi had an accurate picture of the roots of Thompson's suffering, his inability to reach her deepest layers clinically left her with a suppressed feeling of disappointment, which returned with increasing insistence in her later years and led Thompson not only to be far more critical in her attitude toward him than were either de Forest or Severn, but virtually to repudiate his legacy altogether. Highly revealing is the anecdote recounted by Bass (2015) of how, during his analysis with Wolstein, the latter told him of a time during his own analysis with Thompson when he had asked her about the "countertransference basis" of something "she had said or done in a session" (p. 10). Thompson responded that "she would consider his question in her own self-analysis," but that "it didn't belong in his." To this attempt to exclude her own subjectivity from the analytic field, Wolstein replied, "'Well, if it doesn't belong in my analysis, what is it doing in here?'" In contrast to Thompson's classical stance, Wolstein's willingness to share this vignette with his analysand was a truly Ferenczian gesture that encouraged Bass "to take my analysis of his countertransference as far as we were both capable of taking it."

A symptom of Thompson's troubled state of mind with respect to Ferenczi concerns "Confusion of Tongues," which, as we know, she heard him deliver in Wiesbaden—looking "like death" on the platform—though, as she told Eissler, she was unable to understand the paper because it was in German. An English translation had appeared in the *International Journal of Psycho-Analysis* in 1949, but in the interview Thompson (1952a) states, "I don't know whether it still exists or not" (p. 13). Strikingly, however, she had earlier told Eissler that she "got what little she knew" about how Ferenczi became interested in analysis "from reading his notes, those that were published recently in the International Journal" (p. 5), a reference to the extracts from his *Notes and Fragments* that followed immediately after "Confusion of Tongues" in the same Ferenczi issue of the *International Journal*. Even more curiously, in a letter to de Forest two years later about *The Leaven of Love*, on April 26, 1954, Thompson again wondered whether the paper had been published: "I notice you quote from his Wiesbaden paper. Is that in the posthumous publications? I have never run across it" (qtd. in Brennan, 2009, p. 452).

Since Thompson admits that she had seen the issue in which "Confusion of Tongues" was published, her repeated protestations that she was unfamiliar with the paper are uncanny, and Brennan (2015c) is surely correct in deducing that she "dissociated her knowledge of the paper and its key ideas" (p. 85). As Brennan further argues, Thompson's dissociation was in all likelihood motivated by her discomfort with Ferenczi's thesis that "sexual trauma played a role in the etiology of neurosis," since she summarized (1952a) her impression of the paper to Eissler by saying that it dealt with "his favorite theme: that there are no bad patients, there are only bad analysts" (p. 13), with no mention of Ferenczi's resuscitation of Freud's trauma theory. When Thompson's silence on the topic of sexual abuse is combined with the dissociation of her memory of "Confusion of Tongues," it is impossible to escape the conclusion that, in Brennan's (2015c) words, "there is something about trauma that always eludes her" (p. 85), and that her incapacity to confront the unresolved anger stemming from the experience of having been "grossly abused sexually by her father" underlies her drift away from Ferenczi and increasingly critical attitude toward his "whole relaxation theory" in the 1940s and 1950s.

Nevertheless, there can be no doubt that Thompson benefited from her analysis with Ferenczi. Even as she pointed out his "faults" to Eissler, Thompson (1952a) described her time in Budapest, when she was bathed in the Hungarian language so that she "didn't know what people were talking about around me," as her second chance at "growing up in a happy childhood," which was Ferenczi's "fantasy about his method" (p. 11). As she acknowledges, whereas she was formerly a "very detached" and "very schizoid" person, thanks to her "adoption" by Ferenczi she "came to have relationships with people for the first time" in what she describes as "a comfortable sort of way," and her "difficulties with intimacy" were considerably alleviated.

These are important signs of emotional growth that belong on the positive side of the ledger. But her sense of gratitude did not prevent Thompson from informing Jackson about the liberties she had taken with Ferenczi, knowing full well that the tale would be passed on to Freud. She thereby dealt a severe blow to Ferenczi's already-precarious relationship with Freud and became indirectly responsible for much of the damage to his posthumous reputation. In retrospect, however, Thompson (1952a) gave Ferenczi credit for being "very decent" about what had happened when, despite being "very upset," he "finally admitted" that she "was right" in having proceeded "on the theory, well this is what we do, why don't we admit it?" (p. 4).

Although Ferenczi's conscience was clear, Thompson's act of vengeance took its toll. As I noted in the Prelude, the letter in which Freud reprimanded Ferenczi for his "kissing technique" was written on December 13, 1931, while Ferenczi began the *Clinical Diary* on January 7, 1932, leading Bonomi (1999) to remark that it is as if he were "replacing the broken dialogue with Freud" (p. 510). In the same initial entry in which Ferenczi reflects on this incident and links it to Thompson's sexual abuse by her father, he also mentions "that female patient who demanded that the patient should also have the right to analyze the analyst," and admits that "in one case the communication of the content of my own psyche developed into a form of mutual analysis from which I, the analyst, derived much profit" (Dupont, 1985, p. 3). In addition to having been stung by Freud's rebuke over Thompson, therefore, the *Diary* opens in the wake of the inception of his mutual analysis with Severn, and his decision to begin keeping a private journal arises from the convergence of these two momentous developments in his clinical work.

From first to last, Ferenczi's chronicle of his analytic journey in the *Clinical Diary* is set against the backdrop of his life-or-death struggle with Freud. Of all his patients, only Thompson and Severn are juxtaposed in his keynote, "Insensitivity of the analyst," which introduces Ferenczi's critique of Freud, and they are paired again in his post-Wiesbaden finale, where he holds Freud responsible for his "blood-crisis." But whereas the agonizing nature of their termination does not detract from his success with Severn, Thompson's limited gains and qualified praise do not override her predominantly negative verdict on her experience with Ferenczi and his inability to help her heal from her sexual traumas. In contrast to his avowals that he "released R.N. from her torments" and the hopes voiced by Severn for "a *reciprocal* 'honorable' recognition of mutual achievement," he concludes ruefully that Thompson "made herself independent—feels hurt because of the absence of mutuality on my part" (Dupont, 1985, pp. 213–14). "Trampled under foot" by Freud and deprived of a breakthrough with Thompson, Ferenczi found consolation, if not redemption, in his leap of faith with Severn: "*The analyst who is forgiven*: enjoys in the analysis what was denied to him in life and hardened his heart. MUTUAL FORGIVENESS!!—Final success" (p. 202).

Notes

1 Thompson's concept of "'dutiful child' resistance" contains the gist of Bernard Brandchaft's theory of "pathological accommodation" (Brandchaft et al., 2010), though Brandchaft does not cite Thompson in any of the papers in his book.

2 The full title of the manuscript is supplied by Brennan, who saw it years ago at the William Alanson White Institute and quotes brief excerpts in two papers (2011, 2015c). Lamentably, however, the White Institute was unable to locate the manuscript during my own visit in 2015, and it now appears to be irretrievably lost. Like an ancient Greek tragedy that survives only in the fragments quoted by scholiasts, all that remains of the bulk of Thompson's paper are the snippets preserved by Brennan.
3 I had reached this conclusion (Rudnytsky, 2015, pp. 136–37) before reading Brennan's paper, and it has been independently corroborated by Etty Cohen (2015).
4 Fortune (2015) observes that Margaret Severn "defended her mother ferociously against any possible aspersions, knowing there had been detractors, including some of Severn's contemporaries in Budapest, particularly Clara Thompson" (p. 23).

Chapter 11

Beyond Groddeck

As Severn (1952) told Eissler, by the time she landed on Ferenczi's couch in 1925 she had already "been practicing psychoanalysis for a number of years" (p. 1). She had been in treatment with Jelliffe, Ashe, and Rank, not to mention Franklin Leavitt, the theosophical physician who aided her after her 1905 breakdown. But Ferenczi, too, had previously been in analysis, first with Freud for a total of approximately nine weeks in 1914 and 1916, and then on a sporadic and quasi-mutual basis with Groddeck since his first visit to Baden-Baden in 1921.[1] Writing to Groddeck on October 11, 1922, Ferenczi urged him "to come to Budapest and continue here the analysis you have already embarked upon," adding, "whether and how far this will be compatible with the simultaneous analysis of myself, remains to be seen" (Fortune, 2002, p. 31), while Groddeck confirmed in his May 31, 1923 letter to Freud: "Ferenczi was in treatment with me for the first time in September 1921. . . . He was with me again the next year. I treated him again and was analyzed by him about six or seven times" (Giefer, 2008, p. 197). Thus, if Ferenczi was Severn's fourth analyst, she was his third, and their relationship should be seen in the context of its antecedents. It has long been recognized that Ferenczi's friendship with Groddeck served as a catalyst for his emotional detachment from Freud. But what has gone unnoticed is the way this pattern was subsequently re-created when Ferenczi moved closer to Severn and away from Groddeck.

As we have seen, Severn in her first two books had expounded the psychological causes and meanings of organic disease, the same theme that preoccupied not only Jelliffe but also Groddeck, whom Ferenczi (1917b) had lauded even prior to making his acquaintance for being "the first to make the courageous attempt to apply the results of Freud's discoveries to organic medicine" (p. 342). Although Ferenczi did not know Severn when he became enchanted by Groddeck, she was Groddeck's successor in this respect, and her increasing influence over Ferenczi was both a cause and an effect of the diminution of Groddeck's hold over him.

Despite their great affection for one another, intellectual disagreements between Ferenczi and Groddeck surfaced early in their relationship. As Groddeck put it in a letter of November 12, 1922, "I think the difference between us is that you are compelled to want to understand things, whilst I am compelled not to want to understand" (Fortune, 2002, p. 35). Ferenczi concurred with this assessment, and on December 11 tried to convince Groddeck of the inherent contradiction in his anti-intellectual stance:

> I don't, however, deny that I incline towards *wanting to understand*, whilst admitting that *complete* understanding lies in the remote future, and is probably unattainable. . . . If you were right in the characterisation of your scientific method or mode of perception, then logically you would have to content yourself with repeating this one sentence (about the impossibility of knowing the It). . . . You don't do that, however; rather, you are concerned, as we disreputable "academics" indeed are, to understand people, bodies and souls, and to heal them by means of this understanding. . . . It is wrong of you, then, to deny your own method of working and pretend that you work with some mystical, unfathomable daemon, or, to put it more accurately, with an instrument that has nothing to do with logic.
>
> (p. 40)

For several years, however, what Ferenczi termed in a letter on Groddeck's sixtieth birthday, October 13, 1926, the "decided differences between us with regard to the scientific method we employ" remained unclouded by personal conflicts, and the two men, together with their wives, enjoyed "regeneration and exchange of confidences in the intimacy of your home in Baden-Baden" (p. 78) on an annual basis. Prophetically, the first hiatus in this pattern that had begun in 1921 coincides with the first allusion to Severn in their correspondence. Ferenczi writes on July 27, 1928:

> A particularly difficult case that couldn't follow me to Germany was the main obstacle to our visiting you this time. Possibly also an intimation of "discarding" to which you allude, and which I perhaps do not wish to interrupt. I believe that my own ideas are changing, and it is

questionable whether we concur in every point in our views at present. Be that as it may: as individuals we will always remain close.

(pp. 82–83)

Ferenczi clearly desires to preserve his friendship with Groddeck, but the "intimation of 'discarding'" taking place on both sides is palpable, such that his citing of the "obstacle" presented by Severn's condition as an excuse for not being able to come to Baden-Baden seems to be a displacement of their inner strain. He continues by proposing instead that Groddeck should join him and Gizella on a trip to Spain in the autumn, "Wouldn't it be lovely if we could somehow coordinate our plans, or are you of the opinion, dear Georg, that we should go our own separate ways for the time being?" (p. 83). In the event, however, it was not Groddeck but Severn who—to Gizella's consternation—accompanied the Ferenczis to Spain, though, as Severn (1952) told Eissler, "it was extremely difficult for me to live without the analysis," so "it was the lesser of two evils for me. It was terrible . . . I had to go to bed as soon as I arrived, and stay until he chose to move to the next place, then I got up and got on the train and went there and went to bed again" (p. 12).

Nearly a year later, on June 13, 1929, the signs of growing reserve give way to acrimony in the last of Groddeck's three extant letters to Ferenczi:

Quite by chance, or—to be more specific—it was my bookseller who told me about your arbitrary jump [*mutwilliger Sprung*] from the psychic to the organic, and now I'm not sure I know what to do about you. . . . In the first place, there is no question of it having been an arbitrary jump. It was I who introduced you very gently and carefully to these ideas. . . . Secondly, I want to reclaim my property, not that I ever considered this property a personal discovery. . . . But it is none the less my property, because I acquired it in the course of years of work. You can of course claim originality in your skilful arrangement of the wording, for no one else can lay claim to the Genital Theory nor the ghastly expression "Bioanalysis"—but this does not apply to the rest.

(Fortune, 2002, p. 87)

As Fortune points out in an annotation, Groddeck is here referring to Ferenczi's "Masculine and Feminine" (1929a), which had just appeared in the inaugural issue of *Die Psychoanalytische Bewegung* and was published in an English translation the following year in *The Psychoanalytic Review*.

Having been alerted by his bookseller to the new journal, with Ferenczi's contribution, where he offers a précis of his argument in *Thalassa* (1924), Groddeck must then have fired off this letter while still indignant at what he regarded as Ferenczi's appropriation of his intellectual "property." In the offending paragraph, Ferenczi (1929a) had written:

> I have simply transferred purely psychological concepts—such as repression and symbol formation—to organic processes. But I think it is not yet entirely clear whether this wanton leap [*mutwilliger Sprung*] from the psychic to the organic was really an aberration and not rather a successful stroke, which one is accustomed to call a discovery. I am rather inclined to suppose the latter and to see in these ideas the beginning of a new direction of research. In any case, I hastened to give this form of research a name: I called it "bioanalysis."
>
> (p. 46)

That Groddeck is reacting to this paper is clear not only from the date of his letter but also from his pouncing on the phrase "wanton leap" and his disparagement of the term "bioanalysis." He must have been incensed by Ferenczi's claiming to have made a "discovery" and taking credit for "the beginning of a new direction of research" when he had been ploughing these furrows for decades and considered himself to have been the one who had planted their seeds in Ferenczi.

Several years earlier, in his October 1926 letter on Groddeck's sixtieth birthday, Ferenczi had graciously remarked that his friend did not appear "to care excessively about matters of priority" and "was not particularly bothered by being neglected" (Fortune, 2002, p. 78) by psychoanalytic authors, while on April 26, 1927 he assured him from New York, "I never fail to mention and praise Georg in my lectures as the standard bearer of psychoanalysis *in organicis*" (p. 79). Ferenczi likewise paid homage to Groddeck in his published papers. Even though Rank had written in his portion of *The Development of Psycho-Analysis* that "the actual task" of analysis "consists in understanding and interpreting every experience of the patient above all as a reaction to the present analytical situation" (Ferenczi and Rank, 1924, p. 25), Ferenczi affirmed in "Contra-Indications to the 'Active' Psycho-Analytical Technique" (1925a) that "on an unprejudiced examination the credit of priority belongs to Groddeck" for interpreting all analytic material in terms of the "relation of patient to analyst" (p. 225), while in "Present-Day Problems in Psycho-Analysis" (1926b) he recalled that "some time ago" Groddeck "had attempted with success to extend psycho-analysis to certain cases of purely organic illness" (p. 39). Spurred by Groddeck's reproach, Ferenczi once again acknowledged in "The Principle of Relaxation and Neocatharsis" (1930) that in erasing "the distinction between the analysis of children and that of adults" he "was undoubtedly influenced by . . . the work of Georg Groddeck, the courageous champion of the psycho-analysis of organic diseases, whom I consulted about an organic illness" (pp. 122–23).

In view of these reiterated bows in Groddeck's direction, Groddeck's dudgeon at Ferenczi's effusion in "Masculine and Feminine" seems excessive, and Ferenczi's confidence in Groddeck's indifference concerning "matters of priority" equally misplaced. Two months later, on August 16, 1929, Ferenczi was still trying to mend the rupture: "Although you have refused to discuss further certain misunderstandings between us which I find incomprehensible I see no reason for breaking off our friendly relationship" (Fortune, 2002, p. 90). Having attempted to patch things up, Ferenczi proposed himself and Gizella as guests at Marienhöhe, with Severn making three: "I'd also like to put up one of my pupils, whom you know (Severn), in your house if possible, because she is at a critical stage" (p. 90). Strikingly, in her interview with Eissler Thompson (1952a) discloses that she, too, "was in Baden-Baden . . . one summer, 1929," in the course of which Ferenczi showed her Groddeck "in the distance once" (p. 14). Thus, in the same year that Severn stayed in the sanatorium, Thompson had to find accommodations elsewhere in the town and—as with Freud and Helene Deutsch—was prevented by Ferenczi from meeting Groddeck, which would have given her yet another reason to resent both him and Severn.

This visit came off successfully and restored their relationship, at least on the surface, to an amicable footing. "Many thanks again for everything!" Ferenczi wrote to the Groddecks on October 28, 1929, "This year it really was a 'relaxation' for me"—an allusion to his current "relaxation technique"—"thanks to you!" (Fortune, 2002, p. 91). But though all seemed well, things were no longer as they had been in the halcyon days, and Ferenczi lapsed into silence for almost eight months before his next communication.

A bird's eye view of Ferenczi's later letters to Groddeck, starting with his allusion in July 1928 to the "particularly difficult case" that interrupted his string of sojourns, reveals a cascade of references to Severn and his analytic work with her. In the first year, Severn prevents Ferenczi from coming to Baden-Baden, and she takes Groddeck's place on the trip to Spain. The following year, Groddeck lashes out at Ferenczi for failing to credit him and refuses to clear the air in a manner the latter finds "incomprehensible." When Ferenczi nonetheless reaches out and returns with Gizella to Baden-Baden, he asks Groddeck "to put up one of my pupils," who again is Severn. In his note of thanks for the hospitality, Ferenczi refers to Severn in shorthand as the *"Gräfin"* or Countess, an ironic yet honorific title that recurs in subsequent letters: "The journey back went off all right—even the Gr. tried hard not to be unpleasant. We arrived without coming to blows" (p. 92).

After this affectionate but unremarkable letter Ferenczi fades into eight months of silence, and when "the laziest letter-writer in the world" again decides to show "signs of life," on June 15, 1930, his bond with Severn is even more apparent although her name goes unmentioned: "Oh, if only it were true this matter of thought transference! Then you would already be well-informed about everything, would know how often we think of you, and speak of you" (Fortune, 2002, p. 93). Groddeck's mystical leanings did not extend to an interest in telepathy, whereas it was a hobbyhorse of Ferenczi's and even more of Severn's from the time that her belief in the efficacy of "absent treatment" had galvanized the erstwhile mayor of Cape Town when he read *Psycho-Therapy* to her ongoing analysis with Ferenczi, whom she had, in Margaret's (1988) words, "so deeply entangled with all this odd psychic phenomena that he ain't used to considering" (p. 2,097). Thus, when Ferenczi wishes he could communicate with Groddeck via "thought transference," he is functioning as Severn's medium. As he writes of her in the *Clinical Diary*, "She believes in telepathic healing by means of willpower and thought-concentration, but especially through compassion" (Dupont, 1985, p. 158).

In his August 1929 letter asking if he might bring Severn to Marienhöhe, Ferenczi informs Groddeck that he has been in St. Moritz since July, "as usual with patients and students whom I didn't want to treat in the intense heat of Budapest" (Fortune, 2002, p. 90). What stands out is the contrast between the collective reference to "patients and students" who are with him in Switzerland and the naming of Severn, whom Groddeck already "knows." Writing to Freud from the Groddecks' on September 9, 1929, Ferenczi states, "I packed up my belongings (seven patients), and came here on August 27" (Falzeder and Brabant, 2000, pp. 370–71). Thus, Severn and Thompson formed part of an entourage of seven patients Ferenczi brought with him from St. Moritz to Baden-Baden, of whom only Severn was permitted to stay at Marienhöhe. This pattern recurs in Ferenczi's letter to Groddeck on December 21, 1930, which again comes after an interval of more than six months since his "thought transference" letter. In the December letter, Ferenczi first reports on a visit to Freud in Vienna, which had taken place more than a month earlier, saying with relief that "the differences of opinion turned out to be relatively superficial" and that he "encountered pronounced co-operation compared to previous altercations," before turning to news on the clinical front:

> I have to devote four, sometimes nearly five hours daily to my main patient, "the Queen." Hard work, but rewarding. I think I will soon—in the not too distant future—be able to say what it means to finish an analysis. The other patients are busily enacting as well, and confirm daily what I wrote about the need to give due recognition again to traumatogenesis.
> (Fortune, 2002, p. 96)

The last sentence is a reference to his Oxford Congress paper, where Ferenczi (1930) had signaled his return to trauma theory: "Having given due consideration to fantasy as a pathogenic factor, I have of late been forced more and more to deal with the pathogenic trauma itself" (p. 120). In the letter, Ferenczi elevates Severn from "the Countess" to "the Queen" because the immense number of hours he had been spending with her placed her even more unequivocally in a category by herself, separate from the "other patients" whose enactments likewise "confirm daily" the new direction he was taking. Just as Severn is the only one of his patients from the *Diary* whom Ferenczi credits in his published papers, so, too, she is the only one to be mentioned not once but repeatedly in his letters to Groddeck. All this is proof of how much larger she loomed in Ferenczi's mind than any of her compeers, though he gave the full measure of his devotion to each of his patients, as is attested by his reflections on their cases not only in the *Clinical Diary* but also in his *Notes and Fragments*.

The gaps of first eight and then six months between Ferenczi's two letters in 1930 is followed by another break of nearly ten months before Groddeck's birthday, on October 13, which prompts Ferenczi to send greetings from Capri on October 10, 1931, where he is "trying to recover after all the extreme mental and physical exhaustion" by going on holiday without patients "for the first time in years" (Fortune, 2002, p. 98). In the brief missive, which includes a postscript from Gizella, Ferenczi finds time for an update on scientific matters: "I am grappling with the problem of *the trauma* as such: the splitting, indeed, automatisation of the personality invites a stimulating if most complicated game of riddle solving, which brings you perilously close to the problem of death. (Mentally ill people are really half-dead persons)."

Like Ferenczi's allusion to "thought transference," this meditation on the consequences of trauma shows his preoccupation with Severn, to whom he had acknowledged his indebtedness in "The Principle of Relaxation and Neocatharsis" (1930) for teaching him that "a *psychotic splitting off* of a part of the personality occurs under the influence of shock" (p. 121). The connection between "automatisation of the personality" and the "problem of death" is a leitmotif of the *Clinical Diary*, where Ferenczi describes how the shocks experienced by Severn had left her "with a body progressively divested of its soul, whose disintegration is not perceived at all or is regarded as an event happening to another person, being watched from the outside" (Dupont, 1985, p. 9), while Severn, as we have seen, draws on her own experience of soul murder to argue against Freud in *The Discovery of the Self* (1933) that it is "perfectly possible for a person to be psychically 'killed,' or some part of him killed, while he still continues to live in the flesh" (p. 156).

When Ferenczi wrote his Christmas-day 1921 letter to Groddeck, Freud could not have known that Ferenczi had found someone else to whom he could confide his intimate secrets, including his resentment concerning the pressure that Freud had put on him to marry Gizella rather than Elma, as well as over the Palermo incident. Still, Freud might have sensed Ferenczi's growing detachment in his letter of May 11, 1922, in which Ferenczi calls attention to "the fact that I don't give in more often to the impulse to write to you," comments that he has reached the stage of "badly belated weaning," and confesses that he thinks "not without sadness about the time when I was that much more stormy, happy-unhappier" (Falzeder and Brabant, 2000, pp. 79–80). Analogously, it is indicative of Ferenczi's withdrawal from Groddeck that he never entrusted him with the secret of his mutual analysis with Severn or informed him of Freud's recriminations about his "kissing technique," but only dropped hints of what was taking place in his private world in sporadic letters.

Ferenczi's running commentary on his relationship with Severn continues in his penultimate letter to Groddeck, on March 3, 1932, when the *Clinical Diary* was already in progress:

> My "scientific imagination," although "well-disciplined" (Freud), induces me to fly beyond the unconscious at times to the so-called metaphysical, which I find reflected in almost identical form in the material my patients produce. There seems to be a path which leads from dreams to a deeper understanding of the splitting of the personality, and psychoses too. I owe my technical advances to what my patients tell me about their own resistances.
>
> (p. 103)

In saying he is impelled "to fly beyond the unconscious at times to the so-called metaphysical," Ferenczi echoes his entry that same day in the *Diary*, where he records how Severn insists on the uniqueness "of our joint technique, which penetrates into deep metaphysical regions" (Dupont, 1985, pp. 46–47). In soaring "beyond the unconscious," Ferenczi leaves behind not only Freud but also Groddeck, for it is with Severn that his "scientific imagination" finds itself reflected "in almost identical form," and with whom he traveled farthest down the "path which leads to a deeper understanding of the splitting of the personality, and psychoses too."

Writing in his *Clinical Diary* on May 3, 1932, Ferenczi observes that "the interpretation of every detail as expressing a personal affect toward the analyst, which Rank and I perhaps exaggerated, is likely to produce a paranoid atmosphere, which an objective observer could describe as a narcissistic, specifically erotomaniacal delusion of the analyst" (Dupont, 1985, p. 95). Given that Ferenczi had earlier awarded Groddeck "credit of priority" over Rank in his insistence on the ubiquity of transference interpretations, his current willingness to criticize this technique shows how far Ferenczi has moved away from them both. What he describes to Groddeck as his "technical advances" were spurred by what he was able to glean from the "resistances" put up by his patients. In the *Diary*, for example, Ferenczi writes of Alice Lowell that she had made him aware of "the objectionable habit . . . of engaging her occasionally in conversations and discussions, from which she sometimes had to defend herself with an energetic 'shut up'" (Dupont, 1985, p. 30), while unnamed others demanded that "I should just be there; that I should not talk so much" (p. 12). But though Ferenczi is indebted to all his patients, Severn is the only one he singles out by name in "Child-Analysis in the Analysis of Adults" (1931) for admonishing him that "I sometimes disturbed the spontaneity of the fantasy-production with my questions and answers," and that he ought to confine himself "to stimulating the patient's mind to further efforts when it faltered" by offering "general encouragement rather than specific direction" (pp. 133–34).

Ferenczi's final letter to Groddeck, on March 20, 1933, followed more than a year later and was written under the pall of the "extremely dangerous anaemia" that would take his life on May 22, though he mistakenly believed his condition to be "relatively satisfactory now" (Fortune, 2002, p. 105). In addition to explaining that his recent "indisposition in Baden-Baden was the beginning" of the illness "which almost struck me down in France," Ferenczi reiterates what he had affirmed in the final entry of the *Diary* concerning the psychogenic nature of his affliction when he traces "the underlying psychological reason for this decline" back to his "disappointment in Freud, about which you also know" (p. 105). The correspondence with Groddeck thus comes full circle and returns to Ferenczi's lament in his Christmas-day 1921 letter that he "could never be free and open" with Freud because "he expected too much of this 'deferential respect' from me; he was too big for me, there was too much of the father" (p. 8). Even so, and despite the fact that he and Freud "have stopped corresponding for the time being," Ferenczi does not doubt that "both of us are trying to salvage what can be salvaged" and that, "in the end, we will be more or less successful in doing so" (p. 105).

Ferenczi's main theme in this last letter, therefore, is his relationship with Freud, which he desires to preserve even after their disastrous farewell in Vienna and being given the cold shoulder at the Wiesbaden Congress, and he concludes by similarly assuring Groddeck that "this is the first letter in a long time to put me in touch with the outside world, which is no doubt a sign of our indestructible friendship" (p. 106). But even here, apart from bulletins about his family, the only person Ferenczi mentions is Severn: "N.B. Her ladyship, the Countess, is no longer with me" (p. 108). The trend continues in Gizella's grief-stricken letter to Georg and Emmy on January 9, 1934. After voicing her fear that her having "heard nothing from the Freuds" may either be because she "unintentionally did something wrong" or because "the family no longer wants to have anything to do with us, with Sándor and me"—referring to her late husband as though he were still alive—and passing on the news "that Jones, in London, wrote an article in the 'Journal' against Sándor," Gizella brings the Groddecks up to date on " 'Baroness' Severn," who "has apparently also published a book—which won't please the orthodox Freudians" (p. 111). This unpalatable work is, of course, *The Discovery of the Self*, one of the rare allusions to the book by anyone. Continuing the pattern established during Ferenczi's lifetime, neither Thompson nor any other patient warrants Gizella's notice, but only Severn, who again is given an aristocratic title in recognition of her status in Ferenczi's entourage.

Like many other trauma victims, Gizella's impulse is to blame herself for the insensitivity shown by Freud, but with unerring intuition she juxtaposes Jones's article "against Sándor" with Severn's production that is sure to displease "the orthodox Freudians." Indeed, in what Gizella correctly perceived to be his hostile obituary for Ferenczi in the *International Journal*, Jones (1933) not only disparages *Thalassa* by saying that "what many consider as his most impressive work . . . seems to have stunned rather than stimulated the minds of his readers," but he fires the opening salvo in his campaign of defamation by adding that "in his still later writings Ferenczi showed unmistakable signs of mental regression in his attitude towards fundamental problems of psycho-analysis" (pp. 465–66). Jones's epithet "mental regression" conflates a diagnosis of "mental" illness with a censure of Ferenczi's ideological "regression" in daring to rehabilitate what Freud and his loyalists regarded as the discredited paradigm of the trauma theory that had given birth to psychoanalysis.

In his response to Gizella on February 19, 1934, Groddeck made clear how utterly he and Ferenczi had gone their separate ways. "All these last years," Groddeck wrote, "I could only think about Sándor's life with a heavy heart. He became the victim of his own spirit of inquiry, a fate I escaped only because of my insufficient thirst for knowledge" (Fortune, 2002, pp. 112–13). Groddeck's sense of relief at having escaped Ferenczi's fate is ironic, since he himself would die in less than four months, and during his final weeks he suffered a psychotic breakdown that brought him to Medard Boss's sanatorium outside Zurich, where he wrote appeals to Hitler (which were never mailed and have not been preserved) warning him against his anti-Semitic advisers and seeking his assistance in ridding Germany of cancer (Rudnytsky, 2002, p. 163).

Groddeck's contrast between Ferenczi's self-destructive "spirit of inquiry" and his own "insufficient thirst for knowledge" reprises his antithesis near the beginning of their relationship between their respective compulsions "to want to understand things" and "not to want to understand" them. As Groddeck put it to Gizella, he repeatedly tried "to point out the dangers" in Ferenczi's quest "to investigate the human cosmos scientifically," but was unable to stop him; and "however great our friendship, he had already left me far behind in his ascent to the stars, which I couldn't and wouldn't join" (Fortune, 2002, pp. 113–14). In a paradoxical reversal, by his commitment to science Ferenczi ended up being too mystical even for Groddeck, and in recognizing that he had been left "far behind" in his friend's "ascent to the stars" Groddeck unwittingly bequeathed Ferenczi to Severn, whose experience of abuse, in the words of the *Clinical Diary*, resulted not only in "regression of feelings to the embryonic" and "progression of intellect" but also in "the optical representation of a third kind of fragmentation": "the soul passes through a hole in the head into the universe and shines far off in the distance like a star (this would be clairvoyance, which goes beyond understanding the aggressor and understands the entire universe, so to speak, in order to be able to grasp the genesis of such a monstrous thing)" (Dupont, 1985, pp. 206–7).

Thompson's disillusionment with Ferenczi made her sharp-sighted concerning the defects in his character. As she explained to Eissler, Ferenczi "had something of the same attitude toward Groddeck as he had towards Freud—slightly contemptuous admiration for a powerful man" (1952a, p. 14). She continues: "I think at the time that Ferenczi was so involved with him there was also the element of fighting Freud in there; that Groddeck was sort of an antagonist to Freud, at least in Ferenczi's thinking. . . . But apparently Ferenczi always needed to have somebody as an authority beside him" (p. 15). Thompson is correct not only in saying that Groddeck functioned as an "antagonist to Freud" in Ferenczi's mind but also in her insight that Groddeck, too, despite the genuine affection that each felt for the other, nonetheless represented "an authority" for Ferenczi, so that his attitude toward both "powerful" men was a compound of "slightly contemptuous admiration." In a repetition of the pattern, when Severn became the principal magnet for Ferenczi's transference, "there was also the element of fighting" Groddeck mixed in, so that she inherited the place of authority—on the surface paternal but at a deeper level maternal—previously occupied in turn by Freud and Groddeck. Toward Severn, too, he experienced no small measure of ambivalence, even as they jointly ascended to the stars and became a twinned constellation in the psychoanalytic firmament.

Note

1 According to Falzeder (1996), "Ferenczi had three *tranches* of analysis with Freud during the First World War: the first started on October 1, 1914, and lasted for three and a half weeks; the second was from 14 June to 5 July 1916; and the third and last period was between 29 September and 13 October 1916" (p. 246).

Chapter 12
The Evil Genius

Apart from her starring role as R.N. in the *Clinical Diary*, Severn has hitherto been best known to posterity thanks to an oblique reference by Jones (1957) in the third volume of his Freud biography. At the conclusion of his chapter "Occultism," Jones regales his readers with an anecdote from "years ago" in which a lady living a hundred miles away requested that he "devote an hour a day to analyzing her in her absence." Jones reports that he declined with regret, then appends a postscript to his story: "But I should have been more than grieved had I known that just at that time my old friend Ferenczi believed he was successfully psychoanalyzed by messages transmitted telepathically across the Atlantic from an ex-patient of his—a woman Freud called 'Ferenczi's evil genius'" (p. 407).

This passage forms a centerpiece of Jones's propaganda campaign against his "old friend Ferenczi" by making him sound ridiculous, if not delusional, in believing himself to have been "successfully psychoanalyzed" at a distance not of a mere one hundred miles but "telepathically across the Atlantic." Freud does not refer to Severn as "Ferenczi's evil genius" in any of his extant writings, so the phrase must have been one Jones heard him use orally, but the mention of trans-Atlantic telepathy leaves no doubt as to the identity of this woman, whom Jones declines to name. He is drawing on Freud's letter of May 29, 1933 condoling with him on the news of his quondam analyst's death, an earlier portion of which I quoted in Chapter 9 with respect to Jones's publicizing of the narrative in which Ferenczi's "slow process of destruction" is alleged to have been going on "for years" and to have manifested itself not only "organically in pernicious anemia" but also through "a mental degeneration in the form of paranoia." Having diagnosed Ferenczi with paranoia, at the core of which was said to lie the "conviction that I did not love him enough, did not want to acknowledge his work, and also that I had analyzed him badly," Freud proceeds to round off his indictment:

> His technical innovations were connected with this, as he wanted to show me how lovingly one has to treat one's patients in order to help them. These were indeed regressions to his childhood complexes, the main grievance being that his mother had not loved him—a middle child among 11 or 13—passionately or exclusively enough. So he himself became a better mother, even found the children he needed, among them a suspect American woman to whom he often devoted 4–5 hours a day (Mrs. Severn?). After she had left, he believed that she influenced him though vibrations across the ocean, and said that she analyzed him and thereby saved him. (He thus played both roles, was mother and child.) She seems to have produced a *pseudologia phantastica*; he credited her with the oddest childhood traumas, which he then defended against us. In this confusion his once so brilliant intelligence was extinguished. But let us keep his sad end a secret between us.
>
> (Paskauskas, 1993, p. 721)

Uncannily, the anonymous reviewer's (1938) evisceration of *The Discovery of the Self* in *The Psychoanalytic Review* ends on the same note: "But why go on with this pseudologia phantastica-like product, nicely chocolate-coated for the children?" (p. 136). The appearance of the phrase "*pseudologia phantastica*," meaning far-fetched lies intended to impress others, in both Freud's letter to Jones and this condescending polemic, which may have been not only approved by Jelliffe as editor of the journal but actually written by him, is at least a striking coincidence. But since there is no mention of Severn either in Jelliffe's correspondence with Freud or in his correspondence with Jones between the years 1933 to 1937, we have no evidence that Jelliffe knew that Freud had already dismissed Severn's memories of the abuse perpetrated by her father in this fashion, so the recurrence of the epithet is more likely to be a reflection of their shared antipathy to Severn than to any direct—or even indirect—influence.[1]

It is equally noteworthy that Freud appends a question mark to his naming of "Mrs. Severn" as Ferenczi's "suspect American woman," since we know from Severn's interview with Eissler that she had met and spoken with him twice by 1933. That there remained a doubt in Freud's mind as to whether he had fingered the right culprit demonstrates not only the extent to which Severn was on her guard during their second conversation but, more crucially, how much Ferenczi had kept hidden from Freud during his final years. When one recalls the drumbeat of allusions to Severn in Ferenczi's letters to Groddeck, the paucity of her appearances in his letters to Freud speaks volumes. We first hear of her in the two previously cited letters of April 1925 when Ferenczi informs Freud that he has begun treating a patient whom Rank had analyzed in America. He does not name Severn on either occasion, but this is because she has just arrived in Budapest and Ferenczi attaches no particular importance to her beyond her role as a potential informant against Rank. Then, for the only time, in an undated letter in August 1925 she is named when Ferenczi reminds Freud of his agreement "to receive Dr. Severn, an American woman, whom I know as a capable psychologist and who is in analysis with me" (p. 225). This led to Severn's first visit to Freud, which, as we have seen, she told Eissler took place "a few months" after she had commenced her analysis with Ferenczi in 1925.

Thereafter, for all practical purposes, Severn disappears from the correspondence. This is not strictly true, since editorial annotations draw attention to three other allusions, all in 1930. In a pivotal letter of January 17, 1930, after beginning with a parapraxis by addressing Freud as "Dear Friend" instead of "Dear Professor," Ferenczi permits himself to voice his regret that Freud "did not comprehend and bring to abreaction in the analysis the partly only transferred, negative feelings and fantasies," and he gently chides Freud about "the strictness with which you punished my obstinate behavior in the matter of the Schreber book" (pp. 382–83). Ferenczi regrets that he is unable to come immediately to Vienna to discuss their differences because "a difficult case is tying me to Budapest," although he hopes that Freud "won't consider that an excuse" (p. 383). Then, on September 21, he announces a trip with Gizella to Baden-Baden and Paris, on which "a severe case has to go along," adding jocularly that "relaxation therapy is not very comfortable for the doctor" (p. 400). Upon arriving at Groddeck's, Ferenczi reports on October 11, "I am finally getting a rest after a hard year of work—although I had to take along a [female] patient" (p. 401; brackets in original). In all three instances, footnotes identify the patient for the reader as Severn, but she is otherwise absent from Ferenczi's letters.

Because it now seems obvious that Ferenczi is referring to Severn, it is easy to overlook that Freud would not have known that she was the "difficult case" in question or, by extension, have had any clue about Severn's place in Ferenczi's life and thought. By the same token, even when one is aware of Severn's prominence in the *Clinical Diary* it might be possible to conclude from Ferenczi's silence about her in his correspondence with Freud that she was not of great moment to him, at least until the end. But nothing could be further from the truth. Whereas the fact that Ferenczi does not name any of his patients other than Severn in his letters to Groddeck accurately reflects their subordinate status in comparison to the "Queen" of his psychoanalytic court, and thus carries no freight of psychic meaning, the omission of Severn's name after 1925 in Ferenczi's letters to Freud, combined with the nugatory hints of her existence, is indubitably tendentious. Severn is missing not because of her *in*significance to Ferenczi but because he is thinking about her all the time, and his silence attests to how much of what was going on in his inner world he felt that he needed to conceal from Freud.

As Severn (1952) reported to Eissler, when Ferenczi went to Vienna to put before Freud his ideas about analytic love and his conviction that analysts themselves should have a thorough analysis, he did so "without telling him that he had been analyzed by me" (p. 6). If Ferenczi sensed from the beginning that his work with Severn would not be well received by Freud and instinctively kept his own counsel about her, by the time they reached the stage of mutual analysis he had gone almost entirely "underground" and developed the "secret life" of a trauma therapist that, as we have seen, was replicated in Fodor's analytic apprenticeship with Severn. Freud's punitive response to hearing from Jackson about Ferenczi's "kissing technique" with Thompson—even though Ferenczi himself had courageously "made no secret" (Falzeder and Brabant, 2000, p. 422) about his permissiveness in this regard—could only have strengthened Ferenczi's conviction that he was doing the right thing by keeping his mouth shut about Severn.

In a letter of October 3, 1910, one month after the Palermo incident, Ferenczi reported a dream of seeing Freud standing naked before him and voiced the desire for a friendship based on "absolute mutual openness" (Brabant et al., 1993, p. 218). Ferenczi held out this hope—or clung to this fantasy—throughout their relationship. As late as February 14, 1930, as he dealt with the repercussions from having had the temerity to bring up Freud's neglect of the negative transference in his analysis and his pain at how Freud had treated him "in the matter of the Schreber book," Ferenczi explained that he felt obliged to contradict Freud only "on one point:

analytically open talking things out on no account means, in my view, that I am pressing you back into the role of the analyst and in so doing am relinquishing that of the tried-and-true friend. . . . I must admit that I would no longer feel good in the one-sided role of the analysand. Do you consider such mutual openness impossible?" (Falzeder and Brabant, 2000, p. 388).

Ferenczi's pleas, in both 1910 and 1930, for "mutual openness" came from the bottom of his heart. Had Freud been able to respond differently, Ferenczi would have wanted nothing more than to have an "analytically open talking things out" on a basis of equality and respect in which the two of them could speak freely about Severn and everything else. But this was not to be. Just as Freud's approbation depended on Ferenczi's adherence to his own version of Kardiner's (1977) "silent pact," "I will continue to be compliant provided that you will let me enjoy your protection" (p. 59), so when he tried to assert his independence Ferenczi was scolded in the same brutal fashion with which Freud quashed the skeptical rumblings of Joseph Wortis (1954) during their analytic sessions in 1934:

> You want to learn more about human nature (*Menschenkenntnis*) because you are ignorant and I am here to teach you. An analysis is not a chivalrous affair between two equals. . . . But you must learn to absorb things and not argue back. You must change that habit.
> (pp. 50, 114)

This attitude on Freud's part led Ferenczi to develop a "secret life," which after his death left Freud unsure whether Severn was indeed the "suspect American woman" who was mixed up in his "sad end." Jones, in turn, refused to name Severn as "Ferenczi's evil genius," although he knew perfectly well to whom Freud was referring. For Jones, Severn was a nonentity whose sole contribution to psychoanalytic history was to furnish him with a final nail to drive into Ferenczi's coffin. She was of even less consequence than de Forest, whose existence Jones had recognized when he cursorily dismissed *The Leaven of Love* in his review in the *International Journal*.

But though Freud was in doubt whether Severn was the patient who Ferenczi believed had "influenced him though vibrations across the ocean" in the immediate aftermath of his death, he had assuredly confirmed his suspicions by 1935, when he said to Blanton (1971) about "one of Ferenczi's pupils. . . 'She had, I'm afraid, a bad influence on Ferenczi'" (p. 65). In 1929, Freud had seemed pleased when he learned from Blanton that Clara

Thompson had been analyzed by Ferenczi; but in 1935, when Blanton (who had visited Ferenczi in 1930) asked Freud to explain "the kernel of his new idea," Freud replied with a reprise of the indictment he had furnished Jones two years earlier:

> "You cannot understand Ferenczi's method without understanding his whole history. He was one of eleven children. His mother was intelligent and efficient, but naturally she could not give this child much love. He could not be singled out. He was starved for love. That was his secret, which came out when he was analyzed by me. . . . Ferenczi tried to play the part of an overtender father, to give the love he himself had not received and to get love from his patients. That was his secret. He was ill for several years before his death. And during this illness, this tendency to give and get love, because of his childhood starved condition, came out."
>
> (p. 67)

Here Freud portrays Ferenczi as having tried to play the role of an "overtender father" with his surrogate children, instead of, as he put it to Jones, a "better mother," but his critique is otherwise identical.[2] Freud, who had himself been ill with cancer since 1923, again falsely states (as he did in his obituary) that Ferenczi "was ill for several years before his death," and he ascribes what he regards as Ferenczi's pathological "tendency to give and get love" with his patients, originating in Ferenczi's "childhood starved condition," to this supposed fact. But even if every word of what Freud said were true, not only is his tone callous but he reveals to one patient the "secret" of another, "which came out when he was analyzed by me." This betrayal of confidentiality, which stems from Freud's compulsion to discredit Ferenczi, is yet another boundary violation that is more serious than the worst possible construction one could put on Ferenczi's mutual analysis with Severn.

Jones's biography is the sole source for Freud's branding Severn as Ferenczi's "evil genius." But the epithet crops up elsewhere in his writings. In the case of the Rat Man, Freud (1909) describes how, when his obsessional patient would attempt to pray, "'May God protect him,' the Evil Spirit [*der böse Geist*] would hurriedly insinuate a 'not'" (p. 193).[3] Similarly, in the *New Introductory Lectures* (1933a), Freud states that religion represents an advance over animism in its "psychical binding of the fear of daemons," but "nevertheless a vestige of this primaeval age, the Evil

Spirit [*der böse Geist*], has kept a place in the religious system" (p. 166). The term goes back to Descartes' *Meditations* (1641), where the philosopher grounds his refutation of skepticism by hypothesizing the existence of a demonic counterpart to God whose sole purpose is to deceive him. Freud shows his familiarity with its provenance by citing the phrase "evil genius" (*mauvais génie*) in his letter to Maxime Leroy (1929, p. 204) on Descartes' dreams.

Given that the "Evil Spirit" or "Evil Genius" is a malevolent being, the moniker becomes especially pointed when Freud applies it to a specific person. Prior to attaching it to Severn, Freud had employed it to denounce "that evil genius," Alfred Hoche, professor of psychiatry at Freiburg and author of "A Psychical Epidemic among Doctors" (1910), in which Hoche had, as Freud put it in *On the History of the Psycho-Analytic Movement* (1914a), characterized his followers as "a fanatical sect blindly submissive to their leader," and who, during the 1913 Munich Congress, "by a malicious stroke of chance . . . had settled in the very hotel where the meetings were held" (p. 45). It is clear that the phrase haunted Freud's imagination and that he reserved it for those whom he regarded as his most contemptible enemies but who nonetheless posed a mortal threat to his own godlike sway over the psychoanalytic realm.

By calling Severn an "evil genius," therefore, Freud ascribes to her a great influence, as if he could not help recognizing the hold she exerted over Ferenczi's soul, over which the two of them were battling like good and bad angels. Indeed, both in his letter to Jones and to Blanton Freud sets forth his twin indictments of Ferenczi—his "technical innovations," which Freud regarded narcissistically as an attempt to prove to *him* "how lovingly one has to treat one's patients in order to help them," and Ferenczi's willingness to believe in the reality of even the "oddest childhood traumas, which he then defended against *us*," that is, himself and his disciples who fell in line behind his repudiation of the "seduction theory." Nor does Freud hesitate to give Ferenczi's heretical deviations an *ad hominem* interpretation. Inasmuch as it was through his partnership with Severn that Ferenczi elaborated his trauma theory and took to the limit his modifications of standard technique, Freud was right to single out this "suspect American woman" as his greatest antagonist in the struggle not simply over Ferenczi but over the future direction of psychoanalysis. Only now, when the sounds of the silence in which this story has been shrouded can at last be heard, is it possible for Severn's shade to arise from the underworld and shake the Olympian powers.

Notes

1 I am grateful to Bruce Kirby, reference librarian at the Manuscript Division of the Library of Congress, for examining Jelliffe's correspondence with Jones during the relevant years on my behalf.
2 In the "kissing technique" letter itself, Freud had warned Ferenczi "from the brutal fatherly side" against his inclination "to play the tender motherly role with others," namely, his patients (Falzeder and Brabant, 2000, p. 423).
3 I have amended Strachey's translation, "an evil spirit," to "the Evil Spirit," as Freud in German uses the definite article, which makes it clear that he intends a personification.

Part 3

Consequences

Chapter 13

For No Assignable External Reason

1

In response to Ferenczi's letter of January 17, 1930, in which he stated that he was "especially sorry" that his analysis could not be completed because Freud "did not comprehend and bring to abreaction . . . the partially only transferred, negative feelings and fantasies," adding that concern for Freud's health had kept him from "communicating certain reservations which I began to harbor in relation to the one-sidedness in the development of psychoanalysis" (Falzeder and Brabant, 2000, pp. 382–83), Freud on January 20 professed himself to be "amused by some passages of your confession," to wit, "when you reproach me for having neglected the foreseeable negative reactions in your analysis." That undertaking, Freud reminded Ferenczi, "goes back fifteen years," to a time when there was as yet no evidence of such "inimical impulses" as might have endangered their "excellent relationship" (pp. 385–86).

For good measure, addressing Ferenczi's acknowledgment that he had "withdrawn somewhat from the common field of work" due to "disgruntlement about the behavior of Brill and Jones" (p. 383), Freud opined that these protests were attributable to Ferenczi's "presumed slighting" at having been passed over at the Oxford Congress, where he had delivered "The Principle of Relaxation and Neocatharsis," in favor of Eitingon for the presidency of the International Psychoanalytical Association. This affront, according to Freud, "reactivated the remnants of your earlier neurosis," including the "brother complex" that Ferenczi had so "brilliantly corrected" as "leader of the Budapest group," but which still caused him to be unduly sensitive "to the rudeness of the 'brothers'" (p. 386) on the international scene. Finally, because Ferenczi had said he did not share Freud's view "that the process of healing is an unimportant procedure, or one that should be neglected" (p. 383), Freud admitted that "my patience with

DOI: 10.4324/9781315280134-17

neurotics runs out in analysis, and that in life I am inclined to intolerance toward them," before concluding with the observation that by connecting their current "ill feeling" with what had happened in his analysis Ferenczi had "pressed me back into the role of the analyst, which I would otherwise not have reassumed vis-à-vis the tried and true friend" (pp. 385–86), and expressing renewed curiosity about his Oxford lecture, which Freud had not yet seen.

As in a biopsy, everything that ails the Freud–Ferenczi relationship in the crucial final installment that extends from the 11th Congress of the International Psychoanalytical Association in Oxford in July 1929 to the 12th Congress in Wiesbaden in September 1932, and its aftermath, can be diagnosed in this epistolary exchange. On the one hand, we see Ferenczi tentatively putting forth his new ideas, defending his commitment to psychoanalysis as a "process of healing," even reporting "with joy that precisely here a whole series of questions is apparently moved into a different, sharper light, perhaps even the problem of repression!" (p. 383)—an intimation of his insights concerning dissociation in trauma—and struggling to voice his criticisms of Freud on a personal level in the face of his paralyzing fear of Freud's disapproval. On the other hand, Freud not only refuses to take seriously (or even hear) anything Ferenczi is saying, whether about psychoanalytic theory and technique or about the dynamics of their interaction; he also resorts to the tactic of "psychoanalyzing" Ferenczi by interpreting his complaints about his analysis or the "strictness" with which Freud had "punished" him over the Schreber case as symptoms of his "neurosis." Under such circumstances, when one party to a disagreement takes no interest in trying to understand why the other feels the way he does, no genuine dialogue is possible, and this is the basic condition that governs the Freud–Ferenczi stalemate, as is demonstrated time and again by their correspondence as well as by Freud's continued polemics against Ferenczi after his death.

Even in his obituary for Ferenczi, in which Freud (1933b) puts the best possible face on things, he not only rued that Ferenczi had "slowly drifted away from us" after his "summit of achievement" in *Thalassa*, passing over in silence his later writings, and claimed that "a grave organic destructive process" had "probably overshadowed his life for many years already," but he also pathologized Ferenczi's "need to cure and to help" by alleging that it arose "from unexhausted springs of emotion" that had induced him to believe that "one could effect far more with one's patients if one gave them enough of the love which they had longed for as children" (p. 229). As with Freud's allegation concerning Ferenczi's longstanding "destructive process," this explanation of Ferenczi's therapeutic zeal as the byproduct of "unexhausted springs of emotion" constitutes a muted echo of what he had written to Jones (and would tell Blanton) about how Ferenczi's "technical innovations" were "regressions to his childhood complexes, the main grievance being that his mother had not loved him—a middle child among 11 or 13—passionately or exclusively enough" (Paskauskas, 1993, p. 721).

Without explicitly saying so, Freud conveys the impression in the obituary that Ferenczi's efforts in his final period ended in failure. According to Freud (1933b), Ferenczi had "probably set himself aims which, with our therapeutic means, are altogether out of reach today"—which assumes that Ferenczi's "therapeutic means" were identical with Freud's—and he asserts that "wherever it may have been that the road he had started would have led him, he could not pursue it to the end" (p. 229). It is, of course, true that Ferenczi died before having reached his sixtieth birthday, but that is a very different matter from saying that his work was broken off before he had arrived at a rigorously elaborated and profoundly integrated vision of psychoanalysis that differed in essential respects from Freud's own.

That Ferenczi's contributions to psychoanalysis were grounded in personal experience—both in his "childhood complexes" and in his quarter-century agon with Freud—is not something that he himself would have disputed. In the aforementioned letter of January 17, 1930, for example, he says with respect to their conflict twenty years earlier in Sicily over the Schreber case that he appreciates that Freud "wanted to travel with a healthy person and not with a neurotic" (Falzeder and Brabant, 2000, p. 383). Freud's conviction that Ferenczi's "main grievance" was that he had been deprived of love by his mother is likewise anticipated in Ferenczi's Christmas-day 1921 letter to Groddeck, where he begins his self-analysis by describing his pose of "aloof reticence" as "a regression to the infantile," and continues: "Did I want too much attention, or was my mother—the mother of 11 surviving children, of which I was the 8th—too strict? As I remember it, I certainly didn't get enough love, and did get too much severity from her as a child" (Fortune, 2002, pp. 8–9).

Just as with his fatal illness, therefore, where, in Bonomi's (1999) words, Ferenczi "would not have rejected" Freud's interpretation of its psychological dimension but "would have enriched it with further meanings . . . in conformity with the principle of mutuality, as opposed to one-sided analysis" (p. 518), so he would have endorsed the premise that his intellectual creativity could be traced to biographical roots. But he would have offered two caveats. The first is that, whatever might be said about their subjective—and even neurotic—origins, his ideas deserved to be judged on their own merits. In a letter of July 20, 1930, Ferenczi acknowledged that his "exaggerated fearfulness" that Freud would not approve of his "reactionary tendency" to "freshen up the apparently antiquated (at least temporarily cast aside) trauma theory" goes "far back into the infantile" (Falzeder and Brabant, 2000, p. 396). (Ferenczi's self-deprecating reference to his ideas as "reactionary" constitutes an attempt to placate Freud.) He further concedes that "my relationship to you and to the colleagues in the Association is in many respects rooted in father and brother bonds." But he goes on immediately thereafter to assert, "I have the feeling that my, perhaps here also subjectively colored, investigations can also lay claim to a certain objective value."

Similarly, after Freud, in a notably cruel letter of September 18, 1931, bluntly informed Ferenczi that his "inner dissatisfaction" was causing him "to press forward in all kinds of directions which to me seem to lead to no desirable end," and speculated that he could be undergoing a "third puberty," Ferenczi responded with consummate dignity on October 10: "Let us assume that the diagnosis is correct: the value of what is created in this condition should for the moment be judged objectively" (p. 419). He went on to ask, "Do you consider it out of the question that . . . I will be able to produce something that is practically or even theoretically useful?" He reiterated on December 5 that, "above all, the investigation should be predicated on whether the things I have observed are true and whether their interpretation by me is correct," adding that he would "endeavor to keep such purely personal motives (being insulted, infantile rebellion, etc.) in check," but that "it is still possible that some of what I am now experiencing in the analyses also has objective validity" (p. 421).

Ferenczi's second caveat can be summed up in Dostoevsky's apothegm from *The Brothers Karamazov*, which Freud (1928a) himself was fond of quoting, that psychology is "a knife that cuts both ways" (p. 189). In other words, if, as Freud said to Blanton (1971), "'You cannot understand Ferenczi's method without understanding his whole history'" (p. 6), then the same must hold true for Freud. Because of his "exaggerated fearfulness," Ferenczi could not bring himself to give Freud a dose of his own medicine in their correspondence, reserving his psychoanalytic reflections on Freud's character, and how it impacted his theories, for the private pages of the *Clinical Diary*. But the principle is clear, and Ferenczi at least managed to get the point across in his January 17, 1930 letter when, after acknowledging that Freud must have wanted "to travel with a healthy person and not with a neurotic," he posed the follow-up question, "But do you believe that there are people without character difficulties?" (Falzeder and Brabant, 2000, p. 383).

2

When Freud rebuffed Ferenczi's expressions of disappointment about his analysis, he claimed to be "amused" by the notion that he had "neglected the foreseeable negative reactions." This is, however, disingenuous in the extreme. That Freud, on the contrary, felt seriously aggrieved by Ferenczi's protest can be seen by the way it continued to rankle in his disguised clinical vignette in "Analysis Terminable and Interminable" (1937a) about "a certain man, who had himself practiced analysis with great success" (p. 221), Freud's most revealing engagement with his memories of Ferenczi during the final six years that separated the younger man's death from his own.

In Freud's synopsis, because of "neurotic impediments" in his relationships with both men and women, the patient in question entered analysis with someone "whom he regarded as superior to himself" (p. 221). What Freud depicts not as a therapeutic experience but as "this "critical illumination of his own self" had, he claims, "a completely successful result," as shown by the facts that the patient "married the woman he loved and turned into a friend and teacher of his supposed rivals." Here Freud is referring to Ferenczi's marriage to Gizella Pálos in 1919 and his presumed overcoming of what they both understood to be Ferenczi's "brother complex" with respect to his male colleagues in the psychoanalytic movement. But this rosy narrative leaves out the inconvenient truth that Ferenczi had been, as Freud knew full well, in love with Gizella's daughter Elma and only made the decision to renounce the daughter in favor of the mother under pressure from Freud himself, and that he remained conflicted about his choice for many years thereafter. Thus, the representation that Ferenczi's "analysis"—amounting, let us not forget, to a total of nine weeks in 1914 and 1916—was "completely successful" cannot be taken seriously by anyone acquainted with the realities of Ferenczi's life.

What is agitating Freud becomes clear when he turns his attention to his own relationship with Ferenczi. As he tells the story, Ferenczi's attitude toward his "former analyst"—that is, himself—"remained unclouded" for "many years." "But then," he continues, "for no assignable external reason, trouble arose. The man who had been analysed became antagonistic to the analyst and reproached him for having failed to give him a complete analysis," above all because the analyst "should have given his attention to the possibility of a negative transference" (p. 221). This is, of course, the nub of Ferenczi's reproach in his January 17, 1930 letter, which wounded Freud so deeply that he felt obliged to mount a defense seven years later against a criticism that Ferenczi had never voiced publicly. The essence of Freud's apologia is that the "trouble" between the two of them arose "for no assignable external reason"—not, that is, as a result of anything he himself might have done, but due solely to internal processes, presumably of a neurotic nature, which had caused Ferenczi to become "antagonistic" toward his blameless physician.

This one-sided attitude on Freud's part, which foreclosed the possibility of any genuine dialogue or understanding with Ferenczi, recurs throughout their correspondence. A prototypical instance, early in the period we are considering, occurs after Ferenczi, on November 6, 1929, calls attention to "the extreme sparseness and apparent flimsiness of my correspondence," saying that his attention has shifted away from "the psychoanalytic movement (and politics)" and toward "purely scientific problems," and that "a product of this change was the Oxford lecture" (Falzeder and Brabant, 2000, p. 372). Ferenczi acknowledges that his "life drive" may have reacted to a comment made by Freud about his "*premature senility*" with "defiance and contradiction" by throwing "itself zealously upon unsolved problems of psychoanalysis," although he pleads with Freud to consider whether this may be "a case not only of such reaction formation, but also of the reexperiencing of long-repressed intellectual and other strivings, which could also contain and produce something really valuable."

In his response on December 13, Freud tells Ferenczi he does not remember ever having said he looked "prematurely senile," and, after observing that "you have doubtless outwardly distanced yourself from me in the last few years," he goes on to bestow a title that has since become famous: "Inwardly, I hope, not so far that a step toward the creation of a new oppositional analysis might be expected from you, my paladin and secret Grand Vizier" (pp. 373–74). Freud simultaneously elevates Ferenczi by calling him his "paladin and secret Grand Vizier" and warns him against doing anything that might lead to "the creation of a new oppositional analysis." Ferenczi's "intellectual and other strivings" are affirmed insofar as they conform to Freud's conception of psychoanalysis, but as soon as they take him in an independent direction they are stigmatized as "oppositional." Freud thus places Ferenczi in a double bind, at once elevating him to a position of special favor and holding him down by not allowing him to go his own way. Even the seemingly honorific designation "paladin and secret Grand Vizier" casts Ferenczi as inherently subordinate to Freud, who, as the head of the Secret Committee, is paradoxically at once the Christian emperor Charlemagne (with his twelve "paladins") and the Muslim Turkish sultan, both of whom bestowed rings on the highest officials of their respective realms.[1]

Freud again places Ferenczi in a double bind in his "third puberty" letter of September 18, 1931, where he says that his disciple's innovations will "lead to no desirable end." Having just heard from Ferenczi for the first time in three months, Freud's first key move is to comment: "There is no doubt that with this interruption of contact you are distancing yourself from me more and more. I say, and hope not: alienating. I accept it as fate—like so many other things; I know that I am not personally to blame for it; in recent times I also preferred no one else to you" (Falzeder and Brabant, 2000, p. 418). Just as he will do again in "Analysis Terminable and Interminable," Freud portrays Ferenczi's "distancing" as solely a function of his intrapsychic conflicts, not as a response to tensions arising in their intersubjective field. Indeed, Freud ascribes Ferenczi's withdrawal to "fate" and claims to "know" that he is "not personally to blame for it." In seeming to negate the possibility that Ferenczi is "alienating" himself, Freud summons this specter, and he contrives to add to Ferenczi's burden of guilt (and his "brother complex") by assuring him that he has "preferred no one else" to him "in recent times," that is, since the defection of Rank.

In the ensuing paragraph, Freud tells Ferenczi, "But I have . . . always respected your independence and am prepared to wait until you yourself take steps to turn around" (p. 418). These are again contradictory messages. On the one hand, Ferenczi's "independence" is purportedly being "respected." On the other, the only outcome Freud is able to envision with equanimity is that Ferenczi will realize he is headed in the wrong direction and "take steps to turn around" and return to the fold. Seeking to bind Ferenczi to him with the fetters of official recognition, Freud ends by simultaneously tugging at his heartstrings and appealing to his vanity: "But I definitely have to deal with the next, for me, perhaps last, president of the IPA."

After the chastisement of the "third puberty" letter comes the icy blast of Freud's attack on Ferenczi's "kissing technique." Responding to Ferenczi's assertions on December 5 that some of his clinical findings may have "objective validity" and that "honesty obliges me to say that, *up to now*, I don't feel called upon to change *anything essential*," Freud, armed with what he had heard from Edith Jackson about Ferenczi's analysis of Clara Thompson, lets loose on December 13: "If you were unable to decide on any change in your position up to now, then it is certainly very improbable that you will do it later. But that is essentially your affair; my opinion that you have not embarked on any fruitful path is a private matter that doesn't need to disturb you" (pp. 421–22). For Freud, the only one who needs to "change position" is Ferenczi; it is literally inconceivable that he himself might benefit from a modicum of self-criticism. The statement that it "need not disturb" Ferenczi if Freud believes he has "not embarked upon any fruitful path" is yet another double bind, since Freud knows that his opinion is of the utmost importance to Ferenczi, and he hammers it home with insinuations that Ferenczi is seeking "erotic gratifications" from his patients. The metaphor of a "third puberty," which Freud had earlier used to suggest that his fifty-eight-year-old colleague had not yet "reached maturity" (p. 418), now takes on its full erotic meaning as Freud directly impugns Ferenczi's character: "the inclination toward sexual games [*Spielerei*] with patients was not alien to you in pre-analytic times, so that one could put the new technique into context with the old misdemeanor" (p. 423).

Rather than retaliate against Freud, Ferenczi on December 27 once again responds with exemplary dignity and humility. Not denying that he was guilty of youthful "misdemeanors," he says that they have been "overcome and analytically worked through" so that he is now "capable of creating a mild, passionless atmosphere" (p. 424). Above all, he shows himself prepared to engage in the self-criticism that is sorely lacking in Freud, "But since I fear the dangers just as much as you do, I must and will, now as before, keep in mind the warnings you reproach me with, and strive to criticize myself harshly."

3

This brings us to the end of 1931 and, as we turn the calendar, to the year of the *Clinical Diary*—instigated, as we have seen, both by Ferenczi's "broken dialogue" with Freud over his analysis of Thompson and by the inception of his mutual analysis with Severn—as well as of the Wiesbaden Congress. Whether or not Ferenczi will accept the presidency of the

International Psychoanalytical Association remains a central question. The fact that this discussion unfolds with no mention of Ferenczi's health is further proof that, contrary to what Freud wrote in his obituary, no "grave organic destructive process" had "overshadowed his life" through the first eight months of 1932. Annoyed by Ferenczi's vacillations, Freud on May 5, 1932 states that he "would like to insist on" the presidency for him, arguing that assuming the office would "have the effect on you of a drastic measure," much like issuing an edict to a patient or announcing the end of an analysis in the "active technique," which would pull Ferenczi out of "the isolation which you had so brilliantly overcome as a teacher and leader in Budapest" and restore him to his rightful "role as leader" (Falzeder and Brabant, 2000, p. 433) in the psychoanalytic movement. He concludes his attempt at manipulation in especially odious fashion, "But you should leave the island of dreams which you inhabit with your fantasy children and mix in with the struggle of men."

By Ferenczi's "fantasy children," Freud means his patients, who served as substitutes for the biological children Ferenczi never had. To use Ferenczi's childlessness as a weapon against him, when Freud himself was the father of six, was a low blow indeed, just as it was to mock Ferenczi for inhabiting an "island of dreams." On a superficial level, Freud flatters Ferenczi and dangles before him the lure of a high honor, but in actuality he is belittling Ferenczi's ideas as worthless and accusing him of being infantile unless he renounces his devotion to therapy in his Budapest enclave and gives himself over instead to psychoanalytic administration and politics, which Freud equates with taking part in the "struggle of men."

To this onslaught Ferenczi responds on May 19 with characteristic mildness, simply questioning Freud's use of expressions such as "dream-life" and "puberty crisis," while asserting his own belief that "out of the confusion something useful will develop and has already developed," and demurring to the extent of saying that he "can't conceive of the presidency as a drastic measure against an illness which I don't actually recognize as such" (p. 435). Nonetheless, he concludes by informing Freud that, if he is permitted to "continue my present manner of working" and can count on the "active assistance of Anna and the two vice presidents," he will "consider it an honor also to stand for once as president of the society on the founding of which I collaborated and in the activity of which I actively participated for a long time."[2]

Having gained his point, one would think that Freud would be gratified and immediately write to congratulate Ferenczi on his decision. Not only is no such accolade forthcoming, but in the letters of the next three months, which revert to routine matters, the topic of the presidency is not mentioned by either of them. The final reversal, the prelude to Ferenczi's disastrous last visit to Vienna en route to Wiesbaden, occurs in Ferenczi's letter of August 21, 1932. "After long, anguished hesitation," he announces to Freud, "I have decided to renounce my candidacy for the presidency" (p. 441). By way of explanation, he avers that in his effort to conduct his analyses "more deeply and more effectively" he has "gotten into decidedly critical and self-critical waters, which seem to necessitate not only extensions but also corrections of our practical and, in part, also our theoretical views." Such an "intellectual constitution," he continues, "is on no account commensurate with the dignity of a president whose main concern should be conserving and consolidating what already exists, and my inner feeling tells me that it would not even be honest to occupy this position."

To Ferenczi himself, Freud replied three days later in seemingly unruffled fashion, but his true feelings are evident in a letter dispatched that same day to Eitingon, his supremely loyal IPA president since 1927, where he fumed:

> One will scarcely be deceived in presuming that he will go the way of Rank. Perhaps he is considerate enough to wait until I am not around any more; if I am difficult to kill, I will live through it myself. He is in full neurotic regression: enmity with father and brothers, mother-child hanky-panky with his patients. Too bad! But if only I could have lived through one case of theoretical deviation without prior personal motivation! With Fer[enczi] I am for once completely innocent.
> (Schröter, 2004, 2:822)

The motif of Ferenczi as a second Rank who may be "considerate enough to wait" for Freud to die to carry out his treacherous betrayal, but who is no less consumed with murderous desires, is on full display here. Freud diagnoses Ferenczi as being in "full neurotic regression," the proof of which lies in his declining of the presidency, complete with "enmity" toward his psychoanalytic "father and brothers" and "mother-child hanky-panky with his patients," a combined reference to his supposed "sexual games" with Thompson and to his disposition to play the good mother with his "fantasy children." Above all, Freud asserts that he himself is "completely innocent" and has no death wishes toward anyone, whereas Ferenczi's "theoretical deviation" can only be explained by his "prior personal motivation."

After Ferenczi's renunciation of the presidency, the story ends with his Wiesbaden lecture and death eight months later. Again, Freud's visceral response to hearing "Confusion of Tongues" is revealed in his letters to those on whom he could count for solidarity. On the day of their meeting in Vienna, September 2, 1932, Freud telegraphed Eitingon, "Ferenczi lecture read aloud harmless stupid otherwise inaccessible impression unpleasant" (Schröter, 2004, 2:829). The following day, he wrote in greater detail to Anna, who was already in Wiesbaden:

> He has made a complete regression to etiological views that I believed and renounced 35 years ago, that gross sexual traumas of childhood are the regular cause of neuroses . . . including therein remarks on the hostility of patients and the necessity to accept their criticism and to confess one's errors to them. The conclusions are confused, unmistakably overblown. The whole thing is really stupid, or so it appears, because it is so insincere and incomplete. . . . It's the same as with Rank, only much sadder.[3]
>
> (qtd. 2:829; ellipses in original)

To Jones, who had just assumed the presidency of the International Psychoanalytical Association in Ferenczi's stead, Freud wrote on September 12:

> To be sure, Ferenczi's change is most regrettable, but there is nothing traumatic about it. For three years already I have been observing his increasing alienation, his unreceptiveness to warnings about his technical errors, and what is probably most crucial, a personal hostility toward me for which I have certainly given him even less cause than in previous cases. Except perhaps for the fact that I am still here.
>
> (Paskauskas, 1993, pp. 708–9)

Whether Freud might have responded differently had Ferenczi not disappointed him in the matter of the presidency is impossible to determine. As it is, however, "Confusion of Tongues," now hailed as one of the landmarks in the history of psychoanalysis, is dismissed by Freud as "really stupid" and, what is more, "insincere and incomplete." He reiterates his view that Ferenczi is staging a rerun of Rank's defection, "only much sadder," since he himself has given "even less cause" for Ferenczi's "personal hostility" and "increasing alienation," apart from "the fact that I am still here." Freud again maintains, in other words, that he has frustrated

Ferenczi's murderous fantasies by stubbornly refusing to die. On the theoretical plane, Freud has no doubt that Ferenczi is guilty of a "complete regression" to obsolete views about trauma, while in his clinical work he is deaf to Freud's "warnings about his technical errors." For some bizarre reason, according to Freud, Ferenczi thinks it advisable to take seriously the "hostility of patients," to "accept their criticism," and, worst of all, to "confess one's errors to them." In short, there is "nothing traumatic" about "Ferenczi's change," a denial by Freud that this turn of events has had a traumatic effect on him, just as Freud is convinced he has done nothing to instigate it because Ferenczi's "increasing alienation" is due exclusively to his internal conflicts.

Toward Ferenczi himself, only in his letter of October 2, 1932, one month after the event, does Freud lash out with the full force of his wrath. On September 27, as we have seen, Ferenczi had written to Freud to register the "depth of the shock" left in him by their conversation in Vienna, which manifested itself in the "bodily ailments" that transformed what was supposed to be a holiday trip to Baden-Baden and the south of France into "a voyage de lit-à-lit." He likewise specified that what had affected him "in so painful a fashion" was "less the substance of the scientific differences" between them than the "two seemingly extraneous facts" that Freud had brought in Brill, "who doesn't deserve to be a judge between us," to witness their interaction, and that he had asked Ferenczi to "refrain from publication" of his paper (Falzeder and Brabant, 2000, pp. 443–44).

To be fair, even after Ferenczi had received his diagnosis of pernicious anemia from Lévy, neither he nor Freud could have known the gravity of his illness. As late as December 14, Ferenczi reports "favorable things" about his health, including that the "number and shape of the cellular blood components is normal again" (p. 445), and Freud had no reason to worry that Ferenczi's "bodily ailments" might endanger his life. Hence, it is comprehensible that he should have failed to inquire about Ferenczi's condition, and only the suddenness of Ferenczi's demise lends Freud's letter of October 2 its tragic pall. Still, it makes grim reading and illustrates with consummate clarity Freud's refusal to engage in any genuine dialogue with Ferenczi as well as the degree to which he is blinded by narcissistic rage.

Freud begins by defending himself against Ferenczi's "reproach" concerning Brill, pointing out that Brill came in after Ferenczi had begun reading his paper and that Ferenczi had already "talked with him about the same thing a few days before," so there was no question of Freud's having ascribed to Brill "the role of a judge" (p. 444). So far, Freud's vindication seems fair enough. But he becomes less credible when he informs Ferenczi about his own conversation with Brill: "I also knew from him that you don't credit me with more insight than a little boy. [Just as Rank did, back then]" (brackets in original). It it difficult to imagine that Ferenczi, who distrusted Brill, would have spoken to him thus derogatorily about Freud. As the association to Rank confirms, the idea that Ferenczi accused him of having no "more insight than a little boy" is more likely to have been Freud's own projection. He does concede that he and Brill "had a common interest" in seeing to it that Ferenczi's lecture, which was to open the Wiesbaden Congress, would "not produce a sensation," and Freud likewise contends that his "request" that Ferenczi defer publication of his paper "for another year was predominantly in your interest," though, he adds, "I naturally relieve you of your promise" (pp. 444–45).[4]

Even if one gives Freud the benefit of the doubt, his attitude is paternalistic inasmuch as he tells Ferenczi that his paper is an embarrassment and that he knows better than Ferenczi himself what is in his best interest. Freud states that he "didn't want to give up hope that in your continued work you would still recognize yourself the technical impropriety of your procedure and the limited correctness of your results," but now "I don't any longer believe that you will rectify yourself, the way I rectified myself a generation earlier" (p. 445). Ferenczi, therefore, has been written off as hopeless, which leads Freud to say he will "forgo any influence, which I don't possess anyway." But in reality, as can be seen in the final entry to the *Clinical Diary*, written the same day as Freud's letter, Freud's "higher power" continued to loom so large in Ferenczi's mind that he held it responsible for his "blood-crisis," and Freud's claim to forgo the influence he no longer possesses is a form of emotional blackmail stemming from his anger and feeling of helplessness at having—as he mistakenly supposed—been rejected by Ferenczi.

The most devastating portion of Freud's October 2 letter, however, is the third and final paragraph:

> For three years you have been systematically turning away from me, probably developed a personal hostility that goes further than it could express itself. Each of those who were once near to me and then fell away was able to find more to reproach me with than you, of all people. [No, Rank just as little.] The traumatic effect dissipates in me, I am prepared, and used to it. Objectively, I think I would be in a position

to point out to you the theoretical error in your construction, but for what? I am convinced you would not be accessible to any doubts. So, there is nothing left for me but to wish you the best, which would be very different from what is going on at present.

(p. 445; brackets in original)

Again, as in a biopsy at a more advanced stage of the disease, everything is visible here. Freud's reference to "three years" echoes his statement to Jones that he had been observing Ferenczi's "increasing alienation" for "three years already," and it traces the origin of their estrangement back to 1929 and the Oxford Congress paper, where Ferenczi for the first time comprehensively laid out the new directions in his thinking. In another refrain of his September 12 letter to Jones, Freud directly accuses Ferenczi of harboring a "personal hostility" toward him of inexpressible proportions. Ferenczi's "falling away" is assimilated by Freud to all the prior betrayals by his faithless disciples, and he again affirms it to be comparable only to that of Rank in being utterly gratuitous. Thus, Freud says, the "traumatic effect dissipates" in him, since he is so "used to it" that such acts of treachery no longer have any power to wound him emotionally.

In his closing sentences, Freud claims to be able to point out "objectively" to Ferenczi "the theoretical error in your construction," thus denying his own subjectivity and equating his side of their argument with the truth. Yet, Freud shrugs, what would be the purpose of such an exercise since he is "convinced" that Ferenczi "would not be accessible to any doubts"? Thus, all that is left is for Freud to "wish you the best," which is tantamount to telling Ferenczi not to let the door hit him in the rear as he leaves the room.

To invoke a diagnostic category Freud repeatedly used against his opponents, most notably Fliess and Adler, this is classic paranoid thinking. Let us heed Freud's (1905a) own words in the Dora case:

A string of reproaches against other people leads one to suspect the existence of a string of self-reproaches with the same content. All that need be done is to turn back each reproach on to the speaker himself.... In paranoia the projection of a reproach on to another person without any alteration in its content and therefore without any consideration for reality becomes manifest as the process of forming delusions.

(p. 35)

The evidence is clear. It is not Ferenczi who is "not accessible to any doubts" or unwilling to entertain the possibility that there may be a "theoretical error" in his "construction." Nor is it Ferenczi who is driven by "a personal hostility that goes further than it could express itself," or Ferenczi who does not credit Freud with having any "more insight than a little boy." No, "all that need be done is to turn back each reproach on to the speaker himself," and they have collectively so little "consideration for reality" that they may justifiably be called "delusions."

4

According to Peter Hoffer (2010) in his commentary on the disagreement between Freud and Ferenczi, "there was little sign of serious discord between them as late as February 1930" (p. 92), and "a dramatic shift in Freud's position appears to have occurred" (p. 94) in the fall of 1931. This reading of the correspondence is in the service of Hoffer's argument that Freud's "negative reaction" to "Confusion of Tongues," and to the work of Ferenczi's final period in general, "was not in response to its assertion of the reality of infantile trauma, or the prevalence of sexual abuse of children by adults, but rather to the technical measures that Ferenczi employed in the pursuit of that reality" (p. 102). But this is a false dichotomy, as can be seen by Freud's letters to Jones and Anna about the Wiesbaden Congress, as well as to Ferenczi himself, where he rails with equal vehemence against Ferenczi's "technical errors," on the one hand, and his "complete regression to etiological views that I believed and renounced 35 years ago," on the other.[5] For both Freud and Ferenczi, the issues of "the reality of infantile trauma" and of the "technical measures" to be employed by the psychoanalyst constituted two sides of the same coin, and Freud was equally offended by Ferenczi's heresies on both counts.

Indeed, in an earlier letter to Eitingon, on August 29, relaying what he had just heard from Brill and Sándor Radó about their visit with Ferenczi in Budapest, Freud makes it clear that he rejects the pursuit of historical reality and considers the alleged memories of Ferenczi's patients to be nothing more than fantasies stimulated by his faulty technique:

> His source is what the patients say, when he by happenstance transports them, as he himself says, into a hypnosis-like condition. Then he considers that to be the revelation, but what one thereby obtains are the patients' fantasies about their childhood, not history. My first

great etiological error arose in just this way. The patients suggest to him, then he turns it around. A regression to his earlier neurosis as a consequence of aging, I maintain, going on with him for years.

(Schröter, 2004, 2:826)

Not only does Freud regard Ferenczi's technique as inseparable from his theoretical blunder, and object to them both with equal vehemence, but, as is his custom, he interprets Ferenczi's going off the rails in *ad hominem* fashion, as "a regression to his earlier neurosis . . . going on with him for years."

There is, of course, a diachronic aspect to the unfolding of events in the Freud-Ferenczi relationship, a story in which things can be seen progressively to deteriorate over time. There are also periodic efforts to repair the ruptures, as when Freud recalls for Ferenczi, on January 11, 1933, how they have for years enjoyed "an intimate community of life, feeling, and interest," although even here—as we have seen in the Prelude—he cannot refrain from adding that he can now only "conjure this up from memory" while finding consolation in "the certainty" that he has "contributed especially little to this change" and "some psychological misfortune or other has brought it about in you" (Falzeder and Brabant, 2000, p. 446). Hoffer's thesis about a "dramatic shift" in late 1931 does find support to the extent that, in the previously quoted letter of December 5, following a visit to Vienna, Ferenczi alludes to their having had "such a far-reaching and first-time examination of the differences in our views" (p. 421), while, after being bludgeoned by Freud concerning his "kissing technique," he elaborates on December 27, "perhaps it is happening for the first time that factors of not being in agreement are mixing into our relationship in general" (p. 424).

Thus, there is a clear drop-off in late 1931, just as there is a further exacerbation a year later over Ferenczi's declining of the IPA presidency and his Wiesbaden paper. But Hoffer's notion that "there was little sign of serious discord" between Freud and Ferenczi prior to February 1930 overlooks the numerous red flags in earlier letters. These include Ferenczi's distress at Freud's comment about his "*premature senility*," Freud's apotropaic denial that Ferenczi would be capable of creating "a new oppositional analysis," and Ferenczi's protest that Freud had neglected to analyze his negative transference, about which Freud professed to be "amused" once his "trace of annoyance" (p. 385) had dissipated. There is, likewise, Ferenczi's letter of December 25, 1929, in which he admits that his "intention to reply" to Freud "has to struggle with resistances," and that he has "suppressed something for which I didn't think I could expect any agreement or proper understanding on your part" (p. 375). To go back even further, as early as January 30, 1924, in response to a letter in which Freud criticized a lecture Ferenczi had given to the Vienna Psychoanalytic Society containing a portion of *The Development of Psycho-Analysis* as "very strange" and a "derailment in the long-abandoned tracks of the brother complex," Ferenczi made clear how wounded he felt: "Your letter has shaken me considerably. For the first time since our acquaintance, which you soon elevated to friendship, I hear words of dissatisfaction from you" (p. 119).

Although it is illuminating to track the stages in the decline of this relationship, the crucial point is that it is governed by an underlying structure that becomes progressively visible over time. That structure is constituted by the intersubjective reality that whereas Ferenczi was capable of humility and self-criticism, never engaged in personal recriminations, and was prepared to go to heroic lengths in an effort to engage Freud in authentic dialogue, Freud, by contrast, was constantly berating and "analyzing" Ferenczi, never willing to admit that he himself might be wrong intellectually or at fault on a human level, and, in consequence, was incapable of recognizing his interlocutor as a genuine "other" with a point of view no less worthy of respect than his own. Freud, that is, concomitant with his minimizing of the importance of trauma as an etiological factor in mental illness, imported into his dealings with Ferenczi the same "one-person" model that informed his conception of the analytic situation, while Ferenczi was committed to a "two-person" theory, in which the pseudo-objectivity of the detached, "insensitive" analyst was—as he was acutely aware from his experience with Freud—bound to be traumatic for the emotionally vulnerable, fragile patient.

Despite undervaluing trauma on the plane of theory, Freud was by no means immune to it in his own experience. Indeed, he was no less traumatized by the tragic denouement of his relationship with Ferenczi than was Ferenczi himself. Freud's reiterated protestations that there was "nothing traumatic" about their breakup and that the "traumatic effect dissipates" in him constitute attempts to deny the impact of this loss on his own brittle psyche. By virtue of its finality, Ferenczi's unexpected death magnified exponentially—to borrow Ferenczi's own phrase—the "depth of the shock" felt by Freud. In view of the projective nature of Freud's accusations concerning Ferenczi's "personal hostility" toward him, extending to alleged murderous impulses at once aroused and defied by Freud's longevity, the conclusion becomes inescapable that Freud had unconscious death wishes directed against Ferenczi. Following Ferenczi's death, therefore, there would have been activated in Freud the survivor guilt—originating in his response to the death of his infant brother Julius, when he himself was less than two years old (Rudnytsky, 1987, pp. 19–26)—that was a constant refrain in his life, as illustrated by the "*non vixit*" dream in *The Interpretation of Dreams*.

5

What we see depicted in miniature in Freud's obituary of Ferenczi is writ large in "Analysis Terminable and Interminable." Ferenczi is superficially praised but in reality roundly criticized, held to be completely to blame for their estrangement, and subjected to a merciless dissection of his psyche. Indeed, "Analysis Terminable and Interminable" as a whole constitutes a latter-day *History of the Psycho-Analytic Movement*, in which, along with its theoretical polemics, Freud at the close of his life is consumed with settling old scores and avenging himself against those who had, in his estimation, most deeply disappointed and wronged him. Despite being no less shaken than Ferenczi by the conflicts in their relationship, especially by the way everything came apart at the end, Freud was never able to acknowledge that he had been traumatized, whether by Ferenczi or by anyone else going back to his childhood, although the evidence for these wounds can be seen in the dissociated narratives he constantly tells and retells about his experiences of abandonment and rejection, in which nothing is ever his fault.

A recurring leitmotif of Freud's self-exculpations with respect to Ferenczi is to yoke him with Rank. Of all the angels "who were once near to me and then fell away," Freud the Father regarded them as the most ungrateful apostates since he had "adopted" them both (as he had in bygone days "adopted" Jung) and, in his mind, they could not possibly have had any grounds with which to reproach him. This association helps to explain why Freud opens "Analysis Terminable and Interminable" by launching a blistering attack on Rank's *The Trauma of Birth* (1924) for its attempt to shorten the duration of analytic treatment by proposing, in Freud's (1937a) summary, that "if this primal trauma were dealt with by a subsequent analysis the whole neurosis would be got rid of" (p. 216). Freud compares Rank's proposal to the foolishness of firefighters who, when they were "called to deal with a house that had been set on fire by an overturned oil-lamp, contented themselves with removing the lamp from the room in which the blaze had started" (pp. 216–17). Freud's demolition of *The Trauma of Birth* has a hidden agenda since that was the book that had precipitated Rank's defection, an extremely painful loss about which Freud remained embittered. Immediately after dispatching Rank, Freud turns to the Wolf Man, the subject of his most important case history, whose continual relapses belied Freud's belief at the time his treatment had been terminated in 1914 that "his cure was radical and permanent" (p. 217). Other nemeses who make curtain calls in "Analysis Terminable and Interminable" are Adler, Fliess, and Emma Eckstein, the patient who was pivotal in both Freud's initial espousal and subsequent repudiation of the "seduction theory," the "first great etiological error" to which Ferenczi, in Freud's estimation, had made a "complete regression."

Although each of these unlaid ghosts becomes a revenant for Freud, there are qualitative differences among them. Rank and the Wolf Man stand prominently at the outset but are both identified, indicating that the threats they represent have been successfully mastered by Freud. Adler and Fliess, too, are cited by name and summarily dispatched as the text draws to a close. Of all the specters in "Analysis Terminable and Interminable" only Eckstein shares with Ferenczi a truly wraithlike quality in that her case history, which follows immediately after Ferenczi's as a second example of a supposedly "successful analytic treatment" that did not prevent a "fresh outbreak of neurosis" (pp. 222–23) at a later date, is presented anonymously, such that neither could be identified by the reader without inside information. Without James Strachey's footnote, which appeals to Jones's biography to unmask Ferenczi, it would be easy to miss that Ferenczi is the first patient in question, and even Strachey was unable to pierce Freud's disguise of Eckstein, which remained intact until Masson's *Assault on Truth* in 1984.

But it was above all Ferenczi with whom Freud had not made peace, as evidenced by the number of his appearances in "Analysis Terminable and Interminable." Forming a triptych with the disguised case history are two overt references, the first negative, the second positive. In putting forth the view that analysis sets out "to cure neurosis by ensuring control over instinct," which requires increasing its power "to come to the assistance of the ego," Freud (1937a) hearkens back to his earliest days as a therapist:

> Hypnotic influence seemed to be an excellent instrument for our purposes; but the reasons for our having to abandon it are well known.

No substitute for hypnosis has yet been found. From this point of view we can understand how such a master of analysis as Ferenczi came to devote the last years of his life to therapeutic experiments, which, unhappily, proved to be vain.

(pp. 229–30)

On the one hand, Freud hails Ferenczi as a "master of analysis," yet, on the other, he dismisses the "therapeutic experiments" during "the last years of his life" as "vain." This is a reprise of his verdict in the obituary that Ferenczi had "set himself aims which, with our therapeutic means, are altogether out of reach today," as well as of the barb in his "kissing technique" letter that Ferenczi had "not embarked upon any fruitful path." The brush Freud employs to tar Ferenczi is to equate the technique of his final period with hypnosis, the insufficiency of which (due its reliance on suggestion) Freud had taken for granted since he abjured it at the dawn of psychoanalysis.

As we have seen, this analogy also informs Freud's August 29, 1933 letter to Eitingon, where he says that Ferenczi "transports" his patients "into a hypnosis-like condition" and then "considers that to be the revelation," though what he "thereby obtains are the patients' fantasies about their childhood, not history." He spelled out the accusation in greater detail—and explained it in *ad hominem* fashion—in a letter to Eitingon on November 1, 1931, reporting on the visit that had led to the recriminations over Ferenczi's "kissing technique" and brought their rift out into the open. Freud writes:

> I see in his behavior and its theoretical adornment no progress, but rather a piece of involution with a return to old libido positions. A piece of the business is that he has not found among his colleagues the love that he requires out of infantile need, and he therefore places a premium on being loved by his patients. . . . What he achieves with his play of tender roles seems to me therapeutically inconsequential. It seems as though he produces a form of hypnosis, in which the patients act out in lively fashion things that must often be surmised and constructed through our technique. That is certainly very interesting for the analyst, but he concedes that it is an extraordinary burden, and from the experience with hypnosis one knows that even such extremely lifelike reproductions remain completely ineffective since, split off by resistance against the influence of all the superimposed

layers, they can achieve nothing. . . . I am distrustful of these novelties and cannot free myself from the impression that this theory is only a rationalization for the justification of his affectively required activity.
(Schröter, 2004, 2:764–65)

All this is by now familiar, especially the reduction of Ferenczi's devotion to his patients to an "infantile need" for the love that he had not procured from his psychoanalytic brethren. The condemnation of Ferenczi's "play of tender roles" as nothing more than a revival of hypnosis, which is "completely ineffective" because it relies on suggestion instead of working to strengthen the ego, provides the context for Freud's summary judgment against Ferenczi's technique in "Analysis Terminable and Interminable," his final explicit pronouncement on everything that Ferenczi had set out to accomplish in the four-year period framed by the Oxford and Wiesbaden Congresses.

When Freud wants to cite Ferenczi approvingly, by contrast, he goes back to "The Problem of the Termination of the Analysis" (1927b), presented to the 10th IPA Congress in Innsbruck. By Ferenczi's standards, this is an unremarkable performance, giving few signs of the breakthrough to come, and it appealed to Freud precisely because it did not pose a challenge to his reigning paradigm. Freud extracts from it two principal points. First, reading the paper as "a warning not to aim at shortening analysis but deepening it," he endorses Ferenczi's admonition that "success depends very largely on the analyst's having learnt sufficiently from his own 'errors and mistakes' and having got the better of 'the weak points in his personality'" (1937a, p. 247). Conceding that "analysts in their own personalities have not invariably come up to the standard of psychical normality to which they wish to educate their patients," Freud draws the conclusion that "every analyst should periodically—at intervals of five years or so—submit himself to analysis once more, without feeling ashamed of taking this step" (p. 249). Second, in his peroration affirming, against Fliess and Adler, the "paramount importance of these two themes—in females the wish for a penis and in males the struggle against passivity," Freud again appeals to Ferenczi's 1927 paper, where "he made it a requirement that in every successful analysis these two complexes must have been mastered" (p. 251).

In his two explicit references to Ferenczi in "Analysis Terminable and Interminable," Freud first criticizes him severely for the ideas that Freud could not contain within his own system and then praises Ferenczi in a perfunctory manner while deploying him to advance his own agenda. The "good" Ferenczi was for Freud the docile son who existed prior to the Oxford Congress, while the "bad" Ferenczi was the upstart, led astray by his "evil genius," who "fell victim" to "a mental degeneration in the form of paranoia" in his final years. By the end of his life, Ferenczi no longer agreed with the phallocentric outlook he had espoused as late as 1927, though Freud did not acknowledge this when he quoted him after Ferenczi's death. In the *Clinical Diary*, Ferenczi takes Freud to task for "the unilaterally androphile orientation of his theory of sexuality," in which "he was followed by almost all of his pupils, myself included," and admits that a new edition of *Thalassa* would call for "complete rewriting" (Dupont, 1985, p. 187). In a letter from Venice on May 22, 1932, similarly, Ferenczi mentions to Freud that "lively debates" had been taking place in the Hungarian Society "about the female castration complex and penis envy," adding, "I must admit that in my practice these don't play the great role one had expected theoretically. What has been your experience?" (Falzeder and Brabant, 2000, p. 436). Had Ferenczi been able to read "Analysis Terminable and Terminable," he would have had his answer.

Even more revealing than Freud's (1937a) invoking of Ferenczi to support his doctrine of the castration complex, however, is his use of "Termination of the Analysis" to recommend that analysts undergo a periodic reanalysis to ensure that they possess the "psychical normality" and even "superiority" (p. 248) necessary to perform their functions. The irony, of course, is that Freud himself not only did not have a second analysis but refused to allow himself to be analyzed by another human being even once, despite having been urged to do so by both Ferenczi and Groddeck. When he issues this advisory to "every analyst," therefore, he means everyone other than himself. If Freud were conscious of this contradiction between his words and his deeds, then he would be guilty of hypocrisy. But it is more likely, in my estimation, that Freud could go on to proclaim that analysis requires a "love of truth" and "precludes any kind of sham or deceit" only because he lacked any awareness that he had condemned himself out of his own mouth.

As we have seen, when Freud states in the disguised case history that forms the central panel of his altarpiece in "Analysis Terminable and Interminable" that "trouble arose" only after Ferenczi "became antagonistic" and "reproached" him "for no assignable external reason," he is constructing a narrative according to which he himself is "completely innocent" and the sole source of the problem is Ferenczi's "systematically turning away" due to a neurotically motivated "personal hostility." There can be no doubt that Freud believed this version of events, which he had honed both in their correspondence and in his accounts of their rift to his confidants. But, like Oedipus cursing the murderer of Laius, Freud is unable to perceive his own blindness, and this hubristic refusal to admit that he might be the guilty party is the cause of the plague on his psychoanalytic kingdom. Thus, what we have to reckon with in seeking to understand Freud in his final years is less any deliberate deception than it is an unconscious dissociation in which he cannot acknowledge either the extent to which he had been afflicted by his own history of traumatic experiences or his role as an abuser and perpetrator of trauma on others.

Notes

1 See, in this connection, Frank Scherer's (2015) study of how Freud's Jewish identity plays itself out through an ambivalent discourse of "orientalism" in psychoanalysis.
2 It has been almost entirely forgotten that Ferenczi had already been elected the third president of the IPA at the Budapest Congress in 1918 and only asked Jones to serve in his stead "due to the post-war upheaval and turmoil in Hungary, which made international contacts practically impossible" (Falzeder and Dupont, 2000, p. 805). As late as 1996, on his first visit to the IPA headquarters in Broomhills, Horacio Etchegoyen "noticed a glaring omission in the portrait gallery of Presidents—Sándor Ferenczi" (qtd. in Bonomi, 1999, p. 507). What is more, as Falzeder and Dupont remark, citing an "Open Letter" (1920) by Ferenczi in the inaugural issue of the *International Journal of Psycho-Analysis*, it is another forgotten fact that it was actually Ferenczi's idea to "found a distinct journal in the English language," and it was he who invited Jones to become its editor, as well as "to act for me as President of the 'International Psycho-Analytical Association' until the next Congress" (pp. 1–2). In her centennial review of the history of the *International Journal*, Dana Birksted-Breen (2019) effaces the name of Ferenczi, and she compounds her sin of omission by quoting the risible claim of her predecessor as Editor-in-Chief, David Tuckett, that the *Journal* owes to Jones (!) "two of its most important and scientific traditions: its non-partisan approach to controversy and its encouragement of the view that judgements concerning the truth and utility of ideas should be based as far as possible on evidential data" (p. 3; see Tuckett, 1994, p. 1). I am indebted to Mario Beira for bringing to the surface this archipelago of lost islands.
3 See note 5 to Prelude, where I point out how the meaning of the first sentence has been turned upside down in the English translation of the Sigmund Freud—Anna Freud correspondence.
4 As Brennan (2011) has observed, Jones later proposed to Balint that not only "Confusion of Tongues" (1933a) but also other key texts of Ferenczi's final period—"The Unwelcome Child and His Death Instinct" (1929b), "The Principle of Relaxation and Neocatharsis" (1930), and "Child Analysis in the Analysis of Adults" (1931)—should be omitted from the third volume of Ferenczi's

collected papers. On September 12, 1952, Balint reminded Jones that Freud had approved the publication of all but "Confusion of Tongues" in the *International Journal*, "and that to exclude them would be as if we 'wanted to be more Freudian than Freud himself'" (Brennan, 2011, p. 7*n*9).
5 In a paper that does not take into consideration Freud's correspondence with his partisans, Miguel Gutiérrez Peláez (2009) likewise denies that "Freud's anger with Ferenczi was due to the latter's having revived his early trauma theory" (p. 1226).

Chapter 14

Roux's Needle

1

Apart from the obituary and "Analysis Terminable and Interminable," Ferenczi receives only passing mention in Freud's later writings. Two papers on bridge symbolism (Ferenczi, 1921a, 1921c) are cited approvingly in the *New Introductory Lectures on Psycho-Analysis* (Freud, 1933a, p. 24), as is a paper on sexual habits in which Ferenczi (1925b) links the "fear of castration" to "the original anxiety at birth" (qtd. in Freud, 1933a, p. 87). Beyond these overt references, an editorial note to *An Outline of Psycho-Analysis* (1940a) points out that Ferenczi had anticipated Freud in proposing "a connection between the latency period and the glacial epoch" (p. 153n1), while another to the *New Introductory Lectures* (1933a) is indubitably correct in surmising that Freud had Ferenczi in mind in chastising the "therapeutic ambition of some of my adherents," including the endeavor to "unite other forms of influence" with analysis, which Freud describes as "certainly praiseworthy" but, again, "vain" and carrying with it the "danger of being forced away from analysis and drawn into a boundless course of experimentation" (p. 153).

Although dated 1933, the *New Introductory Lectures* was actually published in December 1932, so this oblique reproach of Ferenczi was written before his death and anticipates those in both the obituary and "Analysis Terminable and Interminable."[1] In all three instances, Freud voices his disapproval of the new directions taken by Ferenczi in his final period. All the positive references, by contrast, both the three explicit ones in the *New Introductory Lectures* and the single implicit one in the *Outline*, are to writings by Ferenczi before "The Principle of Relaxation and Neocatharsis," which do not venture beyond Freud's conceptual framework. All this is what we have seen to be characteristic of Freud and what we would

DOI: 10.4324/9781315280134-18

expect. Taken as a whole, however, the casual reader would be likely to conclude that, apart from the retribution exacted in "Analysis Terminable and Interminable," Ferenczi no longer occupies a place of any consequence in Freud's thinking.

Nevertheless, beginning with Haynal (2005), a number of influential commentators have maintained that "the issues and conflicts in this relationship continued to exert an influence in Freud's mind even after Ferenczi's death" (p. 464). Along the same lines, Jacques Press (2006) has argued:

> By entering a dialogue more or less openly before and after death with his friend, who was also a pupil and rebel, Freud was led to a re-elaboration of his theories of trauma. My hypothesis is that in the theses defended by Freud, particularly in *Moses and Monotheism*, one gets a glimpse of the outlines of a new version of trauma and of its effects, which can be linked up in several ways with Ferenczi's descriptions.
>
> (p. 520)

Finally, in a series of seminal papers, Bonomi (2012, 2013, 2015b) has elaborated the proposition that if, in Freud's latest works, there was "a resurfacing of the provocative question related to *what is real*, which lies at the heart of psychoanalysis itself," the reason is above all "because Ferenczi put the issue of traumatic memories at the top of the psychoanalytic agenda" (2012, p. 240).

As we shall see through an examination of four key texts—*Moses and Monotheism*, *An Outline of Psycho-Analysis*, "Constructions in Analysis," and "Splitting of the Ego in the Process of Defence," with a parting glance at "Analysis Terminable and Interminable"—it is indeed true that Freud was consumed with the question of trauma, and this was inseparable from his continuing battle with Ferenczi's ghost. But, for reasons already set forth in Prelude, I differ with these scholars in rejecting the notion that Freud was engaged in any kind of authentic "dialogue" with Ferenczi or that their conceptualizations of trauma can be "linked up" in anything more than a superficial sense. For, just as Freud showed himself to be incapable of genuinely listening to Ferenczi on a personal level in their correspondence, and was equally closed-minded in his posthumous narratives about their relationship, so, too, on the theoretical plane the evidence will demonstrate that, although Freud gave lip service to the importance of trauma, in reality he did not understand it at all, and there is accordingly (as he himself acknowledged in his dismissals of Ferenczi's work) a profound incompatibility between their perspectives.

2

According to Bonomi (2012), who repeats the trope that "Freud pursued a posthumous dialogue through his last works" with Ferenczi, Freud "never denied the relevance of traumatic memories, but . . . he did not believe that they could 'break through' the unconscious" (p. 240). The phrase "break through" alludes to Freud's pivotal letter to Fliess of September 21, 1897, in which he renounces his "seduction theory," giving as one of his reasons that "in the most deep-reaching psychosis unconscious memory does not break through, so that the secret of childhood experiences is not disclosed even in the most confused delirium" (Masson, 1985, p. 265). Citing *Moses and Monotheism*, Bonomi (2012) maintains that, in response to Ferenczi's challenge, Freud's "earlier convictions about the centrality of real trauma were strengthened" (p. 241), with only the proviso that the supervening defensive formations made it impossible to recover the buried memories. From a complementary angle, Bonomi (2013) reiterates that although, in Ferenczi's estimation, "it was ultimately the patient who was abandoned" with Freud's reversal in 1897, "it was certainly not the trauma that Freud abandoned" (p. 271) because, thanks to his belief in a "phylogenetic scenario" in which unconscious fantasies of castration were transmitted to posterity from actual deeds committed in prehistory, "the theory of the real trauma . . . was now relocated in a primeval past that became the container of Freud's own fantasies regarding the brutality of origins" (2015b, p. 41).

Thus, in Bonomi's account, Freud not only did not back away from his "earlier convictions about the centrality of real trauma" in his final texts, but these convictions were "strengthened" as he absorbed Ferenczi's ideas into his own framework, and the fact that he locates the trauma in the "primeval past" is deemed to be inconsequential. But it is clear that Ferenczi would have disagreed with this assessment. In a letter to Freud on February 15, 1930, while lauding *Civilization and Its Discontents* as "essentially unassailable," Ferenczi demurs "on one point," which comes "evidently from the 'traumatic' standpoint" (Falzeder and Brabant, 2000, pp. 388–89). He elaborates:

> Instead of accepting the view of Melanie Klein, would it not be more correct to hold fast to the *individually acquired (i.e., traumatic)* nature,

that is to say, origin, of conscience and of the neurosis, and to maintain that the all too strict conscience (that is to say, inclination to self-destruction) is the result of a *relatively too strict* treatment—i.e., too strict in relation to the individually varied need for love.

(p. 389; first italics added)

By this stage of his career, therefore, the "'traumatic' standpoint" for Ferenczi requires "holding fast" to the "individually acquired" origin of pathology, which leaves no room for flights of "phylogenetic fantasy"—to echo the title given by Axel and Peter Hoffer to their English translation of Freud's (1987) rediscovered twelfth metapsychological paper—of the kind in which he had indulged in *Thalassa*, and to which both Freud and Klein continued to resort. The phrase *"relatively too strict"* was underlined three times by Ferenczi, who chafed against the harsh treatment to which he had been subjected at the hands first of his mother and later of Freud, while recognizing the intensity of his own "need for love"; and this indictment of Freud's theoretical position gains strength from being grounded in Ferenczi's personal experience.

If we turn to the section of *Moses and Monotheism*, "The Analogy," to which Bonomi (2012, p. 241, 2013, p. 374, 2015b, pp. 44–45) repeatedly appeals but never discusses in detail, the slipperiness of Freud's grasp on trauma becomes apparent. Here Freud (1939) seeks to persuade the reader to accept an analogy that is "very complete, and approaches identity" between "the history of the Jewish religion" and "the genesis of human neuroses" (p. 72). He then launches into a discourse on trauma, which, however, begins with the disclaimer, "We may leave on one side the question of whether the aetiology of the neuroses in general may be regarded as traumatic." He thereby sidesteps the question that most urgently requires an answer, and to which both Ferenczi and Severn responded in the affirmative. Freud continues, "The obvious objection to this is that it is not possible to discover in every case a manifest trauma in the neurotic subject's earliest history."

Freud's "objection" to a traumatic theory of "the aetiology of the neuroses in general" is vitiated by the inadequacy of his definition of what constitutes a "manifest trauma." In one of the few fragments to have been preserved from the lost portion of her manuscript, "Evaluation of Ferenczi's Relaxation Therapy" (1933), Thompson had written:

> Through this technique Ferenczi believed that he had rediscovered the importance of actual traumas in the etiology of neurosis. It is possible

that the trauma is not necessarily of a gross sexual nature, but of the more subtle nature of the reaction of the child to parental erotic tensions and guilt; nevertheless this means that the neurosis is formed facing an actual difficulty; in other words, that the child does not suffer from his own Oedipus complex but from that of his parents.

(qtd. in Brennan, 2011, p. 11)

In this profound passage, which anticipates Jean Laplanche's (1987) theory of "general seduction," Thompson recognizes that traumas may be of a "subtle nature" while being nonetheless "actual." Similarly, de Forest (1942), in her overview of the types of circumstances that, according to Ferenczi, "must have actually occurred in the childhood of an individual" to cause a neurosis, includes "a sequence of less intense traumatic experiences" (p. 121). Both these first-generation expositors of Ferenczi grasped the essence of what has since come to be known as "strain" (Kris, 1956), "cumulative" (Khan, 1963), or "micro-" trauma (Crastnopol, 2015), a concept that eluded Freud when he assumed that trauma must originate in a discrete, palpable event. Consequently, Freud's inability to discern the presence of a "manifest trauma" in a patient's childhood does not mean that no such trauma "actually occurred" in "the neurotic subject's earliest history," but is rather a function of the inadequacy of his analyzing instrument.

Having established to his own satisfaction that some cases of neurosis lack a discernible trauma and that there are therefore times when "we have nothing else for explaining a neurosis but hereditary and constitutional dispositions," Freud (1939) unexpectedly pivots and collapses the distinction between traumatic and nontraumatic etiologies he had just posited: "It is quite possible to unite the two aetiological determinants under a single conception; it is merely a question of how one defines 'traumatic'" (p. 73). Freud invokes a "quantitative factor" to argue that since "in every case it is an excess in demand that is responsible for an experience evoking pathological reactions—then we can easily arrive at the expedient of saying that something acts as a trauma in the case of one constitution but in the case of another would have no such effect." What we are left with, accordingly, is the principle of a "sliding 'complemental series'" between heredity and environment, in which "as a rule both factors operate together and it is only at the two ends of the series that there can be any question of a simple motive being at work." The upshot of Freud's reasoning is that, as far as he is concerned, "we can disregard the distinction between traumatic and non-traumatic aetiologies as irrelevant to the analogy we are in search of."

Freud, therefore, ends up where he started, assuring the reader that it is possible to "leave on one side" the question of whether traumas of one kind or another are indeed always the cause of the "neuroses in general." In concluding that "we can disregard the distinction between traumatic and non-traumatic aetiologies," what Freud is *not* saying is that the analyst should be prepared to investigate how (to take several examples from my own practice) being conceived as the result of rape, hearing the gunshots of a murder-suicide in which one's mother was killed by one's stepfather, being beaten on the buttocks by one's father in the presence of one's siblings, and not being allowed to play the flute in the sixth grade are *all* traumatic experiences for the patients in question, which become woven into the entire fabric of a life. What he *is* saying is that it does not matter in the end whether we consider these experiences to be traumatic or not, since everything boils down to a "complemental series" in which all we are doing is adjudicating the relative weight of the "quantitative factors" of nature and nurture.

Thus, although Freud continues to use the language of trauma—and does so eloquently on occasion—he remains removed from the immediacy of traumatic experience, and as a result eviscerates the concept of trauma of any substantive meaning. A perfect illustration is when he writes in the ensuing paragraph, "Our researches have shown that what we call the phenomena (symptoms) of a neurosis are the result of certain experiences and impressions which for that very reason we regard as aetiological traumas" (p. 74). If this statement were taken seriously, it would mean that the analyst should in every case inquire into, and seek to understand, those "experiences and impressions" that have given rise to the observed "symptoms" in a patient, and for that reason constitute "aetiological traumas." As construed by Freud, however, the assertion is entirely tautological. Since, to a sufficiently vulnerable "constitutional disposition," even the slightest stimulus may produce an "excess in demand" that results in "pathological reactions," to call something a trauma is not to give it any explanatory weight. Once again, in Freud's words, "it is merely a question of how one defines 'traumatic,'" and "we can disregard the distinction between traumatic and non-traumatic aetiologies."

It is against this backdrop that we must assess Freud's most insightful and moving sentences later in this same section, which have rightly attracted the attention of Bonomi. As Freud observes, the "later illness" that constitutes the presenting symptoms of a neurosis "may also be looked upon as an attempt at cure—as an effort once more to reconcile with the rest those portions of the ego that have been split off by the influence of the trauma and to unite them into a powerful whole *vis-à-vis* the external world" (pp. 77–78). He continues by noting that the process "ends often enough in a complete devastation or fragmentation of the ego or in its being overwhelmed by the portion which was early split off and which is dominated by the trauma" (p. 78). This admirable passage could easily be mistaken for an excerpt from Ferenczi or Severn. The problem, however, is that the references to "devastation," "fragmentation," being "split off" and "overwhelmed" by trauma are themselves not integrated into the body of Freud's argument. And why is Ferenczi nowhere cited? Thus, even when Freud uses the right words, they remain inert and decontextualized, and he does not enter into any kind of meaningful "dialogue" with Ferenczi. In the remaining pages of "The Analogy," Freud (1939) cites the example of a "little boy" on whom the mother's "threat of castration had an extraordinarily powerful traumatic effect" (pp. 78–79), the sequelae of which resulted in his neurosis. This, and nothing more, is in the final analysis what Freud means by "trauma."

3

The circular reasoning and avoidance of the emotional reality of traumatic experience evident in *Moses and Monotheism* are even more starkly on display in Freud's posthumously published *Outline of Psycho-Analysis* (1940a), of which the crucial chapter is "An Example of Psycho-Analytic Work." Freud immediately gets off on the wrong foot by announcing it to be one of his "chief findings" that "the neuroses (unlike infectious diseases, for example) have no specific determinants," so that "it would be idle to seek in them for pathogenic excitants" (p. 183). With this denial of any identifiable cause of neurosis, Freud precludes himself from seriously considering trauma as an etiological factor in mental illness. Asserting that neurotics have "the same experiences" and "the same tasks to perform" as other people, Freud once again resorts to the abstract notion of "quantitative *disharmonies*" in "the reciprocal action between innate dispositions and accidental experiences" to elucidate "what must be held responsible for the inadequacy and suffering of neurotics."

Thus far, Freud simply repeats the same argument he had already made in *Moses and Monotheism*. Where he adds a new wrinkle is in making clear that by "innate dispositions" he means above all the instinctual drives, which "may be too strong or too weak innately" (p. 183). Indeed, he goes on to specify that "there is in fact one instinctual demand attempts to deal with which most easily fail or succeed imperfectly" (p. 184), which, of course, is that arising from sexuality. The consequence that follows from these assumptions—and the fallacy that undermines Freud's entire theoretical construction—is that traumas can result just as easily from internal as from external sources. As Freud expressly states, "in these circumstances instinctual demands from within, no less than excitations from the external world, operate as 'traumas,' particularly if they are met half-way by certain innate dispositions" (p. 185).

With this suggestion that "instinctual demands from within" can produce traumas to the same extent as "excitations from external world" we reach a parting of the ways between Freud and all relational conceptions of psychoanalysis. For it is axiomatic from a relational standpoint that every person possesses what Winnicott (1965) calls innate "maturational processes," and it is almost always when there has been an intolerable failure of the "facilitating environment," whether of the catastrophic or the cumulative variety, that deformation ensues. Even the major thought and mood disorders, which have a hereditary component—though this has nothing to do with "instinctual drives"—are profoundly influenced by lived experience. Thus, Freud's (1940a) error is to pathologize normal phenomena—especially in the sphere of sexuality—and by extension to presuppose that the "helpless ego" (p. 185) of the infant, even when aided by a loving caretaker, is unable to regulate its endogenous somatic needs.

Freud then employs an analogy to bolster his argument, but which ironically encapsulates the confusion in his thinking:

> The damage inflicted on the ego by its first experiences gives us the appearance of being disproportionately great; but we have only to take as an analogy the differences in the results produced by the prick of a needle into a mass of cells in the act of cell-division (as in Roux's experiments) and into the fully grown animal which eventually develops out of them. No human individual is spared such traumatic experiences; none escapes the repressions to which they give rise.
> (p. 185)

It is crucial to recognize that by "first experiences" Freud still means primarily "instinctual demands from within," and only incidentally "excitations from external world," which is his mechanistic way of referring to the infant's interactions with his or her primary caretakers. The problem with what Freud is saying is *not* his conviction that "the first period of childhood" (p. 184) lays the foundation for what happens throughout the course of a person's life. The stumbling block is rather his equation of "instinctual demands," which are part of the maturational process, with "the prick of a needle"—in this case, one inflicted by the German embryologist Wilhelm Roux—"into a mass of cells in the act of cell-division."

According to Wikipedia (2016), Roux in 1888 performed "defect experiments" in which he "took 2 and 4 cell frog embryos and killed half of the cells of each embryo with a hot needle," with the result that "they grew into half-embryos," leading Roux to surmise that "the separate function of the two cells had already been determined." Roux, that is, did not simply "prick" the cluster of cells, but actually "*killed* half of the cells of each embryo" with his needle, causing them to become monstrously deformed. Without mentioning Roux by name, Ferenczi (1927a) clearly has his research in mind when he writes that "in the early stages of embryonic development a slight wound, the mere prick of a pin, can not only cause severe alterations in, but may completely prevent, the development of whole limbs of the body," in order to make the point that "if, near the beginning of life, you do only a little harm to a child, it may cast a shadow over the whole of its life" (p. 65).

There could be no more graphic illustration of the untenability of Freud's outlook than his claim of an equivalence between the lethal intrusion of an experimenter's needle into a "mass of cells," which is a trauma if there ever was one, and the biological imperatives arising spontaneously within an organism. The latter should rather be compared to the "act of cell-division" that is preprogramed by evolution to occur in every living being, provided, of course, that the environment facilitates rather than impedes this maturational process. The full extent of Freud's befuddlement is displayed when he asserts that "no human individual is spared such traumatic experiences." If we follow his logic, it is as though every frog embryo on earth were fated to be pierced by Roux's needle, so they should all end up as warped creatures, a self-evidently absurd conclusion.

The effect of Freud's twin postulates that trauma is universal and can arise solely from "instinctual demands" becomes evident when he seeks to determine whether there is a "central experience" (p. 187) of early childhood that can be held responsible for "the causation of the neuroses" (p. 186). He first considers "the effects of certain influences which do not apply to all children, though they are common enough," including "the sexual abuse of children by adults, their seduction by other children," and "their being deeply stirred by seeing or hearing at first hand sexual behaviour between adults" (p. 187). This is, of course, a précis of his "seduction theory," and Freud continues to recognize that such experiences "arouse a child's susceptibility and force his own sexual urges into certain channels from which they cannot afterwards depart" (p. 187). But the fact that these factors "do not apply to all children" for Freud perforce means that they cannot be the key to unlocking the riddle of the neuroses. So, rather than abandon his presumption that trauma is universal, he has to find some other explanation that allows him to maintain this axiom.

In this resuscitation of his pre-1897 "seduction theory," Freud finds room within his mature system for his "first great etiological error," to which he believed Ferenczi had made a "complete regression." But in limiting his consideration of these early experiences to their effect on the child's "sexual urges," Freud fails to reckon with the frequently shattering impact of such abuse on his or her developing sense of self and capacity for basic trust. Thus, it is misleading to equate Ferenczi's understanding of trauma, arrived at jointly with Severn, with Freud's ideas at any stage. Indeed, as Guasto (2013) has argued, although Ferenczi continued to recognize the importance of sexuality, his thinking encompassed "far more devastating experiences" than Freud could dream of in his metapsychology, and he "described in a strikingly lucid way the mortal anguish, the psychic shock (*Erschütterung*), of the victim of sexual abuse" (p. 44). Not only does Freud ignore Ferenczi's contributions, but he fails to grasp the radical challenge to his entire worldview posed by Ferenczi's ideas.

Having ruled out anything coming from the external world as the "central experience" of childhood for which he is searching, Freud (1940a) proposes that "a still higher degree of interest must attach to the influence of a situation which every child is destined to pass through," one that "we shall recognize as inevitable" (p. 187). Needless to say, he means the Oedipus complex, to which Freud devotes the remaining pages of his chapter in *An Outline of Psycho-Analysis*. This linchpin of his theory allows Freud to maintain both that "instinctual demands from within" are inherently traumatic—regardless of environmental factors—and that "no human individual is spared such traumatic experiences."

As one reads on, what is most astonishing is how completely Freud devalues what Ferenczi called, in his critique of *Civilization and Its Discontents*, "the individually acquired (i.e., traumatic) nature, that is to say, origin, of conscience and of the neurosis," in favor of phylogenetic templates. He expounds how the mother serves as "the first and strongest love-object for the child":

> In all this the phylogenetic foundation has so much the upper hand over personal accidental experience that it *makes no difference* whether a child has really sucked at the breast or been brought up on the bottle and *never enjoyed the tenderness of a mother's care*. In both cases the *child's development takes the same path*.
>
> (pp. 188–89; italics added)

Again, it is important to be clear that Freud is *not* suggesting, as Winnicott does in his writings, that a bottle-fed baby can experience "good-enough" mothering, so that what matters above all is the quality of love and devotion bestowed on the infant, not whether the milk comes from a breast or a bottle. Rather, he claims that it "makes no difference" whether or not a child has ever "enjoyed the tenderness of a mother's care," and that "the child's development takes the same path" regardless of the quality of its environmental provision.

Not for the first time, this is not only wrong but absurd, and it underscores the gulf between Freud and Ferenczi in their final years. It also lays bare the untenability of Bonomi's contention that, in resorting to a "phylogenetic scenario," Freud's "earlier convictions about the centrality of real trauma were strengthened." On the contrary, by this point in his argument "real trauma" has disappeared entirely from view, along with "personal accidental experience," and all we are left with is a "phylogenetic foundation" that turns out if we stand on it to be a trap door into the void. As a corollary to his premise that it "makes no difference" what sort of care one receives as a child, Freud maintains that "for however long it is fed at the mother's breast," the child "will always be left with a conviction after it has been weaned that its feeding was too short and too little" (p. 189). Just as a neglected child, according to Freud, is no worse off than one that has been genuinely loved, so even one who has had its physical and emotional needs met will be left with a perpetual sense of lack and deprivation. There is, in short, no place in Freud's theory either for "good-enough" experience, on the one hand, or, on the other, for experience that is genuinely traumatic because the environment has not met a minimum threshold of adequacy. Consequently, just as he does in *Moses and Monotheism*, Freud in *An Outline of Psycho-Analysis* ends up sidestepping the decisive "question of whether the aetiology of the neuroses in general may be regarded as traumatic."

Having introduced the Oedipus complex, Freud then brings the chapter to a close with a peroration on the castration complex, one that repeats not only in substance but verbatim what he had already said in the concluding section of "Analysis Terminable and Interminable." Here he affirms in the final paragraph: "If we ask an analyst what his experience has shown to be the mental structure least accessible to influence in his patients, the answer will be: in a woman her wish for a penis, in a man his feminine attitude towards his own sex, a precondition of which would, of course, be the loss of his penis" (p. 194). As Bonomi (2013) has observed, the concept of the castration complex functions as "the synthetic *a priori* of trauma" in Freud's thought, and as such it "has a systemic and all-embracing structure impermeable to compromises: one is forced to either accept it or reject it, to remain inside or outside the system" (p. 371). Bonomi's comparison of the castration complex to Kant's category of "synthetic *a priori*" judgments precisely captures how Freud's doctrine is for him a logically necessary truth that precedes experience. That the castration complex is "impermeable to compromises," and his disciples are "forced to either accept it or reject it," is a manifestation on the level of theory of the double bind Freud imposed on Ferenczi—and indeed on nearly everyone in the psychoanalytic movement—in their personal dealings. The tragic consequence of this arrangement is that the price for remaining "inside the system" is accepting one's own "castration" by confessing the infallibility of Freud's teaching, while the price for asserting one's independence is to be anathematized for practicing "oppositional analysis," and hence also to be "castrated" for having dared to rebel.

Thus, within the authoritarian structure of Freud's universe, the castration complex is inescapable, and Freud may be credited with having created a perfect mechanism for gaslighting others by inflicting a trauma on them that is paradoxically based on a denial of the reality of traumatic experience. It follows that when Freud refers to the real or threatened loss of the penis as "the mental structure least accessible to influence," he is, in dissociated fashion, making a statement that is extremely revealing about himself, but not about patients in analysis or the human condition. It is this kind of thinking that enables Freud (1940a), in describing the "phallic phase" of the boy's "libidinal development," to assert that "from the age of two or three" he "becomes his mother's lover" and "tries to seduce her by showing her the male organ which he is proud to own" (p. 189).

So far have we come from the reality of the sexual abuse of children by adults, and the soul-murdering effects of all forms of trauma, that it is now a child of "two or three"—Freud's own age during his "prehistoric" period in Freiberg—who is now purported to be the "lover" of his mother and the one responsible for trying to "seduce *her*" with his tiny throbbing penis. The mother, of course, knows that this is "not right," and so she threatens the boy by telling him that his father "will cut the penis off," a threat that does not seem credible until the sight of the female genitals convinces the boy that there are indeed unfortunate creatures who "really lack this supremely valued part," which brings on with full force the castration complex that is "the severest trauma of his young life" (pp. 189–90). So hackneyed is this narrative, which persists unchanged from the case of Little Hans, that when we encounter it again not only here in *An Outline of Psycho-Analysis* but also in "Analysis Terminable and Interminable" and *Moses and Monotheism*, the reader may be forgiven for groaning at how boring and predictable this obsession has become in Freud's old age—and perhaps always was, at least after he had ensconced the castration complex as the "synthetic *a priori*" of psychoanalysis.[2]

4

Freud again addresses the issue of trauma in "Analysis Terminable and Interminable" (1937a) when he considers what it would mean to have genuinely finished an analysis. He defines an ideal ending as one where the analyst has helped the patient to achieve "a level of absolute psychical normality" and "succeeded in resolving every one of the patient's repressions and in filling in all the gaps in his memory" (pp. 219–20). In those "few cases which have had this gratifying outcome," Freud cites two conditions as "the determinants of these successes": "The patient's ego has not been noticeably altered and the aetiology of his disturbance had been essentially traumatic" (p. 220). This statement is bewildering because it fails to explain how one could experience a trauma *without* it resulting in an alteration of the ego. It contradicts his recognition, in *Moses and Monotheism*, of the "complete devastation or fragmentation of the ego" and "its being overwhelmed by the portion which was early split off and which is dominated by the trauma." In contrast to *An Outline of Psycho-Analysis*, moreover, Freud also argues that "there is no doubt that an aetiology of the traumatic sort offers by far the more favourable field for analysis." He elaborates:

> Only when a case is a predominantly traumatic one will analysis succeed in doing what it is so superlatively able to do; only then will it, thanks to having strengthened the patient's ego, succeed in replacing by a correct solution the inadequate decision made in his early life. Only in such cases can one speak of an analysis having been definitively ended. In them, analysis has done all that it should and does not need to be continued.

From the antiseptic way that Freud speaks of the goal of analysis as assisting the traumatized patient in "replacing by a correct solution the inadequate decision made in his early life," one would have no idea that victims of trauma experience overwhelming emotions, from the blackness of despair to the white heat of anger, and that the process of recovery involves far more than replacing an "inadequate decision" with a "correct solution." A corollary to this insensitivity is what Freud says about those cases in which it may be impossible for the analyst to deem the treatment to be complete: "A constitutional strength of instinct and an unfavourable alteration of the ego acquired in its defensive struggle in the sense of its being dislocated and restricted—these are the factors which are prejudicial to the effectiveness of analysis and which may make its duration interminable" (pp. 220–21). Paradoxically, and illogically, whereas in "essentially traumatic" cases resulting from "personal accidental experience" Freud believes that the ego remains *unaltered*, which creates "a *favourable* field for analysis," when neuroses are attributable entirely to "a constitutional strength of instinct" there will be an "unfavourable alteration of the ego." The latter condition is what dooms an analysis to be "interminable," and instead of "an enquiry into how a cure by analysis comes about," a topic Freud believes has been "sufficiently elucidated," he directs his attention to the question of "the obstacles that stand in the way of such a cure" (p. 221).

It is against this backdrop that Freud introduces the disguised case histories of Ferenczi and Emma Eckstein examined in the preceding chapter. In addition to his personal motivations for settling old scores with these nemeses, he uses them to mount a theoretical argument that their neuroses were due to an "instinctual disturbance" (p. 223), and that is why neither could be cured by analysis. But, together with Severn, Eckstein is the most traumatized patient in the history of psychoanalysis. Not only was she victimized by Fliess's near-fatal operation on her nose in 1895, but we know from Bonomi (2015a, pp. 102–14) that she underwent a surgical circumcision of one of her labia minora as a young girl. To make matters worse, just as Severn had had her ovaries involuntary removed, Freud (1937a) informs us that more than a decade after the end of her analysis Eckstein developed a myoma—a noncancerous tumor in the uterus—which necessitated a "complete hysterectomy" (p. 222). This series of catastrophes, however, does not prevent Freud from describing Eckstein as having "wallowed in masochistic phantasies" that rendered her "inaccessible to a further attempt at analysis"—for which he bore no particle of blame—and from portraying her "second illness" as "a different manifestation of the same repressed impulses, which the analysis had only completely resolved."

Ferenczi, too, was a massively traumatized human being, as he disclosed to Freud, to Groddeck, and to Severn in ever-increasing depth in the course of his personal and analytic relationships with them. Thus, for Freud to maintain not only that Ferenczi became estranged from him "for no assignable external reason," but also that his anguished history was the result of "instinctual conflict" (p. 223) that caused his ego to become permanently "dislocated and restricted," is of a piece with Freud's evasion of the challenge posed by Ferenczi's insistence on restoring trauma to the heart of psychoanalytic theory. Once it is understood that Freud adduces the case histories of Ferenczi and Eckstein to illustrate why "a constitutional strength of instinct" places certain patients beyond the reach of analysis, while refusing to take environmental factors seriously, it becomes clear why "Analysis Terminable and Interminable" is the lamest of all the late texts in which he is engaged in a supposed "dialogue" with Ferenczi.

5

"Constructions in Analysis" (1937b), by contrast, shows Freud at his finest. We are, for once, spared his obsession with the castration complex, while his discussion of how the validity of an intervention cannot be judged on the basis of the patient's immediate response but depends rather on such "indirect confirmation" (p. 264) as may or may not be forthcoming from subsequent material displays an absence of dogmatism such as we also find in his most brilliant early paper, the covertly autobiographical "Screen Memories" (1899), with which "Constructions in Analysis" has much in common in its sophisticated engagement with the vicissitudes of memory. Only in the final paragraph does Freud divagate into phylogenetic fantasies, asking the reader to join him in believing in the transmission of collective memories from the "forgotten and primaeval past" of the human race, just as the analyst seeks to accompany the "single human individual" (p. 209) in his search for the relics of lost time.

As Press (2006) has pointed out, moreover, "nowhere did Freud express himself in terms so similar to Ferenczi" (p. 532) as he does in "Constructions in Analysis" (1937b) when, toward the end of the paper, he declares that the analyst's recognition of the "kernel of truth" contained in the patient's delusion "would afford common ground on which the therapeutic work could develop," and that this work "would consist in liberating the fragment of historical truth from its distortions and its attachments to the actual present day and in leading it back to the point in the past to which it belongs" (p. 268). This is indeed in Ferenczi's spirit, and Freud is to be applauded for recognizing that what are commonly called "delusions" contain a nucleus of real experience, often going back to early childhood, which it is the task of the analysis to disinter and reconstruct, insofar as this may still be possible at a later date. Also extremely admirable is Freud's statement that the patient "must be brought to recollect certain experiences and the affective impulses called up by them which he has for the time being forgotten" (pp. 257–58), since the mention of "affective impulses" indicates an awareness that the recovery of repressed or dissociated memories is more than an intellectual exercise and bound to involve an emotional experience. It is no wonder John Bowlby, the preeminent psychoanalyst of real-life experience, should have quoted with approval Freud's avowal in "Constructions in Analysis" concerning the purpose of analysis: "What we are in search of is a picture of the patient's forgotten years that shall be alike trustworthy and in all essential respects complete" (p. 258; see Bowlby, 1979, p. 57).

6

Like "Constructions in Analysis," the posthumously published fragment "Splitting of the Ego in the Process of Defence" (1940b) is another late text in which Freud finds himself in Ferenczi's territory, though in neither paper is Ferenczi cited. Bonomi (2012) is therefore mistaken in proposing that this "delayed acknowledgment of Ferenczi's new metapsychology could have been the first step of a vast revision" (p. 242) in Freud's thinking, since Freud ignores Ferenczi entirely in coming to grips with the phenomenon of "a splitting of the ego," which, he says, "seems strange to us because we take for granted the synthetic nature of the processes of the ego" (1940b, p. 276). Freud here tacitly alludes to Herman Nunberg's paper at the Oxford Congress, "The Synthetic Function of the Ego" (1931), an instant classic of ego psychology. As Freud (1940b) notes, this "remarkable" act of splitting on the part of "the ego of a person whom we know as a patient in analysis" manifests itself only "in certain particular situations of pressure," the nature of which he further elaborates by adding that it "occurs under the influence of a psychical trauma" (p. 275).

Thus far, Freud appears to be off to a good start. But the problems quickly mount up. Although Freud does refer to "psychical trauma," the expression "situations of pressure" makes it clear that, no less than in *An Outline of Psycho-Analysis*, he is operating with the premise that an "instinctual demand" (p. 275) can be the instigator of the trauma. Furthermore, once he introduces "an individual case history into this schematic disquisition," Freud again invokes the "threat of castration" that causes a "little boy" who "had already become acquainted with the female genitals by being seduced by an older girl," and who "carried on the sexual stimulation set going in this way by zealously practising manual masturbation" until warned by an "energetic nurse" of the punishment to be carried out on his penis by his father, to confront the realization that "his own genitals may meet with the same fate" as that which had already befallen the girl, and who thereafter "cannot help believing in the reality of the threat of castration" (pp. 276–77).

Thus, the reader is forced to endure yet another of Freud's sermons on his "synthetic *a priori*" doctrine of the castration complex. The "psychical trauma" in this alleged "case history" is not the boy's actual seduction by an "older girl" that led to his precocious masturbation, but rather the "tremendous effect of fright" (p. 276) resulting from the ensuing castration threat. In Freud's schema, however, the "fright" has nothing to do, in Guasto's phrase, with the child's "loss of basic trust" in his caretakers, but is instead due to the "dreaded confirmation" of the fear that he might lose "such a highly prized part of his body" as his penis and consequently become no less mutilated than the female with whose genitals he was already "acquainted" through the seduction. Notwithstanding Bonomi's (2013) assertion that "Freud tried to incorporate and absorb Ferenczi's language of fragmentation" within his system, of which "the trauma of castration remained the pillar" (p. 374), Freud neither acknowledges Ferenczi nor does he contemplate fragmentation in "Splitting of the Ego in the Process of Defence."

Indeed, even what Freud has to say about splitting turns out to be little more than a restatement of his venerable model of compromise formation. As Freud (1940b) tells it, the conflict in the boy's mind between the castration threat and his desire to "proceed with his masturbation undisturbed" leads him to create "a substitute for the penis which he missed in females—that is to say, a fetish. In so doing, it is true that he had disavowed reality, but he had saved his own penis" (p. 277). In developing this fetish, the nature of which Freud does not specify but which evidently allowed the boy "between three and four years of age" (p. 276) to maintain a solitary sex life that would do credit to a grown man, "he effected no more than a displacement of value—he transferred the importance of the penis to another part of the body." Freud's language here echoes his description forty years earlier in "Screen Memories" (1899) of how a seemingly insignificant image retained in the mind "has been to some degree associatively *displaced*" (p. 307) from the important memory for which it serves as a surrogate. As Freud argued at the outset of his career as a psychoanalyst, the "opposing forces do not cancel each other out," but rather "a compromise is brought about, somewhat on the analogy of the resultant in a parallelogram of forces," and "the process which we here see at work—conflict, repression, and the formation of a compromise—returns in all psychoneurotic symptoms and gives us the key to understanding their formation" (pp. 307–8).

Apart from Freud's own fetish with the penis and the constant threats that he believes endanger it, "Splitting of the Ego in the Process of Defence" is commendable as far as it goes. The paper, however, does not go far enough. Any hope that Freud would engage with Ferenczi's "new metapsychology" is dashed by the realization that he remains wedded to a theory in which the mind, as he affirms in "Screen Memories," is the seat of a conflict between "two opposing forces" (p. 307), and everything that the analyst encounters clinically is reducible to a dualistic model. Despite its promise, therefore, "Splitting of the Ego in the Process of Defence," like Freud's other late writings, fails to deliver in this instance above all because he underestimates not only the anguish entailed by a "splitting of the ego"—which should rather be conceptualized as a dissociation and fragmentation of the self in response to the shattering effects of trauma—but also the power of the "synthetic" function that he "takes for granted" as its defining feature.

For an alternative paradigm, we must turn back to Severn (1933), who speaks of nightmares as "records of personal catastrophes, the consequence of which was disruption of the whole mental machinery," but who nonetheless believes that even a psyche that remains "haunted by its tragedy" is "forever seeking to repair and restore its damaged unity and soundness" (pp. 123–24). "Synthesis" for Severn is not merely a capacity belonging to the ego but an expression of her faith in "the innate integrity of every mind" (p. 109).

Notes

1 Information on the publication date derives from Jones (1957, p. 175) and is included by Strachey is his editor's introduction to the *New Introductory Lectures*.
2 See my chapter, "'Mother, Do You Have a Wiwimaker, Too?': Freud's Representation of Female Sexuality in the Case of Little Hans," in *Reading Psychoanalysis* (Rudnytsky, 2002).

Chapter 15

The Antitraumatic in Freud

1

As their lives drew to a close, Freud and Ferenczi engaged in a "reciprocal analysis" in which each sought to lay bare the theoretical and technical errors of the other and to explain these in *ad hominem* fashion as manifestations of neurotic conflicts and psychological blind spots. I call this analysis "reciprocal" rather than "mutual" not only because the two men so often talked past each other in their correspondence, but also because—apart from Freud's attempts to diagnose Ferenczi's character in his letters—their respective impeachments took place in texts that the interlocutor could not have read. Freud expressed his disgruntlement with Ferenczi in communications to his palace guard—Eitingon, Jones, and Anna—and in his jousts with Ferenczi's ghost in the writings of his final years, most notably in the disguised clinical vignette in "Analysis Terminable and Interminable." Ferenczi, for his part, refrained from responding to Freud's provocations and, apart from what he confided to those in his inner circle—including his key triad of American women patients—recorded his thoughts about Freud's character only in the sacrosanct pages of his *Clinical Diary*, the existence of which Freud had no knowledge and which was not published until more than fifty years after Ferenczi's death.

Ferenczi shared with Freud the conviction that it is legitimate to seek to understand all forms of creativity in psychobiographical terms. He thus had no quarrel in principle with Freud's repeated attempts to interpret his contributions to psychoanalysis as outgrowths of his personal struggles. But he would, as I have argued, have offered two caveats: first, the quest to unearth the subjective origins of ideas should not preclude a fair-minded consideration of their objective value; and, second, since psychology is "a knife that cuts both ways," it is equally justified to deploy the tools of psychoanalysis to try to pluck out the heart of *Freud's* mystery. Freud,

DOI: 10.4324/9781315280134-19

therefore, although he was right to a limited extent in what he said about Ferenczi's character, not only could not appreciate Ferenczi's revolutionary insights, but he also lacked humility and could not acknowledge the astigmatism that distorted his own vision. On the plane of theory, Freud's position is flawed and self-contradictory, particularly in his stripping of the concept of trauma of any explanatory power or emotional resonance and in his phallocentric obsession with the castration complex. Having established *how* Freud went wrong, both as a man and as a thinker, I shall now seek to analyze *why* he did so, an inquiry for which the *Clinical Diary* furnishes an indispensable starting point.

2

From the first sentence of his opening entry, on January 7, 1932, where Ferenczi observes that the "mannered form of greeting, formal request to 'tell everything,' so called free-floating attention, which ultimately amounts to no attention at all," is "certainly inadequate to the highly emotional character of the analysand's communications, often brought out only with the greatest difficulty" (Dupont, 1985, p. 1), the *Clinical Diary* constitutes a profound critique of Freud. With utmost perspicacity, Ferenczi outlines how "the patient is offended by the lack of interest" but "looks for the cause of this lack of reaction in himself," with the result that "finally he doubts the reality of the content, which until now he had felt so acutely." Taking his own experience with Freud as a touchstone, Ferenczi distills the process by which traumatized individuals find it easier to blame themselves, and to question the trustworthiness of their perceptions, than to hold the abusers on whom they are emotionally dependent responsible for their actions. Nonetheless, as Ferenczi recognizes, inwardly the patient is reproaching the analyst for his remoteness: "You don't believe me! You don't take seriously what I tell you! I cannot accept your sitting there unfeeling and indifferent while I am straining to call up some tragic event from my childhood." Consequently, the response of an analyst sensitive enough to discern the patient's unspoken accusations ought to be "that we examine in a critical way our own behavior and our own emotional attitudes with respect to these observations and admit the possibility or even the actual existence of fatigue, tedium, and boredom at times." This leads to Ferenczi's endorsement of the *"natural and sincere behavior"* exemplified by Groddeck and Thompson as "the most appropriate and favorable atmosphere in the analytic situation."

Not only is Ferenczi's indictment of the "insensitivity of the analyst" a commentary on Freud, but his exhortation that analysts should respond to patients' protests by looking first at "our own behavior and our own emotional attitudes" sums up what Freud was incapable of doing. Unlike Freud, who saw things only from the analyst's perspective, Ferenczi, as he explains in "The Principle of Relaxation and Neocatharsis" (1930), by virtue of his "double role" in the psychoanalytic movement, became—like Severn—"a kind of cross between a pupil and a teacher" (pp. 108–9), which permitted him to elucidate in unsurpassed fashion the dynamics of trauma, as these are enacted in the analytic situation, at once from the standpoint of the compassionate clinician and of the patient who knows how it feels to be rebuffed by his analyst.

Even when Freud is not named in the *Clinical Diary*, Ferenczi leaves no doubt that he has him in mind in depicting what must impress patients as the "deliberate cruelty" of their analysts: "One receives the patient in a friendly manner, works to establish transference securely, and then, while the patient is going through agonies, one sits calmly in the armchair, smoking a cigar and making seemingly conventional and hackneyed remarks in a bored tone; occasionally one falls asleep" (Dupont, 1985, p. 178).[1] Again, Ferenczi goes on to emphasize that "in one or another layer of his mind the patient is well aware of our real thoughts and feelings"—aware, in other words, that the analyst has taken refuge behind a mask of "*professional hypocrisy*"—but the acute vulnerability of the patient often makes it impossible for him to escape the chains of a sadomasochistic relationship: "As long as the slightest trace of hope exists that his wish for love will be gratified, and since our every word and every gesture acts on him with great power of suggestion, the patient will not be able to free himself from us and look around for other, more real possibilities in life."

Most of the time, however, Ferenczi makes it explicit that his painful lessons were learned in Freud's school: "My own analysis could not be pursued deeply enough because my analyst (by his own admission, of a narcissistic nature), with his strong determination to be healthy and his antipathy toward any weaknesses or abnormalities could not follow me down into those depths, and introduced the 'educational' stage too soon" (p. 62). Also extremely pertinent is his entry of May 1, 1932, which opens many fruitful avenues for exploration:

> Question: Is Freud really convinced, or does he have a compulsion to cling too strongly to theory as a defense against self-analysis, that is,

against his own doubts? It should not be forgotten that Freud is not the discoverer of analysis but that he took over something ready-made, from Breuer. Perhaps he followed Breuer merely in a logical, intellectual fashion, and not with any emotional conviction; consequently, he only analyzes others but not himself. Projection.

(p. 92)

Ferenczi here makes four interrelated points: (1) theory serves Freud as a defense against genuine self-analysis and self-knowledge; (2) psychoanalysis began not with Freud but with Breuer, and Breuer may still have something to offer that was lost with Freud; (3) Freud's version of analysis is purely "logical" and "intellectual," lacking "any emotional conviction"; and (4) Freud's defensiveness leads him to use analysis as a weapon against others while refusing to make himself vulnerable, that is, as a global form of "projection."

Later in this same entry, "Who is crazy, we or the patients? (the children or the adults?)," Ferenczi contemplates how patients are in danger of being harmed rather than healed by their insufficiently analyzed analysts: "Is it not possible, or even probable, that a doctor who has not been well analyzed (and who *is* well analyzed?) will not cure me, but instead will act out his own neurosis or psychosis at my expense[?]" (pp. 92–93). He adds in the next sentence, as "justifying these elements of suspicion" on the part of patients, "some of Freud's remarks he let fall in my presence, obviously relying on my discretion: 'Patients are a rabble' [*Die Patienten sind ein Gesindel*]. (2) Patients only serve to provide us with a livelihood and material to learn from. We certainly cannot help them" (p. 93; brackets in original). When Freud spoke thus unguardedly to Ferenczi, he looked on him as a fellow analyst who could be counted on to share his disdainful attitude toward "psychotics, perverts, and everything in general that is 'too abnormal,' so even against Indian mythology," forgetting that Ferenczi himself belonged to the "rabble" he had just deprecated. "This," Ferenczi now rejoins, "is certainly therapeutic nihilism, and yet by the concealment of these doubts and the raising of patients' hopes, patients do become caught."[2]

Although Freud sought to conceal his "therapeutic nihilism" from patients, he was much more cavalier with those whom he considered colleagues. In an October 9, 1918 letter to the Swiss pastor and psychoanalyst Oskar Pfister, he wrote: "I have found little that is 'good' about human beings on the whole. In my experience most of them are trash" (Meng and

Freud, 1963, p. 61). Almost exactly a decade later, on October 4, 1928, Freud explained to István Hollós, the first Secretary of the Hungarian Psychoanalytic Association and a specialist in the treatment of psychotics, why he experienced a "sort of opposition that was just not readily understandable" to Hollós's book *My Farewell to the Yellow House*:

> I finally had to confess to myself that it came from the fact that I do not love these sick people, that I become angry at them because I feel them to be so far from me and everything that is human. A surprising kind of intolerance, which certainly makes me unsuitable to be a psychiatrist. With the passing of time, I have ceased to find myself interesting, which is certainly analytically incorrect.[3]

Even more "surprising" than Freud's "intolerance" of "sick people" is the protestation that he no longer finds himself interesting, which exempts him from having to analyze his "anger" at the mentally ill, as though they were not part of humanity, and thus might have something in common with himself.

Intriguingly, Ferenczi goes on to propose that, while "originally Freud really did believe in analysis" and "followed Breuer with enthusiasm and worked passionately, devotedly, on the curing of neurotics," since "making the discovery that hysterics lie" Freud "no longer loves his patients" and "has returned to the love of his well-ordered and cultivated superego" (Dupont, 1985, p. 93). From his revisionist perspective, Ferenczi now sees Freud's abandonment of the "seduction" theory, not as a breakthrough, but instead as a response to feeling "first shaken, and then disenchanted" by his patients, which had the effect of reinforcing Freud's turning away from trauma: "Since this shock, this disillusionment, there is much less talk of trauma, the constitution now begins to play the principal role. Of course this involves a certain amount of fatalism." Without having lived to read Freud's final sequence of texts from the *New Introductory Lectures* to *An Outline of Psycho-Analysis*, Ferenczi unerringly pinpoints the replacement of "trauma" by "constitution" that is Freud's fundamental theoretical move and gravest error. As he further notes, Freud's "therapeutic technique, like his theory," is "becoming more and more impersonal (levitating like some kind of divinity above the poor patient, reduced to the status of a mere child, unsuspecting that a large share of what is described as transference is artificially provoked by this kind of behavior), one postulates that transference is created by the patient."

Ferenczi here extends his argument that authoritarian analysts, of whom Freud is the prototype, foist their unanalyzed tendencies onto their patients and thereby "artificially provoke" the responses that they in turn interpret as transference "created by the patient." As he writes in an earlier entry, "the possibility should not be rejected out of hand that the analyst's habit of identifying any obstacle encountered as resistance on the part of the patient can be misused in an equally *paranoid, that is, delusional way* for the *projection or disavowal of his own complexes*" (p. 26; italics added). Without denying that such a technique may be "useful for bringing old material to the surface," and that the interpretation may therefore be "true in part"—just as he did not contest the partial truth of Freud's interpretations of his own behavior—Ferenczi, in a continuation of his dissection of Freud's "narcissistic nature," points out how "comfortable" such an arrangement can be for the doctor, "in which his patients spare him the unpleasure of self-criticism and give him an opportunity to enjoy his superiority, and to be loved without any reciprocity (a situation of almost infantile grandeur), and moreover he even gets paid for it by the patient" (p. 94).

In a brief entry dated July 19, 1932, Ferenczi outlines the trajectory of his relationship with Freud. Initially, having "landed in the 'service of love' of a strong man," he gained a "new impetus" from the "experience of psychoanalysis" that led to "enthusiasm, personal work, a great deal of originality" (p. 159). After this first flush of joy, however, Ferenczi found himself subjected to "literal subordination" and the resentments arising from "secret Grand Vizier ambivalence" (pp. 159–60). He recalls that he felt a "partial relaxation of enthusiasm already in America," when he accompanied Freud and Jung to receive their honorary degrees from Clark University in 1909, but this resulted in "at most, *silence*. Unproductivity" (p. 160). This refers to Ferenczi's decade-long inability to complete *Thalassa* and his inhibition against expressing any of his steadily accumulating dissatisfaction to Freud. Then, from his present vantage point, Ferenczi sums up the results of his analysis of what would today be diagnosed as Freud's narcissistic personality disorder: "Latent disappointment: 'He does not love anyone, only himself and his work' (and does not allow anyone to be original)."[4] Ferenczi credits his gradual "libidinal detachment" with his three "'revolutionary' technical innovations: activity, passivity, elasticity," culminating in "return to trauma (Breuer)," before he ends by literally underscoring his main point: "*In opposition to Freud* I developed to an exceptional degree a capacity for *humility* and for appreciating the clearsightedness of the uncorrupted child (patient). Finally, I even allowed them (1) full insight into my weaknesses (analysis by everyone), (2) into my fraudulent superiority (tranquillity)." Ferenczi's phrase "in opposition to Freud" means not simply "in contrast to Freud" but also "from my struggle with Freud." Writing for his own eyes only, Ferenczi recognizes his "exceptional" capacity for humility, a virtue of which Freud was no less spectacularly bereft.

Together with the final entry in the *Clinical Diary*, where Ferenczi ascribes his "blood-crisis" following the Wiesbaden Congress to the realization that he would be "trampled under foot" by Freud's "indifferent power as soon as I go my own way and not his," and delivers his verdicts on the analyses of Thompson and Severn, the other truly indispensable entry is that of August 4, 1932, "Personal causes for the erroneous development of psychoanalysis," in which Ferenczi poses the question, "Why antitrauma and predisposition?" (p. 184). Why, in other words, did Freud retreat from his original focus on individually experienced traumas as the primary cause of human suffering to a theory centered on "predisposition" or "constitution" as a supposed biological bedrock laid down by our phylogenetic heritage?

In the course of his exposition, Ferenczi reflects on the burden he had to shoulder in succeeding Jung as Freud's "proclaimed crown prince" and "most perfect heir of his ideas" (p. 184). Again, the 1909 trip to America, during which Ferenczi observed Freud's "two hysterical symptoms" of "the fainting spell in Bremen" and "incontinence on Riverside Drive," is recalled as a turning point. Ferenczi thinks back as well to the harshness of Freud's conduct during their 1910 sojourn in Sicily and levels the criticism that Freud "could tolerate my being a son until the moment when I contradicted him for the first time (Palermo)" (p. 185). Acknowledging how he colluded in Freud's demand that he play the role of a "blindly dependent son," for which he was rewarded by gaining "membership in a distinguished group guaranteed by the king, indeed with the rank of field marshal for myself," and by means of which he learned the technique of "calm, unemotional reserve; the unruffled assurance that one knew better," as well as how to find "the causes of failure in the patient instead of partly in ourselves," Ferenczi again quotes Freud's cynical statements that "neurotics are a rabble, good only to support us financially and to allow us to learn from their cases" and that "psychoanalysis as a therapy may be worthless" (pp. 185–86).[5]

In sum, Ferenczi lays the groundwork for a psychoanalytic interpretation of Freud's authoritarian character. In what I would nominate as the most profound sentence about Freud ever written, Ferenczi concludes, "Thus *the antitraumatic in Freud is a protective device against insight into his own weaknesses*" (p. 186; italics added). Going beyond his earlier explanation of Freud's turning away from trauma as an expression of his "shock" and "disillusionment" at the discovery that "hysterics lie," Ferenczi grasps that, although the "essence of psychoanalysis" is "trauma and reconstruction," Freud abandoned his original theory above all because he could not come to terms with the extent to which he himself had been traumatized. As he elaborates, "in his conduct Fr[eud] plays only the role of the castrating god, he wants to ignore the traumatic moment of his own castration in childhood; he is the only one who does not have to be analyzed" (p. 188).

Ironically, by referring to Freud's "castration in childhood," Ferenczi continues to employ the phallic terminology that his own "revolutionary" innovations rendered obsolete, but he means to encompass the full range of Freud's "traumatic moments," which caused him to found "the theory of the parricidal Oedipus, but obviously applied only to others, not to himself," with the concomitant "fear of allowing himself to be analyzed" (p. 185). Whether in the guise of a "castrating god," an "indifferent power," or an analyst "levitating like some kind of divinity above the poor patient," Ferenczi depicts Freud as arrogating to himself the status of a supernal being, but he unmasks this stance as a defensive formation that serves to compensate for an underlying anxiety and feeling of insecurity.

Thus, just as Freud can never admit to being at fault in his personal relationships, so, too, he cannot acknowledge—even to himself—that he had been severely traumatized as a child. In reprehending Freud for "the unilaterally androphile orientation of his theory of sexuality," as instanced by his "castration theory of femininity" according to which "the clitoris develops and functions earlier than the vagina," Ferenczi speculates that Freud may have had a "personal aversion to the spontaneous female-oriented sexuality in women," leading to an "idealization of the mother" (p. 188). Ferenczi ventures further: "He recoils from the task of having a sexually demanding mother, and having to satisfy her. At some point his mother's passionate nature may have presented him with such a task."

Unlike Freud, Ferenczi is keenly aware of the severity of his traumas at the hands of women. As we have seen, through his analysis of and by

272 Consequences

Severn Ferenczi came to appreciate "the source of my hatred of females" in such experiences as the "passionate scenes" with the housemaid who "allowed me to play with her breasts, but then pressed my head between her legs so that I became frightened and felt I was suffocating" (p. 61), as well as the "terrifyingly rough treatment" he received from a nurse in early childhood "after an incident of anal soiling" (p. 36). He likewise recalled having been "cut to the heart" by his mother's accusation, "'You are my murderer.'" Ferenczi writes of how his "almost unbearable superperformance" with Severn was accompanied by "corresponding feelings of hate toward the patient," and explains that "these feelings of hate can at the same time be linked to the highly painful superperformances of youth and childhood, only grasped through reconstruction as compensation for very significant traumata" (p. 26). By "painful superformances" of childhood, Ferenczi means his "endless masturbatory activity" climaxing in "ejaculation up to the sky" (p. 15), and one could not ask for a more forthright recognition of how his greatest feats throughout the life cycle were impelled by the need to cope with "very significant traumata."

3

Ferenczi's hypothesis that Freud's theories of female sexuality might have originated in his having been charged as a boy with satisfying a "sexually demanding mother" finds support in Freud's epochal letters to Fliess of October 3–4 and October 15, 1897, which culminate in his proclamation that being in love with the mother and jealous of the father is "a universal event in early childhood," and this psychic constellation explains "the gripping power of *Oedipus Rex*" (Masson, 1985, p. 272). As is well known, Freud (among other intimate revelations) informs Fliess that many of his earliest memories center on a nursemaid who was arrested for theft and disappeared from his life in Freiberg shortly after the birth of his sister Anna on December 31, 1858. Crucially, Freud describes the nursemaid—and *not* his father—as the "'prime originator'" of his neurosis, adding that "she was my teacher in sexual matters and complained because I was clumsy and unable to do anything," a mortifying experience that Freud believes underlies his present-day sense of "impotence as a therapist" (pp. 268–69).[6]

Thus, although not his biological mother, Freud before the age of three did have a "sexually demanding" female caregiver who made him feel inadequate for being unable to "satisfy" her. Ferenczi's interpretation of the biographical origins of Freud's "castration theory of femininity" is corroborated by Freud's own testimony. Josef Sajner, who on the basis of his archival researches in Freiberg originally proposed (1968) that Freud's nursemaid was Monika Zajíc, a member of the family of locksmiths above whose shop the forty-one-year-old Jacob Freud lived in one room with his twenty-year-old wife Amalia and their newborn son, subsequently discovered (1981) in the nearby spa town of Roznau a register showing that, in June 1857, "Amalie Freud, wool-merchant's wife, with the child Sigmund and the maidservant Resi Wittek" (p. 143), had come for a cure of an intestinal inflammation. It was thus, in all likelihood, the latter woman, Theresa ("Resi") Wittek, who was, in Sajner's (1989) words, "the mysterious 'prime originator' of Freud's self-analysis" (p. 78).[7]

From Freud's description of his nursemaid as his "teacher in sexual matters," there is good reason to believe, as Marianne Krüll (1979) has argued, that Resi may have "manipulate[d] his penis, not simply when teaching him to urinate but on other occasions, too" (p. 121). Krüll bolsters this hypothesis by pointing to passages in his published writings, above all *Three Essays on the Theory of Sexuality* (1905b), that may very well possess a covert subjective resonance. There, Freud declares it to be "well known that unscrupulous nurses put crying children to sleep by stroking their genitals" (p. 180*n*1). He writes even more revealingly:

> A child's intercourse with anyone responsible for his care affords him an unending source of sexual excitation. . . . This is especially so since the person in charge of him, who, after all, is as a rule his mother, herself regards him with feelings that are derived from her own sexual life: she strokes him, kisses him, rocks him and quite clearly treats him as a substitute for a complete sexual object.
>
> (p. 223)

As Krüll (1979) has astutely remarked, "That Freud was thinking of his own experiences may be deduced from the fact that he spoke of 'the person in charge of him . . . as a rule his mother,' a qualification he might not otherwise have added" (p. 121).

The implications of identifying Freud's nursemaid as his "seducer" in early childhood are far-reaching. Indeed, she might be better termed his molester or abuser than his seducer. Commenting on the passage in Freud's letter to Fliess, Mary Marcel (2005) has highlighted how Freud tries "to make the unbearable thing more bearable by calling her his teacher, rather than his molester," and he "rewrites his sexual molestation" at the hands of this woman "as if it were a teenage boy's first visit to a prostitute" (pp. 17–18). In a "confusion of tongues," the imposition of the "passionate" sexuality of the adult on the "tender" psyche of the child was metamorphosed into a scenario in which the innately sexual child projects his desire onto the adult. This shifting of the locus of responsibility is replicated in *An Outline of Psycho-Analysis* (1940a) where, as we have seen, Freud would have us believe that "from the age of two or three" the boy "becomes his mother's lover" and "tries to seduce her by showing her the male organ which he is proud to own" (p. 189), a temptation to which the allegedly horrified mother responds by voicing a threat to have the offending member amputated.

In a further development of her revisionist reading, Marcel interprets Freud's ensuing avowal to Fliess that his "libido toward *matrem* was awakened, namely, on the occasion of the train journey with her from Leipzig to Vienna, during which we must have spent the night together and there must have been an opportunity for seeing her *nudam*" (Masson, 1985, p. 268), in light of his history of sexual abuse.[8] In Marcel's (2005) words, "It was not that he first had sexual thoughts about his mother and was jealous of his father, and that this becomes proof positive of the 'universality' of the Oedipus complex. Rather, his sexual feelings were prematurely aroused by the 'sexual lessons' carried out on him by his nurse" (p. 21). Because of his precociously triggered "sexual thoughts or impulses," merely seeing his mother's body as she changed her clothes on the train would, in little Sigismund's mind, be "associated with sexual acts or stimulation," but "his mother does not act out her expected role of molester. So the toddler is left with his own feelings, about which he now feels guilt and embarrassment." From this perspective, Freud's proclamation that what he would come to call the "Oedipus complex" is "a universal event in early childhood," far from being the discovery of a truth about human nature, is the culmination of a process in which Freud internalizes the "guilt and embarrassment" implanted in him by his adult abuser. Precisely as Ferenczi (1933a) outlines in his valedictory paper, "the most important change, produced in the mind of the child by the anxiety-ridden identification with the adult partner, is *the introjection of the guilt feelings of the adult* which makes hitherto harmless play appear as a punishable offense" (p. 162).

The evidence is compelling that not only Ferenczi but also Freud was sexually abused by a nursemaid in early childhood. Unlike Ferenczi, however, who was able to face his experiences squarely and to declare in his Wiesbaden lecture that "the trauma, especially the sexual trauma, as the pathogenic factor cannot be valued highly enough" (p. 161), Freud took refuge in both autobiographical and theoretical fantasies in which he transformed himself from a molested child into a swashbuckling rake who was initiated into the mysteries of sex by his "teacher" and then "spent the night together" with his mother. As Simon Partridge (2014) has summed up Freud's metamorphosis, he "air-brushed his life-giving but sexually compromised and deeply painful relationship with his nurse . . . and heroically invented a novel idea with supposedly universal appeal. The latter fits with his narcissistic self-reference as the 'conquistador,' a defence . . . against his own childhood feelings of rage, helplessness, and humiliation" (p. 145). Whereas Ferenczi's acknowledgment of his childhood traumas enables him to uncover the roots of not only his own unconscious misogyny but also of Freud's, Freud's psychic retreat is illustrated by his ridiculous claim in "On Narcissism" (1914b) that his comparison of women to "animals which seem not to concern themselves about us, such as cats and the large beasts of prey," is "not due to any tendentious desire to depreciate women," and indeed that any kind of tendentiousness is "quite alien to me" (p. 89).

4

The experience of sexual abuse is only one of many symmetries between the lives of Ferenczi and Freud. Closely connected is the fact that both men had "two mothers," which they recreated in later erotic triangles—Freud with his wife and his sister-in-law, and Ferenczi with his (future) wife and daughter-in-law. A third parallel is early sibling loss. Freud discloses the death of his baby brother Julius in the same October 3, 1897 letter to Fliess where he identifies his nurse as his "teacher in sexual matters" and infers that he "must have" seen his mother naked, saying that this event "left the germ of [self-]reproaches in me" (Masson, 1985, p. 268; brackets in original). The analogous experience for Ferenczi, as he writes in the *Clinical Diary*, is "my sense of guilt at the death of a sister (diphtheria) two years younger than myself" (Dupont, 1985, p. 121). As Judith Dupont points out in a note, Ferenczi's sister, Vilma, who died before reaching her first birthday, was actually not two but four years Ferenczi's junior, and whereas Julius was born immediately after Freud, there was another sibling, a brother, who came between Ferenczi and

Vilma; but the sense of guilt experienced by the two psychoanalysts is otherwise very similar. Strikingly, the death of their siblings is never mentioned by either Freud or Ferenczi in their published writings, but after his second fainting spell in Jung's presence, this time in Munich, Freud did explain to Ferenczi in a letter of December 9, 1912, "All these attacks point to the significance of cases of death experienced early in life (in my case it was a brother who died very young, when I was little more than a year old)" (Brabant et al., 1993, p. 440). Like Ferenczi's, Freud's chronology is imprecise, because when Julius died on April 15, 1858 Freud had almost reached his second birthday, which came on May 6; but, as in his letter to Fliess, Freud again ascribes great psychological significance to his early exposure to sibling loss.

Although Freud twice singled out the death of Julius as a momentous event in his life, in response to a lost letter in which Ferenczi had analyzed a dream having to do with the unconscious roots of his desire to become a doctor, Freud declared on January 10, 1910, "This need to help is lacking in me, and I now see why, because *I did not lose anyone whom I loved in my early years*" (p. 122; italics added). Freud adds that the "inner cause" of his break with Fliess—which, as usual, he insists the latter "effected in such a pathological (paranoid) manner"—was that he had interpreted Fliess's turning "his attention to the nose" as well as his "theory of predetermined dates of death" as responses to the deaths of his father and sister, a "piece of analysis" that was "unwanted by him." Freud's linking of both Fliess's predilection for numerology and his choice of otolaryngology as a medical specialty to the deaths of a parent and a sibling leaves no doubt that the thought of sibling loss was present in Freud's mind as he was writing to Ferenczi, which makes it even more puzzling that he should have forgotten about Julius in seeking to persuade Ferenczi that he did not feel the "need to help" others because "I did not lose anyone whom I loved in my earliest years."

Freud had no difficulty in calling the death of Julius to mind in connection with sibling rivalry, as this was reenacted in his relationships with Fliess and Jung, but he dissociated it in the context of the theme of loss. Because he disavows his losses, Freud is unable to admit that his own "medical tendencies" could have originated in an impetus to make reparation for damage suffered or inflicted, or even that he possessed any "need to help" others in the first place. Thus, just as is true with respect to their having been victims of childhood sexual abuse, both Freud and Ferenczi suffered the blow of early sibling loss, but Ferenczi was able to integrate this trauma into his sense of self and to acknowledge the compensatory function of his sexual and analytic "superperformances," whereas Freud labored ceaselessly to shield himself from this awareness.

At a deeper level, the death of Julius stands as a synecdoche for what Louis Breger (2000) has called the "host of calamities" (p. 11) that befell Freud's family in the period leading up to and following Sigismund Schlomo's birth. These include the death of Jacob Freud's first wife, Sally Kanner Freud, the mother of Freud's adult half-brothers Emanuel and Philipp; the death or disappearance by 1854 of his second wife, Rebekka; and then, less than three months before Freud's birth, the death of Jacob Freud's father Schlomo, in whose memory the boy received his Hebrew name. As Breger comments, while these losses preceding Freud's birth may have been "assimilated by the family" (p. 12), the same cannot be said of the deaths of Amalia Freud's younger brother, Julius Nathansohn, in Vienna on March 15, 1858 of tuberculosis at the age of approximately twenty-two, and then, exactly one month later, of his namesake little Julius Freud.[9] Thus, before Freud was two years old, his mother had been smitten by a double loss, which "created a family atmosphere of mourning and depression."

This pall of familial and, specifically, maternal depression would have been thickened by the crisis resulting in the arrest and imprisonment of Freud's Catholic Czech nursemaid and the family's ensuing departure from Freiberg, whether this was due to an economic reversal or possible anti-Semitic repercussions from this incident—or, as Krüll (1979, pp. 145–46) has speculated, was arranged by Jacob in order to separate Amalia from his son Philipp, with whom she may perhaps been having an affair—while the parade of six siblings who followed Julius meant that his mother was continually pregnant during Freud's first ten years and overwhelmed by the demands of her burgeoning family, rendering her emotionally unavailable to her firstborn.[10] In calling attention to "the mother's lack of availability engendered by this spate of mournings" in Freud's family, Press (2006) asks, "Was not Freud . . . obliged to be the indispensable narcissistic complement to the young Amalia Freud, plunged into mourning for both her second son and her brother?" (p. 522).

Unlike Ferenczi, the eighth of twelve children, Freud stood at the head of the brood of siblings in his immediate family. He did, however, have to contend not only with the existence of his half-brothers but, even more immediately, with that of Emanuel's children, John and Pauline—immortalized as his playmates on the Freiberg meadow in "Screen Memories"—the former being nine months his elder and the latter six months younger than he was. Despite these complications, the sense of being his mother's favorite shaped Freud's self-image and the narratives he fashioned about himself, as when he wrote of Goethe but also in an autobiographical vein, "if a man has been his mother's undisputed darling he retains throughout life the triumphant feeling, the confidence in success, which not seldom brings actual success along with it" (1917, p. 156). He went so far as to proclaim in the *New Introductory Lectures* (1933a) that a mother's devotion to her son is "altogether the most perfect, the most free from ambivalence, of all human relationships" (p. 133). There is no reason to question that Freud was his mother's "golden Sigi." But what remains unconvincing is his depiction of this privileged status as "undisputed" and "free from ambivalence," which flies in the face of his own dogma that women are plagued by penis envy even toward their sons and masks the complex and troubled reality of his emotional experience.

As so often, we get a much more accurate picture of Freud's inner world in one of his dissociated narratives, this time in "Femininity," the same chapter in the *New Introductory Lectures* (1933a) where he idealizes the mother-son relationship but writes of the girl that her "turning away from the mother is accompanied by hostility; the attachment to the mother ends in hate" (p. 121). In Freud's view, "the reproach against the mother which goes back the furthest is that she gave the child too little milk—which is construed against her as a lack of love" (p. 122). He continues:

> The next accusation against the child's mother flares up when the next baby appears in the nursery. If possible the connection with oral frustration is preserved: the mother could not or would not give the child any more milk because she needed the nourishment for the new arrival. In cases in which the two children are so close in age that lactation is prejudiced by the second pregnancy, this approach acquires a real basis, and it is a remarkable fact that a child, even with an age difference of only 11 months, is not too young to take notice of what is happening. But what the child grudges the unwanted intruder and rival is not only the suckling but all the other signs of maternal care. It feels that it has been dethroned, despoiled, prejudiced in its rights; it casts a jealous hatred upon the new baby and develops a grievance against the faithless mother which often finds expression in a disagreeable change in its behaviour. . . . Especially as this jealousy is constantly receiving fresh nourishment in the later years of

childhood and the whole shock is repeated with the birth of each new brother or sister. Nor does it make much difference if the child happens to remain the mother's preferred favourite. A child's demands for love are immoderate, they make exclusive claims and tolerate no sharing.

(p. 123)

Here we have the dark underside of the rosy picture of Freud as his mother's "undisputed darling," basking in a mutual admiration that is "free from ambivalence." Instead he describes a child dealing with "hostility" and "hate" for the mother, one who reproaches her with a "lack of love" and who feels "dethroned, despoiled, prejudiced in its rights" with "the birth of each new brother or sister," a repeated "shock" that is not alleviated even "if the child happens to remain the mother's preferred favourite." This is the true autobiography of Sigmund Freud. His empathy with the bitterness of a child deprived of mother's milk arises from the fact that, as Paul C. Vitz (1988) has calculated, "during the first 32 months of Sigmund's life (i.e., until Anna's birth), his mother was pregnant a total of 18 months," which makes it "unlikely that Sigmund was nursed by his mother for more than a brief period" (p. 7). But, as Breger (2000) points out, Freud "did not connect any of this to himself, or even to male babies as a group; in his essay 'Femininity,' only little girls were presumed to have such feelings" (p. 14).

Thus, notwithstanding their different positions in the sibling order, Freud shares with Ferenczi the fate of being the offspring of a beleaguered, controlling, and depressed mother of either eight or twelve children. But just as is true with respect to their experiences of sexual abuse and early sibling loss, whereas Ferenczi was able to acknowledge to Groddeck that he "certainly didn't get enough love" from his mother "and did get too much severity from her as a child," Freud cannot accept the extent of his own deprivation. Instead, he projects it not only onto girls but also onto Ferenczi, whom he can then disparage by informing Jones that "his mother had not loved him . . . passionately or exclusively enough." At every turn, we find confirmation for Ferenczi's interpretations that "the antitraumatic in Freud is a protective device against insight into his own weaknesses," and that, in arrogating to himself "the role of the castrating god," Freud "wants to ignore the traumatic moment of his own castration in childhood; he is the only one who does not have to be analyzed."

5

In "Origins," the opening chapter of his biography, Jones (1953) terms the universality of the Oedipus complex the "greatest" of Freud's discoveries and suggests that it was "potently facilitated by his own unusual family constellation, the spur it gave to his curiosity, and the opportunity it afforded of a complete repression" (p. 11).[11] As I have sought to demonstrate, however, this supposed "discovery" is better understood as a defensive formation, and what is subject to a "complete repression" is not Freud's oedipal desire but rather the painful reality of what Breger calls, in the title of the opening chapter of *his* biography, "a traumatic childhood." Marcel (2005) throws down the gauntlet in the opening paragraph of her book when she writes that "the Oedipus complex concerns a neurosis, not a trauma," but in order to take Freud's measure what needs to be investigated is "the trauma behind the Oedipus complex" (p. 1).

In his analysis of the consequences for psychoanalysis of "the paranoid strain in Freud's character," David M. Terman (2014) has hypothesized that the genesis of such a structure lies in "significant traumatic narcissistic injuries," though he doubts whether "we know enough to say where—or if—in his early childhood such things may have occurred" (p. 1,012). But we can in fact account convincingly for Freud's "paranoid strain." In addition to the "host of calamities" visited on him in his first three years, Terman himself notes the relevance of two famous "narcissistic injuries" from a later period involving Freud and his father, both reported in *The Interpretation of Dreams* (1900). The first occurred at the age of seven or eight when Sigismund "disregarded the rules which modesty lays down and obeyed the calls of nature in my parents' bedroom while they were present," to which Jacob responded with the crushing words, "'The boy will come to nothing'" (p. 216). Freud describes the reprimand as "a frightful blow to my ambition," adding that "references to this scene are still constantly recurring in my dreams and are always linked with an enumeration of my achievement and successes, as though I wanted to say, 'You see, I *have* come to something.'"

This incident with his father resonates with Freud's experience of being shamed by his nurse for being "clumsy and unable to do anything." Indeed, the behavior that incurred his father's displeasure—urinating in his parents' bedroom—constitutes a repetition of an earlier occasion in which, as Freud (1900) recalls, "when I was two years old I still occasionally *wetted the bed*, and when I was reproached for this I *consoled* my father by promising to buy him a nice *new red* bed" (p. 216). This pattern of incontinence becomes comprehensible when seen as a sequela of Freud's sexual abuse by his nursemaid. As he maintained in "The Aetiology of Hysteria" (1896), the fullest exposition of his "seduction theory," when a child is molested his "performance of the sexual activities assigned to him is often interrupted by his imperfect control of his natural needs," and he names the "painful need to urinate" as the first in a "set of exceedingly common hysterical symptoms" that his analyses had shown "to be derivatives of the same childhood experiences" (pp. 214–15). Marcel (2005) is unquestionably right to read these passages as dissociated autobiography and to infer that by "imperfect control of his natural needs" Freud means, in the case of a boy, that "the child might urinate when his penis was stimulated" (p. 18), which lends credence to Krüll's hypothesis that one of the occasions on which Resi Wittek "manipulated" her young charge's penis was "when teaching him to urinate."

Thus, when Jacob Freud humiliated his eight-year-old son by telling him he would "come to nothing," the event was not only traumatic in itself but was superimposed on Sigismund's reproaches and abuse by his nurse, and his offense against "the rules which modesty lays down" was already a "hysterical symptom" in which was encoded his somatic memory of that ancient indignity. Urinary incontinence was a neurotic symptom that plagued Freud throughout his life. As we have seen, Ferenczi in the *Clinical Diary* recalled Freud's "incontinence on Riverside Drive" during the trip to America, and we know from the corroborating testimony of Jung that this occurred immediately after Freud had called a halt to Jung's attempt to analyze one of Freud's dreams having to do with his love triangle with his wife and sister-in-law by uttering the fateful words, "I could tell you more but I cannot risk my authority."[12] Ferenczi in the *Diary* recollects Freud's "American vanity" and how he seemed "ridiculous, when almost with tears in his eyes he thanked the president of the university for his honorary doctorate" (Dupont, 1985, p. 184). This sign of international renown made the 1909 voyage to America the supreme proof for Freud that he *had* "come to something," but the little boy inside was still wounded by his father's "blow to his ambition," as evidenced by his once again involuntarily obeying the "calls of nature," while the further connection of this same "hysterical symptom" to Freud's dream about his wife and sister-in-law shows that the trip to America was likewise when the chickens came home to roost for his affair in 1900 with Minna Bernays.

The second, still more famous, episode involving his father is a mirror image of the first. As Freud (1900) recalls in his dream book, when he had reached the age of "ten or twelve" the two of them went walking in Vienna and his father recounted how, as a young man, he had gone walking in the streets of Freiberg and a Christian knocked off his "new fur cap" and yelled, "'Jew, get off the pavement!'" (p. 197), to which Jacob responded by going into the roadway and picking up his cap. Whereas in the previous incident Sigismund was humiliated by his father, now it is his father—described by Freud as a "big strong man"—whom the son inwardly reproaches for his "unheroic conduct," and the "little boy" who identifies with Hannibal and wishes that he could "take vengeance on the Romans" (p. 197).

Thus, just as when he promised to buy his father "a nice *new red* bed," or when he transformed his molestation by his nurse into an oedipal romance, Freud copes with an experience of humiliation by casting himself in a heroic role. In so doing, he adopts an "antitraumatic" stance that functions as "a protective device against insight into his own weaknesses." Had his father not shamed him by saying he would "come to nothing," Freud would not have needed to retaliate by debasing his father and—at literally the drop of a hat—to engage in a "superperformance" by vowing "to take vengeance on the Romans."

As Ferenczi grasped by the time of the *Clinical Diary*, Freud suffered from a narcissistic character disorder that stemmed from the unhealed wounds of his childhood. Although he was unaware of the *Diary*, Fromm, like Ferenczi, understood that Freud's tragic flaws were the "personal causes for the erroneous development of psychoanalysis." In *Sigmund Freud's Mission* (1959), Fromm argued that "dependency and insecurity are central elements in the structure of Freud's character, and of his neurosis" (p. 23). Because he could not face his own traumas, Freud repudiated his dependency needs and wanted to play "only the role of the castrating god." This made him unable to imagine the possibility of a relationship not based on dominance and submission, in which two people meet as equals in a spirit of mutual love and respect. Consequently, Fromm describes Freud as "a *rebel* and not a *revolutionary*," because a rebel is someone "who fights existing authorities but who himself wants to be an authority," whereas a revolutionary "achieves true independence and overcomes his desire for the domination of others" (p. 64). Dismissing as psychologically naive the denials by Jones and other "faithful worshipers" of "any authoritarian tendency in Freud," Fromm pries open the vise of the double bind that Freud sought to impose on his followers. As Fromm explains, in the authoritarian character "there is an *unconscious* dependence in which a dominant person is dependent on those who are dependent on him" (p. 52), and it is because Freud "was so dependent on unconditional affirmation and agreement by others" that he could be "a loving father to submissive sons," but became "a stern and authoritarian one to those who dared to disagree" (p. 71).

When Ferenczi rues that Freud "is the only one who does not have to be analyzed," his point is not that Freud would have gained greater insight into himself through being the beneficiary of someone else's "pedagogical" interpretations. It is, rather, that because of his need to control everyone else Freud was unwilling to entrust himself to the care of another human being to whom he would have to expose his vulnerabilities, and thus was never able to experience the transformative and healing power of psychoanalysis. In the death agony of his relationship with Freud, Jung wrote to him on December 18, 1912, "You know, of course, how far a patient gets with self-analysis: *not* out of his neurosis—just like you" (McGuire, 1974, p. 535), while fifteen days earlier he had pleaded, "It is only occasionally that I am afflicted with the purely human desire to be understood *intellectually*, and not be measured by the yardstick of neurosis" (p. 526).

In his wrath and sorrow, Jung turned against Freud the double-edged sword of psychoanalysis and sought to parry his authoritarianism with the same ripostes that would later be pivotal to Ferenczi's side of his "reciprocal analysis" with Freud. Both "crown princes" beseeched their royal father to acknowledge his own fallibility and pleaded that they might be "understood *intellectually*," instead of being "measured by the yardstick of neurosis." But whereas Jung flung his reproaches in Freud's face and paid the price of being excommunicated from the fold, Ferenczi kept his most critical thoughts private and defended himself to Freud only in the mildest fashion, thereby preserving the thread of their relationship and bequeathing to posterity a truly "revolutionary" vision of psychoanalysis. As Fromm (1935) had the wisdom and courage to recognize, even while Freud was still alive, "The example of Ferenczi shows, however, that the Freudian attitude need not be that of all analysts" (p. 163).

Notes

1 Compare Severn's (1933) description, quoted in Chapter 4, of how Rank "sat and looked out of his window with a vacant, bored expression, without a single word of response, while listening to the tragic tale which a distressed and anxious person was struggling to tell him" (p. 86).

2 Compare Angelika Frink's comments about Freud's "completely selfish" treatment of others quoted in the Prelude and the remarks about a homosexual attributed to Freud by Clara Thompson in Chapter 8.
3 I am indebted to Bryony Davies at the Freud Museum, London, for supplying me with a typescript of the German original of Freud's (1928b) letter. A complete French version is given by Eva Brabant-Gerő (1986, p. 9) in her introduction to the French translation of Hollós's book published by *Le Coq-Héron*.
4 According to the *DSM-IV-TR*, "The essential feature of Narcissistic Personality Disorder is a pervasive pattern of grandiosity, need for admiration, and lack of empathy that begins by early adulthood and is present in a variety of contexts" (American Psychiatric Association, 2000, p. 714).
5 So indelibly did Freud's words impress themselves on Ferenczi's memory that he cites them for a third time on June 12, 1932, "*Freud*: 'rabble,' 'only good for making money out of, and for studying.' (Is true, but must be admitted to the patients.) They feel it in any case and produce resistance. (When it is admitted—trust increases)" (p. 118).
6 As Mario Beira has noted in a personal communication, the German word "*Urheberin*," which Masson translates as "prime originator," could be rendered more literally as "primal raiser" in order to suggest that his nursemaid's ministrations caused the very young Freud to have an erection.
7 The existence of yet another maidservant, the twenty-nine-year-old Anna Hrazek, who accompanied Amalia Freud and her two children, Sigismund—as he was named until 1875, when (according to the Biographical Note in the Freud Archives) he began to call himself Sigmund—and Anna, from Freiberg to Leipzig in August 1859, but of whom there is no trace following the family's arrival in Vienna in October 1859, has been established from travel documents (Schröter and Tögel, 2007, p. 206; O'Donoghue, 2019, pp. 133-34). Freud's mother's name is spelled both "Amalia" and "Amalie" in contemporary records (see, e.g., Sajner, 1968, p. 176); but since, as Beira points out in a personal communication, the Latin form appears both on the certificate of her marriage to Jacob Freud and on the tombstone erected in Vienna by her children, I have used "Amalia" throughout.
8 Noting the qualification implied by Freud's repeated use of the phrase "must have been," as well as the fact that he claimed to have been "between two and two and a half years" (Masson, 1985, p. 268), whereas "he was in actuality nearly three and a half when, in October 1859, they traveled from Leipzig to Vienna," Diane O'Donoghue (2019) judiciously cautions against assuming the veridicality of his memory. But even if we cannot rely on "the attending specifics," O'Donoghue acknowledges that Freud's account does indicate "his internal, libidinal response" (pp. 125–26).
9 Although Breger (2000), basing himself on the following passage quoted from "Femininity," states that Freud was "just eleven months old" (p. 11) when his brother was born, Julius Freud was born in October 1857, which makes Freud seventeen months old at the time.
10 At the time that Amalia went to Roznau with Sigismund and Resi Wittek, she was approximately four months pregnant with Julius (Sajner, 1989, p. 78), while she was "in her fifth month of pregnancy with Freud's second sister, Rosa" (O'Donoghue, 2019, p. 144), at the time of the reconstructed *matrem*

nudam incident on the train from Leipzig to Vienna. What is more, the family's departure from Leipzig was delayed by two months by the illness of Freud's first sister Anna, who recalled having suffered from scarlet fever and dropsy; and, as O'Donoghue has documented, "by the age of ten Freud had lived in nine places in three different central European locations" (p. 6; see p. 146).

11 This sentence is copied verbatim from *Freud and Oedipus* (Rudnytsky, 1987, p. 15). While I remain committed to the indispensability of biography in understanding Freud and the history of psychoanalysis, my current vantage point is 180 degrees from what it was in my first book.

12 For complete documentation of Freud's urinary incontinence in New York, see my *Rescuing Psychoanalysis from Freud* (Rudnytsky, 2011, pp. 42–52). The quoted sentence is taken from Jung's 1957 interview with John M. Billinsky (1969, p. 42).

Chapter 16

New Veins of Gold

1

One of the accusations most frequently leveled by proponents of psychoanalytic orthodoxy against rival schools is that, whereas the traditional framework derived from Freud is capable of including all the alternative perspectives, the dissidents offer no more than slivers of the truth encompassed in Freud's grand theory. A classic statement to this effect is Leo Rangell's (1988) declaration that all the elements that "have served as nodal points of alternative theories are included in this total unitary theory, whereas the converse is not true" (p. 317). Rangell (1982) perpetuates Freud and Jones's tactic of diagnosing intellectual adversaries by insisting that "indefensible arguments . . . are invariably the glue which binds a new group together" (p. 31), and that self psychology and allied challenges to mainstream thinking are "pathological developments" (p. 33) that reflect "a negative transference to psychoanalysis itself" (p. 35).

What, to quote Fromm (1935) again, "the example of Ferenczi shows" (p. 163) with consummate clarity, however, is that the choice between his version of psychoanalysis and Freud's is not a choice between a "partial theory" and a "total theory," but rather one between two comprehensive visions that, while they do overlap at some points, are in the end radically divergent. And just as Ferenczi recorded for posterity his answer to Freud's attempts to analyze him in the *Clinical Diary*, so, too, he sets forth in the writings of *his* final period, of which his two greatest papers stand as bookends, an integrated conception of psychoanalytic theory and technique that I believe to be demonstrably superior to Freud's.

The first hint of the paper that Ferenczi would deliver in July 1929 at the eleventh congress of the International Psychoanalytical Association in Oxford under the title "Advances in Psychoanalytic Technique," published the following year as "The Principle of Relaxation and Neocatharsis," is found in his letter to Freud on January 10, 1929, where he announces, "I seem to have penetrated to a kind of technique which allows one to work calmly and successfully; at the same time, a number of theoretical connections become clearer without any strain. Perhaps I will write something about this for the next Congress" (Falzeder and Brabant, 2000, p. 359). Although Ferenczi did not send Freud a copy of his lecture until February 14, 1930, he outlined its main points in a letter of December 25, 1929. These start with the reports that "in *all* cases, in which I penetrated deeply enough, I found the traumatic-hysterical basis for the illness," and that "where I and the patient succeeded in this, the therapeutic effect was much more significant" (p. 379). While avowing that he "can confirm everything that modern ego psychology has brought about," by which Ferenczi means the new directions charted by Freud in *The Ego and the Id* (1923a) and *Inhibitions, Symptoms and Anxiety* (1926a), he nonetheless faults these tendencies because of their "overestimation of fantasy—and the underestimation of the traumatic reality in pathogenesis," and admits that he does not "place these investigations . . . so very much in the center of theoretical and technical interest" (p. 376).

Ferenczi (1930) opens his Oxford Congress paper by commenting on the irony of using the word "progresses" or "advances" (*Fortschritte*) in his title, since he recognizes that what he is about to say "might more fittingly be termed retrogressive or reactionary" (p. 108). This was, of course, Freud's aspersion when he accused Ferenczi, prior to their final meeting before the Wiesbaden Congress, in a letter to Eitingon of having repeated his own "first great etiological error" (Schröter, 2004, 2:826); and Ferenczi (1930) percipiently defends himself by defining his aim not as seeking to cast out the new in favor of the old, but rather as highlighting "where we are tending to be one-sided, and, without foregoing what is good in the new teaching, to plead that justice shall be done to that which has proved its value in days past" (p. 109). Or, as he puts it at a later stage of his argument, "The sudden emergence in modern psycho-analysis of portions of an earlier technique and theory should not dismay us; it merely reminds us that . . . we must constantly be prepared to find new veins of gold in temporarily abandoned workings" (p. 120).

Ferenczi's depiction of his aspiration as one of restoring a balance between earlier and more recent standpoints in psychoanalysis doubtless reflects his genuinely held conviction. But in assessing this stance it should not be forgotten how difficult he always found it to express any opposition to Freud, and how much internal pressure he felt to present himself as a "dutiful child" of his mentor. Thus, in his next paper, "Child Analysis in the Analysis of Adults" (1931), delivered at the Vienna Psychoanalytic Society on the occasion of Freud's seventy-fifth birthday, Ferenczi scolds, "Over and over again one hears irresponsible remarks about the intolerance, the 'orthodoxy' of our master. It is said that he will not suffer any of his associates to criticize any of his theories, and that he drives all independent talent out of his circle in order tyrannically to impose his own will in matters scientific" (p. 126).[1] He continues by hailing *The Interpretation of Dreams* as "so polished a gem, so closely knit in content and in form, that it withstands all the changes of time and of the libido, so that criticism scarcely ventures to approach it" (p. 127).

To be sure, a birthday celebration is hardly the venue for remonstrances, but Ferenczi's inveighing against those who would upbraid Freud for his "intolerance" and propensity to drive "all independent talent out of his circle in order tyrannically to impose his own will in matters scientific" is irreconcilable with his arraignments in the *Clinical Diary* of Freud's "narcissistic nature," his willingness to tolerate Ferenczi's "being a son until I contradicted him for the first time," his playing "only the role of the castrating god" in his conduct (Dupont, 1985, pp. 62, 185, 188), and so forth. The only explanation for this contradiction between what he says in public and in private is that Ferenczi's authentic feelings are those consigned to the *Diary*, while his official pronouncements are symptomatic of the very problems caused by Freud's authoritarian character he forthrightly denounces in his solitary musings. Similarly, Ferenczi's protestation that *The Interpretation of Dreams* contains eternal verities is belied by his challenge to Freud's wish-fulfillment theory in "On the Revision of the *Interpretation of Dreams*," dated March 26, 1931, included in his posthumously published *Notes and Fragments* (1920, 1930–1932), the abstract of which he sent to Freud, along with that for a second paper that eventually became "Confusion of Tongues," on May 31, 1931, the same month and year in which he delivered his birthday encomium in Vienna.[2]

Starting from the premise that "the day's (and, as we may add, life's) residues are indeed repetition symptoms of traumata," Ferenczi argues that "instead of 'the dream is a wish-fulfillment' a more complete definition of the dream function would be: every dream, even an unpleasurable one, is an attempt at better mastery and settling of traumatic experiences" (1920, 1930–1932, p. 238). Allied to this accentuation of what Ferenczi terms the "traumatolytic function of the dream" (p. 240) is his contention that the "return of the day's and life's residues" should not "be considered as mechanical products of the repetition instinct," but that these are rather to be understood as the expression of "a tendency (which should be called psychological) towards a new and better settlement, and the wish-fulfillment is the means which enables the dream to achieve this aim more or less successfully" (p. 239).

Far from regarding *The Interpretation of Dreams* as impervious to "all the changes of time and of the libido," Ferenczi—like Severn in *The Discovery of the Self*—proposes an inversion of explanatory paradigms whereby Freud's wish-fulfillment theory, while not discarded entirely, is subordinated to his concept of "the traumatolytic function of the dream." He rejects Freud's postulate of the repetition compulsion as a biological instinct, and instead explains repetition as an attempt to achieve "a new and better settlement" of unresolved emotional conflicts. Responding to Ferenczi's letter of May 31, 1931 proposing that "sleep state and dream seek to unburden the psychic system also by reexperiencing traumatic day's and life's residues" (Falzeder and Brabant, 2000, p. 412), Freud claims that Ferenczi is not saying anything original because "the so-called second function of dreams is certainly its first (mastery, see Beyond the Pleasure Principle)" (p. 413). He also trivializes Ferenczi's idea, the germ of "Confusion of Tongues," that, as Freud had done with neurotics, "one could also take seriously as psychic reality the mechanisms, which are of a different nature and rather universal, behind the productions of psychotics and those who have been traumatically shocked." As examples of such mechanisms, Ferenczi cites a "fragmentation and atomization of the personality; sequestration" (p. 412). Just as Freud had told Ferenczi on September 16, 1930 that his "new views about the traumatic fragmentation of mental life . . . seem to me to be very ingenious and have something of the great characteristic of the Theory of Genitality" (p. 399), all he can say now is that Ferenczi's extension of psychoanalytic metapsychology possesses "that characteristic which is so inestimable to me, which I respect so very much, like your theory of genitality" (p. 413).

Far from being Ferenczi's "summit of achievement" (p. 229), as Freud (1933b) called *Thalassa* in his obituary, Ferenczi recognized in the *Diary* that this venture in "bioanalysis" would require "complete rewriting" (Dupont, 1985, p. 187) if it were to be rescued from obsolescence. Smarting under the lash, Ferenczi plucked up his courage on September 21, 1930 to try to make clear to Freud why the comparison to *Thalassa* is off-base:

> I was pleased to hear that you find my new views "very ingenious"; I would have been much more pleased had you declared them correct, probable, or even only plausible. The comparison with the "theory of

> genitality" is perhaps only a superficial one. The "theory of genitality" was the product of pure speculation at a time when, far removed from any practice, I totally gave way to contemplation (military service). The newer views, only fleetingly alluded to, originate from the practice itself, were brought to the surface by it, extended and modified daily; they proved to be not only theoretically but practically valuable, that is to say, usable.
>
> (p. 400)

Unlike *Thalassa*, which was "the product of pure speculation" and imbued with Freud's zeal for phylogenetic fantasies, his later views are anchored in clinical experience and, for that reason, "not only theoretically but practically valuable." Similarly, on June 14, 1931, Ferenczi acknowledges that what he had hypothesized to be the function of dreams had been understood by Freud in *Beyond the Pleasure Principle* to be "characteristic of the dreams of traumatics," but he adds that he had been led once again by clinical experience "to emphasize this point of view more strongly" than Freud had done in *The Interpretation of Dreams*, that is to say, he was seeking "to generalize somewhat the point of view of mastery of trauma in sleep and dream" (Falzeder and Brabant, 2000, p. 414).

Given Ferenczi's extreme inhibition about voicing public criticism of Freud, as well as his reluctance to stand up to him even in private, it is not surprising that he should wish to present his ideas in "The Principle of Relaxation and Neocatharsis" (1930), not as a radical challenge to Freud's teaching, but rather as the modest redressing of a temporary one-sidedness. But in his letter of December 25, 1929 Ferenczi did affirm categorically that "in *all* cases, in which I penetrated deeply enough, I found the traumatic-hysterical basis for the illness," and in the paper itself he manages to be nearly as forthright:

> The precautions of the hysteric and the avoidance of the obsessional neurotic may, it is true, have their explanation in purely mental fantasy-formations; nevertheless the first impetus towards abnormal lines of development has always been thought to originate from real psychic traumas and conflicts with the environment. . . . Accordingly, no analysis can be regarded (at any rate in theory) as complete unless we have succeeded in penetrating to the traumatic material.
>
> (p. 120)

Despite Ferenczi's delicacy, the contrast with Freud could not be sharper. Whereas Freud, in *Moses and Monotheism* (1939), seeks to "leave on one side the question of whether the aetiology of the neuroses in general may be regarded as traumatic" and opines that "we can disregard the distinction between traumatic and non-traumatic aetiologies" (pp. 72–73), Ferenczi asserts without qualification—and here I supply the italics—that *"no analysis can be regarded as complete . . . unless we have succeeded in penetrating to the traumatic material."*

In his effort to relegate trauma to an ancillary role, furthermore, Freud claims in *Moses and Monotheism* that there are cases when "we have nothing else for explaining a neurosis but hereditary and constitutional dispositions" (p. 73). Ferenczi (1930) preemptively rebuts this position when he writes:

> Having given due consideration to fantasy as a pathogenic factor, I have of late been forced more and more to deal with the psychogenic trauma itself. It became evident that this is far more rarely the result of a constitutional hypersensitivity in children (causing them to react neurotically even to a commonplace and unavoidable painful experience) than of really improper, unintelligent, capricious, tactless, or actually cruel treatment.
>
> (pp. 120–21)

Ferenczi reiterates this critique at the outset of "Confusion of Tongues" (1933a) when he couples his renewed attention to "the traumatic factor in the pathogenesis of neurosis which had been unjustly neglected in recent years" with the proposition that "insufficiently deep exploration of the exogenous factor leads to the danger of resorting prematurely to explanations—often too facile explanations—in terms of 'disposition' and 'constitution'" (p. 156).

2

The cornerstone of Ferenczi's "alternative theory," accordingly, is that analysis entails a search for the "traumatic material" that lies at the root of the patient's suffering. The corollary to this axiom is that the analyst must participate emotionally if the patient's traumatic memories are to be recovered. In "The Principle of Relaxation and Neocatharsis" (1930), Ferenczi defines the clinical method against which he is reacting when he states that the "successive advances" in psychoanalytic technique caused what had been the "highly emotional relation between physician and patient, which resembled that in hypnotic suggestion," to be "gradually cooled down to a kind of unending association experiment," so that "the process became mainly intellectual" (p. 110). Ferenczi's makes his dissatisfaction with this approach even more explicit in the *Clinical Diary* where, as we have seen, he surmises that Freud "followed Breuer merely in a logical, intellectual fashion, and not with any emotional conviction." He likewise recalls that his own analysis became stymied because Freud "could not follow me down into those depths, and introduced the 'educational' stage too soon," and he ironically thanks Freud for teaching him "the calm, unemotional reserve; the unruffled assurance that one knew better" (Dupont, 1985, pp. 92, 62, 185).

Ferenczi spells out his conception of therapeutic action in the January 31, 1932 entry to the *Clinical Diary*, "The catharsis gets bogged down, and how to remedy it." Anticipating the direction taken by Freud in "Constructions in Analysis," Ferenczi begins by remarking, "One would think that the perpetual repetition in analysis of the traumatic experience, stressing first one factor and then another, would in the end result in a mosaic-like reconstruction of the whole picture" (p. 24). The problem, however, as he observes in "The Principle of Relaxation and Neocatharsis" (1930), is that while efforts "to reconstruct the repressed causes of the illness from the disconnected fragments of the material acquired through the patient's associations" may be compared to "filling in the spaces in an extremely complicated crossword puzzle," such an approach—no matter how elegant the solution—is bound to result in "disappointing therapeutic failures" (p. 110). In the *Diary* entry, he elaborates that while a "mosaic-like reconstruction" may indeed be obtained, it remains on the level of speculation and does not enable the patient to gain "the firm conviction that the events were real" (Dupont, 1985, p. 24). The challenge for the analyst, accordingly, is that "'something' more is required to transform the intellectual coherence of the possible or probable into the more solid cohesion of a necessary or even obvious reality."

The notion that there must be "'something more' than interpretation" in psychoanalytic therapy has passed into common currency with the work of the Boston Process of Change Study Group (Stern et al., 1998), and Ferenczi offers his own impassioned summation of these mutative factors in the *Clinical Diary*:

> It appears that patients cannot believe that an event really took place, or cannot fully believe it, if the analyst, as the sole witness of the

events, persists in his cool, unemotional, and, as patients are fond of stating, purely intellectual attitude, while the events are of a kind that must evoke, in anyone present, emotions of revulsion, anxiety, terror, vengeance, grief, and the urge to render immediate help: to remove or destroy the cause or person responsible; and since it is usually a child, an injured child, who is involved (but even leaving that aside), feelings of wanting to comfort it with love, etc., etc.

(Dupont, 1985, p. 24)

Ferenczi, crucially, is here speaking not about any *actions* on the part of the analyst, but rather of the "attitude" or "emotions" that being the "sole witness" of the patient's agony awakens in him. The consequence, for Ferenczi, follows ineluctably and receives its fullest expression in his mutual analysis with Severn:

To take really seriously the role one assumes, of the benevolent and helpful observer, that is, *actually to transport oneself with the patient into that period of the past* (a practice Freud reproached me with, as being not permissible), with the result that *we ourselves and the patient believe in its reality*, that is, a present reality, which has not been momentarily transposed into the past.

(italics added)

Here we have the heart of the matter: Ferenczi's belief in the possibility—indeed, the necessity—that the analyst should allow himself to be "transport[ed] . . . with the patient into that period of the past" when the traumas took place, with the paradoxical result that the past comes to life once again as a "present reality."

Ferenczi is the furthest thing imaginable from naive. Not only does he recognize that his innovations are castigated by Freud as "not permissible," but he has no difficulty in articulating the argument that detractors, such as Freud or Thompson, could mount against his procedure: "The objection to this approach would be: after all we do know that the whole episode, insofar as it is true, is not taking place now. Therefore we are dishonest if we allow the events to be acted out dramatically and even participate in the drama" (p. 24). He then mounts his rebuttal:

But if we adopt this view, and contrive right from the beginning to present the events to the patient as memory images that are unreal in the present, he may well follow our line of thought but will remain on an intellectual level, without ever attaining the feeling of conviction. "It cannot be true that all this is happening to me, or someone would come to my aid"—and the patient prefers to doubt his own judgment rather than believe in our coldness, our lack of intelligence, or in simpler terms, our stupidity and nastiness.

(pp. 24–25)

Ferenczi restates this guiding principle of technique later in the *Clinical Diary*, "A purely intellectual reconstruction by the analyst does not appear to be sufficient for this task. The patient must feel that the analyst shares his pain and would also gladly make sacrifices to relieve it" (p. 121).

Given the insufficiency of a process that "remains on an intellectual level," and that a paramount aim of therapy is to foster in the patient a "feeling of conviction" concerning the reality of the events that have led to his suffering, the question becomes, first, how best to do this and, second, how to ascertain when one has reached the nucleus of the patient's trauma. In "Confusion of Tongues" (1933a), Ferenczi writes, "We talk a good deal in analysis of regressions into the infantile, but we do not really believe to what great extent we are right. . . . The patient gone off into his trance is a *child indeed* who no longer reacts to intellectual explanations, only perhaps to maternal friendliness" (p. 160). Integral to Ferenczi's "relaxation technique," jointly elaborated with Severn, is that the traumatized patient needs to fall into a trance—or what might be described today as a reverie—in order to access his dissociated memories.

In his 1931 note "On the Revision of the *Interpretation of Dreams*" (1920, 1930–1932), Ferenczi connects his view of the "traumatolytic function of the dream" with his emphasis on the importance of trance states in clinical work. Because "the repetition tendency of the trauma is greater in sleep than in waking life," it follows that "in deep sleep it is more likely that deeply hidden, very urgent sensory impressions will return which in the first instance caused deep unconsciousness and thus remained permanently unsolved" (p. 240). Analogously, in the analytic setting the imperative to access preverbal memories "justifies the experiments of searching for the experiences of shock in intentionally induced absorption in trance" (p. 239).

Without recognizing his affinity with Ferenczi, Winnicott explains in his posthumously published paper, "Fear of Breakdown" (1974), how analysis can permit the patient to "remember" a catastrophe that must have taken place in the past but has not yet been "experienced":

> The patient needs to "remember" this but it is not possible to remember something that has not yet happened, and this thing of the past has not yet happened because the patient was not there for it to happen to. The only way to "remember" in this case is for the patient *to experience this past thing for the first time in the present*, that is to say, in the transference. . . . This is the equivalent of remembering, and this outcome is the equivalent of the lifting of repression that occurs in the analysis of the psychoneurotic patient.
> (pp. 91–92; italics added)

This is precisely how Ferenczi (1920, 1930–1932) believes it is possible for a patient to recapture the state of "complete paralysis" that ensues when the ego is anesthetized by "an unexpected, unprepared for, overwhelming shock":

> No memory traces of such impressions remain, even in the unconscious, and thus the causes of the trauma cannot be recalled from memory traces. If, in spite of this, one wants to reach them, which logically appears to be almost impossible, then one must repeat the trauma itself and under more favourable conditions one must bring it *for the first time* to perception and to motor discharge.
> (pp. 239–40)

He restates his understanding of the purpose of dream analysis—and by extension of all analysis of trauma—in the following words: "The therapeutic aim of the dream analysis is the restoration of direct accessibility to the sensory impressions with the help of a deep trance which regresses, as it were, behind the secondary dream, and brings about the re-living of the events of the trauma in the analysis" (p. 242).

Just as he offers a far-reaching modification of Freud's wish-fulfillment theory of dreams, Ferenczi's re-vision of psychoanalysis prompts him to question the "fundamental rule" of free association. The point is not only, as he remarks in the *Diary*, that "free association, by itself, without these new foundations for an atmosphere of trust, will thus bring no real healing. The doctor must really be involved in the case, heart and soul" (Dupont, 1985, p. 170). It is also, as Ferenczi explains in a 1931 note, "Attempt at a Summary," that the patient's dedication to free association, and the analyst's corresponding reliance on interpretation, may actually *interfere* with the state of absorption they are intended to promote:

> *Absorption* in the real sphere of emotional experience inevitably demands as complete as possible an abandonment of present reality. In principle so-called free association is in itself such a diversion of attention from actual reality, yet this diversion is rather superficial and is maintained at a rather conscious, at the most pre-conscious, level both by the intellectual activity of the patient and by our attempts to explain and interpret following one on the other in more or less rapid succession.
> (1920, 1930–1932, p. 232)

It is because Ferenczi believes regression is indispensable in order to gain access to "the real sphere of emotional experience" that he is committed to trying to help the patient achieve a trance state during the analytic session. There is, however, a crucial difference between nocturnal dreaming and regression in analysis, namely, the presence of another person who is "really involved in the case, heart and soul," and can serve as a companion and witness. As Ferenczi elaborates in the same note, "What one calls a trance is, therefore, a kind of a state of sleep in which communication is yet kept up with a reliable person" (p. 233).

On the core issue of how one knows when one has uncovered the patient's "traumatic material" and by extension whether one can rely on memories to be trustworthy, Freud and Ferenczi once again gravitate toward diametrically opposed positions. Freud's view, at its starkest, is expressed in his previously quoted August 29, 1932 letter to Eitingon where he accuses Ferenczi of repeating his own "first great etiological error" by believing "what the patients say, when he by happenstance transports them, as he himself says, into a hypnosis-like condition," which Ferenczi, according to Freud, then "considers that to be the revelation, but what one thereby obtains are the patients' fantasies about their childhood, not history" (Schröter, 2004, 2:826). From this standpoint, Freud's abandonment of the "seduction theory" leads him to maintain that "patients' fantasies" have no basis in external reality but are rather spontaneous emanations from the unconscious. Ferenczi's view, conversely, in agreement with Severn that "nightmares are real," is that

> the hallucinations of the insane, or at least a part of them, are not imaginings but real perceptions, stemming from the environment and from

the psyches of other human beings, which are accessible to them—precisely because of their psychologically motivated hypersensitivity—whereas normal people, focusing only on immediate matters of direct concern to them, remain unaffected.

(Dupont, 1985, p. 58)

As he reiterates in the *Diary*, "perhaps there are no hallucinations, but only an illusionary working through of real events" (p. 140).

3

This debate between Freud and Ferenczi is played out against the backdrop of the history of psychoanalysis, with Ferenczi giving a markedly different spin to his narrative of Breuer's role in private from the one he presents in public. The public version is encapsulated in "The Principle of Relaxation and Neocatharsis" (1930), where Ferenczi defines "Breuer's remarkable contribution to psychotherapy" in twofold fashion: "Not only did he pursue the method indicated by the patient, but he had faith in the *reality* of the memories which emerged, and did not, as was customary, dismiss them out of hand as the fantastic inventions of a mentally abnormal patient" (p. 109). But he forthwith qualifies this praise by noting that "Breuer's capacity for belief had strict limitations," and "upon the first manifestations of uninhibited instinctual life he left not only the patient but the whole method in the lurch." It remained "for a man of stronger calibre" to make the decisive breakthrough. When Freud came to doubt his initial conviction that "in every case of neurosis a *conditio sine qua non* is a sexual trauma," Ferenczi continues, it took all his "intellectual acumen" to save psychoanalysis "from the imminent danger of being once more lost in oblivion" when he "perceived that, even though certain of the statements made by patients were untrue and not in accordance with reality, yet the psychic reality of their lying remained an incontestable fact" (p. 110). Thus, Ferenczi concludes, Freud displayed exceptional strength of mind and character when he was able to free himself "from disturbing affects and pronounce the deceptive unveracity of his patients to be hysterical fantasy, worthy as a psychic reality of further consideration and investigation."

This is the received version of psychoanalytic history, with Breuer given limited credit but chastised for fleeing from Anna O., and Freud hailed for his heroism in rejecting the seduction theory and according unprecedented respect to "psychic reality." Ferenczi, however, tells a very different story in the *Clinical Diary*. Off the record, as we have seen, Ferenczi states, "It should not be forgotten that Freud is not the discoverer of analysis but that he took over something ready-made, from Breuer" (Dupont, 1985, p. 92). Indeed, Freud "followed Breuer merely in a logical, intellectual fashion, and not with any emotional conviction"; consequently, "he only analyzes others but not himself" and displays "a compulsion to cling too strongly to theory as a defense against self-analysis, that is, against his own doubts."

Instead of praising Freud for understanding the "deceptive unveracity of his patients" as "hysterical fantasy" that deserves to be taken seriously as a "psychic reality," as he did in the Oxford Congress lecture, Ferenczi turns this on its head in the *Diary* by citing Freud's "discovery that hysterics lie" as the turning point following which he "no longer loves his patients," and by interpreting "this shock, this disillusionment" as the reason why there is now "much less talk of trauma" in psychoanalysis and "constitution now begins to play the principal role." Ferenczi takes his critique further by arguing that Freud's transformation led him to "a certain amount of fatalism"—in other words, to the pessimism that reaches its apogee in "Analysis Terminable and Interminable"—as a result of which "he sees almost nothing of the subjective" and "remains attached to analysis intellectually but not emotionally." This reversal on the plane of theory, moreover, resulted in a "modification of his therapeutic method" in which the "impersonal" analyst, "levitating like some kind of divinity above the poor patient," does not suspect that "a large share of what is described as transference is artificially provoked by this kind of behavior," and therefore mistakenly "postulates that transference is created by the patient."

In contrast to this indictment of Freud, there is not one negative word about Breuer in the *Clinical Diary*.[3] Even when he acknowledges his own reliance on "observations made by Freud, according to which no delusional idea is devoid of at least a grain of truth," when Ferenczi goes on to recount how he "resolved to search more intensively for the reality contained in such apparently delusional concepts" and "to identify myself for a good long time with those presumed insane," he specifies that his "model for this process" is the no longer timorous but now admirably courageous "Dr. Breuer, who did not shrink from seeking and finding the truth in the most nonsensical statements of a hysteric, whereby he had to rely both theoretically and technically on the hints and suggestions of the patient" (p. 58). In this alternative account, it is Breuer who remains committed to "finding the truth" in everything imparted by the patient, and Freud who withdraws emotionally from the mentally ill and regards their "fantastic inventions" as lies. Ferenczi sums up his personal and theoretical odyssey in the realization that Freud " 'does not love anyone, only himself and his work,' " an awakening that led to "libidinal detachment" and "permitted 'revolutionary' technical innovations," culminating in "Return to trauma (Breuer)." The ensuing words bear repeating: "*In opposition to Freud* I developed to an exceptional degree a capacity for *humility* and for appreciating the clearsightedness of the uncorrupted child (patient)" (p. 160).

Not only does Ferenczi acknowledge his debt to Breuer both in his espousal of a trauma theory and in his willingness to identify himself even "with those presumed insane," but his experience with Severn replicates that of Breuer with Anna O. at the dawn of psychoanalysis. As he describes in the *Diary*, when he yielded to Severn's importunities by giving her extra sessions, taking her on vacation trips, and implementing the relaxation technique, "we arrived at the point where the evidently traumatic infantile history could emerge, in the form of states of trance, or attacks" (p. 97). Severn accompanied Ferenczi and his wife to Spain in the summer of 1928, so the foregoing account describes where the treatment stood before the Oxford Congress lecture, in which Ferenczi (1930) avers, "In certain cases these hysterical attacks actually assumed the character of *trances*," so that one was "forced to compare" the resulting "autohypnotic" states "with the phenomenon of the Breuer-Freud *catharsis*" (p. 119). Despite Ferenczi's "extreme exertions," however, the analysis remained stymied and "without further progress for another two years," though by the time of the *Diary* he was persuaded that "the most significant turning point" had occurred when "the patient conceived the plan, or reported her conviction, that in the course of the summer, on the dates corresponding to her infantile trauma, according to the calendar, she would repeat and remember the whole event" (Dupont, 1985, p. 98). Although Ferenczi does not note the resemblance, Severn's day-by-day reenactment of her "infantile trauma" parallels—and even outdoes—Breuer's report in *Studies on Hysteria* of how Anna O., in her "alternating states of consciousness," could be "induced by any sense-impassion" to go back in time from 1881–1882 to 1880–1881, as "she lived through the previous winter day by day" (Breuer and Freud, 1895, p. 33), which Breuer confirmed both from memories retrieved under hypnosis and from a diary that had been kept by Bertha Pappenheim's mother.

4

Fundamentally, therefore, Freud and Ferenczi adopt antithetical positions. Ferenczi starts by accepting the reality of traumatic experience and the need for the analyst's emotional participation in the therapeutic process to bring about the reliving that is necessary for healing; Freud starts with fantasy and constitution and conceives of analysis as leading by interpretation to the replacement by a "correct solution" of the "inadequate decision" made by the patient in his childhood. At the same time, both thinkers are capable of nuance and attempt to accommodate the outlook of the other. Freud, as we have seen, is at his most Ferenczian in "Constructions in Analysis" (1937b), where he writes that the patient "must be brought to recollect certain experiences and the affective impulses called up by them which he has for the time being forgotten," and that "what we are in search of is a picture of the patient's forgotten years that shall be alike trustworthy and in all essential respects complete" (pp. 257–58), but even here he does not mention trauma or acknowledge the delicate and hazardous nature of any attempt to reanimate dormant "affective impulses."

The challenge faced by Ferenczi, on the other hand, is set forth by Freud in his letter of September 16, 1930, in which he compares Ferenczi's views on "the traumatic fragmentation of mental life" to *Thalassa*, adding that "one can hardly speak of the extraordinary synthetic function of the ego without treating the reactive scar formation along with it. The latter, of course, also produces what we see; we must make the traumas accessible" (Falzeder and Brabant, 2000, p. 399). Although Freud here appears to admit the possibility of uncovering buried traumas, he cautions that they will necessarily emerge in a distorted form; and in his September 21, 1897 letter to Fliess renouncing the "seduction theory," he goes so far as to maintain that "unconscious memory does not break through, so that the secret of childhood experiences is not disclosed even in the most confused delirium" (Masson, 1985, p. 265). Consequently, as Bonomi (2012) emphasizes, Freud's overriding message is that "traumatic memories are condemned to remain forever opaque, because what is allowed to resurface has to be regarded as a *composite structure*," and, when all is said and done, "Ferenczi's request to penetrate the traumatic material is an illusion" (p. 241).

As Ferenczi demonstrates in the *Notes and Fragments* (1920, 1930–1932), however, he is cognizant of the imperative to take into account the "reactive scar formation" or defenses that encase the "traumatic material" and must be peeled away before the underlying wound can be treated. Insisting that "we must make an exact differentiation between that part of catharsis which appears spontaneously when approaching the pathogenic material and that which, as it were, can only be elicited by overcoming strong resistances," Ferenczi explains that in his version of "neo-catharsis" the "single cathartic outbreak" simply indicates

> the place where further detailed exploration has to begin, that is to say, one must not content oneself with what is given spontaneously, which is somehow adulterated, partially displaced, and quite often attenuated; one must press on (of course as far as possible without suggesting contents) to obtain from the patient more about his experiences, the accompanying circumstances, and so on.
> (p. 223)

Elsewhere, he poses the same fundamental question raised by Freud: "Here is the problem: how much of the reproduction is fantasy and how much reality; how much *subsequent* displacement to *persons and scenes which only later become significant?* How much 'historical dressing up' of a real-life situation?" (p. 259). Complementing this awareness of the workings of retroactive signification (*Nachträglichkeit*) in psychic life is Ferenczi's recognition that, in some cases, "the 'mental' events of the past (childhood) may have left their memory traces in a language of gestures, un-understandable to our cs.," so that "only *fragments* of the external (traumatic) events can be reproduced" (p. 264). "If this is so," he continues, "then some memories of childhood cannot be ever raised as such into the cs, and even in physical symptoms and hallucinations are always mixed with dreamlike (wish-fulfilling) distortions of defence and turning into the opposite."

These statements make it clear that Ferenczi did not minimize the difficulty of recovering memories of childhood trauma. In some instances, this may be possible only to a limited extent, while in others it may not be possible at all. But he differs radically from Freud in maintaining that the ultimate source of suffering almost always lies in "external (traumatic) events" and in his conviction that analysis should aspire to bring these events to light, while distinguishing between the memories themselves and the "distortions of defence" with which they have become entwined. After noting that what is at first spontaneously produced by the patient may be "adulterated, partially displaced, and quite often attenuated," Ferenczi explains that the cathartic probes must be sent down "innumerable times until the patient feels, as it were, surrounded, and cannot but repeat before our eyes the trauma which had originally led to mental disintegration" (p. 224). In "The Principle of Relaxation and Neocatharsis" (1930), he insists:

> There is all the difference in the world between this cathartic termination to a long psycho-analysis and the fragmentary eruptions of emotion and recollection which the primitive catharsis could provoke and which had only a temporary effect. The catharsis of which I am speaking is, like many dreams, only a confirmation from the unconscious, a sign that our toilsome analytic construction, our technique of dealing with resistance and transference, have finally succeeded in drawing near to the aetiological reality.
>
> (p. 119)

All these passages are congruent with his declaration that the purpose of dream analysis is "the restoration of direct accessibility to the sensory impressions with the help of a deep trance which regresses, as it were, behind the secondary dream, and brings about the re-living of the events of the trauma in the analysis" (1920, 1930–1932, p. 242).

In a more extended iteration of this theme, Ferenczi argues that, "without actually giving him direct hints," it is possible to obtain from the patient "details of his emotional and sensory processes and of the exogenic causes of those traumas and sensations, and of the defences against them" (p. 234). When the analyst puts "all these formulations to the patient" and urges him "to combine them into a whole, we may experience the re-emergence of a traumatic scene with distinct indications of the time and place at which it occurred." Such a return of the repressed, far from blurring the boundary between fantasy and reality, may allow the survivor of trauma to distinguish between the two for the first time:

> Not infrequently we succeed in differentiating the autosymbolic representation of the mental processes after the trauma (e.g. fragmentation as falling to bits, atomization as explosion) from the real external traumatic events, and in this way reconstruct the *total picture of both the subjective and the objective history*. There often follows, then, a state of calm relaxation, with a feeling of relief.
>
> (italics added)

But even a catharsis that occurs in the wake of an accurate reconstruction "of both the subjective and the objective history" is unlikely to bring about a permanent resolution. Rather, "the next day we may find the patient in full rebellion or desolation again, and often it is only after some days' effort that we may succeed in getting near once more to the painful point, or in getting out of the depths new painful points which are interwoven with the previous ones as it were in a traumatic web."

5

Despite the sophistication of his position, Ferenczi's emphasis consistently falls on the primacy of real-life events, above all those involving childhood sexual abuse, in the etiology of mental illness, and on the possibility of recovering authentic memories in analysis. The note, dated October 30, 1932—nearly a month after he had abandoned the *Clinical Diary*—in which Ferenczi acknowledges the possibility that "some memories of childhood cannot be ever raised as such into the cs" is titled "The Two Extremes: Credulity and Scepticism." Echoing Severn, who in the closing pages of *The Discovery of the Self* (1933) had introduced the terms *"psychognosis"* and *"psychosophy"* (pp. 148–49), Ferenczi begins: "'Psychognostic': '*Gnosis*' = the view that it is possible to reach by correspondingly deep relaxation to the direct experience of the past, which may then be accepted as true without any further interpretation" (1920, 1930–1932, p. 263). Ferenczi's outlook is dialectical, and his recognition that "all thoughts and ideas must be examined very critically," because they may represent either "absolutely nothing of the real happening" or "a very distorted version of it," does not preclude his commitment to achieving a "direct experience of the past" that transcends interpretation. As he declares in "The Principle of Relaxation and Neocatharsis" (1930), "hysterical fantasies do not lie when they tell us that parents and other adults do indeed go to monstrous lengths in the passionate eroticism of their relation with children" (p. 121). From a complementary standpoint, he affirms in "Confusion of Tongues" (1933a) that "trauma, especially the sexual trauma, as the pathogenic factor cannot be valued highly enough," citing as corroboration not only the reports of patients who had been the victims of abuse but also, unexpectedly, "the number of such confessions, e.g. of assaults upon children, committed by patients actually in analysis" (p. 161).

In a trenchant commentary on the concept of introjection, originally propounded by Ferenczi in "Introjection and Transference" (1909), Franco

Borgogno (2010) has drawn attention to the way that it entails the realization that "even from the earliest stages of life it is possible to 'eat shit' and be poisoned *by parents* who . . . were by no means 'good by definition'" (p. 176). He aptly characterizes Ferenczi as "the 'introjective psychoanalyst' *par excellence* in the history of psychoanalysis" (p. 171). This epithet is no less applicable to Severn, who, in the opening chapter of *The Discovery of the Self* (1933), underscores how, in the first three years of life, the child's mind is "the constant recipient of the words, actions, and behavior (and I believe also thoughts) of those in his environment" (p. 28). As Borgogno (2010) distills Ferenczi's mature conceptualization of the therapeutic process, "it is necessary for the *intra*psychic (which was produced by the *extra*psychic in the very early stages of life) once again to become *interpsychic* within the 'here and now' of the analytic relationship" (p. 180).

In Ferenczi's (1930) own words, while his conception of psychoanalysis continues to recognize the importance of "intrapsychic forces," he does not consider these forces to be innate, but understands them rather as "the representatives of the *conflict originally waged between the individual and the outside world*" (p. 125). This is the point of his previously quoted assertion that "the precautions of the hysteric and the avoidance of the obsessional neurotic may, it is true, have their explanation in purely mental fantasy-formations; nevertheless the first impetus towards abnormal lines of development has always been thought to originate from real psychic traumas and conflicts with the environment" (p. 120). Ferenczi relies on the same principle in "Confusion of Tongues" (1933a) when he explains that through the child-victim's "identification, or let us say, introjection of the aggressor" the perpetrator of abuse "disappears as part of the external reality, and becomes intra- instead of extra-psychic; the intra-psychic is then subjected, in a dream-like state as is the traumatic trance, to the primary process" (p. 162). Ferenczi clearly recognizes the power of the "primary process" to distort—and at times even to render unrecognizable—what has been introjected, but he never abandons the premise that there must have been a "real happening" in the patient's early history that, under favorable conditions, can be relived "interpsychically" in the analysis.

As part of his argument against, as he put it to Freud on December 25, 1929, the prevalent "overestimation of fantasy—and the underestimation of the traumatic reality in pathogenesis" (Falzeder and Brabant, 2000,

p. 376), Ferenczi makes a further seminal observation in a post-Wiesbaden note on November 4, 1932:

> Traumatogenesis being *known*; the doubt, whether reality or fantasy, remains or can return (even though everything points at reality). Fantasy theory = an escape of *realization* (amongst resisting analysts too). They rather accept their (and human beings') mind (memory) as unreliable than believe that such things with *those* kinds of persons can *really* have happened. (Self-sacrifice of one's own mind's *integrity* in order to save the parents!)
> (1920, 1930–1932, p. 268)

In the wake of trauma perpetrated by parents or other loved adults, who then collude in denying the reality of the experience, it becomes easier for the child to doubt the reliability of her own memory than to "believe that such things with *those* kinds of persons can *really* have happened." Such an "escape of *realization*" on the part of "resisting analysts" can be seen when Freud and Jelliffe (or whoever reviewed *The Discovery of the Self*) dismiss Severn as the purveyor of "*pseudologia phantastica*."

Similarly, as Ferenczi observes in "Confusion of Tongues" (1933a), it is common for patients to "deteriorate into an extreme submissiveness because ... of a fear of occasioning a displeasure in us by their criticism," and in a recapitulation of their previous "introjection of the aggressor," "instead of contradicting the analyst or accusing him of errors and blindness, the patients *identify themselves with him*" (p. 158). What happens to a traumatized person who prefers to sacrifice his "own mind's integrity in order to save the parents" is ratified on the plane of theory by the tendency of analysts to resort to fantasy "even though everything points at reality," a reflex that can be traced back to Freud's disastrous wrong turn in 1897 to "antitrauma and predisposition," which was unconsciously motivated by his need to deny how severely he had been traumatized and thereby served as "a protective device against insight into his own weaknesses" (Dupont, 1985, p. 186).

Central to Freud's attack on Ferenczi for reverting to his own "first great etiological error" is the claim that Ferenczi was engaged in a process of mutual suggestion with his patients, in which, as he wrote to Eitingon, they "suggest to him, then he turns it around" (Schröter, 2004, 2:826). But just as Ferenczi is anything but naive in his approach to fantasy or in his emphasis on the analyst's obligation to become more than a spectator of the patient's drama, so, too, is he aware of the dangers of suggestion. In his note "On the Revision of the *Interpretation of Dreams*," he emphasizes "the difference between 'suggestion of content' in the earlier hypnoses and the *pure suggestion of courage* in the neo-catharsis: the encouragement to feel and think the traumatically interrupted mental experiences to their very end" (1920, 1930–1932, p. 243; italics added). Publicly thanking Severn for what he has learned from her, Ferenczi reiterates in "Child-Analysis in the Analysis of Adults" (1931) that "suggestion, which is legitimate even in analysis, ought to be of the nature of general encouragement rather than special direction" (p. 134). By empathically joining with the patient, Ferenczi bestows the "pure suggestion of courage" while refraining from implanting ideas in the other person's mind. Freud, by contrast, while espousing "a sympathetic, friendly objectivity," betrays his own ideal because "*forcing one's own theory* is not objective—a kind of tyranny. Also the whole attitude is somewhat *unfriendly*" (1920, 1930–1932, p. 262). Paradoxically, therefore, because Ferenczi recognizes the inescapability of the analyst's influence on the patient, he is able to use that power in a benign and unobtrusive way, whereas Freud, in professing to be objective, denies the extent to which he is imposing his own preconceptions and in so doing turns analysis into "a kind of tyranny."

In addition to the charge of suggestion, another criticism frequently directed against Ferenczi, as it continues to be against relational analysts and self psychologists, is that he fails to confront the ferocity of the patient's aggression. Ferenczi's answer is two-pronged. First, as he reminds his colleagues in "The Principle of Relaxation and Neocatharsis" (1930), notwithstanding his advocacy of indulgence, "I have remained faithful to the well-tried analytical principle of frustration as well, and I try to attain my aim by the tactful and understanding application of *both* forms of technique" (p. 123). The preservation of a dialectical sensibility ensures that "practice does not outrun discretion," and "however great the relaxation, the analyst will not gratify the patient's actively aggressive and sexual wishes or many of their other exaggerated demands. There will be abundant opportunity to learn renunciation and adaptation" (p. 123). Second, Ferenczi observes in "The Elasticity of Psycho-Analytic Technique" (1928) that the analyst must be prepared to "accept for weeks on end the role of an Aunt Sally on whom the patient tries out all his aggressiveness and resentment" (p. 91).[4] He goes even further in the *Clinical Diary*, where he cautions that although the analyst "may take kindness and relaxation as far as he possibly can, the time will come when he will have to repeat with his own hands the act of murder previously perpetrated against the patient," with the vital difference being that the analyst, unlike the parent, "is not allowed to deny his guilt" (Dupont, 1985, p. 52).[5]

Ferenczi's acceptance of the inevitability that the patient's trauma must be reenacted in the analysis as part of the cure—and that the analyst must consequently be cast in the role of the "murderer"—means that he both does and does not view analysis as a "corrective emotional experience." On the one hand, as we have seen, he would agree with Alexander's (1946) contention that "the patient, in order to be helped must undergo a corrective emotional experience suitable to repair the traumatic influence of previous experiences," and that "this can be accomplished only through actual experience in the patient's relationship to the therapist; intellectual insight alone is not sufficient" (pp. 66–67). But he would, on the other hand, have reservations about his compatriot's recommendation that "the analyst should assume intentionally a kind of attitude which is conducive to provoking the kind of emotional experience in the patient which is needed to undo the pathogenic effect of the original parental attitude" (1950, pp. 268–69), though even in this later formulation Alexander cautions that his technique "does not consist in artificial play acting but in creating an atmosphere which is conducive to undoing the effects of early family influences" (p. 275).

The crucial difference between Ferenczi and Alexander, as Lewis Aron (1996) has grasped, is that Ferenczi goes "far beyond the simplistic notion that the analyst needs to be a 'good object' or better parent to the patient" (p. 168). Unless the analyst also becomes the "bad object," but without "denying his guilt," the toxicity at the root of the patient's pathology can never be eradicated. Despite his best efforts, the analyst must in some preordained way fail the patient as the parent had previously done, and it is the analyst's *response* to this failure—his willingness, as Ferenczi writes in the *Clinical Diary*, "to admit to all his negative emotional impulses, and thereby free the patient from the feeling that he is hypocritical" (Dupont, 1985, p. 204)—that breaks the vicious cycle. Ferenczi's more profound understanding of the concept of the corrective emotional experience again uncannily foreshadows Winnicott's thesis in "Fear of Breakdown" (1974) that the patient's agony "experienced in the transference, in relation to the analyst's failures and mistakes," is what enables him to recollect "the original failure of the facilitating environment" (p. 91).

That the analyst's humility is indispensable in making possible the transformation of a traumatic repetition into a new beginning is a prominent theme throughout the texts of Ferenczi's final period. Arguing in "The Principle of Relaxation and Neocatharsis" (1930) that *while the similarity of the analytical to the infantile situation impels patients to repetition, the contrast between the two encourages recollection*" (p. 124), Ferenczi spells out the essence of this contrast in "Confusion of Tongues" (1933a):

> The setting free of his critical feelings, the willingness on our part to admit our mistakes and the honest endeavour to avoid them in the future, all these go to create in the patient a confidence in the analyst. *It is this confidence that establishes the contrast between the present and the unbearable traumatogenic past*, the contrast which is absolutely necessary for the patient in order to enable him to re-experience the past no longer as hallucinatory reproduction but as an objective memory.
>
> (p. 160)

In highlighting the imperative to transform "hallucinatory reproduction" (or "repetition") into "objective memory" (or "recollection"), Ferenczi expresses his continued concurrence with Freud's conviction in "Remembering, Repeating and Working-Through" (1914c) that the analyst "celebrates it as a triumph for the treatment if he can bring it about that something that the patient wishes to discharge in action is disposed of through the work of remembering" (p. 153), though he would add the qualification that emotionally charged repeating is often a necessary precondition for remembering traumas.

Indeed, in *The Development of Psycho-Analysis*, Ferenczi and Rank (1924) jointly affirm that "we must connect directly with Freud's last technical work" (p. 3). Anticipating Ferenczi's later formulations, they make the twofold argument that while it is "not only absolutely unavoidable that the patient should, during the cure, repeat a large portion of his process of development," especially "just those portions which cannot be really experienced from memory, so that there is no other way open to the patient than that of repeating" (p. 3), yet "in the end remembering still remains the final factor of healing and the actual problem is constantly to transform one—as it were organic—kind of repeating, the reproducing, into another form of repeating, the remembering" (p. 26). As de Forest recognized in calling her book *The Leaven of Love*, what is distinctive about Ferenczi is his insistence that interpretation alone is never enough, and only when, as he puts it in the *Clinical Diary*, the patient also comes to feel "the kindness and energy of the analyst" does it become "possible to avoid the explosion on contact between the worlds of emotion and thought, so that *at last recollection can take the place of repetition*" (Dupont, 1985, p. 204; italics added). Fittingly, the title of the German edition of the *Diary*, *Ohne Sympathie keine Heilung*, is taken from the following credo: "Understanding is necessary in order to employ sympathy in the right place (analysis), in the right way. Without sympathy: there is no healing. (At most, insight into the genesis of the illness)" (p. 200).

Just as in their "reciprocal analysis," where Freud's paranoid insistence that Ferenczi is solely to blame for the deterioration in their personal relationship must be deplored when weighed against the genuine humility with which Ferenczi recognized his own shortcomings (while also unerringly dissecting those of Freud), so, too, Freud's oblique efforts after Ferenczi's death to parry the challenge posed by his rehabilitation of trauma theory are abortive when compared to the latter's brilliant breakthroughs with Severn. By virtue of what Freud could see only as a "retrogressive or reactionary" movement, Ferenczi succeeded in rethinking both the history of psychoanalysis and its most fundamental concepts. Thanks to his labors, the wish-fulfillment theory of dreams, free association, the repetition compulsion, and the nature of psychic reality are all placed on a firmer foundation, while "the idea of the death instinct" is prototypical of the blunders that must be rectified because it "goes too far, is already tinged with sadism" (p. 200).

Ferenczi does not exempt the Oedipus complex from scrutiny, though, as we have come to expect, he refrains from avowing publicly what he entertains in his private thoughts. In "The Principle of Relaxation and Neocatharsis" (1930), he declares, "To-day I am returning to the view that, beside the great significance of the Oedipus complex in children, a deep significance must also be attached to the *repressed incestuous affection of adults, which masquerades as tenderness*" (p. 121). This is a step forward, but it still pours his new wine into Freud's old bottle. Only in the *Clinical Diary* does Ferenczi dare to pose the question, "Is the *Oedipus complex* also a consequence of adult activity—passionate behavior?" (Dupont, 1985, p. 173), instancing the "certainly not rare" cases "in which fixation on parents, that is, incestuous fixation, does not appear as a natural product of development but rather is implanted in the psyche from the outside" (p. 175). As Thompson affirmed more categorically in the lost portion of her unpublished 1933 paper, "Evaluation of Ferenczi's Relaxation Therapy," "the child does not suffer from his own Oedipus complex but from that of his parents" (qtd. in Brennan, 2011, p. 11).[6]

What Ferenczi understood but was unwilling to say aloud it was left to the founders of object relations theory and self psychology to proclaim in their writings. According to Fairbairn (1944), "the role of ultimate cause, which Freud allotted to the Oedipus complex, should properly be allotted to the phenomenon of infantile dependence," and it is possible to "dispense with" this supposed shibboleth altogether as an "explanatory concept" (p. 120). For Kohut, too, the Oedipus complex no longer possesses "universal applicability" (1977, p. 223), while castration anxiety should be viewed as a pathological development and not "as a feature of the oedipal phase of the healthy child of healthy parents" (1984, p. 14). By his return to the "temporarily abandoned workings" of Freud's earliest inspirations, Ferenczi bequeathed to future generations a gold mine for further psychoanalytic prospecting.

Notes

1 Along the same lines, it is ironic that, in *The Development of Psycho-Analysis*, Ferenczi and Rank (1924) should write of those analysts whose resistances have not been properly analyzed that "the practice of psycho-analysis seems to have been a symptom of their own neuroses," and that "some supporters, while consciously recognizing analysis, simply reacted with their latent neurosis out of which they then created their resistances in the form of scientific objections" (p. 23n10), since this is precisely what Freud would say of them when first Rank and then Ferenczi began to raise their "scientific objections" to his conception of psychoanalysis.
2 Both papers were intended for a Congress in 1931 that was canceled, and the International Psychoanalytical Association did not meet between the 1929 Oxford Congress and the 1932 Congress in Wiesbaden.
3 The same contradiction is evident in the contrast between the praise of Breuer in the *Clinical Diary* and Ferenczi's statement in "Freud's Influence on Medicine" (1933b) that "it was certainly no accident that Breuer," despite having been the discoverer of the cathartic method, "soon lost interest in these problems and no longer associated himself with Freud or his further studies" (p. 143), as well as between his critique of Freud in the *Diary* and his encomium in the published paper that "there was no other Hercules" than Freud "to bring order into this Augean stable" of "the aberrations of sexual life" and "the animal aggressive instincts" (p. 151).
4 This passage is quoted by Michael Parsons (2009) as part of a masterful defense against the Kleinian accusation that "Independent analysts 'soft-pedal' their patients, neglect the negative transference, and so on" (p. 195).
5 See my exposition of this theme, "The Analyst's Murder of the Patient," in *Reading Psychoanalysis* (Rudnytsky, 2002, ch. 7).

6 Although they appear to be unaware that "Laius's forgotten story, itself embedded in a whole generational story of children betrayed," has been much more rigorously expounded by John Munder Ross (1982, p. 171), who links his groundbreaking work to Ferenczi's, as well as by Marie Balmary (1979), Carol Gilligan and Naomi Snider (2018) argue similarly that to take the Oedipus myth "as a template for the human condition, as Freud and others have done, to carry forward the name of Oedipus while forgetting the origins of his story in trauma, holds the danger of regarding murder and incest as natural impulses rather than impulses that arise in the wake of abuse and abandonment" (p. 19).

Finale
A Whole Soul

On July 7, 1932, Ferenczi recorded in the *Clinical Diary* that Severn experienced a "frequently recurring form of dream" in which "two, three, or even several persons represent, according to the completed dream-analysis, an equal number of component parts of her personality" (Dupont, 1985, p. 157). He had already described Severn's fragmentation into "two, three, or even several persons" in his January 12 entry chronicling the series of "shocks" she had undergone at the ages of one and a half, five, and eleven and a half, the reverberations of which in her nightmares are familiar to us from *The Discovery of the Self*. In the present instance, "the dreamer herself receives a written message from the beloved person who is closest to her, which reads: 'Here I am. I am here.'" Severn then "attempts to tell this to a third person, a man, but she can contact him only indirectly, by a long-distance telephone call," which makes "the whole conversation" sound "very indistinct, as if coming from an immense distance." In the course of the dream, "the difficulty increases to the point of a nightmarish and helpless struggle because the text of the message cannot be read directly: the dreamer sees it only in mirror writing."

It is not difficult to deduce that the "beloved person who is closest" to Severn must be Margaret, while the "third person" to whom Severn struggles to communicate the "written message" is Ferenczi. The way that the "text of the message" takes the inverted form of "mirror writing" conveys how the traumas of childhood can only be deciphered and overcome through the reverse temporality of *Nachträglichkeit*, that is, by being repeated and, in Winnicott's (1974) words, experienced "*for the first time in the present*, that is to say, in the transference" (p. 92). Ironically, Margaret's message, which is intended to assure her mother that she is with her in spirit in Budapest—despite being physically in Paris—can be relayed to Ferenczi "only indirectly, by a long-distance telephone call," in which the conversation seems to be "coming from an immense distance." Just as the writing, which "cannot be read directly," is transformed into words spoken to someone who can likewise only be reached "indirectly," there is a reversal in the dream not only of time but also of space, since far becomes near and near becomes far. Severn's sense that she is speaking to Ferenczi at "long distance," even though they are in the same room, exemplifies Borgogno's (2014) insight that both patient and analyst are always "coming from afar" in their sessions, having each traversed a journey through life to reach the present moment.

Ferenczi's commentary on the dream charts manifold vectors of the analytic field, beginning with Severn's history with her abusive father and how she projects this onto himself in the transference:

> Her inability to make herself understood is linked by association in the analysis to (a) her despair over the fact that I, the analyst, could have misunderstood her for so long. . . . (b) This behavior on my part reproduces the moment when she despaired of ever regaining the love her father had once shown her. She recognizes that his true nature is blind and mad (twisted) rage, anger, and cruelty. (c) Furthermore, it is interwoven with the diabolical idea, which he in fact carried out, of making the patient totally defenseless and transforming her into an automaton by various poisons. The man in the dream who is so hard to reach is on the one hand this tormentor; on the other hand he represents me, the stubborn analyst.
> (Dupont, 1985, pp. 157–58)

Although extremely profound, Ferenczi's interpretation thus far remains focused on Severn's inner world, but he then extends it to include the countertransference aroused "interpsychically" in him by being the recipient of her "long-distance telephone call": "The historical analysis of the male figure leads (a) to her own infantile life story. . . (b) to similar infantile experiences suspected in the analyst (drunkenness and abuse)" (p. 158).

Just as the dream shows how he and Severn come to each other "from afar," Ferenczi must also, as Borgogno (2014) elucidates, "temporarily become the patient without knowing it." From this point on, his exposition lures us into mystical waters:

> The most comprehensive interpretation of this nightmare, however, is that this personality, shattered and made defenseless by suffering and

poison, is attempting, over and over again but always unsuccessfully, to reassemble its various parts into a unit, that is, to understand the events taking place in and around her. But instead of understanding herself (realizing her own misery) she can only display in an indirect and symbolic way the contents that relate to her and of which she is herself unconscious: she must concern herself with analogous mental states in others (the reason for her choice of career), perhaps in the secret hope that one day she will be understood by one of these sufferers.

(Dupont, 1985, p. 158)

Severn's "choice of career" as a psychoanalyst, Ferenczi apprehends, was impelled by an attempt, as Polonius would say, by indirections to find directions out. In order to succeed in reassembling the "various parts" of her "shattered" self "into a unit," which she could not do by "understanding herself" because she was "herself unconscious" of her traumas, Severn had to find them mirrored in "an indirect and symbolic way" by the "analogous mental states in others," in the "secret hope" she could finally be "understood by one of these sufferers" whose history of "misery" was an inverted image of her own.

Ferenczi's explication of Severn's choice of a vocation as a quest to find—to refract the title of Harold Searles's (1975) classic paper—a therapist willing to become her patient is no less applicable to himself. He continues:

Her hypersensitivity—as says the association—goes so far that she can send and receive "telephone messages" over immense distances. (She believes in telepathic healing by means of willpower and thought-concentration, but especially through compassion.) As she links her own life history with that of the analyst, she suspects that even as a child she found the analyst, who is subject to similar suffering, "over a long distance" by means of telepathy, and after some forty years of aimless wandering has now sought him out.

(Dupont, 1985, p. 158)

Severn's belief in "telepathic healing," even "over immense distances," to which she adhered from the outset of her career, made her a laughingstock for Freud and Jones. But in Ferenczi's telling, Severn's nightmare, far from seeming ridiculous, becomes explicable in light of the "hypersensitivity" that is a consequence of her traumatic history. As he had written previously, it was "with the aid of an omnipotent intelligence" that, even "at the time of the principal trauma," Severn "scoured the universe in search of help," so that "her Orpha" prophetically tracked Ferenczi down "as the only person in the world who owing to his special personal fate could and would make amends for the injury that had been done to her" (p. 121).

Ferenczi completes his exegesis of Severn's dream by showing how his agreement to embark on a mutual analysis vindicated her intuition about the affinities between "her own life history" and "that of the analyst," and thereby made possible not only her healing but also his own:

> However, the obstacles and amnesia in the analyst himself have delayed the emergence of an understanding (in the analyst; see her complaints about my erroneous judgments), and only now, as I begin to realize my mistakes and recognize and exonerate her as an innocent and well-intentioned person . . . are we approaching the possibility of fitting the fragments of her personality together and of enabling her, not only indirectly but also directly, to recognize and remember the actual fact and causes of this disintegration. Until now, she could read (know) about her own circumstances only in mirror-writing, that is, in the analogous suffering of others. Now, however, she has found someone who can show her, in a, for her, convincing manner, that what she has uncovered about the analyst she must acknowledge as a distant reflection of her own sufferings.
>
> If this succeeds, then the former disintegration, and consequently the tendency to project (insanity) will in fact be mutually reversed.
>
> (pp. 158–59)

By virtue of Ferenczi's openness to acknowledging the "obstacles and amnesia" in himself, and concurrently to "recognize and exonerate" Severn's essential goodness, it became possible for the two of them to begin to reassemble "the fragments of her personality," and for Severn "not only indirectly but also directly, to recognize and remember the actual fact and causes of this disintegration." But this breakthrough could only take place in circuitous fashion, when Ferenczi was prepared to confirm that "what she has uncovered" in him was indeed "a distant reflection of her own sufferings." Thus, the "former disintegration" and resulting "tendency to project" was "mutually reversed" not only because they did it together but because Severn became Ferenczi's analyst even as he continued to be hers.

Another dream of Severn's, preserved by Ferenczi in the *Clinical Diary* on January 19, leads us into the hall of mirrors in which the mutual analysis is embedded: "R.N.'s dream. Former patient Dr. Gx. forces her withered breast into R.N.'s mouth. 'It isn't what I need; too big, empty—no milk.' The patient feels that this dream fragment is a combination of the unconscious contents of the psyches of the analysand and the analyst" (p. 13). Although the unknown "Dr. Gx." who "forces her withered breast into R.N.'s mouth" is *Severn's* "former patient," when Ferenczi says "the patient feels" that "this dream fragment is a combination of the unconscious contents of the psyches of the analysand and the analyst," he presumably means Severn in her capacity as *his* patient, just as it is Severn who "demands that the analyst should 'let himself be submerged,' even perhaps fall asleep," according to their shared commitment to the "relaxation principle." Severn's hallucination of Gx.'s "withered breast" sodomizing her mouth serves as a nodal point for the condensation of these two distinct analytic dyads.

Ferenczi proceeds to track the reverberations of Severn's dream of her patient's depleted breast being forced into her mouth not only in her psyche but also in his own:

> The analyst's associations in fact move in the direction of an episode in his infancy (*száraz dajka* [= nurse] affair, at the age of one year); meanwhile the patient repeats in dream scenes of horrifying events at the ages of one and a half, three, five, eleven and a half, and their interpretations. The analyst is able, for the first time, to link *emotions* with the above primal event and thus endow that event with the feeling of a real experience. Simultaneously the patient succeeds in gaining insight, far more penetrating than before, into the reality of these events that have been repeated so often on an intellectual level.
>
> (pp. 13–14)

In a parallel process, Severn repeats in her dream the "scenes of horrifying events" at four pivotal moments in her childhood, while Ferenczi is led by *his* "associations" to *her* dream to summon a "primal event" from his own infancy. By allowing himself to become "submerged" in Severn's dream, Ferenczi "for the first time" links his traumatic memory of abuse at the hands of his nurse, whether at the age of one or later in his childhood, with his hitherto dissociated "*emotions*." He thereby manages to "endow that event with the feeling of a real experience," while Severn "succeeds in gaining insight, far more penetrating than before, into the reality of these events that have been repeated so often on an intellectual level."[1]

Like the sundered beings of Aristophanes' speech in Plato's *Symposium*, Ferenczi and Severn found in each other the missing counterparts they had been seeking, and through their bidirectional exchange of "ideas" and "emotions" they healed the internal splits by which both had been riven:

> It is as though two halves had combined to form a whole soul. The emotions of the analyst combine with the ideas of the analysand, and the ideas of the analyst (representational images) with the emotions of the analysand; in this way the otherwise lifeless images become events, and the empty emotional tumult acquires an intellectual content.
>
> (p. 14)

As Ferenczi conceptualizes their psychic twinship, "the common attribute, the identity between the analyst and the analysand," resides in the way that they "both had been forced to do more and endure more sexually than they had in fact wanted to" (p. 15). Compared to Ferenczi's "infantile traumata," which he compresses into the "affair of the nurse, plus housemaid," however, the violence to which Severn was subjected by her father was infinitely more horrific. He quotes her summary of "the combined result of the two analyses":

> "Your greatest trauma was the destruction of genitality. Mine was worse: I saw my life destroyed by poisons and suggested stultification, my body defiled by the ugliest mutilations, at a most inappropriate time; ostracism from a society in which no one wants to believe me innocent; finally the horrendous incident of the last 'experience of being murdered.'"
>
> (p. 14)

Although Sándor was "cut to the heart" by his mother's accusation, "'You are my murderer'" (p. 61), Leota's "'experience of being murdered'" appears, as we have seen, to have been grounded in her participation in an actual manslaughter at the age of eleven and a half, followed by the "sudden desertion" by her father, who "as a kind of farewell, cursed the child" (p. 10). The Orphic destiny that drew Severn and Ferenczi to one another emanates from the symbiosis that allowed him to re-create in her his metaphorically murdering mother, while she found in him her literally homicidal father.

In their capacity as analysts, both Severn and Ferenczi had "to repeat the act of murder previously perpetrated against the patient," with the life-saving difference that neither was "allowed to deny his guilt" (p. 52). As Ferenczi writes of himself in the third person:

> His hatred of his mother in his childhood had almost led to matricide. At the dramatic moment in the reproduction of this scene he, so to speak, violently throws the knife away from himself and becomes "good." The "woman analyst" discovers from this that in order to save his mother the "patient" has castrated himself and become "good."
> (p. 110)

From the repudiated "hatred of his mother," Ferenczi's distillation of what transpired in his analysis with Severn turns to his conflicted bond to men, for which the template was chiseled by his grandfather:

> Even his relationship to men (father) is in fact compensation for a still more deeply repressed murderous rage. The entire libido of this man appears to have been transformed into hatred, the eradication of which, in actual fact, means self-annihilation. In his relationship to his friend the woman "analyst," the origins of guilt feelings and self-destructiveness could be recognized *in statu nascendi*.

Although Freud's name is not mentioned, Ferenczi's avowal of a "deeply repressed murderous rage" toward men can have no one else in its sights. Toward both sexes, his "entire libido" was "transformed into hatred," but this secondary hatred then underwent "eradication" by being turned inward in the form of "guilt feelings and self-destructiveness" that culminated in "self-annihilation." What Severn endured far exceeded Ferenczi's traumas, but his "destruction of genitality" was likewise a soul murder in which his very existence was at stake.

If the relationship of Ferenczi and Severn proved to be a marriage of true minds, it arrived at this comic ending only by reliving the ancient tragedies of incest and parricide. As Ferenczi observes, "the extraordinary analogy between my fate (neurosis) and the psychosis of her own father" enabled Severn to forge with Ferenczi a "total community of soul and spirit," as a consequence of which "sometimes she maintained that she lived in the head of the father, at other times that the father lived in the head of the patient" (p. 85). But Severn's father, "because of his insanity," did not realize that "all the infamous acts against the daughter are in fact meant for the mother," and "the final, atomizing trauma," which "occurred at a moment of mutual sobriety," involved a "desperate act of incest" (pp. 85–86). Following this catastrophe, he "withdrew from his daughter emotionally, in order to vilify her henceforth for life," and Severn's "atomization came about when she suddenly became aware of the impossibility of getting her father to admit his insane acts and sins" (p. 86).

In their joint pilgrimage through the underworld, Ferenczi and Severn reached what, since Freud's self-analysis, has always been the bedrock of psychoanalysis. But even Oedipus can now be seen to have been an abused, abandoned, and adopted child, as well as the victim of an inherited curse; and this hero and heroine of relational theory and practice teach us that our fates should no longer be ascribed to universal fantasies in the minds of children. In concert with our throw of the genetic dice and the accidents of personal experience, they are in large measure shaped by the legacies bequeathed by our mothers and fathers, who are themselves links in the endlessly receding chains of history and embedded in the widening gyres of culture and our increasingly precarious natural world. To follow in the footsteps of Ferenczi and Severn makes it possible to envision therapy as a process whereby all forms of trauma can be transfigured through emotionally charged repetitions into recollections and "MUTUAL FORGIVENESS" (p. 202). They leave us to ponder the questions: "Is the purpose of mutual analysis perhaps the finding of that common feature which repeats itself in every case of infantile trauma? And is the discovery or perception of this the condition for understanding and for the flood of healing compassion?" (p. 15).

Note

1 See the searching commentary on this and the ensuing passage from the *Clinical Diary*, with attendant clinical examples, by Juan Tubert-Oklander (2004), who foregrounds Ferenczi's "emphasis on emotional experience as the living core of the psychoanalytic experience, and on the complex unconscious interaction between analyst and patient" (p. 183).

References

Adler, Gerhard, ed. 1973. *Experimental Researches: Including the Studies in Word Association*. In *The Collected Works of C. G Jung*. 20 vols. Trans. R. F. C. Hull. Princeton: Princeton University Press, 1953–1979. Vol. 2.

Alexander, Franz. 1946. The Principle of Corrective Emotional Experience. In *Psychoanalytic Therapy: Principles and Application*. Eds. Franz Alexander, Thomas Morton French et al. New York: Ronald Press, 1946, pp. 66–70.

———. 1950. Analysis of the Therapeutic Factors in Psychoanalytic Treatment. In *The Scope of Psychoanalysis: Selected Papers of Franz Alexander, 1921–1961*. New York: Basic Books, 1961, pp. 261–75.

American Psychiatric Association. 2000. *Diagnostic and Statistical Manual of Mental Disorders: DSM-IV-TR*. Washington, DC: American Psychiatric Association.

Anonymous [Smith Ely Jelliffe?]. 1938. Review of *The Discovery of the Self: A Study in Psychological Cure*, by Elizabeth Severn. *Psychoanalytic Review*, 25(1):134–36.

Aron, Lewis. 1991. The Patient's Experience of the Analyst's Subjectivity. In Aron 1996, pp. 65–91.

———. 1996. *A Meeting of Minds: Mutuality in Psychoanalysis*. Hillsdale, NJ: Analytic Press.

Aron, Lewis, and Adrienne Harris, eds. 1993. *The Legacy of Sándor Ferenczi*. Hillsdale, NJ: Analytic Press.

Balint, Michael. 1956. Interview with Kurt R. Eissler. November 4. Freud Archives, Library of Congress, Washington, DC. 14 pp. Unpublished.

———. 1968. *The Basic Fault: Therapeutic Aspects of Regression*. London: Tavistock.

Balmary, Marie. 1979. *Psychoanalyzing Psychoanalysis: Freud and the Hidden Fault of the Father*. Trans. Ned Lukacher. Baltimore: Johns Hopkins University Press, 1982.

Baranger, Madeleine, and Willy Baranger. 2008. The Analytic Situation as a Dynamic Field. In Lisman-Pieczanski and Pieczanski 2015, pp. 21–60.

Baranger, Madeleine, Willy Baranger, and Jorge Mom. 1983. Process and Non-Process in Analytic Work. In Lisman-Pieczanski and Pieczanski 2015, pp. 64–86.

Barnett, Alan J. 2013. The Psychoanalytic Review: One Hundred Years of History. *Psychoanalytic Review*, 100(1):1–56.
Bartlett, Robert, Adrienne Harris, and Lauren Levine. 2018. Afterword to Bokanowski 2011, pp. 111–24.
Bass, Anthony. 2015. The Dialogue of Unconsciouses: Mutual Analysis and the Uses of the Self in Contemporary Relational Psychoanalysis. *Psychoanalytic Dialogues*, 25:2–17.
Berman, Emanuel. 1981. Multiple Personality: Psychoanalytic Perspectives. *International Journal of Psycho-Analysis*, 62:283–300.
———. 1997. Mutual Analysis: Boundary Violation or Failed Experiment? *Journal of the American Psychoanalytic Association*, 45:569–71.
———. 2004a. *Impossible Training: A Relational View of Psychoanalytic Education.* New York: Routledge, 2014.
———. 2004b. Sándor, Gizella, Elma: A Biographical Journey. *International Journal of Psychoanalysis*, 85:489–520.
———. 2015. On "Polygamous Analysis." *American Journal of Psychoanalysis*, 75:29–36.
Billinsky, John M. 1969. Jung and Freud (The End of a Romance). *Andover Newton Quarterly*, 10:39–43.
Birksted-Breen, Dana. 2019. 100 Years of the International Journal of Psychoanalysis. *International Journal of Psychoanalysis*, 100:1–6.
Blanton, Smiley. 1971. *Diary of My Analysis with Sigmund Freud.* New York: Hawthorn Books.
Blum, Harold P. 2004. The Wise Baby and the Wild Analyst. *Psychoanalytic Psychology*, 21:3–15.
Bohleber, Werner. 2010. *Destructiveness, Intersubjectivity, and Trauma: The Identity Crisis of Modern Psychoanalysis.* London: Karnac Books.
Bokanowski, Thierry. 2011. *The Modernity of Sándor Ferenczi: His Historical and Contemporary Importance in Psychoanalysis.* Trans. Andrew Weller. New York: Routledge, 2018.
Bone, Harry. 1957. Letter to Erich Fromm. November 19. Fromm Archives, Tübingen, Germany. Unpublished.
Bonomi, Carlo. 1999. Flight into Sanity: Jones's Allegation of Ferenczi's Mental Deterioration Reconsidered. *International Journal of Psycho-Analysis*, 80:507–42.
———. 2012. Freud, Ferenczi, and the "Disbelief" on the Acropolis. *International Forum of Psychoanalysis*, 21:239–48.
———. 2013. "So It Really Does Exist—The Sea-Serpent We've Never Believed In!" Freud's Influence on Ferenczi Revisited. *American Journal of Psychoanalysis*, 73:370–81.
———. 2015a. *The Cut and the Building of Psychoanalysis, Volume 1: Sigmund Freud and Emma Eckstein.* New York: Routledge.
———. 2015b. The Penis on the Trail: Re-Reading the Origins of Psychoanalysis with Sándor Ferenczi. In Harris and Kuchuck 2015, pp. 33–51.

Borgogno, Franco. 2010. Ferenczi, the "Introjective Analyst." In Harris and Kuchuck 2015, pp. 171–86.
———. 2014. "Coming from Afar" and "Temporarily Becoming the Patient without Knowing It": Two Necessary Analytic Conditions according to Ferenczi's Later Thought. *American Journal of Psychoanalysis*, 74:302–12.
Bowlby, John. 1979. Psychoanalysis as Art and Science. In *A Secure Base: Clinical Applications of Attachment Theory*. London: Routledge, 1989, pp. 39–57.
Boyle, John. 2021. From Metapsychology to Magnetic Gnosis: An Esoteric Context for Interpreting Traumatic Modes of Transcendence in Sándor Ferenczi's *Clinical Diary* and Elizabeth Severn's *Discovery of the Self*. *Psychoanalysis and History*, in press.
Brabant, Eva, Ernst Falzeder, and Patrizia Giampieri-Deutsch, eds. 1993. *The Correspondence of Sigmund Freud and Sándor Ferenczi. Volume 1, 1908–1914*. Trans. Peter T. Hoffer. Cambridge, MA: Harvard University Press. German edition: *Sigmund Freud—Sándor Ferenczi Briefwechsel. Band I/1.1908–1911*. Wien: Böhlau Verlag, 1993.
Brabant-Gerö, Eva. 1986. L'ami des fous. Introduction to *Mes adieux à la maison jaune*, by István Hollós. Trans. from the Hungarian by Judith Dupont. *Le Coq-Héron*, 100:3–14.
Brandchaft, Bernard, Shelley Doctors, and Dorienne Sorter. 2010. *Toward an Emancipatory Psychoanalysis: Brandchaft's Intersubjective Vision*. New York: Routledge.
Breger, Louis. 2000. *Freud: Darkness in the Midst of Vision*. New York: Wiley.
Brennan, B. William. 2009. Ferenczi's Forgotten Messenger: The Life and Work of Izette de Forest. *American Imago*, 66:427–55.
———. 2011. On Ferenczi: A Response—from Elasticity to the Confusion of Tongues and the Technical Dimensions of Ferenczi's Approach. *Psychoanalytic Perspectives*, 8:1–21.
———. 2015a. Decoding Ferenczi's *Clinical Diary*: Biographical Notes. *American Journal of Psychoanalysis*, 75:5–18.
———. 2015b. The Medium Is the Message: Turning Tables with Elizabeth Severn. Paper presented at the conference of the International Sándor Ferenczi Society, Toronto. 8 pp. Unpublished.
———. 2015c. Out of the Archive/Unto the Couch: Clara Thompson's Analysis with Ferenczi. In Harris and Kuchuck 2015, pp. 77–95.
Brenner, Ira. 2016. A Psychoactive Therapy of DID: A Multiphasic Model. In Howell and Itzkowitz 2016, pp. 210–20.
Breuer, Josef, and Sigmund Freud. 1895. *Studies on Hysteria*. In *The Standard Edition of the Complete Psychological Works of Sigmund Freud*. 24 vols. Eds. and trans. James Strachey et al. London: Hogarth Press, 1953–1974. Vol. 2.
Bromberg, Chaim E., and Lewis Aron. 2019. Disguised Autobiography as Clinical Case Study. *Psychoanalytic Dialogues*, 29:695–710.
Bromberg, Philip. 1998. *Standing in the Spaces: Essays on Clinical Process, Trauma, and Dissociation*. New York: Psychology Press, 2001.

---. 2011. *The Shadow of the Tsunami and the Growth of the Relational Mind*. New York: Routledge.

Burnham, John C. 1983. *Jelliffe: American Psychoanalyst and Physician & His Correspondence with Sigmund Freud and C. G. Jung*. Ed. William McGuire. Chicago: University of Chicago Press.

Burrow, Trigant. 1926. The Laboratory Method in Psychoanalysis, Its Inception and Development. In Pertegato and Pertegato, 2013, pp. 143–55.

Cassullo, Gabriele. 2014. Splitting in the History of Psychoanalysis: From Janet and Freud to Fairbairn, Passing through Ferenczi and Suttie. In *Fairbairn and the Object Relations Tradition*. Eds. Graham S. Clarke and David E. Scharff. London: Karnac Books, 2014, pp. 49–58.

---. 2018. Ferenczi before Freud. In *Ferenczi's Influence on Contemporary Psychoanalytic Traditions:—Lines of Development—Evolution of Theory and Practice over the Decades*. Eds. Aleksandar Dimitrijevic, Gabriele Cassullo, and Jay Frankel. New York: Routledge, 2018, pp. 18–24.

---. 2019a. Janet and Freud: Long-Time Rivals. In Craparo, Ortu, and Van der Hart 2019, pp. 43–52.

---. 2019b. On Not Taking Just One Part of It: Janet's Influence on Object Relations Theory. In Craparo, Ortu, and Van der Hart 2019, pp. 66–74.

Cincinnati Enquirer. 1934. The Psycho-Analysis of Today. April 29 and May 10. Severn Archives. Library of Congress, Washington, DC.

Cohen, Etty. 2015. The "Method of Game": Sándor Ferenczi and His Patient Dm./Clara Thompson. *American Journal of Psychoanalysis*, 77:295–312.

Conci, Marco. 2012. *Sullivan Revisited—Life and Work*. 2nd ed. Trans. Laurie Cohen and David Lee. Trento: Tangram Edizioni Scientifiche.

Contributors to this Issue. 1958. *Psychoanalytic Review*, 45A(1/2):160–61.

Cook, Lavinia Cole. 1918. Letter to Elizabeth Severn. November 21. Severn Archives. Library of Congress, Washington, DC. Unpublished.

Craparo, Giuseppe, Francesca Ortu, and Onno van der Hart, eds. 2019. *Rediscovering Pierre Janet: Trauma, Dissociation, and a New Context for Psychoanalysis*. New York: Routledge.

Crastnopol, Margaret. 2015. *Micro-Trauma: A Psychoanalytic Understanding of Cumulative Psychic Injury*. New York: Routledge.

Daily Herald. 1912. The Higher Thought in Practice [Report on a lecture by Elizabeth Severn at the Higher Thought Centre]. December 14, p. 3.

---. 1913. The Faults of Women. [Report on a lecture by Elizabeth Severn at the Higher Thought Centre]. February 15, p. 3.

Davies, Jody Messler. 1998. Repression and Dissociation—Freud and Janet: Fairbairn's New Model of Unconscious Process. In *Fairbairn Then and Now*. Eds. Neil J. Skolnick and David E. Scharff. Hillsdale, NJ: Analytic Press, 1998, pp. 53–69.

Davies, Jody Messler, and Mary Gail Frawley. 1994. *Treating the Adult Survivor of Childhood Sexual Abuse: A Psychoanalytic Perspective*. New York: Basic Books.

de Forest, Izette. 1942. The Therapeutic Technique of Sándor Ferenczi. *International Journal of Psycho-Analysis*, 23:120–39.

———. 1954. *The Leaven of Love: A Development of the Psychoanalytic Theory and Technique of Sándor Ferenczi*. New York: Da Capo Press, 1984.

———. 1957. Letter to Erich Fromm. February 18. Fromm Archives, Tübingen, Germany. Unpublished.

Descartes, René. 1641. *Meditations on First Philosophy*. In *The Philosophical Works of Descartes*. 2 vols. Trans. Elizabeth S. Haldane and G. R. T. Ross. Cambridge: Cambridge University Press, 1975, 1:131–99.

Dupont, Judith, ed. 1985. *The Clinical Diary of Sándor Ferenczi*. Trans. Michael Balint and Nicola Zarday Jackson. Cambridge, MA: Harvard University Press, 1988. German edition: *Ohne Sympathie keine Heilung: Das klinische Tagebuch von 1932*. Frankfurt: S. Fischer, 1988.

———. 1988. Ferenczi's "Madness." Trans. Bernard Ehrenberg. *Contemporary Psychoanalysis*, 24:250–61.

Eastman, Max. 1948. *Enjoyment of Living*. New York: Harper and Brothers.

Edmunds, Lavinia. 1988. His Master's Choice. *Johns Hopkins Magazine*, 40–2(April):40–49.

Ellenberger, Henri F. 1970. *The Discovery of the Unconscious: The History and Evolution of Dynamic Psychiatry*. New York: Basic Books.

Everett, Patricia R. 2016. *Corresponding Lives: Mabel Dodge Luhan, A. A. Brill, and the Psychoanalytic Adventure in America*. London: Karnac Books.

———. 2021. *The Dreams of Mabel Dodge: Diary of an Analysis with Smith Ely Jelliffe (1916)*. New York: Routledge.

Fairbairn, W. R. D. 1944. Endopsychic Structure Considered in Terms of Object-Relationships. In Fairbairn 1952, pp. 82–136.

———. 1949. Steps in the Development of an Object-Relations Theory of the Personality. In Fairbairn 1952, pp. 152–61.

———. 1952. *Psychoanalytic Studies of the Personality*. London: Routledge, 1986.

Falzeder, Ernst. 1996. Dreaming of Freud: Ferenczi, Freud, and an Analysis without End. In Falzeder 2015, pp. 245–55.

———. 1998. Family Tree Matters. In Falzeder 2015, pp. 77–102.

———, ed. 2002. *The Complete Correspondence of Sigmund Freud and Karl Abraham, 1907–1925*. Trans. Caroline Schwarzacher with the collaboration of Christine Trollope and Klara Majthényi King. London: Karnac Books.

———. 2015. *Psychoanalytic Filiations: Mapping the Psychoanalytic Movement*. London: Karnac Books.

Falzeder, Ernst, and Eva Brabant, eds. 2000. *The Correspondence of Sigmund Freud and Sándor Ferenczi. Volume 3, 1920–1933*. Trans. Peter T. Hoffer. Cambridge, MA: Harvard University Press.

Falzeder, Ernst, and Judith Dupont. 2000. Sándor Ferenczi: President of the International Psychoanalytical Association (1918–1920) and Founder of the International Journal of Psycho-Analysis. *International Journal of Psychoanalysis*, 81:805.

Ferenczi, Sándor. 1899. Spiritism. Trans. Nandor Fodor. *Psychoanalytic Review*, 50A(1963):139–44.
———. 1909. Introjection and Transference. In *Sex in Psycho-Analysis* [= Contributions to Psycho-Analysis]. Trans. Ernest Jones. New York: Dover, 1956, pp. 30–79.
———. 1912a. Exploring the Unconscious. In Ferenczi 1955, pp. 308–12.
———. 1912b. Suggestion and Psychoanalysis. In Ferenczi 1926a, pp. 55–68.
———. 1913a. Belief, Disbelief, and Conviction. In Ferenczi 1926a, pp. 437–50.
———. 1913b. The "Grandfather Complex." In Ferenczi 1926a, pp. 323–24.
———. 1916–17. Two Types of War Neuroses. In Ferenczi 1926a, pp. 124–41.
———. 1917a. My Friendship with Miksa Schachter. Trans. Boriz Szegal. *British Journal of Psychotherapy*, 9(1993):430–33.
———. 1917b. Review of "Die psychische Bedingtheit und die psychoanalytische Behandlung organischer Leiden," by Georg Groddeck. In Ferenczi 1955, pp. 342–43.
———. 1920. Open Letter. *International Journal of Psycho-Analysis*, 1:1–2.
———. 1920 and 1930–1932. *Notes and Fragments*. In Ferenczi 1955, pp. 216–79.
———. 1921a. Bridge Symbolism and the Don Juan Legend. In Ferenczi 1926a, pp. 356–58.
———. 1921b. Contribution to Symposium on War Neuroses. Trans. Ernest Jones [?]. In Ferenczi, Abraham, Simmel, and Jones 1921, pp. 5–21.
———. 1921c. The Symbolism of the Bridge. In Ferenczi 1926a, pp. 352–56.
———. 1924. *Thalassa: A Theory of Genitality*. Trans. Henry A. Bunker. New York: Norton, 1968.
———. 1925a. Contra-Indications to the "Active" Psycho-Analytical Technique. In Ferenczi 1926a, pp. 217–30.
———. 1925b. Psycho-Analysis of Sexual Habits. In Ferenczi 1926a, pp. 259–97.
———. 1926a. *Further Contributions to the Theory and Technique of Psycho-Analysis*. Ed. John Rickman. Trans. Jane I. Suttie et al. New York: Brunner/Mazel, 1980.
———. 1926b. Present-Day Problems in Psycho-Analysis. In Ferenczi 1955, pp. 29–40.
———. 1927a. The Adaptation of the Family to the Child. In Ferenczi 1955, pp. 61–76.
———. 1927b. The Problem of the Termination of the Analysis. In Ferenczi 1955, pp. 77–86.
———. 1928. The Elasticity of Psycho-Analytic Technique. In Ferenczi 1955, pp. 87–101.
———. 1929a. Männlich und Weiblich: Psychoanalytische Betrachtungen über die "Genitaltheorie," sowie über sekundäre und tertiäre Geschlechtsunterschiede. *Die Psychoanalytische Bewegung*, 1:41–50. English version: Masculine and Feminine: Psychoanalytic Observations on the "Genital Theory" and

on Secondary and Tertiary Sex Characteristics. Trans. Olga Marx. *Psychoanalytic Review*, 17(2)(1930):105–13.

———. 1929b. The Unwelcome Child and His Death Instinct. In Ferenczi 1955, pp. 102–7.

———. 1930. The Principle of Relaxation and Neocatharsis. In Ferenczi 1955, pp. 108–25.

———. 1931. Child-Analysis in the Analysis of Adults. In Ferenczi 1955, pp. 126–42.

———. 1933a. Confusion of Tongues between Adults and the Child: The Language of Tenderness and of Passion. In Ferenczi 1955, pp. 156–67.

———. 1933b. Freud's Influence on Medicine. In Ferenczi 1955, pp. 143–55.

———. 1955. *Final Contributions to the Methods and Problems of Psycho-Analysis*. Ed. Michael Balint. Trans. Eric Mosbacher et al. New York: Brunner/Mazel, 1980.

Ferenczi, Sandor, Karl Abraham, Ernst Simmel, and Ernest Jones. 1921. *Psycho-Analysis and the War Neuroses*. Trans. Ernest Jones [?]. London: Forgotten Books, 2012.

Ferenczi, Sandor, and Otto Rank. 1924. *The Development of Psycho-Analysis*. Trans. Caroline Newton. New York: Dover, 1956.

Field, Dorothy S. 1941. Letter to Elizabeth Severn. July 8. Severn Archives. Library of Congress, Washington, DC. Unpublished.

Field, Manning C. 1941. Letter to Elizabeth Severn. May 23. Severn Archives. Library of Congress, Washington, DC. Unpublished.

Fodor, Nandor. 1944. A Personal Analytic Approach to the Problem of the Holy Name. *Psychoanalytic Review*, 31(2):165–80.

———. 1949. *The Search for the Beloved: A Clinical Investigation of the Trauma of Birth and Pre-Natal Condition*. Hyde Park, NY: University Books.

———. 1951. *New Approaches to Dream Interpretation*. Hyde Park, NY: University Books.

———. 1955. Freud and the Poltergeist. *Psychoanalysis: Journal of Psychoanalytic Psychology*, 4(2):22–28.

———. 1958. *On the Trail of the Poltergeist*. New York: Citadel Press.

———. 1959. *The Haunted Mind: A Psychoanalyst Looks at the Supernatural*. New York: Helix Press.

———. 1963. Jung, Freud, and a Newly-Discovered Letter of 1909 on the Poltergeist Theme. *Psychoanalytic Review*, 50B(2):119–28.

———. 1968. *The Unaccountable*. New York: Award Books.

Fodor, Nandor, and Frank Gaynor, eds. 1958. *Freud: Dictionary of Psychoanalysis*. New York: Fawcett Premier.

Fonagy, Peter, and Mary Target. 1997. Perspectives on the Recovered Memory Debate. In *Recovered Memories of Abuse: True or False?* Eds. Joseph Sandler and Peter Fonagy. London: Karnac Books, 1997, pp. 183–216.

Fortune, Christopher. 1993. The Case of "RN": Sándor Ferenczi's Radical Experiment in Psychoanalysis. In Aron and Harris 1993, pp. 101–20.

———. 1994. A Difficult Ending: Ferenczi, "R.N.," and the Experiment in Mutual Analysis. In *100 Years of Psychoanalysis: Contributions to the History of Psychoanalysis*. Eds. André Haynal and Ernst Falzeder. *Cahiers Psychiatriques Genevois*, special issue, 1994, pp. 217–23.

———, ed. 2002. *The Sándor Ferenczi-Georg Groddeck Correspondence, 1921–1933*. Trans. Jeannie Cohen, Elisabeth Petersdorff, and Norbert Ruebsatt. New York: Other Press.

———. 2015. Thwarting the Psychoanalytic Detectives: Defending the Severn Legacy. *American Journal of Psychoanalysis*, 75:19–28.

Freud, Sigmund. 1896. The Aetiology of Hysteria. In *The Standard Edition of the Complete Psychological Works* (hereafter *S.E.*). 24 vols. Ed. and trans. James Strachey et al. London: Hogarth Press, 1953–1974, 3:191–221.

———. 1899. Screen Memories. *S.E.*, 3:303–22.

———. 1900. *The Interpretation of Dreams*. *S.E.*, 4 and 5.

———. 1901. *The Psychopathology of Everyday Life: Forgetting, Slips of the Tongue, Bungled Actions, Superstitions and Errors*. *S.E.*, 6.

———. 1905a. Fragment of an Analysis of a Case of Hysteria. *S.E.*, 7:7–122.

———. 1905b. Three Essays on the Theory of Sexuality. *S.E.*, 7:130–243.

———. 1909. Notes upon a Case of Obsessional Neurosis. *S.E.*, 10:155–249.

———. 1910. Five Lectures on Psycho-Analysis. *S.E.*, 11:9–55.

———. 1912. Recommendations to Physicians Practising Psycho-Analysis. *S.E.*, 12:111–20.

———. 1914a. On the History of the Psycho-Analytic Movement. *S.E.*, 14:7–66.

———. 1914b. On Narcissism: An Introduction. *S.E.*, 14:73–102.

———. 1914c. Remembering, Repeating and Working-Through (Further Recommendations on the Technique of Psycho-Analysis II). *S.E.*, 12:147–56.

———. 1917. A Childhood Recollection from *Dichtung und Wahrheit*. *S.E.*, 17:147–56.

———. 1923a. *The Ego and the Id*. *S.E.*, 19:12–66.

———. 1923b. Two Encyclopaedia Articles. *S.E.*, 18:233–60.

———. 1924. A Short Account of Psycho-Analysis. *S.E.*, 19:189–210.

———. 1925. *An Autobiographical Study*. *S.E.*, 20:7–74.

———. 1926a. *Inhibitions, Symptoms and Anxiety*. *S.E.*, 20:87–172.

———. 1926b. *The Question of Lay Analysis*. *S.E.*, 20:183–258.

———. 1928a. Dostoevsky and Parricide. *S.E.*, 21:177–94.

———. 1928b. Letter to István Hollós. October 4. Freud Museum, London. Unpublished.

———. 1929. Some Dreams of Descartes': A Letter to Maxime Leroy. *S.E.*, 21:203–4.

———. 1931. Female Sexuality. *S.E.*, 21:225–44.

———. 1933a. *New Introductory Lectures on Psycho-Analysis*. *S.E.*, 22:5–182.

———. 1933b. Sándor Ferenczi. *S.E.*, 22:227–29.

———. 1937a. Analysis Terminable and Interminable. *S.E.*, 23:216–53.

———. 1937b. Constructions in Analysis. *S.E.*, 23:257–70.

———. 1939. *Moses and Monotheism: Three Essays*. *S.E.*, 23:7–138.
———. 1940a. *An Outline of Psycho-Analysis*. *S.E.*, 23:144–208.
———. 1940b. Splitting of the Ego in the Process of Defence. *S.E.*, 23:275–78.
———. 1987. *A Phylogenetic Fantasy: Overview of the Transference Neuroses*. Ed. Ilse Grubrich-Simitis. Trans. Axel Hoffer and Peter T. Hoffer. Cambridge, MA: Harvard University Press.
Friedman, Lawrence J., assisted by Anke M. Schreiber. 2013. *The Lives of Erich Fromm: Love's Prophet*. New York: Columbia University Press.
Frink, Angelica [*sic*] Bijur. 1952. Interview with Kurt R. Eissler. June 19. Freud Archives, Library of Congress, Washington, DC. 7 pp. Unpublished.
Fromm, Erich. 1935. The Social Determinants of Psychoanalytic Therapy. Trans. Ernst Falzeder with Caroline Schwarzacher. *International Forum of Psychoanalysis*, 9(2000):149–65.
———. 1955. Love Stood between Him and Freud. Review of *The Leaven of Love*, by Izette de Forest. *New York Times*, August 7. Section BR, p. 19.
———. 1957. Letter to Elizabeth Severn. December 12. Fromm Archives, Tübingen, Germany. Unpublished.
———. 1958. Freud, Friends, and Feuds. 1. Scientist or Fanaticism? *Saturday Review*, June 14, pp. 11–13, 55.
———. 1959. *Sigmund Freud's Mission: An Analysis of His Personality and Influence*. New York: Grove Press, 1963.
Gabbard, Glen O. 1995. The Early History of Boundary Violations in Psychoanalysis. *Journal of the American Psychoanalytic Association*, 43:1115–36.
———. 1997. Letter: Glen O. Gabbard Replies. *Journal of the American Psychoanalytic Association*, 45:571–72.
Gargiulo, Gerald. 2020. Reik: Yesterday and Today. *Theodor Reik Archive Newsletter*, 2. November 1, pp. 3–4.
Geoffrey of Monmouth. 1999. *History of the Kings of Britain*. Trans. Aaron Thompson, rev. J. A. Giles. Cambridge, ON: In Parentheses Publications.
Giefer, Michael, ed. 2008. *Briefwechsel Sigmund Freud—Georg Groddeck*. In collaboration with Beate Schuh. Frankfurt: Stromfeld.
Gilligan, Carol, and Naomi Snider. 2018. *Why Does Patriarchy Persist?* Cambridge: Polity Press.
Green, Maurice R. 1964a. Her Life. In Green 1964b, pp. 347–77.
———, ed. 1964b. *Interpersonal Psychoanalysis: The Selected Papers of Clara M. Thompson*. New York: Basic Books.
Groddeck, Georg. 1913. *Nasamecu. Der gesunde und kranke Mensch gemeinverständlich dargestellt*. Ed. Michael Giefer. Frankfurt: Stroemfeld, 2014.
———. 1923. *The Book of the It*. Trans. V. M. E. Collins. Mansfield Centre, CT: Martino Publishing, 2015.
———. 1926. Bowel Function. In *Exploring the Unconscious*. Trans. V. M. E. Collins. London: Vision Press, 1989, pp. 81–110.
———. 1934. On the Psychic Conditioning of Cancer Sickness. In *The World of Man*. Trans. V. M. E. Collins. London: Vision Press, 1951, pp. 150–70.

Guasto, Gianni. 2013. Trauma and the Loss of Basic Trust. *International Forum of Psychoanalysis*, 23:44–49.
Gurevich, Hayuta. 2016. Orpha, Orphic Function, and the Orphic Analyst: Winnicott's "Regression to Dependence" in the Language of Ferenczi. *American Journal of Psychoanalysis*, 76:322–40.
Gyimesi, Júlia. 2012. Sándor Ferenczi and the Problem of Telepathy. *History of the Human Sciences*, 25(2):131–48.
Hainer, Marianne L. 2016. The Ferenczi Paradox: His Importance in Understanding Dissociation and the Dissociation of His Importance in Psychoanalysis. In Howell and Itzkowitz 2016, pp. 57–69.
Hale, Nathan G., Jr. 1971. *Freud and the Americans: The Beginnings of Psychoanalysis in the United States, 1876–1917*. New York: Oxford University Press, 1995.
———. 1995. *The Rise and Crisis of Psychoanalysis in the United States. Freud and the Americans, 1917–1985*. New York: Oxford University Press.
Harris, Adrienne. 1998. The Analyst as (Auto)biographer. *American Imago*, 55:255–75.
Harris, Adrienne, and Lewis Aron. 2017. The Work of Elizabeth Severn: An Appreciation. In Severn 1933, pp. xii–xviii.
Harris, Adrienne, and Steven Kuchuck, eds. 2015. *The Legacy of Sándor Ferenczi: From Ghost to Ancestor*. New York: Routledge.
Haynal, André E. 2002. *Disappearing and Reviving: Sándor Ferenczi in the History of Psychoanalysis*. New York: Routledge, 2018.
———. 2005. In the Shadow of a Controversy: Freud and Ferenczi 1925–33. *International Journal of Psychoanalysis*, 86:457–66.
Haynal, André E., and Ernst Falzeder. 1991. "Healing through Love"? A Unique Dialogue in the History of Psychoanalysis. In Falzeder 2015, pp. 3–18.
Health Record and Psycho-Therapeutic Journal, The. 1913a. Colours and Their Meaning. Abstract of Lecture Given by Dr. Elizabeth Severn before the Psycho-Therapeutic Society. 12(May–June), p. 46.
———. 1913b. Psycho-Therapeutic Society. [note on a lecture by Dr. Elizabeth Severn, Mental States in Relation to the Causes and Cure of Disease.] 12(November), p. 100.
Herman, Judith Lewis. 1992. *Trauma and Recovery*. New York: Basic Books, 1996.
Hoche, Alfred. 1910. Eine psychische Epidemie unter Ärzten. *Medizinische Klinik*, 6:1007–10.
Hoffer, Peter T. 2010. From Elasticity to the Confusion of Tongues: A Historical Commentary on the Technical Dimension of the Freud/Ferenczi Controversy. *Psychoanalytic Perspectives*, 7:90–103.
Hoffer, Peter T., and Axel Hoffer. 1999. Ferenczi's Fatal Illness in Historical Context. *Journal of the American Psychoanalytic Association*, 47:1257–68.
Howell, Elizabeth F. 2005. *The Dissociative Mind*. New York: Routledge.
Howell, Elizabeth F., and Sheldon Itzkowitz, eds. 2016. *The Dissociative Mind in Psychoanalysis: Understanding and Working with Trauma*. New York: Routledge.
Jelliffe, Smith Ely, and Elida Evans. 1916. Psoriasis as an Hysterical Conversion Symbolization. *New York Medical Journal*, 104:1077–84.

Jelliffe, Smith Ely, and William Alanson White. 1917. *Diseases of the Nervous System: A Text-Book of Neurology and Psychiatry*. 2nd ed. Philadelphia: Lea and Febiger.

Jones, Ernest. 1933. Sandor Ferenczi, 1873–1933. *International Journal of Psycho-Analysis*, 14:463–66.

———. 1953. *The Life and Work of Sigmund Freud: Vol. 1, The Formative Years and the Great Discoveries, 1856–1900*. New York: Basic Books.

———. 1956. Review of *The Leaven of Love. A Development of the Psychoanalytic Theory and Technique of Sandor Ferenczi*, by Izette de Forest. *International Journal of Psycho-Analysis*, 37:488.

———. 1957. *The Life and Work of Sigmund Freud: Vol. 3, The Last Phase, 1919–1939*. New York: Basic Books.

Kardiner, A[bram]. 1977. *My Analysis with Freud: Reminiscences*. New York: Norton.

Khan, M. Masud R. 1963. The Concept of Cumulative Trauma. *Psychoanalytic Study of the Child*, 18:286–306.

Kirshner, Lewis A. 1993. Concepts of Reality and Psychic Reality in Psychoanalysis as Illustrated by the Disagreement between Freud and Ferenczi. *International Journal of Psychoanalysis*, 74:219–30.

Kohut, Heinz. 1971. *The Analysis of the Self: A Systematic Approach to the Treatment of Narcissistic Personality Disorders*. New York: International Universities Press.

———. 1977. *The Restoration of the Self*. Madison, CT: International Universities Press, 1984.

———. 1984. *How Does Analysis Cure?* Eds. Arnold Goldberg and Paul E. Stepansky. Chicago: University of Chicago Press.

Kris, Ernst. 1956. The Recovery of Childhood Memories in Psychoanalysis. *Psychoanalytic Study of the Child*, 11:54–88.

Krüll, Marianne. 1979. *Freud and His Father*. Trans. Arnold Pomerans. New York: Norton, 1986.

Kuhn, Philip. 2017. *Psychoanalysis in Britain, 1893–1913: Histories and Historiography*. Lanham, MD: Lexington Books.

Laplanche, Jean. 1987. *New Foundations for Psychoanalysis*. Trans. David Macey. Oxford: Blackwell, 1989.

Leavitt, C. Franklin. 1900. *Leavitt-Science: The Power-Path to Mental and Physical Poise and Achievement*. Chicago: Privately published.

———. 1914. *Mental and Physical Ease and Supremacy; Being a Practical Adaptation of Leavitt-Science to Individual Use*. Chicago: Rogers and Hall.

Lévy, Lajos. 1957. Letter to Erich Fromm. November 30. Fromm Archives, Tübingen, Germany. Unpublished.

———. 1998. Trois Lettres sur la maladie de Sándor Ferenczi. Trans. from the German by Stéphane Michaud. *Le Coq-Héron*, 149:23–26.

Lewis, Nolan D. C. 1966. Smith Ely Jelliffe, 1866–1945: Psychosomatic Medicine in America. In *Psychoanalytic Pioneers*. Eds. Franz Alexander, Samuel Eisenstein, and Martin Grotjahn. New York: Basic Books, 1966, pp. 224–34.

Lipskis, Peter. 1981. *Dance Masks: The World of Margaret Severn*. Berkeley: University of California Extension Media Center. Film. YouTube. 32 minutes, 18 seconds.

———. 1991. *Childhood Chapters. Two-part video recording of Margaret Severn reading chapters 1 and 2 of* Spotlight. YouTube. 34 minutes.

———. 1992. *Portrait of an Artist as a Young Woman (1914–1919)*. Film. YouTube. 26 minutes, 54 seconds.

———. 2018. Why Margaret Severn Was the Most Fascinating Person I Ever Knew. *The Wise Baby* [*Il poppante saggio: Rivista del rinascimento ferenziano*], 1:113–19.

Lizman-Pieczanski, Nydia, and Alberto Pieczanski, eds. 2015. *The Pioneers of Psychoanalysis in South America: An Essential Guide*. In Collaboration with Karla Loyo. New York: Routledge.

Luhan, Mabel Dodge. 1936. *Movers and Shakers: Volume Three of Intimate Memories*. New York: Harcourt, Brace.

Lynn, David J. 2003. Freud's Psychoanalysis of Edith Banfield Jackson, 1930–1936. *Journal of the American Academy of Psychoanalysis*, 31:609–25.

Marcel, Mary. 2005. *Freud's Traumatic Memory: Reclaiming Seduction Theory and Revisiting Oedipus*. Pittsburgh: Duquesne University Press.

Maroda, Karen. 1998. Why Mutual Analysis Failed: The Case of Ferenczi and Rn. *Contemporary Psychoanalysis*, 34:115–32.

Masson, Jeffrey M. 1984. *The Assault on Truth: Freud's Suppression of the Seduction Theory*. New York: Farrar, Straus and Giroux.

———, ed. and trans. 1985. *The Complete Letters of Sigmund Freud to Wilhelm Fliess 1887–1904*. Cambridge, MA: Harvard University Press.

Mastery. Issued Monthly for the New Education Centre. 1914. Summer School, 1913, by G. C. S. [Guy Clifford Stanley]. January, pp. 45–46.

Mayer, Elizabeth Lloyd. 2007. *Extraordinary Knowing: Science, Skepticism, and the Inexplicable Powers of the Human Mind*. New York: Bantam Books, 2008.

McGuire, William, ed. 1974. *The Freud/Jung Letters: The Correspondence between Sigmund Freud and C. G. Jung*. Trans. Ralph Manheim and R. F. C. Hull. Princeton: Princeton University Press.

Meigs, Kathleen E. 2017. The Failure of Clara Thompson's Ferenczian (Proxy) Analysis of Harry Stack Sullivan. *American Journal of Psychoanalysis*, 77:313–31.

Menaker, Esther. 1989. *Appointment in Vienna: An American Psychoanalyst Recalls Her Student Days in Pre-War Austria*. New York: St. Martin's Press.

———. 2001. Anna Freud's Analysis of Her Father: The Assault on the Self. *Journal of Religion and Health*, 40:89–96.

Meng, Heinrich, and Ernst L. Freud, eds. 1963. *Psychoanalysis and Faith: The Letters of Sigmund Freud and Oskar Pfister*. Trans. Eric Mosbacher. New York: Basic Books.

Meyer-Palmedo, Ingeborg, ed. 2006. *Correspondence 1904–1938. Sigmund Freud and Anna Freud*. Trans. Nick Somers. Malden, MA: Polity Press, 2014.

Mucci, Clara, Giuseppe Craparo, and Vittorio Lingiardi. 2019. From Janet to Bromberg, via Ferenczi: Standing in the Spaces of the Literature on Dissociation. In Craparo, Ortu, and Van der Hart 2019, pp. 75–92.

Nelson, Marie Coleman. 1964. Nandor Fodor: 1895–1964. *Psychoanalytic Review*, 51B(2):155–57.
New York Times. 1964. Nandor Fodor, 69, A Psychoanalyst; Author of Theory to Explain Poltergeists is Dead. May 19, p. 37.
Nin, Anaïs. 1945. The Voice. In *Winter of Artifice: Three Novelettes*. Athens, OH: Swallow Press, 1999, pp. 87–130.
Nunberg, H[erman]. 1931. The Synthetic Function of the Ego. *International Journal of Psycho-Analysis*, 12:123–40.
O'Donoghue, Diane. 2019. *On Dangerous Ground: Sigmund Freud's Visual Cultures of the Unconscious*. New York: Bloomsbury.
Parsons, Michael. 2009. An Independent Theory of Clinical Technique. In *Living Psychoanalysis: From Theory to Experience*. New York: Routledge, 2014, pp. 184–204.
Partridge, Simon. 2014. The Hidden Neglect and Sexual Abuse of Infant Sigmund Freud. *Attachment*, 8:139–50.
Paskauskas, R. Andrew, ed. 1993. *The Complete Correspondence of Sigmund Freud and Ernest Jones 1908–1959*. Cambridge, MA: Harvard University Press.
Peláez, Miguel Gutiérrez. 2009. Trauma Theory in Sándor Ferenczi's Writings of 1931 and 1932. *International Journal of Psychoanalysis*, 90:1217–33.
Perry, Helen Swick. 1982. *Psychiatrist of America: The Life of Harry Stack Sullivan*. Cambridge, MA: Harvard University Press.
Pertegato, Edi Gatti, and Giorgio Orghe Pertegato, eds. 2013. *From Psychoanalysis to Group Analysis: The Pioneering Work of Trigant Burrow*. London: Karnac Books.
Press, Jacques. 2006. Constructing the Truth: From "Confusion of Tongues" to "Constructions in Analysis." *International Journal of Psychoanalysis*, 87:519–36.
Prince, Morton. 1906. *The Dissociation of a Personality: A Biographical Study in Abnormal Psychology*. 2nd ed. New York: Longmans, Green, 1913.
Putnam, J[ames]. J[ackson]. 1909. Personal Impressions of Sigmund Freud and His Work. With Special Reference to His Recent Lectures at Clark University. In Putnam 1921, pp. 1–30.
———. 1915. *Human Motives*. Boston: Little, Brown.
———. 1921. *Addresses on Psycho-Analysis*. London: Hogarth Press, 1951.
Rachman, Arnold W. 2018. *Elizabeth Severn: The "Evil Genius" of Psychoanalysis*. New York: Routledge.
Rangell, Leo. 1982. Transference to Theory: The Relationship of Psychoanalytic Education to the Analyst's Relationship to Psychoanalysis. *Annual of Psychoanalysis*, 10:29–56.
———. 1988. The Future of Psychoanalysis: The Scientific Crossroads. *Psychoanalytic Quarterly*, 57:310–40.
Rank, Otto. 1924. *The Trauma of Birth*. Trans. from the German. New York: Dover, 1993.
Righter, James V. 2015. On Elizabeth Severn's Couch: Reflections of a Patient. Lecture presented at the conference of the International Sándor Ferenczi Society, Toronto. Unpublished.

Rosenzweig, Saul. 1969. Sally Beauchamp's Career: A Psychoarchaeological Key to Morton Prince's Classic Case of Multiple Personality. *Genetic, Social, and General Psychology Monographs*, 113–1(February):15–60.
Ross, John Munder. 1982. Oedipus Revisited—Laius and the "Laius Complex." *Psychoanalytic Study of the Child*, 37:169–200.
Rudnytsky, Peter L. 1987. *Freud and Oedipus*. New York: Columbia University Press.
———. 2002. *Reading Psychoanalysis: Freud, Rank, Ferenczi, Groddeck*. Ithaca: Cornell University Press.
———. 2011. *Rescuing Psychoanalysis from Freud and Other Essays in Re-Vision*. London: Karnac Books.
———. 2015. The Other Side of the Story: Severn on Ferenczi and Mutual Analysis. In Harris and Kuchuck 2015, pp. 134–49. Rpt. as Introduction to Severn 1933, pp. 1–20.
———. 2019a. *Formulated Experiences: Hidden Realities and Emergent Meanings from Shakespeare to Fromm*. New York: Routledge.
———. 2019b. Series Editor's Foreword to Craparo, Ortu, and Van der Hart, pp. ix–xiii.
Rudnytsky, Peter L., Antal Bókay, and Patrizia Giampieri-Deutsch, eds. 1996. *Ferenczi's Turn in Psychoanalysis*. New York: New York University Press.
Sajner, Josef. 1968. Sigmund Freuds Beziehungen zu seinem Geburtsort Freiberg (Příbor) und zu Mähren. *Clio Medica*, 3:167–80.
———. 1981. Drei dokumentarische Beiträge zur Sigmund Freud-Biographik aus Roznau. *Jahrbuch der Psychoanalyse*, 13:143–52.
———. 1989. Die Beziehungen Sigmund Freuds und seiner Familie zu dem mährischen Kurort Roznau. *Jahrbuch der Psychoanalyse*, 24:73–96.
Schatzman, Morton. 1973. *Soul Murder: Persecution in the Family*. New York: Random House.
———. 1990. Another Soul Murder. *New York Review of Books*. Letter to the Editor, November 8.
Scherer, Frank. 2015. *The Freudian Orient: Early Psychoanalysis, Anti-Semitic Challenge, and the Vicissitudes of Orientalist Discourse*. London: Karnac Books.
Schröter, Michael, ed. 2004. *Sigmund Freud—Max Eitingon. Briefwechsel 1906–1939*. 2 vols. Tübingen: edition diskord.
Schröter, Michael, and Christfried Tögel. 2007. The Leipzig Episode in Freud's Life (1859): A New Narrative on the Basis of Recently Discovered Documents. *Psychoanalytic Quarterly*, 76:193–215.
Searles, Harold. 1975. The Patient as Therapist to His Analyst. In *Countertransference and Related Subjects: Selected Papers*. New York: International Universities Press, 1979, pp. 380–459.
Severn, Elizabeth. 1913. *Psycho-Therapy: Its Doctrine and Practice*. 2nd ed. London: Rider and Son, 1914. University of California Library reprint, n.d.
———. 1917. *The Psychology of Behaviour: A Practical Study of Human Personality and Conduct with Special Reference to Methods of Development*. New York: Dodd, Mead. Kessenger Legacy Reprints, n.d.

———. 1921(?). *Crystals. A Novel.* Severn Archives. Library of Congress, Washington, DC. Unpublished.

———. 1933. *The Discovery of the Self: A Study in Psychological Cure.* Ed. Peter L. Rudnytsky. New York: Routledge, 2017.

———. 1937a. Mental Catharsis: A Means of Cure. Lecture presented at the Practical Psychology Club, London. November 23. Severn Archives. Library of Congress, Washington, DC. 24 pp. Unpublished.

———. 1937b. What Is a Psychic Injury? Lecture presented at the Practical Psychology Club, London. November 16. Severn Archives. Library of Congress, Washington, DC. 19 pp. Unpublished.

———. 1952. Interview with Kurt R. Eissler. December 20. Freud Archives. Library of Congress, Washington, DC. 24 pp. Unpublished.

———. 1957. Letter to Erich Fromm. November 29. Fromm Archives, Tübingen, Germany. Unpublished.

———. n.d.a. *65 Degrees of Psychological and Mental Healing.* Severn Archives. Library of Congress, Washington, DC. Unpublished.

———. n.d.b. *An Analysis of Love and Sex: A Psychological Study of Love, Sex and Marriage, with some Counsel to Lovers.* Severn Archives. Library of Congress, Washington, DC. Unpublished.

Severn, Margaret. 1988. *Spotlight: Letters to My Mother.* Margaret Severn Collection. New York Public Library for the Performing Arts. 3,099 pp. Unpublished.

———. 1992. *Letter to Agnes de Mille.* June 2. Margaret Severn Collection. Library of the Performing Arts, New York City. Unpublished.

Shapiro, Sue A. 1993. Clara Thompson: Ferenczi's Messenger with Half a Message. In Aron and Harris 1993, pp. 159–74.

———. 2000. The Unique Benjamin Wolstein as Experienced and Read. *Contemporary Psychoanalysis*, 36:301–41.

Shaw, Daniel. 2014. *Traumatic Narcissism: Relational Systems of Subjection.* New York: Routledge.

Shengold, Leonard. 1989. *Soul Murder: The Effects of Childhood Abuse and Deprivation.* New Haven: Yale University Press.

Simmel, Ernst. 1921. Contribution to Symposium on War Neuroses. Trans. Ernest Jones [?]. In Ferenczi, Abraham, Simmel, and Jones 1921, pp. 30–43.

Simon, Bennett. 1992. "Incest—See under Oedipus Complex": The History of an Error in Psychoanalysis. *Journal of the American Psychoanalytic Association*, 40:955–88.

Smith, Fred. 1918. Letter to Elizabeth Severn. April 14. Severn Archives. Library of Congress, Washington, DC. Unpublished.

Smith, Nancy A. 1998. "Orpha Reviving": Toward an Honorable Recognition of Elizabeth Severn. *International Forum of Psychoanalysis*, 7:241–46.

———. 1999. From Oedipus to Orpha: Revisiting Ferenczi and Severn's Landmark Case. *American Journal of Psychoanalysis*, 59:345–66.

Spraggett, Allen. 1969. Nandor Fodor: Analyst of the Unexplained. *Psychoanalytic Review*, 56A(1):128–37.

Stern, Daniel N. 1985. *The Interpersonal World of the Infant: A View from Psychoanalysis and Developmental Psychology.* New York: Basic Books.

Stern, Daniel N., Louis W. Sander, Jeremy P. Nahum, Alexandra M. Harrison, et al. 1998. Non-Interpretive Mechanisms in Psychoanalytic Therapy: The "Something More" than Interpretation. *International Journal of Psychoanalysis*, 79:903–21.

Stern, Donnel. 1997. *Unformulated Experience: From Dissociation to Imagination in Psychoanalysis*. Hillsdale, NJ: Analytic Press.

———. 2010. *Partners in Thought: Working with Unformulated Experience, Dissociation, and Enactment*. New York: Routledge.

Stern, Steven. 2017. *Needed Relationships and Psychoanalytic Healing: A Holistic Relational Perspective on the Therapeutic Process*. New York: Routledge.

———. 2021. Analytic Adoption of the Psychically Homeless. *Psychoanalysis, Self and Context*, 16:24–42.

Strindberg, August. 1887. *The Father*. In *Seven Plays*. Trans. Arvid Paulson. New York: Bantam Books, 1972, pp. 6–56.

Summerscale, Kate. 2020. *The Haunting of Alma Fielding: A True Ghost Story*. London: Bloomsbury Circus.

Taft, Jessie. 1957. Letter to Izette de Forest. November 22. Fromm Archives, Tübingen, Germany. Unpublished.

Tartakoff, Helen. 1956. Recent Books on Psychoanalytic Technique—A Comparative Study. *Journal of the American Psychoanalytic Association*, 4:318–43.

Terman, David M. 2014. Self Psychology as a Shift away from the Paranoid Strain in Classical Analytic Theory. *Journal of the American Psychoanalytic Association*, 62:1005–24.

Thompson, Clara. 1931. "Dutiful Child" Resistance. In Green 1964b, pp. 103–10.

———. 1933. Ferenczi's Relaxation Method. In Green 1964b, pp. 67–71.

———. 1938. Development of Awareness of Transference in a Markedly Detached Personality. In Green 1964b, pp. 111–21.

———. 1943. "The Therapeutic Technique of Sándor Ferenczi": A Comment. *International Journal of Psycho-Analysis*, 24:64–66.

———. 1950. *Psychoanalysis: Evolution and Development*. New Brunswick, NJ: Transaction Publishers, 2003.

———. 1952a. Interview with Kurt R. Eissler. June 4. Freud Archives. Library of Congress, Washington, DC. 24 pp. Unpublished.

———. 1952b. Sullivan and Psychoanalysis. In Green 1964b, pp. 83–94.

———. 1957. Letter to Erich Fromm. November 5. Fromm Archives. Tübingen, Germany. Unpublished.

Thompson, Nellie L. 1987. Early Women Psychoanalysts. *International Review of Psycho-Analysis*, 14:391–406.

———. 2001. American Women Psychoanalysts 1911–1941. *Annual of Psychoanalysis*, 29:161–77.

Trilling, Lionel. 1957. Suffering and Darkness Marked the Last Years of Triumph. Review of *The Life and Work of Sigmund Freud: Vol. 3, The Last Phase, 1919–1939*, by Ernest Jones. *New York Times Book Review*. October 18, pp. 7, 36.

Tubert-Oklander, Juan. 2004. The Clinical Diary of 1932 and the New Psychoanalytic Clinic. In *The One and the Many: Relational Psychoanalysis and Group Analysis*. London: Karnac Books, 2014, pp. 181–205.

---. 2018. Ferenczi and Group Analysis. *Group Analysis*, 52:23–35.
Tuckett, David. 1994. The 75th Volume. *International Journal of Psychoanalysis*, 75:1–2.
Van der Hart, Onno. 2016. Pierre Janet, Sigmund Freud, and Dissociation of the Personality: The First Codification of a Psychodynamic Depth Psychology. In Howell and Itzkowitz 2016, pp. 44–56.
Van der Hart, Onno, Ellert R. S. Nijenhuis, and Kathy Steele. 2006. *The Haunted Self: Structural Dissociation and the Treatment of Chronic Traumatization*. New York: Norton.
Van der Kolk, Bessel. 2014. *The Body Keeps the Score: Brain, Mind, and Body in the Healing of Trauma*. New York: Penguin Books, 2015.
Vida, Judith E. 2015. Treating the "Wise Baby." *American Journal of Psychoanalysis*, 65:3–12.
Vitz, Paul C. 1988. *Sigmund Freud's Christian Unconscious*. New York: Guilford Press.
Warner, Silas L. 1994. Freud's Analysis of Horace Frink, M.D.: A Previously Unexplained Therapeutic Disaster. *Journal of the American Academy of Psychoanalysis and Dynamic Psychiatry*, 22:137–52.
Wikipedia. 2016. Wilhelm Roux. Last modified April 5, 2016, https://en.wikipedia.org/wiki/Wilhelm_Roux.
Winnicott, D. W. 1960. Ego Distortion in Terms of True and False Self. In Winnicott 1965, pp. 140–52.
---. 1965. *The Maturational Processes and the Facilitating Environment: Studies in the Theory of Emotional Development*. New York: International Universities Press, 1966.
---. 1969. The Use of an Object and Relating through Identifications. In *Playing and Reality*. London: Tavistock, 1985, pp. 86–94.
---. 1974. Fear of Breakdown. In *Psycho-Analytic Explorations*. Eds. Clare Winnicott, Ray Shepherd, and Madeleine Davis. Cambridge, MA: Harvard University Press, 1992, pp. 87–95.
Wortis, Joseph. 1954. *Fragments of an Analysis with Freud*. New York: Simon and Schuster.
Zitrin, Arthur. 2012. Why Did Freud Do It? A Puzzling Episode in the History of Psychoanalysis. *Journal of Nervous and Mental Disease*, 200:1,080–87.

Index

Abraham, Karl 37, 41, 123
abuse, childhood sexual 1, 15, 58–60, 82, 95, 97, 99, 103–4, 107, 142, 146, 191, 194, 235, 253–4, 257, 272, 273–6, 281, 303, 319; *see also* Ferenczi, Sándor; Freud, Sigmund; Severn, Elizabeth; Severn, Margaret; Thompson, Clara
"Adaptation of the Family to the Child, The" (Ferenczi) 253
Adler, Alfred 234, 239, 241
"Aetiology of Hysteria, The" (Freud) 10, 281
Alchemical Society 34
Alexander, Franz 11, 77, 307
American Institute of Psychoanalysis 140
American Psychoanalytic Association (APsaA) 23n3, 65, 144, 186
American Psychological Association 144
Ames, Thaddeus 6
"Analysis Terminable and Interminable" (Freud) 78, 225–7, 238–43, 245–6, 256–9, 264, 298
Anna O. *see* Breuer, Josef; Pappenheim, Bertha
Apparently Normal Personality, and Emotional Personality 100, 107, 125
Armstrong, Robert (Severn's mother's first husband) 29

Aron, Lewis 15, 87n1, 307
Asch, Joseph 37, 40, 67, 69, 75–6, 197
Autobiographical Study, An (Freud) 12
autobiography, disguised 16, 44, 56–60, 99, 102, 185, 187–8, 190–1, 259, 264, 273, 279

Bad Homburg Congress (IPA) 23n3
Balint, Alice 23n2
Balint, Michael 4, 23n2, 16–19, 61n3, 141, 175, 243–4n4
Balmary, Marie 311n6
Baranger, Madelon, and Willy Baranger 61n6
Barnett, Alan 158n4
Bartlett, Robert 61n6
Bass, Anthony 4, 8, 140, 193
Battey, Robert 57
Bauer, Ida 16; *see also* Dora case (Freud)
Beira, Mario L. 243n2, 284n6, 284n7
"Belief, Disbelief, and Conviction" (Ferenczi) 185
Bergson, Henri 66
Berkeley, George 56
Berman, Emanuel 2, 4–5, 25n8, 25n13, 135
Bernays, Minna (Freud's sister-in-law) 6, 276, 281
Beyond the Pleasure Principle (Freud) 71, 289–90

Bijur, Abraham 6
Billinsky, John M. 22, 285n12
bioanalysis 199–200, 289
Bion, Wilfred 86
Birksted-Breen, Dana 243n2
Blanton, Margaret 188
Blanton, Smiley 136, 188–9, 214–16, 223–4
Blum, Harold P. 2–3
Bohleber, Werner 19
Bokanowski, Thierry 56n6, 100n3
Bone, Harry 181n1
Bonomi, Carlo 15, 21, 57–8, 172, 178–9, 181n8, 195, 223, 246–8, 250, 255, 260–1, 300
Borgogno, Franco 303–4, 313
Boss, Medard 207
Boston Process of Change Study Group 292
Bowlby, John 260
Boyle, John 23n1, 43n3, 145, 158n3
Brabant, Eva 156, 284n3
Brandchaft, Bernard 21, 195n1
Breger, Louis 24n6, 277, 279–80, 284n9
Brennan, B. William 7, 23n3, 40, 56, 58, 61n8, 88, 126, 135–7, 139–40, 154, 156, 169, 173, 186–7, 189, 191, 193–4, 196n2, 196n3, 243–4n4, 248–9
Brenner, Ira 15
Breuer, Josef 12, 23n2, 62, 68n1, 267, 269, 292, 297–8, 310n3; and Anna O. 14–15, 65, 72, 299
"Bridge Symbolism and the Don Juan Legend" (Ferenczi) 245
Brill, A. A. 38, 55, 174, 176, 217, 232–3
Bromberg, Chaim E., and Lewis Aron 25n11, 41, 123, 187
Bromberg, Philip 12, 50, 53, 142
Brown, Harriet Maria Mann (Severn's mother) 29, 32

Brown, Leota Loretta *see* Severn, Elizabeth
Brown, Marcus M. (Severn's father) 29, 104, 124–6, 128, 150, 152, 157, 166, 313, 317–19
Brücke, Ernst 23
Bryan, Douglas 36
Budapest Congress (IPA) 24n6, 243n2
Bull, Nina 55, 60n2
Burlingham, Dorothy Tiffany 136, 158n2, 189
Burn, Patty 119
Burnham, John 60n2, 159n7
Burrow, Trigant 23–4n3, 61n5, 159n9

Carrington, Hereward 146–7
Cassullo, Gabriele 25n9
Charcot, Jean-Martin 14, 32
"Child Analysis in the Analysis of Adults" (Ferenczi) 84, 186, 205, 243n4, 288, 306
Christian Science 30, 55–6
Cincinnati Enquirer 41, 103
Civilization and Its Discontents (Freud) 247, 254
Clinical Diary (Ferenczi) 1, 3; beginning of 21, 195, 228; on Breuer 14, 267, 269, 292, 298–9, 310n3; dictated to secretary 175; on Freud 20, 75, 178–9, 195, 224, 265–9, 283, 286, 310n3; German title of 309; and "insensitivity of the analyst," 184; on mediums 51, 132n8, 202, 208, 296–7; patients in 7, 135, 187, 203, 205; Severn's recurring dreams in 312; and *passim*
Cohen, Etty 196n3
Conci, Marco 139
"Confusion of Tongues between Adults and the Child" (Ferenczi) 10, 91, 99–100, 105, 193, 274–5, 288, 291–2; attacked by Freud 146, 174, 176, 231–3, 235, 243–4n4; cited by

Severn 81; on duration of training analyses 87n4; and introjection of the aggressor 91, 185, 274, 304–5; original title of 81; and "precocious maturity," 93; publication of 137; read aloud to Freud 174, 176; and *passim*
"Constructions in Analysis" (Freud) 246, 259–60, 292, 300
"Contraindications to the 'Active' Psycho-Analytical Technique" (Ferenczi) 200–1
Cook, Lavinia Cole 45
corrective emotional experience 11, 77, 307
Craparo, Giuseppe 24n6
Crastnopol, Margaret 249

Dabo, Leon 42, 43n10
Dahl, Nikolai 32
Davies, Bryony 284n3
Davies, Jody 25n18; and Mary Gail Frawley 25n18
death instinct 93, 309
de Forest, Alfred 136
de Forest, Izette 22, 110–12, 135–6, 181n1, 186, 189–90, 193, 214; affair with Pierce 137; and Alice Lowell 139; "Certificate" from Ferenczi 140, 145; on Ferenczi 137–41, 181, 308–9; on Ferenczi's last encounter with Freud 176–7; never acknowledges Severn 140; as pastoral counselor 140
de Forest, Judith 136, 158n2
de Mille, Agnes 119
Descartes, René 216
Deutsch, Felix 49
Deutsch, Helene 155, 201
Development of Psycho-Analysis, The (Ferenczi and Rank) 11, 40, 111, 200, 237, 308, 310n1
Discovery of the Self, The (Severn) 41; and analysis with Ferenczi 81; on analytic adoption 70, 183; approved by Ferenczi and Margaret 16, 78, 89; case of Ferenczi in 89–99, 165; case of Margaret in 103–7; and *Clinical Diary* 1, 10, 21, 70; on contrast between Freud and Ferenczi 69, 71, 75, 81; critique of Freud 73; disguised case histories in 1, 16; on dreams 84, 289; on Ferenczi 74; on Jung 87n2; on limitations of psychoanalysis 73–4, 79, 148; lone review of 147, 158n4, 211, 305; mentioned by Gizella Ferenczi 205; on nightmares 86, 127–8, 263, 296, 312; on reliving traumatic events 11, 83–5; subjective dimension of 69; on transference and free association 72; writing of 81; and *passim*
dissociation 25n8, 65; and enactment 19; and repression 15, 50, 99; and split or multiple personality 72, 82, 99–100, 101, 124, 312; term coined by Janet 83; and trauma 12, 14–16, 20, 22, 50, 66, 102, 107, 128, 142, 222, 243, 262, 294; *see also* trauma
Dodge, Mabel 38–9, 48, 55, 64, 80
Dora case (Freud) 234
Dormandi, Olga Kovács 23n2
Dostoevsky, Fyodor 224, 264
dramatic participation of the analyst 11, 83, 85–6, 94, 105, 127, 138, 186–7, 291, 293, 300
dreams, traumatolytic function of 85–6, 288–90, 294–5, 309
Dupont, Judith 23n2, 129, 181n2, 275; *see also* Falzeder, Ernst

Eastman, Max 55–6, 60n2
Eckstein, Emma 15–16, 58, 65, 239, 258–9
Eddy, Mary Baker 30; *see also* Christian Science

Edmunds, Lavinia 24n4
Ego and the Id, The (Freud) 287
ego psychology 135, 261, 287
Eissler, Kurt R. 2, 7, 158n8; and Margaret Severn 103; never met Freud 87n3; *see also* Severn, Elizabeth; Thompson, Clara
Eitingon, Max 221, 230–1, 235, 240, 264, 287, 296, 305
"Elasticity of Psychoanalytic Technique, The" (Ferenczi) 306
Ellenberger, Henri F. 11
Emerson, Ralph Waldo 56
Etchegoyen, Horacio 243n2
Evans, Elida 48
Everett, Patricia R. 38, 60n2
"Exploring the Unconscious" (Ferenczi) 13–14

Fairbairn, W. R. D. 12–14, 15, 25n8, 310
Falzeder, Ernst 25n10, 156, 209n1; and Judith Dupont 243n2; *see also* Haynal, André E.
Ferenczi, Gisela (sister) 94, 96
Ferenczi, Gizella (wife) 94, 96, 110, 131n3, 131n4, 161–2, 174, 199, 202, 204–5, 212; abortion of 168; accompanies Sándor on last visit to Freud 181n4, 181–2n8; as Ferenczi's lover 2, 168; letter to Georg and Emmy Groddeck 173, 206–7; marries Ferenczi 5, 169–70, 225; on Severn 206–7; urges Ferenczi to divorce her and marry Elma 169
Ferenczi, Lajos (brother) 170
Ferenczi, Sándor: and 1909 trip to America 23n3, 40, 269–70, 281; "adopted" by Freud 93, 168, 238, 269–70; and aggression 306–7; aggression against Gizella 181–2n8; alleged insanity of 2, 89, 91–2, 97, 160, 172–82, 207, 210; analysis with Freud 3, 75–6, 78, 90, 197, 209n1, 212–13, 221, 225–6, 236, 259, 266, 292; on analytic love 88, 106, 138–9, 167, 185–6, 190, 192, 213, 293; on "analytic third," 68n2; approves of Severn's analysis of Margaret 112, 122; between Freud and Severn 146, 216, 242; bizarre behavior of 170–1, 172; on Breuer 297–8; childhood traumas of 94–7, 99, 100n1, 100n2, 168, 223, 259, 271–2, 274–5, 279, 316–17; childlessness of 93, 169, 229; commitment to healing 222; death of 1, 82, 155, 173, 186, 205, 210, 214, 223, 231–2; desire for openness with Freud 213–14; "double role" of 265; fall in Paris 174, 176; on Freud's view of patients 168, 267–70, 274n5, 298; and Gizella's abortion 168–9; and grandfather 97–8, 103–4, 178, 318; as "Grand Vizier," 226–7, 269; and household servants 94–5, 272, 316; humility of 17, 75, 84, 185, 194, 224, 228–9, 237, 269–70, 299, 308–9; and hypocrisy 184–5, 266; and Janet 13–14, 100; on Jung 18–19; love triangle with Gizella and Elma Pálos 4–5, 94, 96, 131n4, 168–70, 182n8, 204, 226, 275; masturbation of 168, 272; meets Freud 13; mixed-up family situation of 170; and mother 92, 94, 96–7, 248, 272, 275, 317–18; and "Palermo incident," 168, 171n2, 204, 213, 270; perceives Nazi menace 174; pernicious anemia of 161, 172–82, 223, 232–3, 270; physical symptoms of 89, 97, 173, 195; and presidency of IPA 221, 227–30, 236, 243n2; and psychognosis 303; psychosomatic symptoms of 153, 177–9; and "pure suggestion of courage,"

306; refuses to shake Rank's hand 178; relationship with Freud as enactment 18–19; relationship with Freud not "dialogue," 16–18, 21–2, 25n13, 168, 222, 226, 232, 235, 237, 246, 259; relationship with Groddeck 3, 21, 49, 168, 171, 174–5, 179, 185–6, 197–209, 212, 223, 259; "relaxation principle" of 84, 101, 149, 185–6, 189, 192, 194, 201, 294; rescue fantasies of 96–7; says Freud stole his ideas about homosexuality 171n2; second trip to America 40, 111, 131n3, 136, 141; as Severn's father 313, 318–19; and sibling loss 275–7; silence concerning Severn with Freud 212–13; and Society for Psychical Research 35; submission to Freud 19, 185, 224, 287–8, 290; suicide of patient 5; "superperformances" of 91, 272, 277; and telepathy 60–1n3, 202, 204–5, 296; tensions with Groddeck 198–201, 204, 207–8; on teratomas 64, 84, 91; traumatized by Freud 20–1, 89, 99, 152, 167–8, 174, 177, 205, 214, 222, 232–3, 237, 256, 265–6, 269; tributes to Severn 84, 166, 179, 195, 202–3, 205, 213, 270, 306; tribute to Thompson 186, 265; visits to Freud 76, 88, 167, 174, 177, 181n4, 203, 205, 213, 230, 232; on war neuroses 25n6; at Wiesbaden Congress 174, 193, 270; writings of final period 10, 74, 84, 222, 241, 245, 286, 308; *see also* Freud, Sigmund; mutual analysis; Pálos, Elma; Severn, Elizabeth; Severn, Margaret; Thompson, Clara; titles of works; and *passim*
Ferenczi, Wilma (sister) 275
Ffytch, Matt 23n1

Field, Manning C., and Dorothy Field 129
Fielding, Alma 141–3, 145, 158n3
field theory 54, 61n6
Flexner Report 33
Fliess, Wilhelm 10, 58, 234, 239, 241, 272–6, 300
Fodor, Nandor 34, 50, 61n3, 141–8, 158n3, 158n4, 158n6, 213
Fonagy, Peter, and Mary Target 22, 86
Fortune, Christopher 15, 37, 39, 70, 88, 103, 131n2, 141, 148, 165–6, 196n4
Fowler, Clara N. 61n4
free association 295–6, 309
Frenkel, Wolf Aron (Ferenczi's grandfather) 98
Freud, Amalia Nathanson (mother) 271, 275, 277–9, 284n7, 284–5n10
Freud, Anna (daughter) 10, 24n5, 41, 123, 158n2, 181n4, 189, 229, 231, 235, 243n3, 264
Freud, Anna (sister) 272, 279, 284n7, 285n10
Freud, Emanuel (half-brother) 277
Freud, Jacob (father) 272–3, 275, 277, 280–2
Freud, John (half-nephew) 277–8
Freud, Julius (brother) 238, 275–7, 284n9, 284n10
Freud, Martha (wife) 275
Freud, Martin (son) 189
Freud, Pauline (half-niece) 277–8
Freud, Philipp (half-brother) 277
Freud, Rebekka (father's second wife) 277
Freud, Rosa (sister) 284n10
Freud, Sally Kanner (father's first wife) 277
Freud, Schlomo (grandfather) 277
Freud, Sigmund: analysis of Anna 41, 123; analyzes, belittles, or blames Ferenczi 10, 17, 76, 176, 215–16, 221–34, 236–8, 240, 243, 245,

258, 279, 289, 296, 309, 310n1; archeological metaphor of 86; on Asch 37; attacks Rank 238–9, 310n1; authoritarianism of 18–19, 25n12, 179, 181n7, 227–8, 237, 246, 256, 264, 269–70, 282–3, 288; on castration complex 241–2, 247, 251, 256–7, 259, 261–2, 264, 271, 273, 278–9; childhood abuse and traumas of 273–7, 279–82; and Clara Thompson 188–9, 214–15, 228; conduct in "Frink affair," 5–7, 135, 189; death wishes toward Ferenczi 238; denies being traumatized 19, 231–4, 237, 243, 270, 275, 277, 279, 282, 305; denies people dream of their own death 128, 204; does not understand trauma 246–58, 261–2, 264, 268; fainting episodes of 147, 270, 276; and father 280–2; as Ferenczi's grandfather 98–9; on Ferenczi's "premature senility," 167, 226, 236; and Fodor 142–3, 145–6; in Freiberg 257, 272–7, 279; involvement in Ferenczi's love triangle 5, 204, 226; on libido 66; love triangle of 6, 22, 275, 281; and mother 271, 273–4, 277–9; name of 274, 277, 284n7; narcissism and narcissistic rage of 75, 232, 266, 269, 275, 281–2, 288, 299; and nursemaids 272–5, 277, 281, 284n7; as Oedipus 243; paranoid thinking of 234–5, 237, 267, 269, 279–80, 309; professes objectivity 306; profiteers from Jackson 189; on psychoanalysis of organic diseases 49; refuses to shake Ferenczi's hand 176, 178; reprimands "kissing technique," 4, 20, 167, 188, 195, 204, 213, 217n2, 227–8, 230, 235, 240; self-analysis of 8, 283, 319; on Severn 47, 77, 210–11, 214–15, 305, 314; and sibling loss 275–6; and Society for Psychical Research 35–6; survivor guilt of 238, 275–6; train journeys to Leipzig and Vienna 274, 277, 284n7, 284n8, 284–5n10; on unconscious communication 50, 63; unwillingness to be analyzed 22, 242, 270, 279, 283, 298; urinary incontinence of 270, 280–1, 285n12; violates confidentiality 189, 215; wrongly dates Ferenczi's illness 179–80, 210–11, 215, 222, 242; *see also* Ferenczi, Sándor; "seduction theory"; titles of works; and *passim*

"Freud's Influence on Medicine" (Ferenczi) 310n3
Friedman, Lawrence J. 157
Frink, Angelika Wertheim Bijur 5–7, 135, 137, 284n2
Frink, Doris 6–7, 135
Frink, Horace 5–7, 135
Fromm, Erich 17–19, 22, 25n12, 137, 141, 157–8, 160, 172–4, 176–7, 181, 181n1, 181n3, 181n7, 282–3, 286
Fromm, Henny Gurland 157–8

Gabbard, Glen O. 2–4, 18
Gargiulo, Gerald 145, 158n5
Gates, Ruth 111–13, 120, 122
Gaynor, Frank 158n6
Geoffrey of Monmouth 42n2
Gilligan, Carol, and Naomi Snider 311n6
Goethe, Johann Wolfgang von 278
"Grandfather Complex, The" (Ferenczi) 98
Green, Maurice R. 186–7, 191
Groddeck, Emmy 173–5, 205–6
Groddeck, Georg 22, 23n3, 47–9, 70, 169, 173–5, 197–209, 265, 279; breakdown and death of 207; letter to Gizella Ferenczi 207–8; *see also* Ferenczi, Sándor

Gross, Otto 23n3
group analysis 23–4n3, 61n5, 156, 158n1, 159n9
Guasto, Gianni 11, 100n1, 254, 261
Gull, William 46
Gurevich, Hayuta 132n10
Gutiérrez Paláez, Miguel 244n5
Gygi, Ota 110, 117
Gyimesi, Júlia 61n3

Hague Congress (IPA) 48
Hainer, Marianne 13
Hale, Nathan G., Jr. 135
Hallam, Arthur 34–5
Harris, Adrienne 15, 25n11
Haynal, André E. 25n10, 246; and Ernst Falzeder 16–17
Health Record, The 35
Hegar, Alfred 57
Herman, Judith Lewis 20–1, 54, 155
Heywood, Charles Kenneth (Severn's husband and Margaret's father) 23n2, 29, 56, 107, 113, 132n5
Heywood, Harriet S. (Severn's mother-in-law and Margaret's grandmother) 117
Heywood, Harvey S. (Severn's father-in-law and Margaret's grandfather) 30, 104, 114–18, 124, 126
Higher Thought Centre 34–5
Hitler, Adolf 207
Hoche, Alfred 216
Hoffer, Axel, and Peter Hoffer 177, 181n7, 182n9, 248
Hoffer, Peter 235–6
Hollós, István 61n3, 268, 284n3
Horney, Karen 16, 140
Howell, Elizabeth 25n8; and Sheldon Itzkowitz 25n8
Hrazek, Anna 284n7

Inhibitions, Symptoms and Anxiety (Freud) 287
Innsbruck Congress (IPA) 241

International Institute for Psychical Research 41, 141–3
International Journal of Psycho-Analysis 137, 140, 148, 193, 207, 214, 243n2, 244n4
International Psychoanalytical Association (IPA) 10, 23n3, 43, 49, 84, 221–2, 224, 227–31, 236, 243n2, 286, 310n2
Interpretation of Dreams, The (Freud) 71, 238, 280, 282, 288–90
introjection 91, 274, 303–4; *see also* "Confusion of Tongues between Adults and the Child"
"Introjection and Transference" (Ferenczi) 304

Jackson, Edith Banfield 188–9, 192, 194, 228
Janet, Pierre 11–13, 24n6, 25n8, 50, 66, 83, 100, 142
Jelliffe, Smith Ely 37–9, 48–9, 55, 60n2, 63, 65, 67, 79–80, 144, 148, 158n4, 197, 211, 217n1, 305
Jones, Ernest 36, 146–7, 177, 179, 181n1, 188, 217n1, 221, 223, 231, 234–5, 239, 243n2, 263n1, 264, 279–80, 282; on de Forest 140–1, 214, 314; on Ferenczi 3, 17–18, 91, 160, 172–3, 177, 180–1, 181n2, 181n7, 206–7, 210, 243–4n4; on Severn 47, 210, 214
Journal of the American Psychoanalytic Association 141
Jung, C. G. 18, 22, 23n3, 41, 55, 61n7, 87n2, 123, 147–8, 238, 269–70, 276, 281, 283, 285n12
Jung, Emma 148, 159n7

Kahn, Otto Hermann 118
Kant, Immanuel 256–7, 261
Kardiner, Abram 78–9, 152, 214
Khan, M. Masud R. 249
Kirby, Bruce 217n1

Klein, Melanie 41, 86, 123, 247–8, 310n4
Kohut, Heinz 15, 16, 77, 310
Kovács, Frédéric 169–70
Kovács, Wilma 155, 160–1, 169
Kris, Ernst 249
Krüll, Marianne 273, 277, 281
Kuhn, Philip 35–7, 43n4

Laplanche, Jean 249
Laurvik, John 5, 169
Lawton, George 147
Leavitt, C. Franklin 30, 45, 58, 197
Leonard, John 158n4
Leroy, Maxime 216
Lévy, Kata 176
Lévy, Lajos 176–8, 181n6, 181–2n8, 232
Lewis, Nolan D. C. 60n2
Lipskis, Peter 2, 22, 43n10, 102–3, 118–19, 132n7
Little Hans case (Freud) 257
London Psycho-Therapeutic Society 34–6
Lowell, Alice 23n3, 88, 110, 135, 139, 156, 186, 205
Luhan, Mabel Dodge *see* Dodge, Mabel
Lynn, David J. 189

Marcel, Mary 273–4, 280–1
Maroda, Karen 3
"Masculine and Feminine" (Ferenczi) 199–201
Masson, Jeffrey M. 23n2, 70, 87n3, 103, 107, 239, 284n64
Mayer, Elizabeth Lloyd 51–3
Meigs, Kathleen E. 1, 42n1, 139
Menaker, Esther 123, 139–40
Menaker, William 139
"Mental Catharsis: A Means of Cure" (Severn) 41
Miller, Orlando Edgar 35
Miller, Teddie 156, 171n1

Milton, John 42n2
Mitchell, T. W. 36
Möbius, August Ferdinand 14
Moltzer, Maria 23n3
Mom, Jorge 51n6
Moore, Hattie (Severn's father's second wife) 30, 132n5
Moses and Monotheism: Three Essays (Freud) 246–51, 255, 257, 291
Mucci, Clara 13
Munich Congress (IPA) 216
mutual analysis: altruism of 7; arrangements of 23n3, 152–4; concealed from Freud 75, 88, 213; concealed from Groddeck 204; concealed in *The Discovery of the Self* 84, 89, 102; crisis in 162; defense of 4, 18, 87n1, 215; denunciations of 2, 17–18; disclosed by Margaret 88; Ferenczi agrees to 91, 150–2, 195, 315; known to de Forest 137; known to Lowell and Thompson 88, 138, 149; and "love child," 68; precedents for 23n3, 159n9, 197; as relational paradigm 8, 11, 15, 19; reliving of traumas in 94–5, 102, 105, 127, 166–7, 293, 315, 318–39; risks of 154, 156; and *passim*
Myers, Frederic W. H. 36, 50, 142

Nachträglichkeit 301, 312
Narcissistic Personality Disorder 269, 284n4
Nathanson, Julius (Freud's uncle) 277
National Psychological Association for Psychoanalysis 144–5, 158n5
Naumberg, Margaret 40–1, 43n8, 56, 61n8
Nederhoed, Roberta Morphet 88, 110, 135
Nelson, Marie Coleman 144
New Introductory Lectures on Psycho-Analysis (Freud) 215, 245, 263n1, 268, 278–9, 284n9

New School for Social Research 40, 111, 136
New Thought 30, 35, 55–6, 63
Nietzsche, Friedrich 47, 56, 67
Nin, Anaïs 80
Notes and Fragments (Ferenczi) 85, 175, 193, 203, 288, 300–1; and *passim*
Nunberg, Herman 261

object relations theory *see* relational psychoanalysis
O'Donoghue, Diane 284n7, 284n8, 284–5n10
Oedipus complex 76, 249, 254, 256, 274, 280, 309–10, 311n6
Oedipus Rex 243, 272, 319
"one-person" and "two-person" models 237
"On Narcissism: An Introduction" (Freud) 275
On the History of the Psycho-Analytic Movement (Freud) 216, 237
Orpha 125, 129–31, 132n10, 166, 315, 317
Outline of Psycho-Analysis, An (Freud) 245, 251–7, 261, 268, 274
Oxford Congress (IPA) 10, 21, 84, 185, 203, 221–2, 241–2, 261, 286, 310n2

Pálos, Elma 94, 96, 168–70, 226; analysis with Ferenczi 2, 5, 100n3, 170, 168; marriage of 5
Pálos, Géza 168–9
Pálos, Gizella *see* Ferenczi, Gizella (wife)
Pálos, Magda 170
Pappenheim, Bertha 15–16, 299; *see also* Breuer, Josef
Parsons, Michael 310n4
Partridge, Simon 42n2, 275
Perry, Helen Swick 139

Pertegato, Edi Gatti, and Giorgio Orghe Pertegato 24n3
Pfister, Oskar 267
Phylogenetic Fantasy: Overview of the Transference Neuroses, A (Freud) 248
Pierce, Frederick 137
Plato 317
"Present-Day Problems in Psycho-Analysis" (Ferenczi) 201
Press, Jacques 246, 260, 277
Prince, Morton 14, 50, 61n4, 72–3, 82, 101
"Principle of Relaxation and Neocatharsis, The" (Ferenczi) 10, 84, 185, 201, 203, 221–2, 224, 234, 243n4, 245, 266, 287, 297, 299, 302–3, 306, 308–9; title of 86n5, 286–7, 291–2
Problem of Lay-Analysis, The (Freud) *see Question of Lay Analysis, The*
"Problem of the Termination of the Analysis, The" (Ferenczi) 241–2
"Psycho-Analysis of Sexual Habits" (Ferenczi) 245
"Psychoanalysis of Suggestion and Hypnosis, The" (Ferenczi) 36
Psychoanalytic Review, The 144, 147–8, 158n4, 186, 200, 211
Psychology of Behaviour, The (Severn) 14–15, 38, 72–3, 79, 148; on "analytic third," 67; on dissociation 65; on Freud 62, 64
Psycho-Medical Society 34, 36
Psychopathology of Everyday Life, The (Freud) 71
Psycho-Therapy (Severn) 14, 34–6, 63–5, 67, 72, 99, 107, 131n1, 202; autobiography in 44–6, 52, 56–60, 102; on Freud 51, 55; letters from readers 45; Severn's later views of 46–7; and New England transcendentalism 56
Putnam, James Jackson 65–6, 68n1, 72–3

Question of Lay Analysis, The (Freud) 71, 108–9, 144
Quimby, Phineas 30

Rachman, Arnold W. 2, 23n2, 32, 42, 43n7, 102–3, 118, 129, 131n1, 163
Rachmaninov, Sergei 32
Radó, Sándor 235
Radó-Révész, Erzsébet 100n2
Rangell, Leo 286
Rank, Otto 11, 17, 37, 39, 67, 69, 74–5, 91, 111, 158n6, 160, 172, 178, 181n1, 197, 200, 205, 212, 227, 230–1, 233–4, 238–9, 283n1, 310n1
Rat Man case (Freud) 215
Read, Herbert 61n5
"Recommendations to Physicians Practicing Psycho-Analysis" (Freud) 63
Reich, Wilhelm 139–40, 187, 192
Reik, Theodor 144–5, 158n5, 158n6
relational psychoanalysis 8, 10–11, 13, 15, 25n9, 42, 135, 252, 306, 310, 319
"Remembering, Repeating and Working-Through" (Freud) 308
repetition compulsion 71, 85, 288–9, 309
Rickman, John 61n3, 110, 177
Righter, James V. 41, 43n9
Rippner, Maxine L. 159n8, 171n3
Rogers, Natalie 110
Rosenzweig, Saul 61n4
Ross, John Munder 311n6
Roux, Wilhelm 252–3
Rudnytsky, Peter L. 23n3, 24n6, 25n10, 25n12, 49, 70, 89, 100n1, 100n2, 132n8, 196n2, 207, 238, 250, 263n2, 285n11, 285n12, 310n5
Ruskin, John 56

Sajner, Josef 273, 284n7, 284n10
Sander, Lewis 9
"Sándor Ferenczi" (Freud) 180, 207, 222–3, 235, 289

Schachter, Miksa 13
Schatzman, Morton 132n9
Scherer, Frank 243n1
Schreber case (Freud) 132n9, 168, 171n2, 212–13, 222–3
Schröter, Michael, and Christfried Tögel 284n7
"Screen Memories" (Freud) 259, 262, 277
Searles, Harold 314
"seduction theory" 10, 15, 17, 41, 51, 54, 145, 216, 239, 247, 254, 268, 300; *see also* trauma
self psychology 15, 139, 286, 306, 310
Severn, Elizabeth: accompanies Sándor and Gizella to Spain 152, 161, 199, 202, 299; administered narcotics 126, 317; alleged *pseudologia phantastica* 211, 305; and Anna O. 299; on analytic love 76–8; and art therapy 41; begins analysis with Ferenczi 39–40, 136, 212; birth and marriage 29, 41, 56; breakdowns of 30, 37, 40, 45, 57–8, 67, 113, 130, 150–1, 162, 165, 197; claims title of "Dr." 33, 41, 157; in Colorado and Washington, D.C. 33, 131n1; and the occult 22, 34, 40, 54, 205, 208; death of 42; on death of Géza Pálos 168; decision to become a healer 31; desertion by father 124–6, 166, 317, 319; discretion of 154; on dissociation 14–15, 50, 66, 82, 99, 101–2, 107; eating disorder of 46; as "evil genius," 210–17; farewell to Budapest 40, 81, 160–71, 192; "feelings of hate" in Ferenczi 3, 76, 90, 150–2, 272, 318; on Ferenczi's analysis with Freud 40, 76; as Ferenczi's mother 96, 318; final years in New York 122, 143, 167; forgives Ferenczi 167, 195; as Groddeck's successor 197–8, 204–5, 208; and Hinduism 35, 54; history of abuse 15, 29, 63,

104, 108, 124–9, 150, 152, 157, 165–6, 208, 312–13, 316–17, 319; influence on Ferenczi 78, 84, 149, 179, 204; interview with Eissler 2, 8, 32, 37, 39–40, 42, 69–70, 73, 75–6, 81, 88, 98, 103, 124, 150–3, 160, 166–7, 169–70, 197, 199, 211; issue of fees with Ferenczi 113, 153–4, 163–4; lectures in London 35–6, 40–2, 44; meetings with Freud 75–6, 78, 146, 211–12; misses the mark concerning Elma 168; name of 1, 29, 32, 42n1, 148, 159n7, 159n8, 171n3; and object relations theory 42; obtains divorce 32; as Orpha 129–30; ovariotomy of 56–7, 59, 64, 126, 259; participates in a homicide 126–7, 317; psychic twinship with Ferenczi 130–1, 205, 208, 312–19; and psychognosis 303; and psychosomatic medicine 47–9, 109, 197; refutes Jones's allegations against Ferenczi 174, 176, 181n3; returns from United States with Sándor and Gizella 131n3; in San Antonio 31–3, 45, 115; sails to England 34; sails to New York 37; seeks analytic therapy 37; and telepathy 36, 47, 49–50, 52, 60, 65, 120, 130, 202, 210–11, 312, 314; tributes to Ferenczi 3, 8; unpublished works of 42; *see also* Ferenczi, Sándor; Freud, Sigmund; Jones, Ernest; Severn, Margaret; Thompson, Clara; titles of works; and *passim*

Severn, Margaret: administered narcotics 126; affair with Peter Lipskis 118–19; analysis with Ferenczi 1, 109–10; analysis with mother 1, 41, 59, 102–3, 112–13, 122–3, 131n1; analysis with Ruth Gates 111–13, 120; attitude toward parents 30, 117, 120; birth of 29, 113, 130; and Christopher Fortune 37, 131n2, 165–6, 196n4; on Clara Thompson 196n4; as dancer 32, 107, 115–16, 119, 122, 132n6; death of 2, 123; dislike of Sigray 154–5; eating disorder of 103, 110, 118, 127; on Ferenczi 163–5; and Izette de Forest 110–11, 136; kidnapping of 30, 57, 107, 114–15; name of 29–30, 115, 124; nightmares of 104–5, 107, 115; relives traumas 105–6; rescue of 31, 45, 58–9, 115–17, 121, 126; sexual abuse by grandfather 60, 103–4, 108, 114–18, 124, 126; unhappy love affairs of 101, 106, 110, 117–18; weaning of 41, 103, 106, 113, 126; *and passim*
Shakespeare. William 43n2, 59
Shapiro, Sue A. 140, 191–2
Shaw, Daniel 21, 77–8
Shengold, Leonard 132n9
Shields, Clarence 23n3, 159n9
Sigray, Harriot 23n3, 110, 132n8, 154–6, 164
Simmel, Ernst 24n6
Simon, Bennett 20
Smith, Fred 45, 202
Smith, Nancy A. 37, 61n9, 63, 132n10
Society for Psychical Research 34, 36, 49–50
Somers, Nick 24n5, 243n3
soul murder 127, 132n9, 204, 257, 318
Spenser, Edmund 42–3n2
"Spiritism" (Ferenczi) 36, 147
"Splitting of the Ego in the Process of Defence" (Freud) 246, 260–3
Spotlight (M. Severn) 2, 40, 46, 60, 102, 119, 132n7, 152, 161; insight into psychoanalysis in 108; as love letter to mother 120–1; and *passim*
Stern, Daniel 22, 292
Stern, Donnel 12, 18–19, 25n8
Stern, Steven 8–10, 11, 18, 21, 78, 87n1

Strachey, James 217n3, 263n1
Strindberg, August 92–4, 96, 105, 107, 127
Studies on Hysteria (Freud and Breuer) 12
Sullivan, Harry Stack 12, 139
Summerscale, Kate 41, 142, 144–5, 158n3
Swedenborg, Emanuel 56
"Symbolism of the Bridge, The" (Ferenczi) 245

Taft, Jessie 181n1
Tartakoff, Helen 141
Terman, David M. 15, 280
Thalassa: A Theory of Genitality (Ferenczi) 200, 207, 222, 242, 269, 289–90, 300
Thompson, Clara 13, 110, 135, 265, 284n2; accompanies Sándor and Gizella to Wiesbaden Congress 174; analysis with Ferenczi 2–3, 23n3, 139, 187–92, 194–5, 215, 270; aware of mutual analysis 88, 149, 189–91; career of 140; childhood of 187–92; conflicts with Severn 136, 149, 157, 161, 180; confusion over "Confusion of Tongues," 193–4; critique of Ferenczi 138–9, 154–5, 187, 190, 192–4, 208, 293; discouraged from meeting Freud and Deutsch 155, 201; does not meet Groddeck 201; and "'dutiful child' resistance," 183–5, 190, 195n1; early endorsement of Ferenczi 183–6, 190–1, 248–9, 309–10; envy of Severn 3, 154–6, 171n1, 189–91, 201; on Ferenczi and Groddeck 208; financial struggles of 154, 156; interview with Eissler 2–3, 75, 140, 149, 154–7, 158n2, 160, 167–70, 172–4, 180–1, 185, 188–94, 201, 208; involvement with Teddie Miller 156; loses virginity 188; odor of 187–8, 191–2; other analyses of 137, 157–8; permitted to kiss Ferenczi 167, 187–8, 191; present near end of Ferenczi's life 155, 170; refutes Jones's allegations against Ferenczi 173, 176; retaliates against Ferenczi 190, 192, 194; and Severn's departure from Budapest 160–71; sexual abuse of 191–2, 194–5
Thompson, Joseph Cheesman 137, 157–8
Thompson, Nellie L. 135
Three Essays on the Theory of Sexuality (Freud) 273
trauma: and analytic technique 235, 287, 291, 293–5, 298, 300, 306; and catharsis 24n6, 65, 299, 301–3; disagreement between Freud and Ferenczi as 19; and "extraordinary knowing," 51–2; and fantasy theory 16, 27, 80, 82–3, 86, 102, 108, 127, 203, 235–6, 256, 287, 290–1, 296, 301, 304–5; and fragmentation 82, 97, 99, 107, 124–8, 130, 145, 204, 208, 251, 254, 257, 261–2, 289, 302, 312; intergenerational transmission of 1, 54, 102, 124, 127; reliving of, in analysis 138, 150, 186, 190, 260, 295, 300, 302, 307–8, 319; theory of 10–11, 14, 137, 194, 224, 247–9, 300–2; (abandoned by Freud 16, 103, 237, 239, 268, 270–1, 296, 298, 305; created by Ferenczi and Severn 15, 20, 41, 80, 83, 91, 127, 207, 222, 254, 259, 269, 290–1, 303, 309; dissociated in psychoanalysis 20); *see also* dissociation; dramatic participation of the analyst; Freud, Sigmund
Trilling, Lionel 162

Tubert-Oklander, Juan 158n1, 319n1
Tuckett, David 243n2

Umansky, Olga 43n9
"Unwelcome Child and His Death Instinct, The" (Ferenczi) 93, 243n4

Van der Hart, Onno 12, 100
Van der Kolk, Bessel 11, 83, 87n6
Vida, Judith E. 129
Vienna Psychoanalytic Society 237, 288
Vitz, Paul C. 279

Waelder, Robert 177, 181n6, 182n8
Warner, Silas L. 24n4
"What Is a Psychic Injury?" (Severn) 41–2, 64
White, William Alanson 48, 148

Whitman, Walt 56
Wiesbaden Congress (IPA) 10, 76, 81–2, 88, 146, 174, 178, 205, 222, 228, 233, 235, 241, 287, 310n2
William Alanson White Institute 140, 196n2
Wilshire, Mary 163, 165
Winnicott, D. W. 42, 92, 132n10, 174, 252, 255, 294–5, 307, 312
Wittek, Theresa 273, 281
Wolf Man case (Freud) 239
Wolstein, Benjamin 140, 193
World War I 24n6, 37, 42, 209n1
World War II 42, 122, 135, 143
Wortis, Joseph 214

Zajíc, Monika 273
Zitrin, Arthur 24n4

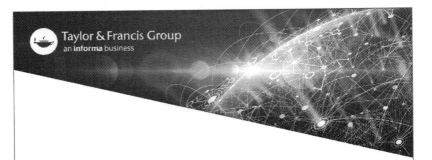

Printed in the United States
by Baker & Taylor Publisher Services